Contents

KU-492-901

Part One: Masterclass: Get Your Book Published

	Introduction	3
1	The publishing world	5
2	What are they looking for?	29
3	Persistence	53
4	Legalities and practicalities	77
5	In production	105
6	Self-publishing	123
7	Ebooks and epublishing	151
8	Promotion and publicity	169
9	Selling the book	203
10	Being a writer	233
	Resources	249

Part Two: Get Started in Self-Publishing

	Introduction: Self-publishing – a revolution	267
1	Begin at the beginning…	271
2	Research	285
3	Redrafting	299
4	Preparing your manuscript for publication	313
5	Print and print on demand	329
6	Self-publishing ebooks	343
7	Publication	359
8	Case studies	369
9	Marketing your book	387
10	Setting up and running a website	399

11	Post-publication	413
12	The continuing need for self-development	423
13	What next?	437
	Resources	449
	Index	452
	Acknowledgements	456

Teach® Yourself

The Insider's Guide to Publishing

Katherine Lapworth, Kevin McCann and Tom Green

First published in Great Britain in 2015 by John Murray Learning. An Hachette UK company.

British Library Cataloguing in Publication Data: a catalogue record for this title is available from the British Library.

ISBN: 978 1 47362 373 6

1

Typeset by Cenveo® Publisher Services.

Printed and bound in Great Britain by CPI Group (UK) Ltd., Croydon, CR0 4YY.

John Murray Learning policy is to use papers that are natural, renewable and recyclable products and made from wood grown in sustainable forests. The logging and manufacturing processes are expected to conform to the environmental regulations of the country of origin.

John Murray Learning
Carmelite House
50 Victoria Embankment
London EC4Y 0DZ
www.hodder.co.uk

Part One

Masterclass: Get Your Book Published

Katherine Lapworth

Introduction

The number of people who claim to 'have a book in them' runs to hundreds of thousands; the people who actually do something about it and produce a book – considerably fewer. If you are reading this, it is because you have written or are writing something that you feel is worth getting published. That is the first successful step to publishing your book.

The second step is to start thinking like a publisher rather than a writer. Publishing is a curious mix of creativity, literary appreciation and hard-nosed financial decisions. You need to look at your work in the same way an editor or literary agent would; is there a market for it and will people buy it in sufficient quantities to cover the costs of getting it into print?

Along with practical information and guidance, this book features insider advice from literary agents and publishers and talks to writers who have successfully been published or have published themselves – everything that you need to know to see your book in print.

Whether you are writing what you hope will be a blockbuster novel or you want to see your poetry or memoirs in print so that your friends and family can have your books on their shelves, there are some definitive dos and don'ts to observe on the road to being published. This book helps guide you along that road. Each chapter features an in-depth case study, key ideas and focus points as well as key quotes from a range of people working in the industry – from writers to editors and agents to booksellers. You can read the book from cover to cover or dip in and out, choosing the chapters that relate to the stage you are at with your manuscript.

It also covers the latest developments in publishing, and, in particular, the rise of self-publishing and the digital revolution that has taken publishing by storm. In the past, self-publishing was seen as a last-ditch attempt by authors who had failed to persuade a publishing house to take them on and print their book. That is no longer the case. Affordable print-on-demand and ebook publication have been a gift to writers. And there has been a seismic shift in the perception of self-publishing; literary agents, publishers *and* the book-buying public regard self-published works as being on a par with the more traditional print books. More importantly, self-publishing allows an author to be in complete control of their work. This book looks at the various stages of self-publishing, examines where you can get help and shows how to set the price of your book.

The rise of the self-published author has been helped by the equally revolutionary development of epublishing. It is estimated that ebooks account for around 25 per cent of the market. Whether you choose to use an epublisher to produce your book or do it yourself, epublishing is a popular choice for writers. This book looks at the options available to authors, how to prepare your manuscript and what tools are available to successfully epublish your work.

The book explains the publishing world, how it is set up and what publishing houses and their editors are looking for. You will learn about whom to approach, what to send and, just as importantly, what not to send. The art of submitting your manuscript, writing a synopsis and a covering letter is explained. We look at working with agents and editors, preparing your manuscript for print and meeting deadlines.

Remember that writing comes with a price – rejection. *Every* writer gets rejected at some point. The book examines why submissions are rejected, how best to deal with rejections and what you can learn from them to improve your work. It also considers the legalities and practicalities of writing, including what to expect to see in a publishing contract.

Writing is a solitary process, but promoting a book demands that the writer steps out of the shadows and into the limelight. Shy writers don't sell many books. Promotion is crucial if you want to sell your work; the more you promote, the more copies you will sell. The book looks at how to promote your work once it is published, what to expect from a publishing house and how you can successfully be your own publicist. You will also learn how to manage your sales, for both print and ebooks. The book explains the sales process, including how books get into bookshops and are stocked with online retailers such as Amazon.

Being able to sustain yourself as a writer is just as important as being able to write well. The book explores what it is to be a writer, the discipline of writing and about writing as a business.

Having a talent for writing and being able to master the techniques of the craft are fundamental skills for a writer. This book is not about teaching you how to write. There are other books in the Teach Yourself Creative Writing series that will help you with that. This is about getting your book into print, either as an actual printed book or as an ebook, with the help of a publishing house or going it alone as a self-publisher.

Mastering the techniques of the craft and improving one's writing talent should be the goals of every writer. To see your book in print will require hard work, determination, perseverance and a dose of good luck. The only sensible thing you *can do is to write.*

1

The publishing world

Jules Renard, a French novelist and playwright, said, 'Writing is the only profession where no one considers you ridiculous if you earn no money.' That may be true of the act of writing but getting published is quite different. Then it becomes a matter of business.

Literary agents, editors and publishing houses do not exist to make writers feel good about themselves; they are there to make money – for themselves and the author. Of course, they love books in all their forms and they are always on the lookout for something exceptional but they cannot do this for love alone. And that is what you have to bear in mind, whether you are trying to get your manuscript accepted by an agent or publishing house or whether you have decided to self-publish. You have to stop thinking like a writer and start thinking like a publisher, and to do that, you need to understand the publishing world.

How publishing is set up

Many of the famous imprints were founded in the nineteenth and early twentieth centuries; Andrew Chatto and W.E. Windus were business partners who published, among others, Mark Twain, Wilkie Collins and Aldous Huxley. Publishing houses were privately owned, usually by the family whose name was over the door. Editors decided which books to publish and worked with authors to that end.

In the 1960s and 1970s literary agents came on the scene, representing authors and dealing with publishing houses on their behalf. As the 1970s turned into the 1980s, the family-run firms were being acquired by publishing and media businesses.

As bookshop chains expanded, the importance of publicity grew and a close relationship developed between the publishing industry and retailers. The importance of sales really began to influence which books were being published; now discussions at a publisher's acquisition meeting not only look at the relative artistic merits of a book but also focus on how well that book might do after publication. The world of the publisher is one driven by the marketplace.

Publishing houses are now made up of one or several imprints. Imprints are brands, the trade names under which books are published. Each imprint will have its own style and specialize in certain genres. Mergers and acquisitions are as rife in the publishing industry as any other area of business. Many of the publishing houses are now owned by a handful of multinationals such as Random House, CBS and Hachette.

Despite these large publishing groups, literary agents will still submit proposals to editors of particular imprints, rather than to the larger group. That means that when it comes to acquiring books some imprints within a group may be in direct competition with each other.

The development of digital has caused another seismic shift in the publishing industry. Amazon, which changed the face of bookselling across the world, is now not only a bookseller and distributor but a publisher as well. Digital has also had a major impact on book publishing with ever more writers opting to self-publish their work, either as a printed book (pbook) or an electronic book (ebook).

Nearly all the publishing houses have, if not embraced the new digital format, begun to engage with it. Smartphones, Kindles, NOOKs, iPads and Sony Readers have helped change the reading experience. It is not yet clear whether ebooks will increase the overall market or replace sales of printed books; what is certain is that epublishing is here to stay.

The biggest domestic market for books is the United States (well over 300,000 new titles are published a year; that is almost 6,000 new books coming out each week), followed by Germany, Japan, China and the UK. The UK produces over 150,000 new titles a year, well ahead of Japan, Germany, Russia, France, Italy and Spain.

Three hundred thousand-plus titles in the United States and 150,000 in the UK seems to suggest that getting a book published is quite easy. Sadly, the numbers that are being published are a fraction of the books that their authors hoped would get into print.

Orna Ross, founder and director, Alliance of Independent Authors

www.allianceindependentauthors.org

'You're publishing to a global audience and therefore [the Alliance] has to be a global organization; it wouldn't make sense otherwise. I think it's about 35 per cent UK members, a similar number in the US and then the rest are all over the world. We have members in Australia, Canada, Africa, India… all six continents in fact. And that's really a part of what makes author publishing so vibrant because as well as bringing their own personal experience, people bring their geographical experience.'

Front and backlists

In publishing, you will hear references to 'backlist' and 'front list'. These are the lists of books that a particular publishing house or imprint produces:

- **The backlist** is made up of a publishing house's long-lasting titles which sell at a steady rate and therefore keep revenue coming in. A strong backlist is the backbone of many publishing houses.
- **The front list** are its new books. Most of a publisher's marketing and promotion will go on front-list books. Many books have a relatively short shelf life. Peak sales of most books happen in the first year of publication, often within the first three or four months. Some publishers have a greater reliance on their front list (for example, publishers who deal in TV tie-in books), while

others rely on their backlist, constantly revising editions (as the Teach Yourself series does), rebranding or redesigning covers and so on.

Agent or publisher?

Very few large publishing houses will take unsolicited manuscripts nowadays. The more traditional route is for authors, certainly those writing fiction, to approach literary agents with their submission. If an agent likes their work, they will try to sell it on to a publishing house on behalf of that author. In effect, the agents are acting as a filter for the publishers.

 Key idea

Always be professional when you deal with agents, publishers, publicity people, bookshops (be polite, on time, etc.). Publishing is like any other business; if you act like a professional, you come over as reliable – that is a positive for anyone considering investing in you and your work.

Some publishers will look at unsolicited work; if they do so, they will say so on their website. This can change from month to month if the publisher is over-subscribed; they will state whether they are not currently taking submissions.

A few publishers are now taking a different approach to finding new authors and manuscripts; for example: HarperCollins 'authonomy' in the UK and Penguin's Book Country:

- **authonomy** (www.authonomy.com) invites unpublished and self-published authors to post their manuscripts online; they must put at least 10,000 words available for people to read. Visitors to the site can then comment on those submissions and recommend their favourites. The more recommendations a book receives, the higher its ranking on the site. It also ranks the visitors who consistently recommend the best books in its most influential trend-spotters listing. It costs nothing to upload your book or recommend books. Once a month, the top five books are read by the HarperCollins Editorial Board who will send their comments to the individual authors of those books.
- **Book Country** (www.bookcountry.com) – similar to authonomy, writers can post and critique each other's work. It

has a wide international reach and lists 60 genres. Uploading your book is free. There is a range of publishing options, tied in with Author Solutions, a Penguin subsidiary, and there is a free package that offers distribution to online bookstores (authors earn 85 per cent of the list price), but they can also publish their book elsewhere.

The publisher

Doug Young, publishing director, Sport & Entertainment, Transworld

www.transworldbooks.co.uk

'I still come across writers who turn their back on the fact that this is a commercial transaction and think that it's all about art. It isn't.'

Someone once described publishers as eternal optimists with short memories, constantly searching for and expecting success, believing that future rewards would surpass previous losses. They are certainly a curious mix of the business and the creative worlds. They have to be. Publishers are the link between the writer and the reader, looking for good books (the creative) that sell (business).

A publisher…

- researches and understands the market
- looks for new authors and works to maintain a relationship with current authors
- adds the authority of their brand/imprint to a writer's work
- assesses the quality of a written work
- works out costs, schedules and potential sales
- finances the production and marketing of a book
- brings design and production values to the look of a book
- buys and oversees print production
- develops new technology
- works with wholesalers/retailers to promote and sell books
- fulfils orders and distributes books
- keeps stocks of books to meet demand
- collects royalties and distributes them.

Carole Welch, publishing
director, Sceptre

www.hodder.co.uk

'Judging whether to publish a manuscript involves a number
of factors for an editor. Critical assessment is one – is it well
written, involving, entertaining, etc.? – though inevitably
personal taste comes into this. Personal passion, too. You
might admire a manuscript, but if it doesn't excite you in
any way, you're not likely to get other people excited about
it. You also have to consider it in the context of the list – do
we already have something too similar, either in terms of
the subject, the author, the audience or all three? And the
market – is it unusual enough to stand out from the crowds
of already published or forthcoming books? Can you envisage
making people want to read it with just a brief description of
it? Particularly in the case of non-fiction, is the subject one
that enough people are going to want to read about, might be
out of date by the time the book is published, has already been
well covered in the press or would be better as an extended
magazine article? Is the author well qualified to write on the
subject? And if there is only a proposal to consider and it's
the author's first book, what evidence is there that they will
be able to deliver a finished script as good as the proposal
promises. That's what an editor does: takes all such factors
into account and judges whether to take something on.

'The next stage can involve a lot of time and effort. In
theory, if an editor likes something and wants to make
an offer for it – whether there is an auction running or
not – they will usually ask colleagues (in sales, marketing,
publicity) to read it too. If it's a book to which you might
be able to acquire world rights or, at least, serial rights,
which can be particularly important with non-fiction, you
would need to involve the rights department as well. What
you want, ideally, is for them all to agree that the script
or proposal is fantastic. Of course, you aren't always met
by unanimous enthusiasm but that doesn't preclude you
from taking the book on anyway. But you have to take
into account other people's views; if, for example, a sales
colleague is saying "It's your call but, personally, I'm a bit

lukewarm about it," they're going to do their best when it comes to selling the book but perhaps not with quite the heartfelt enthusiasm they would have for something they felt passionate about – and that kind of enthusiasm can make a crucial difference. If a rights colleague says they don't think they could sell the book in the US or to foreign publishers, or serial rights to a newspaper, that doesn't mean you shouldn't publish the book but does affect what you should be offering for it.

'So the process of preparing to offer for a debut book (or deciding not to, after all) can take time. It involves researching the competition, gathering people's opinions, having discussions and calculating the advance based on projected sales figures and rights income. It can involve putting together a publishing plan with details of how your company would publish the book, from format to marketing to publicity, and presenting that plan in a meeting with the author and their agent. And sometimes, usually when it's a book other publishers are going after, you can go through all that and still not end up with the book.'

A publishing house relies on its editors to keep a constant flow of publishable books coming in. Editors are constantly under pressure to acquire titles that will be successful, bringing profit to the company.

A commissioning (or acquiring) editor takes on a book and champions it in the company; senior commissioning editors are also responsible for developing the list in general (called 'list building'). Editors sometimes commission books themselves – that is, they have an idea and actively seek a suitable author to write the book (as in textbook publishing) or they will buy work from authors' agents.

At the editorial meeting, the commissioning editor pitches a book to other departments in the publishing house (including sales, marketing, publicity and rights). The manuscript is circulated to other departments for their input. To get approval for a new book, decisions have to be made on established sales figures, likely production costs, the author's track record and so on. The editor will prepare a costing to show the book's profitability because they have to balance the actually physical cost of producing the book (advance, production costs, etc.) against what the market is doing. It is not a straightforward process; a lot of people have to be convinced of a book's suitability for a publishing house.

AUCTIONS

Auctions are a gift to an author. This is when several publishing houses enter into a bidding war to secure an author's book (generally a work of fiction). The auction takes place on the phone and can take a few days.

 ## Annie Ashworth & Meg Sanders, authors who write as 'Annie Sanders'

www.anniesanders.co.uk

AA *'There were the big advances for the celebrity autobiographies which put publishing in a bad place. The knock-on effect is that publishers have got to earn back somewhere so they offer small advances to people like us. They do now acknowledge that it was silly money, don't they? There will be a handful that will undoubtedly have earned out and earned out handsomely. I know Peter Kay's first biography paid for the entire bonuses of the publishing house that year and I have a girlfriend who works at Transworld who thinks Dan Brown is god because that's who pays her salary. But if you are a publisher with £1 million worth of unearned advance (which there will be with those figures), authors further down the line will have advances that get chopped and chopped.'*

MS *'There is a popular belief among authors that if you get a large advance, the publishing house put more effort into publicity because they've got to make sales to try to justify that advance. But publicity isn't everything; it doesn't guarantee astronomical sales. Looking at it for the long term, it's better to have a slow build over time and several books, rather than go up like a rocket and fall like a stick.'*

CONSUMER (OR TRADE) PUBLISHING

Consumer or trade books are aimed at the general reader. The hope is to publish books that will appeal to the widest number of people. You get the bestsellers in trade publishing but there are also books that the publishers had high hopes for but that didn't sell well. Trade publishers often have to respond quickly to trends, such as the popularity of a genre, personality or a topical issue (for example, biographies of Michael Jackson, many of which appeared immediately after his death).

CHILDREN'S PUBLISHING

These are fiction and non-fiction books aimed at the very young to young adult.

ACADEMIC, TEXTBOOK AND EDUCATIONAL PUBLISHING

These publishing houses tend to specialize in academic and textbooks for schools, colleges, universities and libraries. The lead times on academic and textbooks publishing can, on average, be longer than trade books.

Textbooks are commissioned, designed and priced to meet teaching and learning needs. There are differences between the UK and the United States when it comes to publishing educational books. US textbook publishers look closely at the curriculum needs because US professors will adopt a particular book for a course from which they will teach. In the UK there has been a slightly different approach; professors have been less likely to adopt one particular book for their course and would instead produce a suggested reading list.

STM (SCIENTIFIC, TECHNICAL, MEDICAL)

Professional books are usually aimed at helping professionals in their work – for example managers, lawyers, financiers and healthcare workers.

BOOK PACKAGING

A book packager will deliver a complete book, written, edited, designed and illustrated – and sometimes printed – to their customer, a publishing house. The promotion and selling of the book is then down to the publisher, not the book packager.

Book packagers work in many different genres, predominantly children's and young adult and especially in illustrated non-fiction. Working Partners is one such packager in the UK. They are popular with books that are considered labour-intensive, such as books with lots of illustrations and diagrams, a high proportion of photographs, numerous authors or novelty books.

A book packager will commission an author to write the text for them. They are generally paid a fixed fee rather than an advance and royalties; although terms differ from packager to packager. (There is more information on book packaging in Chapter 4.)

SELF-PUBLISHING PROVIDERS

Self-publishing is now widely accepted and has been enthusiastically taken up by many writers. While it is possible to do pretty much everything a commercial publisher would do yourself, there are author services companies who offer to do some or all of the jobs for you. We look at self-publishing in more detail in Chapter 6.

Agents

In *Get Started in Creative Writing* (available in this series) Stephen May says that having a good agent is like having a native guide through hostile territory. They know the editors in the various publishing houses; they know what they are looking for, where the gaps in the lists are, whether editors are looking to expand their list, develop into new genres and so on.

Agents will send manuscripts to selected editors; either one at a time or, if they wish to conduct an auction because they feel the book will sell really well, simultaneously to several editors at once. Equally, editors will get in touch with agents if they have an idea or project that they need an author for.

Many agents are either member of the Association of Authors' Agents (AAA) in the UK or the Association of Authors' Representative (AAR) in the United States. Members adhere to a code of practice. You can identify those who are members by the asterisk against their name in the *Writers' & Artists' Yearbook*; guides in the States also identify members of the AAR.

Do not be put off if an agent is not a member. It may be that they have just set up their agency and have therefore not been practising for the three years that the AAA requires of its members (two years for the AAR) or its revenue may be under £25,000.

WHAT AN AGENT DOES

 ## Sarah Davies, literary agent, The Greenhouse Literary Agency

www.greenhouseliterary.com

'You have to remember that dealing with queries is only a small part of what agents actually do. I think a lot of aspiring writers feel that we just sit there reading submissions all day

and that is not the case. My first duty is to my existing clients. I send their manuscripts out and work on getting them a deal. A writer may think one contract is amazing but, as an agent, I see my job much more as trying to assist them to have a long-term writing career which can be a challenge. So there's the challenge of the first contract and then the challenge of staying under contract and I work hard to make sure they are kept under contract with a publisher. Someone who has written a great first story doesn't always follow it up with an equally commercial concept second time around, so there can be a lot of advising and revising on new work.

'So, I'm doing a lot on behalf of my existing clients, including liaising with my sister company which sells foreign rights, dealing with all things financial or answering a myriad of questions from authors, publishers and colleagues. I also do a lot of preparation and travel for conferences (critiques and speeches), website maintenance, and interviews.

'Submissions have to be fitted around all these other responsibilities – in the evenings, at weekends, on the train, in coffee shops. But also in specially set-aside slabs of time when I try to ignore the phone and constant demands of email. Submissions have to be treated very seriously and looked at with real focus – a potential gem may be among them.'

Being a literary agent involves:
- assessing the quality and marketability of a writer's work
- giving editorial guidance to their writers
- giving advice about trends, market conditions, practices and contracts
- marketing an author's work
- devising strategies for getting an author's work accepted by a publisher
- negotiating deals and getting the best terms for their authors
- reviewing licensing agreements
- checking advance payments and royalties
- reviewing royalty statements, chasing money and keeping the author informed about financial matters.

Literary or author's agents earn money only when their clients do; in other words, when they sell a book or rights to a publishing house. That means that they will only take on authors who they feel have something that is marketable. Agents put a lot of unpaid work, time and effort in on behalf of their clients – they need to feel confident that all that work is worth while.

Literary agents will negotiate terms with the publishers on behalf of their clients. They know the market, both at home and abroad, and will therefore ensure that they get the best terms possible for an author's work. More to the point, they understand publishing contracts, which is an art in itself.

Agents sell and license the rights to various media (book publishers, TV, film, etc.) at home and abroad on behalf of their authors. They negotiate what rights a publisher can have and what rights they retain on behalf of their author. For example, they might withhold foreign-language translation or merchandising rights. They can sell to US publishers, film and TV companies, Europe or other overseas agents. Equally, a UK agent may represent an American author on behalf of their American agents in the UK.

Agents receive a commission, on average 15 per cent of the author's earnings from sales of their books at home; this can rise to around 20 per cent for overseas sales. Commissions for TV or film are around 15–20 per cent. So, if an agent secures an advance of £3,000 and charges 15-per-cent commission, their share will be £450.

Publishers do not have time to read through the 'slush pile' – the unsolicited submissions sent in by aspiring authors because it does not make them money. Agents *will* tackle the slush pile; it may be a fairly junior person going through it or it will be an in-house reader whose job it is to look at unsolicited work, but manuscripts will get looked at.

Learn about the market

 ## Kate Parkin, publisher, Hodder

www.hodder.co.uk

'Most publishers would be honest enough to not take on a book they didn't really like or enjoy just because they thought it was commercial. And many publishers turn down books that subsequently go on to be best sellers. It doesn't mean they are bad books, it means that they just weren't right for them. Or it wasn't right for the publishing house. If you've got an incredibly good sex and shopping type of commercial women's fiction, don't try to send it to Faber. And the same would go for agents. Be sensible; look at agents' and publishers' websites to see the sorts of authors they are interested in. Do your homework.'

Learn about the publishing world; so you know what is selling, where to send your work and, perhaps more importantly, where *not* to send it. Agents and editors continually complain about getting incorrect submissions; with the reference material and information that is available to authors, there should be no excuse for this.

There are some extremely useful publications and websites that list all the agents, publishing houses and general resources for writers. They contain information on:

- literary agents – both home and abroad; what genres they work in; list of clients; commission charged
- publishing houses – both at home and abroad; what genres they publish books in
- self-publishing
- epublishing and ebooks
- book packagers – what genres they work in; what services they offer
- societies, organizations and clubs
- art agents – what they specialize in; commission charged
- picture agencies and libraries
- prizes and awards
- literature festivals
- libraries
- creative writing courses
- trade journals.

Useful books include:

- *Writers' & Artists' Yearbook* (UK)
- *The Writers' Handbook* (UK)
- *Writer's Market* (US)
- *Media Bistro* (US)
- *Writer's Digest* (US)
- *The Writer* (US)

Magazines (some of which are subscription only) include:

- *The Author* (www.societyofauthors.org)
- *Poets & Writers* magazine (www.pw.org/magazine) (US)
- *Writers' Forum* (www.writers-forum.com) (UK)
- *The Writer Magazine* (www.writermag.com) (US)
- *Writers' News* (www.writersonline.co.uk)

- *The Bookseller* (www.thebookseller.com) – this weekly trade publication in the UK has listings of books that will be published over the next six months. You can also see who is moving to which company and who has left to set up their own agency/press.
- *Publishers Weekly* (US) – similar to *The Bookseller*, this provides publishing news, gossip and statistics (www.publishersweekly.com)
- *Bookbrunch* (www.bookbrunch.co.uk).

 Key idea

Make sure you use an up-to-date version of a yearbook. Addresses and details change as do the requirements for submissions.

Book fairs

Literary festivals are about books and writing. Book fairs are about the business of books; in particular, they are key venues for the business of selling foreign rights. If you want to learn about the industry, it is worth attending the London and Frankfurt (and Bologna – if you are interested in children's fiction) book fairs or BookExpo America. There is a range of free seminars on a variety of useful topics; you can see what ideas, subjects and genres are popular and topical; you will get to meet useful companies (especially if you are considering self-publishing) such as printers, wholesalers and packagers.

The main book fairs take place in:
- Beijing (www.bibf.net/websiteen/home/default.aspx)
- Bologna (children's book fair) (http://www.bookfair.bolognafiere.it/home/878.html)
- Frankfurt (www.book-fair.com)
- London (www.londonbookfair.co.uk)
- United States (www.bookexpoamerica.com).

Don't expect to land a book deal by turning up at a book fair and cornering an agent or editor. These are industry get-togethers; ideal places for agents and publishing houses to do deals. The last thing they want is to be buttonholed by an author.

TIPS FOR AUTHORS GOING TO BOOK FAIRS
- Draw up a shortlist of publishing houses that publish your kind of work and visit their stand to see what they have to offer; are they interested in taking on a new book in that genre?

- Find out what is popular and selling right now.
- Get the contact details of the right people to approach.
- Get ideas.
- Go on a Sunday, which is the best day for the public.
- Dress smartly – you want to look like a publisher, not like an author.
- Don't put 'author' on your name badge; use a company name – otherwise industry professionals will try to avoid you.
- Take business cards (or some other kind of promotional artefact – like a bookmark) to leave with people.

> ## Key idea
>
>
> Avoid sending in submissions before and after Christmas, before and after the book fairs. The slush pile has the least priority then.

The marketplace

Fiction categories can be divided into:
- commercial / mass-market
- literary
- action/adventure
- children's and young adult
- sci-fi, fantasy, horror
- crime, thriller, mystery
- romance
- erotica/adult
- historical
- war
- Western

…plus variations on the above, such as 'historical crime'.

Non-fiction can be divided into:
- art/photography/fashion
- autobiographies/biographies/ memoirs
- business/economics
- computer/Internet
- cookery/food/drink
- education/academic
- gardening
- health/beauty/fitness
- history/politics/current affairs
- home front

- humour/gift books
- language and literature
- mind, body and spirit (MBS)
- natural history/pets
- personal development/self-help
- popular science
- psychology/sociology
- reference
- sport
- television/film/TV tie-ins
- travel.

We will assume that you know what genre you are writing in. If you don't and it is too muddled, it will be hard to market. And if it is hard to market, agents/publishers are not likely to want to take it on.

The best way to categorize what you are writing is to think where it would be put if it were being sold in a bookshop. If you struggle to find the right shelf, imagine how difficult it would be for an agent/publisher to sell something like that.

A good writer is a good reader. Read widely so you know your market. Look at different categories, series, genres, publishers' imprints (to help you find a suitable publisher). Look at recent titles published (ask for a catalogue from the marketing department of a publishing house or imprint). The trade press, such as *The Bookseller*, is a good source of information on what new books are coming out and when.

New genres are being invented and cross-fertilized all the time. Part of your job as a writer is to keep up with the trends in the industry. That means reading publications that deal with books, publishing and writing; go into bookshops and see what is selling; attend literary festivals.

Large vs. small

 Robert Forsyth, publisher, Chevron Publishing

www.chevronpublishing.co.uk

'Someone said that the worst place to be is a medium-sized publisher because the big houses have got bigger and are snapping up more and more imprints. They are the only ones who can ride through economic slowdowns; they compete against each other to get the next big bestseller, like Dan Brown; they operate at the super-league level. In the middle are medium-sized publishers; they have overheads like everybody but they find it very tough because they have to

compete against the big boys. At the other end, you've got the independent publishers who can take decisions quickly, who will chase an author they really want, who can slip under the wire, if you like. It's economies of scale – they want one or two good authors with bankable books; that means that the author is a big fish in a small pond, which is nice for the author because they feel wanted and looked after. The rise of the independent is on the up, I think.

'If I was starting to do this now, I would consider an independent publisher. They will say "No" just as easily as one of the bigger publishing houses but I think that their antennae are much more finely tuned; they are more receptive, welcoming; they are on the lookout for new authors because they have to survive.'

Big is not better than small and vice versa. There are pros and cons to working with a large or small publisher and/or a large or small agency. It will depend on what is important to you and what you want from the relationship with your agent/editor.

The large agencies have a range of agents, each of whom will have a particular area of expertise and interest. They will usually have a separate rights department whose sole aim is negotiating rights around the world. The large agencies, such as Curtis Brown, will have offices in the UK and the United States as well as contacts in Hollywood.

Large publishing houses enjoy economies of scale. It means that they can sometimes get press coverage more readily than smaller firms. They may also have close links with large bookshops around the country and a large sales force to service those retailers. Large houses can offer more resources in designing and editing the book and in selling and promoting it. They have bigger budgets and often offer larger advances

However, they are huge corporations, with the focus more on the bottom line; they are increasingly phasing out the niche titles that do not sell as many copies. It can take a long time to get a decision because several people will have to be consulted. You may get asked for your opinion but, with a large publisher, what they say ultimately goes. You will have a relationship with an agent or editor, not with the company itself.

Camilla Goslett, literary agent, Curtis Brown

www.curtisbrown.co.uk

People like to go with the big agencies because they come with a lot of extras. For instance, the different departments we have at Curtis Brown [theatre, film, television, actors, presenters] can be very helpful to certain writers. Having all that in-house means there's a lot of creative cross-over within the departments. But then some authors don't need that. A boutique, small agency, where they are one of a small number of authors, is also very nice. I think it's horses for courses and what suits you as an individual.'

With a smaller publishing house or agency, you will often deal directly with the person who can make a decision. As an author, you are a much bigger fish in a smaller pond. You will potentially have more of an input into areas such as design and price. You will have a relationship with the people who actually run the company. The budgets will not be as large.

Smaller publishing houses and agencies are able to move quickly to seize opportunities and operate efficiently in difficult market conditions. They are often more willing to publish books that will instantly go to the backlist, rather than target front-list books. A smaller house may be more suitable for a particular genre or non-fiction writer because some publishers tend to specialize; a couple of examples of publishing houses who specialize are Mills & Boon in romantic fiction in the UK and Prufrock Press in the States which publishes titles for parents of children with special needs.

Sarah Davies, literary agent, The Greenhouse Literary Agency

www.greenhouseliterary.com

'Make a short list – a mix of large and small agencies – and don't just necessarily base it on the big names. Younger agencies are often incredibly driven and hardworking, and that can be to your advantage. Plus, a newer agent may just be starting to build their list, so will be more open to submissions and the possibility of taking on new clients.'

Timing

The trouble with publishing is that a book will come out that is tremendously successful. It strikes a chord with the buying public and agents/editors will look to jump on that successful bandwagon. But it's a law of diminishing returns – only the first few will be successful. Then you will be told that there is no market for your book because the subject has been over-published. Take heart – the market will always come back. It may not return in the next few months but if writing in that style or genre is something that is important to you – stick to that rather than try to second-guess what you think will sell. Having a passion for your work is a more reliable way of getting published than trying to follow what you think the market wants.

The time it takes to get a book to publication can vary; it usually depends on the genre. A few months from commission for a non-fiction book to 18 months to two years for a novel. Doug Young, Publishing Director, Sport & Entertainment at Transworld rarely has projects that last longer than a year. As he points out, the more commercial you get, the more time specific you have to be; particularly if the book is tied in to a television series or something similar.

What is predictable is the *annual* timetable for books, and publishers are very aware of timing certain books to meet these dates. There may be a particular sporting event or anniversary (the Olympics or the World Cup, for example) that they would want to tie books into. Seasons come round, obviously, once a year. Almost three-quarters of books sold are bought in the run-up to Christmas. Christmas is good for cookery books and presents; the New Year for dieting, self-improvement and gardening publications; Mother's Day, Valentine's Day and Father's Day are also all useful dates where particular books will do well; travel books are popular in early summer. Hardbacks get good media coverage in the autumn (during the run-up to Christmas) and spring (there are a lot of literary festivals at that time).

Case study: Maria McCarthy

The Girls' Guide to Losing Your L-Plates: How to Pass Your Driving Test and *The Girls' Car Handbook* (both Simon & Schuster)

www.mariamccarthy.co.uk

'As I was working on a non-fiction book, I just did a synopsis and three chapters. It's easier to sell non-fiction on a partial; I think it's virtually impossible these days to get fiction sold just on three chapters. Novels can so easily start well and then sink in the middle like a Victoria sponge. But if a non-fiction author can produce some good initial chapters it's far more likely they'll be able to keep it going.

'It felt quite weird because, as a journalist, I'm used to getting commissions from newspapers and magazines up front, so I know in advance that I'm going to get paid for everything I write. Writing three full chapters not knowing if it was ever going to sell felt rather unnerving but I felt so committed to writing a book about learning to drive (*The Girls' Guide to Losing Your L-Plates*) that I just went ahead anyway.

'I looked in the *Writers' & Artists' Yearbook* and I searched for agents who seemed to handle the popular non-fiction, as opposed to something like learned biographies or children's fiction. I narrowed it down to a number of agencies. They say time spent in reconnaissance is never wasted. I had also read in *The Bookseller* that Luigi Bonomi, formerly of the respected agency Sheil Lands had left together with a colleague to set up a new agency (LBA). That happens with reasonable frequency and it's a good 'window of opportunity' to approach them, as they're more likely to be looking for new clients at that point.

'So I put my first three chapters and synopsis in the post to them. In my covering letter, I think I came across as practical and down to earth. I mentioned where I'd been published before and said why I thought the book would work. I also did a selling outline; this was a number of pages: what the market was, why I was entirely the right person to write the book and an analysis of what the competing books in the field were and why mine would be better!

'I approached LBA and got an email the very next day saying they were interested. Naturally, I was over the moon! Then I went up to London for an initial chat. At a first meeting with an agency, they just want to meet you and make sure that you are not the sort of person who is going to throw temper tantrums if things don't go your way. They obviously look at your writing to see if that works but they need to see what kind of person you are; your personality does matter. That doesn't mean you have to waft in and be terribly glamorous or assertive; I think just coming across as pleasant and down to earth will do.

'Publishing can be a rocky road and there are times when things go well and times when they don't. You need to be able to get on with people, to negotiate and keep talking to each other, even if things are going badly.

'I think they also need to see you to work out how you will fit in with the potential marketing and publicity of the book. If you turned up and you were ravishingly beautiful and had a celebrity footballer boyfriend waiting outside in his Aston Martin, that would obviously gain you some extra points but don't feel you have to have that in order to be taken on.

'It is worth taking a bit of trouble with your appearance. As a working writer, I tend to sit around most days wearing trackie bottoms and no make-up. When I meet my agent or publisher, I like to look a bit more groomed; I think it's more professional.

'I wanted an agent who was businesslike and capable and I very much got those vibes at that first meeting with LBA and was delighted when they offered to represent me. After our meeting my agent drew up a contract and popped it in the post and I signed it a few days later.

'I worked with my agent to tidy up the manuscript a bit and by that point it was late November so rather than send it out in the frantic run up to Christmas it was decided to wait until January.

'My agent told me that we would get some acceptances and some rejections. Did I, she asked, want to be told about them as they came in or leave it to the end? I asked to be told at the end. I sort of guessed that there would be rejections and I thought it would be too depressing to hear about them one by one.

'Then came the news that Simon & Schuster were interested. The editor who accepted it had failed her own driving test eight times and that is often how it works in publishing. I think sometimes the difference between a "yes" and a "no" can be as ephemeral as that – whether or not the editor feels a personal connection.

'I was invited in for a meeting with Simon & Schuster, along with my agent. We just had a general chat. I was told beforehand not to mention money or expect any decision there and then. They just wanted to look me over and see what sort of person I was. So I went in and was very friendly, pleasant and low key. I spoke when I was spoken to, told a few stories about learning to drive and then I shut up. I was lively but not pushy. Then I went off shopping in London while the decision was made. I actually got the call from my agent that they'd offered me a contract while I was washing my hands in the ladies' loo in Selfridges. Afterwards, I turned to the other women and said, "I've just got a book deal." I hope they believed me and didn't think I was just some deranged person who loitered in toilets claiming to have book deals.

'My agent emailed the contract over and then talked me through it on the phone so I knew what I was signing up to. I was given a deadline for delivery of manuscript by the end of May; the contract was signed in January. With my journalism work, I was having to juggle the book to fit it in. It was hard, hard work with a lot of hours and lot of research. My editor, Edwina, was brilliant; she held my hand all the way through. I would send in a chapter at a time to her and get feedback. It felt really good; it didn't feel like I was on my own. The agent had, in a sense, done her bit and from now it was down to my editor and myself.

'We had a fantastic relationship. She really got the book and she understood me. She would tell me when I'd repeated myself, would say if my jokes weren't funny but also not destroy me in the process. She was very good at pointing me in the right direction. Not all editorial relationships are necessarily going to be like that; I was very lucky that mine was.

'Although I had submitted the book chapter by chapter, there was still lots of work to do when I sent the last one in. The editor read it through to check for repetitions and so forth and then there was more work to be done on it. The final checking of proofs didn't end till July.

'The book came out in January 2007. The timing was good because it tied in with all that New Year's resolution mindset. The publicity went very well and I did a lot of radio interviews. I had the advantage of a time specific link to the book; it is potentially quite a funny topic and I had lots of amusing stories about driving test disasters. For publicizing non-fiction work, it does help if you can pull out lots of little anecdotes, either funny stories or things that other people would find interesting or entertaining.

'Publicists are quite overstretched so the more you can do yourself, the better. I think it's quite a good idea to ask to see your press release in advance, have a chat with your publicist about what you feel you can do. You could offer to write press releases and distribute them locally to newspapers, magazines and so on, you could approach local radio. I also approached various literature festivals and offered myself as a speaker at those. That's something I've continued – so far I've appeared at Bath, Birmingham, Ilkley, Daphne du Maurier and Warwick Words literature festivals – it's a great way to get to see the country!

Publishers quite like you to do your subsequent books in the same field because they can build you as a brand. So, it felt quite natural for me to go on and do another car book (*The Girls' Car Handbook*).

'The path to publication can have its ups and downs. Your editor may move to another job in the middle of your edits, you might not like your book jacket, you may have writer's block. It's important to realize that a completely smooth ride is the exception rather than the norm and to work with your agent and publishers to tackle any problems in a level-headed manner. Save your angst for your nearest and dearest!'

Focus points

- Very few publishing houses will now look at unsolicited submissions, especially for writers of fiction. Agents *will* look at the slush pile.
- Taking on a book is a mix of business (will the book sell?) and personal preference. A book is championed by a commissioning editor in a publishing house; it is their job to convince their colleagues (in sales, marketing, rights, etc.) to take the book on.
- There are useful annual yearbooks that contain contact details for publishers, agents, packagers, newspapers, magazines and so on that should be on every writer's bookshelf. Make sure that you have the most up-to-date version, though.

Next step

Now you have an idea of the layout of the publishing landscape, you need to know what people are looking for so you can target your submissions effectively. In the next chapter, we will look at who you should approach and how and what to send them to maximize your chances of your submission being read.

2

What are they looking for?

'All good writing is swimming under water and holding your breath.'
F. Scott Fitzgerald

To see your book into print, whether it is traditionally published or a digital version, self-published or published by a more traditional route, you need to be determined and focused. And what route should you take? Agent, publisher or doing it yourself? In this chapter, we will look at what literary agents and publishers are looking for; we will deal with how you can self-publish in Chapter 6. Whatever route you decide to take, remember that publishing is not a race. Get your work in as good a shape as possible before you try to get it published.

Then, stop thinking that agents and publishers need you. Of course, agents have to have authors with work to sell on to the publishing houses who need to acquire books – otherwise they wouldn't make any money. But publishing *is* a business. Remember, too, that agents and publishing houses have existing authors whom they already know and represent. They will not just drop an existing author in order to take on somebody new. A new author is a high risk for a publisher.

What makes a publisher publish a book?

 ## Carole Welch, publishing director, Sceptre

www.hodder.co.uk

'With fiction in particular, we take the attitude that we're taking on an author rather than a book. The idea being that we will continue to publish them and help develop their career. There are always exceptions but, in general, we take someone on with a view to publishing their next book and beyond. Sometimes, it turns out that they only write one book! Sometimes, their second book is rejected and they move to another publisher. And sometimes they recognize that their second book should be put in the bottom drawer and they come back with one we do want to publish.'

A publisher will weigh up the following factors when considering a book:

- Does it fit the company's list?
- The author – can they write? Are they reliable? Are they promotable? What is their motivation for writing?
- USP (unique selling point) – what makes this book different from any other? Is it the author, the subject matter, the way it's produced? Is there a link to an event, a television series, the author's status (i.e. are they a celebrity?)? Is it experimental?
- The marketplace – who will buy the book?
- Competition – what are the competing books like?
- Price/appearance – length of book, size, binding, production, how much it will cost?
- Front list or backlist – how long is its shelf life?
- Investment – how much money will be required (for the advance, marketing, promotion against projected sales)? Has it got earning power?

What the publisher wants, the literary agent wants as well. They can sell an author and their manuscript only if it looks like being a marketable commodity. With debut authors, agents and publishers are looking for something new and fresh, so make sure that you get that new, fresh feeling in your synopsis and sample chapters.

If you are writing fiction, don't send in anything until your book is finished and you have a completed manuscript. An editor or agent may suggest revisions at a later stage but don't submit a 'work in progress'. Literary agents have sold partial manuscripts in the past but they have been *exceptionally* good. A completed manuscript is preferred.

You may only have to send the first three or four chapters to an agent or editor but, if you've got a complete manuscript, it has proved you can finish a project. It makes you more marketable because, if you have already got one manuscript under your belt, you are able to start on a second.

If you are writing non-fiction, it is much easier to sell the *idea* of the book before you have written it. For non-fiction, you can approach a commissioning editor directly with your idea, rather than go via an agent.

Whom should you approach?

Research the agencies and publishing houses to find one that feels like a good match for you and your work. Look at the writers you like or aspire to be like and see who represents them.

Check the websites of the agencies and publishing houses; they will tell you what they expect to see (for example, Sarah Davies at The Greenhouse Literary Agency accepts only electronic submissions, while the MBA literary agency prefers email submissions but will accept them by post). Follow the submission guidelines *to the letter.*

Then find the right person in the organization to send your submission to. If necessary, make a phone call to the company and ask who that person is. Never send a submission to 'Dear Sir/Madam', 'The Managing Director' or 'The Editor'; always address your submission to a named person.

This is not difficult. Again, the yearbooks and the websites are your best resource. There is no point sending your romantic novel to an agency/publishing house that specializes in children's fiction. Equally, it is no good sending your submission to the right agency but the wrong person. Within agencies, people have their own areas of speciality. For example, at the Caroline Sheldon literary agency, Caroline Sheldon is mainly interested in 'women's fiction, children's books and compelling non-fiction stories', whereas her colleague Penny Holroyde shares that interest in children's books but also wants to see memoirs and novels with historical settings.

The Writer's Workshop has launched a new agent and publisher database service called 'Agent Hunter', which has a list of all literary agents and publishers in the UK. You can sign up for free and look around. Full access costs around £12 a year, with a free seven-day trial. The information is detailed and often shows what agents are currently looking for.

It seems such an obvious piece of advice to send your work to agents and publishers who deal in your kind of fiction or genre but practically every agent interviewed for this book made the same point which means that would-be authors are still sending out their work to the wrong people.

 # Heather Holden Brown, literary agent, hhb Agency Ltd

hhbagency.com

'I always tell people to start with the Writers' & Artists' Yearbook, *the latest edition. You would not believe the number of people who are using out of date editions! It's a very easy book to use, it's not expensive and it's a real bible that has a lot of names in it that aren't usually on websites. So, if you want to be systematic about it, go through the* Yearbook, *pick out a shortlist and then work through the individual agency websites for further, up-to-date information. What people tend to do nowadays is to go straight to the website and I wouldn't say that is the most sensible way of getting the best overall picture.'*

What should you send?

Before you send anything out, make sure that you have got it absolutely to the best standard you can.

Agents will find it easier to say 'no' to your manuscript if you haven't sent what they asked for. A new author requires a huge amount of time and effort from both an agent and a publisher; that means adding to their already considerable workload so it is understandable why saying 'no' is so tempting.

It is highly unlikely that you will be asked to send in a complete manuscript, so don't. You will be asked to either send some sample chapters or a set number of pages. Agencies and publishing houses do not have room for them and they do not have time to read through every full manuscript. You should, however, mention whether you have completed your manuscript or not.

If you can, give the impression that you have more than one book in you. Series don't go out of print like stand-alone novels. Agents/editors like to think there will be more to come because they invest a huge amount of time and effort in selling a first book. A second, third, fourth book makes the effort worth while.

The majority of literary agencies will *not* charge a reading fee for looking at unsolicited manuscripts; the Association of Author's Representatives, for example, prohibits its members from charging a fee. Agencies should state this on their website.

Submissions

Kate Parkin, publisher, Hodder

www.hodder.co.uk

'I have a book on my list that I am really pleased with and that has had some wonderful reviews. But it was submitted to me by an agent with an almost unreadable first chapter. If I hadn't been ill at home, rather than busy in the office, I don't think I would have persisted. But there must have been something about it because I picked it up again half an hour after I had given up on it and I kept going. Then I realized "Oh my goodness, this is brilliant!" So really think about the opening. What is going to attract someone's attention?*

It's all about making someone want to turn the page. And that pertains to literary fiction, just as much as it does to commercial fiction. You've got to give the reader a reason to turn the page.'

Agencies and those publishing houses that accept them can receive around 30–50 unsolicited submissions in the post or by email each day; that's anything from 150 to 200 a week and some agencies receive a lot more. Imagine all those submissions landing on desks and into inboxes, all of them believing they are worthy of being published. If there is anything about a submission that makes it hard to read, it will swiftly go to the rejection pile.

A submission represents you. It needs to be well set-out, clean and clear with accurate spelling, grammar and punctuation. If you can show that you care about what you are doing and that you are approaching the job in a professional way, you encourage the agent/editor to have confidence in its contents, even before they start reading. You are, after all, putting yourself forward as a professional writer so make sure your submission is professional.

Submissions will vary slightly from company to company. Literary agents Lutyens & Rubenstein ask for up to 5,000 words or the first three chapters, a covering letter and a short synopsis. Curtis Brown will not take paper or email submissions. You have to submit your work via their Curtis Brown Creative website; here, they want a covering letter, a synopsis of up to 3,000 words and sample material of up to 10,000 words. Blake Friedmann also want the first three chapters or 10,000 words and a covering letter, but state that the synopsis should be no longer than 500 words. If you are submitting non-fiction, your proposal should consist of a detailed synopsis of up to 500 words, a chapter plan and two sample chapters (usually including an introduction or opening chapter). The agencies give *very* clear guidelines. In general, they will comprise the following:

- a **covering letter**
- the **first few chapters** (the *first*, not random chapters; if the number of chapters is not specified, send the first three)
- a synopsis.

Add to that:

- a **stamped addressed envelope if** the agent/editor asks that you do – why should you expect them to pay for the postage? Use a new envelope; not a used one. However, if an SAE is not specified, don't send one. Firstly, it's too much of a temptation to an agent/editor and, secondly, you should not be reusing these submissions, so is a large sae really necessary?

- a **stamped postcard** that the agency/publisher can put in the post to acknowledge receipt; as well as your address, add the title of your book (just in case it gets separated from your submission).

If you are sending by email, add a 'read receipt' to check whether your email has been received or not.

Agents and editors want to see well-presented submissions (no stains, paw prints or smells of cigarette smoke). If it is presented perfectly, it will get noticed for all the right reasons. You should use a computer; do not handwrite your submission. Make sure that your printer produces clear, sharp and easy-to-read text.

In this day and age, it really should be a computer rather than a typewriter. Apart from the fact that it is so much easier to edit your work if it is word-processed, agents and publishers communicate by email; information can be found on the Internet and often it is a requirement of the contract that your manuscript be submitted on a PC compatible disk or via a service like Dropbox.

If you are submitting a hard copy, use a good-quality A4 paper. It doesn't have to be the most expensive paper but it needs to be robust enough to be handled by (potentially) several people and survive being sent in the post.

MULTIPLE SUBMISSIONS OR ONE AT A TIME?

Sarah Davies, literary agent, The Greenhouse Literary Agency

www.greenhouseliterary.com

'If I want to see more of a particular submission, I usually ask a writer to send me a complete manuscript as a Word document. So, while I am getting stacks of new submissions in as emails, I also have a shortlist of ten or so full manuscripts that I am trying to read. Of course, while you're reading the full manuscripts, another 50 or so submissions will come in. It's a tough business that operates completely differently from most "conventional" types of work. The fact is, it would be quite possible to work like crazy for a year and not sell anything. Using your time in the optimum way, focusing on absolutely the right projects, is one of the biggest challenges we face as agents.'

Ask most industry professionals and they will tell you that agents and publishers prefer to be approached one at a time. Ask an author the same question and the response is very different. An author can spend a very long time waiting for a response. If you sent your submission to 20 agents, one at a time, and waited, on average, eight weeks for a decision from each of them, you could spend over three years before you heard from the twentieth.

So, for authors, multiple submissions make sense. Opinion is divided on whether you own up to this or not. Some (mainly writers) feel that you do not have to let the agent/editor know that you are submitting to others; however, if you get a response and are asked whether anyone else is looking at your submission, you should be honest. If they are asking you that question, it shows that they have an interest in your work. Others (industry professionals) feel that it is only common courtesy to let the agent/editor know that you are approaching others.

KEEPING TRACK OF SUBMISSIONS

While one hopes that the number of submissions you make don't run into the hundreds, it makes sense to keep a record of where you sent your work, on what date you sent it out, whether you received your acknowledgement of receipt from the agent/publisher, whether it was rejected and, if so, what kind of rejection it was (a straightforward 'no thanks' letter or one with a bit of helpful advice).

 Trevor Dolby, publisher,
Preface Publishing, an imprint
of Random House
www.prefacepublishing.co.uk

'Inevitably, a lot of common sense comes into this. Do your research. Make sure you know the individual that you are going to contact; "know" in the sense that you've looked up what they've already published in the past, what their taste is and where they fit into the whole system. That's the absolute minimum that you should know. Just spraying around ideas (and proposals) willy-nilly is a waste of time. You should have your script well mapped out in your mind before you approach anyone. People want to know in a nutshell what your proposal is about. It's just like the old Hollywood 25-word pitch. Anyone who has to pitch a proposal should watch the opening scene of Altman's film The Player. *It's very funny but about right.*

'I think the pitch is also a measure of the mindset of the individual who is pitching to me. Obviously, it's important that they can write and that they have a good idea. But is it something I can pitch well in turn – in my acquisition meeting? You pitch to me, if I "get it", I can make sure everyone else around me gets it and they can sell it effectively to the retailers and, one hopes, the retailers can then sell it on to the consumer. The more crafted the package, the easier it can be passed on from one to the other and the more likely it is that you will get a publishing deal.'

The introductory or query letter

Everybody will read your query or covering letter. If you are lucky, they will go on to read your synopsis and maybe even the sample chapters, but they will *all* look at the letter. This is effectively page one of your submission.

Your covering letter needs to give a sense of who you are, your ambitions, what genre you are pitching at and a brief pitch of the book you are trying to submit. Nowadays, the writer is very much part of the package of a published book, so you need to give a sense of yourself in the letter. You should be pleasant, direct, simple and straightforward.

The letter is also a business proposal. You are hoping to sell a product to an agent/editor. You should show that you have knowledge of the company that you are writing to; do not send out a generic covering letter.

Writing a query letter is an art form in itself. You have to get quite a lot of information on to, ideally, *one page*. That can be quite a daunting thought but if you can manage to compact the following information into an interesting and enticing format, you stand a greater chance of grabbing the attention of an agent or editor.

Key idea

Think of the query letter as a shortened version of the conversation you would like to be having face to face with the agent in terms of the information you want to get across. Be businesslike and to the point.

Your letter should include the following:

- the title, subject of your book and the angle you will take
- roughly how many words it contains (see the section on 'Word count' in Chapter 4)
- why people will want to read the book
- why you are the right person to write this book (Do you have a suitable background, relevant qualifications – especially needed if you are writing non-fiction – media experience? What is interesting about you? Do you have any publishing history?)
- whether your book is the first in a series or whether you have other ideas to follow up on this one
- whether the subject matter is topical
- a benchmark against bestselling authors.

The aim is to give the key idea of your book. To do this, think of the 30-second rule. Sales reps have, at most, 30 seconds to sell a book into the shops. Anything that takes longer than that… they will have moved on to the next book.

Having a constraint on your writing can force your creativity. Try to encapsulate your book into one or two sentences. Think Twitter if you like. There is a (probably apocryphal) story that the film *Alien* was sold to Hollywood as '*Jaws* in space'. It's pithy and to the point, and you get an immediate sense of what the film is about.

 # Camilla Goslett, literary agent, Curtis Brown

www.curtisbrown.co.uk

'It's always good to have some kind of pitch (such as "It's a cross between Dan Brown and Jilly Cooper", or whatever) and an uncomplicated synopsis. You can then gauge immediately what you're reading – which is a good thing when we have around 50 unsolicited manuscripts coming in each week. When a writer is submitting, they should always look at it as if the agent was wandering round a bookshop and reading the blurb on a back of a book; that's what you're really aiming for. That immediate hook so that you know what you're in for and want to start the book.'

The title

An eye-catching title is a major part of a book's success. People spend around eight seconds looking at the cover of a book before they make a decision whether to buy it or not. If you are lucky, they spend 12 seconds reading through the blurb and the opening page. You will need to put careful thought into your title.

Shorter titles tend to do better; yes, there are exceptions to the rule (*Salmon Fishing in the Yemen*, *A Short History of Tractors in Ukrainian*, etc.) but shorter titles are more memorable.

If you are writing non-fiction, you should consider having a clear and explanatory title; many people look for books on the Internet and a title that clearly states what the book is all about (*Teach Yourself Spanish*, for example) is more likely to get picked up.

Also for non-fiction, a benefit-spelling-out strapline or subtitle that goes with your title is also helpful. Lynne Truss's book *Eats, Shoots & Leaves* had the strapline 'The Zero Tolerance Approach to Punctuation'. Good straplines will appear on Amazon and Google.

If you are still not convinced that you have the right one, put [working title] after the main title.

The author biography

The agent/editor needs to know a little bit about you. Include whether you have had anything published before (this shows you have a track record at writing), and anything that may be of interest and that can make you a saleable author. Put in any writing or public speaking experience that is relevant to the book. If you have a website or blog, put that down; that shows you are able to self-promote and potentially already have a following.

This has to be condensed into one paragraph of your covering letter. If you feel that there are other elements in your CV that are worth mentioning or expanding upon, have a separate sheet of paper.

Why are you the best author to write this book?

This is useful for the publishers to know from a publicity point of view. Do you have any endorsements? If you know a published fiction writer who has looked at your work and is prepared to say something positive about it, then use that. You have only a short time to sell yourself, so you need all the help you can get. That is not to say that you *must* have an endorsement, and positive comments from your mother, best friend or neighbour will not count either.

Do not:

- grovel, demand or gush – it's a business letter
- use capitals – this is the written equivalent of shouting
- tell the recipient that they are going to love your book / you are the best thing since Rowling/Nabokov/Cussler – you are just setting the reader up to be disappointed
- ask for feedback
- tell them what you want the cover of the book to look like
- say that your work is copyrighted or include a copyright symbol on your manuscript
- do not crack jokes – humour is subjective
- send in a photograph of yourself.

Do:

- write a coherent, enticing, professional friendly letter
- make use of paragraphs (and bullet points if you feel they help get the information over clearly and quickly)
- explain why you sent your submission to that particular agent (you liked their authors, their website, etc.) – it shows that you are interested and have done your homework on the company
- say that you will wait to hear back from them before sending it elsewhere or explain that you have sent it to x other agents but will keep them informed of any developments
- get someone to read it through for you; another pair of eyes is always useful.

THE SYNOPSIS

 ## Kate Parkin, publisher, Hodder

www.hodder.co.uk

'I would be very unlikely to take on a novelist for just one book. It's such a lot of work to develop a relationship with a new writer, to get their books to sell… you don't want to invest all that effort just one book. When I was at Random House, we published the crime writer Karin Slaughter. When her first novel turned up, it was accompanied by four or five brilliantly worked-out plots for the next books in her

proposed series. And she said she had more. It was clear that this was a completely professional and dedicated writer; she had entered her world so completely. We offered her a multi-book contract, which is extremely unusual for a first-time writer. 'It is all about confidence, about the sense that an author has stories in them, who wants to write and who has other ideas that interest them. That suggests a fertile imagination, an engagement in the craft and a willingness themselves to commit themselves to a future as a writer.'

A synopsis is not a blow-by-blow account of what happens in each chapter. A synopsis means 'a brief description of the contents of something'. It has to be detailed enough to grab the reader's attention but short enough to make them want to read more.

This is also an opportunity to show that you know your work really well; that you are in control of it, that you know how to plot its structure and that you are a good-enough writer to break it down to its component parts.

A synopsis is like the extended blurb at the back of a book but with the ending (if it is a work of fiction). This is not the place to be coy about the twist in the tail; the agent/editor needs to be able to judge the book as a whole so tell them how it ends. Equally, you do not have to list every twist and turn of the narrative. The main aim is to intrigue the reader, grab their interest and make them want to read the book.

Writing a synopsis is a skill but it is one that can be learned. If you are writing fiction, have a look at the *Oxford Companion to Literature*. There you will find a large number of brief summaries of well-known works. Also look at film reviews, which are also good examples of how to summarize a creative idea.

Key idea

Make writing a synopsis a positive experience. Show that you really know your work. Use it as an opportunity to go back, study what you have written and improve it, if necessary.

Always submit what the agency or publishing house is asking for. If they want a one-page synopsis, give them one page; if they want three, do three and so on. If you give them what they want, you reduce the annoyance factor and the chance that your submission gets put to one side before they have read it through completely.

If there is no specific guideline as to length of synopsis, then it is down to you. It depends very much on the type of book you are writing. A book on how to learn Spanish may well only take one page to get all the relevant points in, while a literary novel may take a few pages and an academic book even longer. You are aiming to get all the important points of the book in a clear, logical style.

This may, of course, mean that you have to produce several versions of your synopsis, some slightly longer than the others. This should not be a problem, though; you are a writer after all.

TIPS FOR THE SYNOPSIS (FICTION)

- The synopsis needs to be double-spaced (and printed on one side of A4 if submitted by post).
- Introduce the main characters and any other characters pivotal to the plot (but not all).
- Introduce the main plot.
- Highlight the high points.
- Sketch out where and when it is set.
- Say how it ends.
- There's no need for a chapter-by-chapter breakdown.
- Write it in the present tense, even if the book is set in the past tense.
- Say whether you have a particular format in mind. Are there illustrations?
- Indicate your target market – provide facts and figures.
- Say whether there are there tie-ins with anniversaries/special events.

TIPS FOR THE SYNOPSIS (NON-FICTION)

- The synopsis needs to be double-spaced (and printed on one side of A4 if submitted by post).
- Provide an overview of your book's central argument or theme (i.e. the subject and how you will develop it).
- Provide a table of contents.
- Give a breakdown covering the main points of each chapter (typically, no more than a paragraph per chapter); this shows you can plot the book and that you have enough material to produce a decent book on the subject.
- Indicate the competition, providing comparison with other similar books on the market.
- Say whether you have a particular format in mind. Are there illustrations?

- Indicate your target market – provide facts and figures.
- Say whether there are there tie-ins with anniversaries/special events.

Maria McCarthy, author

www.mariamccarthy.co.uk

'If you are writing non-fiction, agents and editors aren't necessarily going to know much about your subject. So what you need to do is give them an overview of it and convince them that there is room for another book on whatever your particular subject is. If you wanted to write a book about asthma, for example, you could give an idea of how many people there are in the country who suffer from asthma. By doing that, you are instantly giving the agent or publisher an idea of the potential purchasers of the book.'

MARKET POTENTIAL AND READERSHIP

It is not enough to hope that your manuscript will speak for itself – it won't. You need to present a good argument that your book will sell. Give agents and, therefore, editors, all the information they need to make a positive decision. Who is going to buy this book and why? You will have mentioned this briefly in your covering letter; now you need to expand on this.

No one will take on a book, however well written, unless they know that it is going to sell in requisite quantities. You will be describing the primary market for your book; in other words, where it is going to sell the greatest numbers. Do not rely on 'the general reader' as the person who will buy your book. The publishers need to know that there is a specific audience who are the potential buyers. There is no need to try to match your book to lots of different markets; for example, if the book is about learning to do ballroom dancing, the main audience would be people who wanted to learn to dance. You don't have to throw in young adults, people who want to lose weight, the newly retired… and any other group you think might be remotely interested in ballroom dancing.

If you believe that the book will have a substantial secondary market (an academic course or a professional organization, for example), then give the details as well. If you feel that your book will have an international audience, then say so.

THE COMPETITION

List similar titles in the marketplace. That there are other books on the same subject as yours is not a problem. Competition is a good thing. Agents and editors are often wary of books that have no competition at all; it is much more comforting to know that it fits into a recognizable genre or subject matter that has already proved successful with the buying public. What you must do is explain why your book will be different and will improve on these other competing titles.

 Key idea

If the choice is between two similar books, the agent/editor will go with the writer that has a ready-made potential readership. If you can provide information on who may buy your book, your submission will look more attractive.

ANNIVERSARIES/TIE-INS

This will not apply to every book. However, if you can link your book to an anniversary or event, then you are already providing a useful hook that could generate media interest.

Sample chapters/opening pages

 Amy Vinchesi, editor, Watson-Guptill, an imprint of Random House

www.randomhouse.com

'A big turn-off is a proposal that is sloppy, incomplete, poorly assembled, and hasn't been proofread/copy-edited; if I see tons of spelling mistakes or it's poorly written, it's an immediate rejection.'

The first chapter is always important in a book. But so is the first paragraph and the first sentence. The first page of a novel should be brilliant if it is to jump off the slush pile.

The reader, in this instance the agent or the publisher, will want the interest that they felt on reading your covering letter and synopsis to be underlined. These chapters will show the quality of your writing.

You need to grab the attention and interest of your reader from the start. It's no good if the story really gets going by Chapter 5 – if that's the case, maybe you should consider getting rid of chapters 1 to 4.

SOME TIPS FOR SAMPLE CHAPTERS

- Chapters should start on a new page.
- Justify the left-hand side of the text only.
- Don't use blank lines between paragraphs; instead, indent the first line of each new paragraph (except the first in a chapter or section). Blank lines should be used for a change of subject, or time, or scene or viewpoint.
- Use spellings, capitalization, subheadings and so on consistently. For example, decide whether you're using '-ise' or '-ize' verbal forms.
- Organize the pages (publishers call them folios) – number them straight through from beginning to end; don't start each chapter with page 1.
- Put your name and the title of your book on each page – use the 'header' or 'footer' option and use a small type size.
- For poetry, present your poems in exactly the way they would appear in the printed version.
- Illustrations/diagrams – if your work requires illustrations, maps or diagrams and you expect to provide them yourself, include a selection with your sample chapters. You could send a rough copy/example with your submission, rather than spend time and money on high-quality originals (which run the risk of getting lost while out with an agent/editor). Unless your book is about photography, you would want to give an *idea* of the quality; copies will be fine for that.

Sarah Davies, Literary Agent, The Greenhouse Literary Agency

www.greenhouseliterary.com

'I think an important tip for anyone who wants to get published is always to go to the agency website. All too often writers submit work that is outside our interests and specialisms – for example, age groups or genres we just *don't represent. This is something that drives all agents mad. Aspiring writers need to take time and trouble to target their work correctly. And it makes me tear my hair out because it means that around 15 per cent of material that comes in is simply not relevant to me and that is such a huge time-waster.*

'When I receive material that just isn't for Greenhouse, I often write back to the sender to enquire where they read about us, with the aim of getting that listing removed or corrected. Usually the answer is: "Oops, sorry, my fault. I misread the information."

'So one thing I would say to aspiring writers is do your homework, go straight to the website for up-to-the-minute instructions because agencies' submission guidelines are subject to change and you want to make sure you don't waste either your time or theirs.'

DOS AND DON'TS

Don't:

- send a synopsis without sample chapters and vice versa
- try to stand out by using coloured paper or coloured text
- use italics or comedy fonts
- use fancy folders, ring binders or plastic folders (too slippery)
- try to be gimmicky; you are aiming for 'professional', not wacky
- condense your text
- staple your work together (it's difficult to read stapled pages) – similarly, don't use paperclips (too easy to pick up extra pages that don't belong to the manuscript when it's been lying on a desk) or pins (they can draw blood)
- try to catch agents/editors out by putting in a trap to check that they have actually read through the submission
- be tempted to stray too far from these layouts – they are used because they work, are easy to read and work for agents and publishers
- suggest your own illustrator – agents/editors like to choose their own so this could put them off
- produce a mock-up of the book.

Do:

- print on one side of the paper
- leave a decent margin (at least 4 centimetres/1½ inches all around text) – editors need the space to make corrections, amendments and instructions to the printer.

- use 12-point type and a font that's easy to read (e.g. Arial, Times); use black ink
- indent the first line of each paragraph
- make sure the pages have printed straight
- have a title page with your contact details (i.e. your name or pen name, your address) in the bottom right-hand corner
- use a couple of rubber bands to bind your papers together
- put the pages into a wallet-type folder (more than one if necessary)
- put the title of the book and your name and address on the outside of folder.

A proposal should be no more than 20 pages long; that is short enough to speed-read but long enough to get an idea of the writer's style and the book's potential.

When you have finished your letter and got your chapters and synopsis ready, print them all off and then read them through again before sending them out. Proofreading off a printed page is very different from reading from a screen.

Key idea

When proofreading, read from the bottom of the page up, a line at a time. Cover up the lines that you have checked as you work up the page. This helps to pick out any typos or spelling errors that you might miss if you read the text conventionally.

Checklist

Before you send anything out, go through the following checklist:
- People's names are spelt correctly. Check *everything* is spelt correctly. If you don't get it right, it doesn't give the reader a feeling of trust and confidence in the writer. ☐
- Grammar, punctuation, syntax are all correct. ☐
- Your covering letter is businesslike and gets to the point. ☐
- The presentation is clean and professional. ☐
- You have a copy of your submission letter, your sample chapters and your synopsis – don't send your only copy. ☐

The closer you get to sending your proposal out, the harder it is to let it go. But it has to go out at some point. Get it to the best standard you can and then send it on its way.

 ## Camilla Goslett, literary agent, Curtis Brown

www.curtisbrown.co.uk

'As an agent, you have to be very straight with people and I think writers appreciate that. If you do believe something is terrible, you've just got to say that you don't think it's working and give your reasons why. It's up to the writer to take that away and either agree with you and see that you've got a point or fight for what they believe in. I think anyone appreciates honesty. Ultimately, you have to get on with each other; you have to like your authors or admire them in some way. This has to work as a relationship because, hopefully, it's one that's going to last for quite a long time; if all goes well it can last decades.'

Case study: Isabel Losada

New Habits (Hodder), *The Battersea Park Road to Enlightenment* (Bloomsbury), *For Tibet with Love: A Beginner's Guide to Changing the World* (Bloomsbury), *100 Reasons To Be Glad* (Summersdale), *Men! Where the **** are they?* (Virgin – Random House), *The Battersea Park Road to Paradise* (Watkins)

www.isabellosada.com

'I'd once edited a book but now I had one that I was writing myself. The compulsory first three chapters were finished and I started to write to agents with what has since been called "misguided eternal optimism". You can imagine my excitement when I was taken on by an enthusiastic agent at one of the three top London literary agencies. She was fantastically positive about the book I was writing (*The Battersea Park Road to Enlightenment*); experienced in the business, and was interested not only in selling the book but also in helping me make it as good as possible. I very quickly came to adore her.

'I had just submitted Chapter 6, the "Tantric Sex" chapter, when she called me in for a meeting. She closed the door and told me she had been fired by the agency because she hadn't been turning over profit quickly enough. I was stunned; halfway through the book and I didn't have an agent any more. I approached practically every other agent in London, none of whom were interested. So I went back to the umbrella company of the first agency and said, "It's not my fault you fired this agent. Don't you have an obligation to represent me?"'

'They agreed and one of the other agents took me on. She was very old school in that she submitted to one publishing house at a time and told me, "Under no circumstances do I ever follow up the submission in any way; I wait for them to get back to me." This method is very respectful of the publishing houses but makes the poor author contemplate their old age pension.

'I think she submitted my book in various forms to practically every single publishing house in London. But because she wouldn't let me speak to any of them, I had no idea why it was being rejected. "They said it wasn't for them," she'd say if I enquired.

'After 18 months of this and with about 18 rejections from publishing houses, she told me to give up, "Put it down to experience; put the book aside and good luck with life." She showed me the door. I still had a book that, bizarrely perhaps, I was convinced that everybody would want to read but I seemed to be alone in this view since I now had no publisher, no agent and enough rejection letters to form a collection. However I found there were advantages to *not* having an agent too. Freed from the shackles of representation, I was able to phone all the editors that had rejected the book and find out why they had turned it down.

'I discovered that, first of all, they remembered the title, then they remembered the content; they were very complimentary about my writing and usually the book had got as far as the editorial meeting. I had known nothing of this when I was with an agent as I had been forbidden to speak to any of the editors.

'I managed to get all the various rejection letters sent through to me and what I noticed is that they all contradicted each other. For example:

'*Rejection A:* "We absolutely loved this book but we felt that the author should have inserted more information about the various subjects that she explored."

'*Rejection B:* "We absolutely loved this book but we felt that the author had included too much information and not enough personal narrative."

'*Rejection C:* "We found that there was too much personal narrative in this book and that she really needed to concentrate on varying the ending of her book."

'*Rejection D:* "We felt that, although she was a wonderful authorial voice, this would be more suitable as a series of magazine articles."

'All this was completely contradictory and left me feeling completely bewildered. I thought: "Right, I need to get myself another agent." But obviously that was difficult because I'd already had rejections from every publishing house in London and no agent will take on a book that everybody has already turned down.

'So I took myself off to the London Book Fair whereby, if you are blessed with the gift of the gab, you can manage to get yourself into areas where authors are not supposed to be... which I did. I met two fabulous agents, both of whom invited me to send them my manuscript, both of whom read the manuscript, asked me who had rejected it and showed me the door again when I was honest about where it had been submitted. Agents obviously don't like something that's already been touted round.

'I set about going back to the 18 publishing houses that had turned it down, resubmitting it myself. If it had been submitted as one chapter, I submitted the whole book; if it had been submitted as a whole book, I submitted one chapter. Basically, I did the opposite of what had been done previously. Eventually, some unknown reader at Bloomsbury read it and got excited. She split up the chapters and passed it around and then everyone got excited, they interviewed me and eventually sent a large bunch of flowers and an offer. They were one of the publishers that had originally rejected the book. But I didn't remind them. I went back to one of the agents, told them I'd got the deal and, unsurprisingly as I had an offer in my hand, they were then willing to take me on.

'It was about two years from the time that I had finished writing the book until I eventually had a publishing deal and an agent but it had been a long hard slog and the really hard work starts at that point.

'One of the problems with my book is that the category was something like "narrative non-fiction – semi-autobiographical humour MBS [mind, body, spirit] and travel". This doesn't help. If I'd give one tip now it would be that, before you even start writing your book, you should go into the bookshop and work out where it's going to be found. If it's not fiction, you may have a problem. And if you've written something really original, then you've definitely got a problem. Books have got to go on a shelf somewhere, but if you've written something that is difficult to put in a category then it's also difficult to market.

'Much as I would love a shelf, in a bookshop, which specifically says "Best selling works by Isabel Losada", I have to rely on my books being put in among other subjects. My books have appeared in "Religion", "Travel", "Popular Psychology", "Mind, Body, Spirit" and "Biography"; they've also appeared (misplaced) in "Fiction". They've literally appeared all over the shop and that has been a huge problem. In fact, one of my titles was so lost in one of the sections, it was retitled; it then appeared in "Philosophy" where it disappeared altogether. So my first advice to prospective authors is to write fiction. OK, if you're not a fiction writer, make sure which part of a shop your books are going to go into. My second piece of advice is persistence – joy, persistence – joy, persistence – joy, persistence – joy…

'If you are *sure* your book is going to sell (because you know who to and why), then you can persevere. One of my inspirations was that I'd read that *Jonathan Livingstone Seagull* had been turned down 98 times; so at 18 rejections I felt I was just starting. In the end, the book that no one wanted did fantastically well. It earned out the advance before publication and went on to sell 100,000 copies and be published in 16 languages.

'Selling subsequent books has not been easier… but that's another story.'

Focus points

- Explain why you have targeted a particular agency or publishing house; it shows that you have done your homework and have an interest in what they do.
- The first instinct of an agent or publisher will be to reject your work so you need to stand out and show them that they can make money from you. Literary agents will only take on a manuscript that they feel passionate about. If they don't have strong feelings for it, it makes it very difficult for them to go on to sell it.
- The covering letter has to convince an agent/editor that this is a person they want to work with. Try reading the letter back to yourself, pretending that you don't know this person. Do you like what you see? Are you intrigued?

Next step

You have worked out whom to approach and worked hard on your covering letter and synopsis. You sent in your submission two months ago and you haven't heard a thing. What should you do? The next chapter looks at persistence and rejection, and how to deal with and learn from them.

3

Persistence

'It is impossible to discourage the real writers – they don't give a damn what you say, they're going to write.'
Sinclair Lewis

Joanna Trollope once said it had taken her 20 years to become an overnight success. She stuck at her writing and refused to give up. Successfully published authors are resilient and tenacious. Many writers have had a great book but it was the wrong time for it; others have had bad books but the timing was just right. Things can go wrong for a variety of reasons but these writers just kept plugging away. You need to have these qualities to survive as an author.

This will not be a fast process. It takes time. Even when you get taken on by an agent and editor, the wheels of the publishing industry grind rather slowly. It *is* frustrating but be prepared to wait for a decision.

While you are waiting for people to get back to you, start working on your next project. It could be an article for the local magazine or newspaper; it might be the outline for your next book. Whatever it is, don't waste time and energy worrying about what is happening to your submission; channel it into something positive.

 ## Sarah Davies, literary agent, The Greenhouse Literary Agency

www.greenhouseliterary.com

'Don't bombard an agent. There's a kind of etiquette here; you send your very best work, and if you are rejected, you don't immediately go back with another one. If you are rejected, you might ask, 'In the future, would you be interested in reading something else?' You certainly shouldn't swamp agents with multiple submissions.

'Never write back to an agent on rejection and say, "That's your loss!" as I have had some people do. Do not write to an agent, telling them you are brilliant or how exactly like Tolkien or Philip Pullman you are because you are setting yourself up to for a disappoint. Just set out your stall clearly and simply and let your writing do your work for you – because it all comes down to the writing in the end.'

 ## Key idea

The larger the agency or publishing house, the more people there are who may have to be convinced to take on you and your book.

On average, the wait for a response is around two to three months; some companies will take longer though. You should be polite and allow the agent/editor enough time to get to your submission and read it through; after all, they have busy jobs, working with their existing authors, and the slush pile can be quite large. Equally, if you have been waiting for a long time, it is perfectly reasonable to either ask for your submission back (if you want it returned) or explain that you will be approaching other companies from now on (even if you have sent your submission out to more than one company).

Agents and editors do receive a tremendous amount of unsolicited work every week (it is not unusual for some of the larger agencies to get over 1,300 submissions each month). They work hard to keep on top of the slush pile. However, it is important to remember that just reading through unsolicited submissions is not their main job; they have many more pressing concerns, not least the authors they already represent. It is also worth realizing how courteous agents and editors are; they actually bother to write back when it would be much easier to just bin the submissions they don't like without even contacting the people who sent them in.

BE PREPARED FOR REJECTION

Writing comes with a price – rejection. *Every* writer gets rejected at some point. If you meet an author who claims that they have never had a rejection, they are either the most extraordinary exception to the rule or they are not being entirely truthful with you. You may have read of the (now) famous authors whose work was rejected time and time again, among them Beatrix Potter, George Orwell and Agatha Christie. C.S. Lewis received over 800 rejections before he sold any of his writing; *Zen and the Art of Motorcycle Maintenance* was rejected 121 times; while the *San Francisco Examiner* rejected Rudyard Kipling's submission in 1889, explaining that they were sorry but 'You just do not know how to use the English language.' Rejections are not pleasant but they will not kill you and you can learn from them.

It is not known whether D.H. Lawrence learned from Heinemann's rejection of *Sons and Lovers* in 1912 because its 'want of reticence makes it unfit… for publication in England'. Lawrence was not happy and wrote back: 'Curse the blasted, jelly-boned swines, the slimy, the belly-wriggling invertebrates… the snivelling, dribbling, dithering, palsied, pulseless lot that make up England today.'

At least Lawrence was given a reason why they turned his manuscript down. Other authors are not as lucky. Don't expect to be given reasons for rejection. If there are any complements (or criticisms) about your work – take them at face value. Editors and agents tend not to give praise if they don't mean it. If they have taken the time and trouble to give an indication of what they think about your work (even if it is a fairly negative comment), take it as a good sign. It is easier and quicker to send out a standard 'thank you but no thank you' letter; anything else is a positive. If there is advice that comes with rejection, take it and learn from it. Don't send an angry or sarcastic letter/email back. Publishing is a small world and word will get round if you are abusive and unhelpful.

Equally, if you have had a rejected submission:

- do not keep resubmitting it in its 'improved' version to the same agent/editor – unless specifically asked to do so
- don't phone up asking to discuss your book
- do not use the phrases from one rejection letter in your approach to another agent/editor (for example, 'my book did not fit the list at Curtis Brown') – phrases such as 'does not fit our list' are conventional
- give yourself a bit of time to feel demoralized, miserable and unwanted, and then pull yourself together and do something positive with your book.

Reasons for rejection

In practical terms, literary agencies and publishing houses have to turn down most of what is sent to them; partly because they would not be able to take on 50 or 60 new authors each week. And partly because they are trying to peer into the future a year or two ahead and guess what will be selling in the book world then – and they do not always get it right.

A rejection is not personal. It is an *individual* reader's response to what you sent in to them at that time. Generally, manuscripts are turned down because they are not what *one* person is looking for at that *particular* moment.

 Key idea

Give distance to the rejection before you do anything about it. Read your manuscript in a different place from where you wrote it. This gives you some perspective.

If you realize that rejection is part of the job, how you deal with it can become a positive and enriching experience. One writer no longer uses the word 'rejection'; she calls them 'remarketing opportunities'. Try not to dwell on the negativity of the rejection. Treat it as a red alert, warning you that something is not quite right yet.

So try to work out why you didn't succeed. Read between the lines of the rejection; it is not easy if you have had a 'thanks but no thanks' response but ask yourself the following:

- Was it *really* the best it could be in every way?
- Were all the facts (contact details etc.) correct?

- Did you check that the agency/publisher was taking unsolicited submissions?
- Was your presentation professional, clean and tidy?
- Was your pitch strong enough?
- Had you researched the market properly?
- Were there any spelling mistakes and were the grammar and punctuation spot on?

Doug Young, publishing director, Sport & Entertainment, Transworld

www.transworldbooks.co.uk

'It is important to do your research about the publishing company. If an author comes in and says they don't know anything about Random House, I think that a) their agent hasn't done a very good job of preparing them and b) I'm not impressed that they have made no effort themselves. It's a bit like a job interview really. If someone goes for an interview and hasn't bothered to do any research about the company, it always strikes me as a bit odd.'

It is not necessarily that your writing is not good enough. It could be that your work was just too similar to an author's the agent or publisher already has on its books. Why would they want something identical to a book they have just sold? If they tell you that they already have a similar author on their list, you should be greatly encouraged by that. It means that they can see potential in your work.

It may be that your work is not right for the market right now. Publishing houses will not be buying the kind of books that are currently in the bestseller lists; they will be looking for something different. You have to be original and write from your heart. Agents and editors can tell when you are writing what you love or feel strongly about.

If they said they enjoyed reading your submission but they just didn't feel strongly about it, again, you should feel encouraged. Maybe your work just didn't 'speak' to that person. There is no point in an agent representing an author whose books they do not like. They need to feel passionate about a book in order to sell it. It is very much about individual tastes and preferences. If one person didn't like it, another may love it.

If they said that the plot didn't engage them or that they found it hard-going, or slow or any similar comment, then you really need to do a rewrite.

It may be that you have written something good but that it is not the right book to launch your career as a published author. Helen Corner (Cornerstones Literary Consultancy) refers to this in greater detail later in this chapter. It is very easy to think of your current work as the best thing you have ever done but it may be the book that helps you develop as a writer – in which case, it was not a waste of time. You may need to consider putting it to one side and begin to work up your next project.

So, take a long hard look at what you sent out, be prepared to rework it and send it out again or put it aside and start anew. Agents and editors tend not to want to work with writers who may have a book in them but it is just not there yet. They want as near to the finished article as possible. Michael Ridpath wrote and rewrote his first thriller, *Free to Trade*, three times before he sent out a synopsis to agents. It was picked up by literary agent Carole Blake, who got five publishing houses bidding for it in an auction (won by Heinemann for a six-figure deal) and sold the rights in 35 territories.

Key idea

Good writers of great books get rejected – many times. Even when they are published, they will get their fair share of bad reviews. Rejection goes hand in hand with success.

Know your craft

Heather Holden Brown, literary agent, hhb Agency Ltd

hhbagency.com

'Writing is terribly hard and lonely and authors have to be highly disciplined. They have to write regularly and, in order to get it "to market" (whether that means to literary agents or publishing houses), writers have to totally absorb themselves in their work. The authors that are getting work accepted by publishers are sometimes doing six, seven, even eight drafts of their book to get it to a high-enough standard.'

Writing is a craft and something that you can learn about and improve on all the time. Reading, whether books that are similar to yours or not, also helps to format the shape of your work in your head. What worked for you? What didn't work? Learn what makes them successful – or not.

The other books in the Creative Writing series are full of advice on technique and crafting your work. Understand that one of the joys of being a writer is that you cannot write the perfect book, so you are always learning. And if you are learning, you are improving. Never be complacent about your work and never stop learning.

Being your own editor

Helen Corner, Cornerstones Literary Consultancy

www.cornerstones.co.uk

'For first-time writers in particular, self-editing is an imperative part of writing a book that is often overlooked when they first start out. It can be a labour-intensive and lengthy process but as long as the author feels like they're improving and we see that they're improving, then it's a worthwhile and rewarding thing to do.'

Whether you are still working on getting your book accepted by an agent or editor, or you have been picked up by someone, you need to develop your skills as your own editor. Of course, you will get help when your book is picked up by an agent/editor. Many literary agents will work with their authors to shape their work, especially to help them turn a good idea into a great commercial idea. Equally, editors will work with writers to edit their work. But you need to get your work in the best shape it can be, whether you are putting it in front of agents/editors for consideration or you have been asked to rework something.

There is no such thing as a bad first draft – it is *first* a draft. The good thing is that you've actually put your words down in some shape and form. Now you can begin to work on it to improve it. Writing and editing are two very different skills and are best kept separate; don't try to edit while you write your first draft and vice versa.

Key idea

When you are editing your work, pretend it is someone else's. Break your editing into 20- to 30-minute sessions.

Network

Children's Editorial Group, HarperCollins US

www.harpercollins.com

'We do expect authors to revise their own manuscript on their own and get it into the best shape they possibly can before seeking publication – writing and critique groups can be an invaluable resource for that type of revision.'

Writing is very solitary but you need people to become a better writer. Listen and observe others; look at things from different angles, be aware of other beliefs and soak up ideas. Don't spend all your time sitting in front of your computer or scribbling in your notebooks.

One way to get out and meet people is to attend literary festivals and writers' groups. Not only do you learn about the craft of writing but you can meet agents and editors, learn about the publishing industry, exchange news, information and advice with like-minded people. Your name starts to become known to people, both within the industry and with the reading public. It is much easier and more effective to start a query letter with 'We met at the such and such festival/fair…'

TIPS FOR NETWORKING

- **Attend writers' groups/workshops:** you will meet like-minded people who understand what you are about.
- **Join associations and societies:** such as the Romantic Novelists' Association, the Society of Authors, the Authors Guild. Katie Fforde, for example, found her agent while she was on the New Writers' Scheme of the Romantic Novelists' Association.
- **Enrol on creative writing courses:** Ian McEwan was one of the first writers on the University of East Anglia's MA course on creative writing, run by Malcolm Bradbury and Angus Wilson. Marina Lewycka's first novel, *A Short History of Tractors in Ukrainian*,

was picked by a literary agent when she did a course at Sheffield Hallam University. Going on a writing course is not necessarily a short cut to getting published, but you will meet like-minded people and being in a creative atmosphere is extremely stimulating.

- **Writing in any format** (blog, local paper, articles) puts your name in front of people.
- **Offer to give talks or interviews** on local radio or television programmes; again, your name is becoming known as a writer to a wider circle.

Feedback

Katherine T. Owen, self-published author of *It's OK to Believe*

'Be very clear about what you are asking of a friend when they read your manuscript. Proofreading is work – you are asking them to draw back from the content to look for typos and grammatical errors and so on. It is a much lesser task to say: "Here's the introduction – can you give me a first impression? Do you think it makes an impact? Does it represent my work in the right way?" You'll have friends who have different levels of interest in the content of your book, and different strengths when it comes to appraising your work, so use them accordingly.'

Most authors lead a rather solitary existence when they are writing so it can be helpful to look outside of your study, shed or garret and get the opinions of others. Ideally, get someone whose judgement you trust and who is interested in and appreciates writing. You could ask another writer; it can help if their work is different from yours, rather than being in direct competition. Be specific about what you want from this person. Ask them:

- Where do you think it is good?
- Where do you think it is bad?
- Where do you think it is slow?

If you have asked someone for feedback, make sure that they actually do get back to you with their comments within a reasonable period of time. It may help to put it on a slightly more businesslike footing. Rather than asking them to comment on your work as a favour, offer them a bottle of wine or a meal. Make it a business transaction.

If writing for children, offer to give a reading at a school or library:

- Did you hold the children's attention?
- Did they understand the language?
- Have you pitched it at the right age group?

If you would prefer not to use your friends, you could try 'crowd-editing'. Platforms such as wattpad.com allow writers to produce their work in public online and get live feedback on what they have written.

As with any feedback, what you choose to do with it is up to you. You can ignore it, disagree with it or take it on board and review your work. Just don't get so much feedback that you begin to drown in it!

 ## Maria McCarthy, author

www.mariamccarthy.co.uk

'The usefulness of writer's groups? It depends. If you just want to write as a hobby, then writers' groups can be great. I think it's very important to be clear in your mind whether you are doing it as a hobby or you want publication. If it's the latter, writers' groups can sometimes throw you off course; I've heard of people writing far too much to please their group rather than being true to themselves and keeping commercial focus.'

 ## Key idea

When rewriting, read your work out loud. Rewrite if you find it difficult to read or stumble over words; it will be just as difficult for a reader.

Literary consultants

 ## Bryony Pearce, author

www.bryonypearce.co.uk

'Nowadays I think the literary consultancy is another useful step, a way of winnowing the wheat from the chaff for the agents. There are so many manuscripts around that a third step is needed

and the literary consultancy helps you get your work right before you send it to the agent. I think it is money well spent. If you're really confident in your book, then yes, you could send it out straight to agents and publishers because you never know – it might just fall on the right desk at the right time and get bought without you having to spend the money. But after that first round of almost inevitable rejection, it is worth sending it to a consultancy and spending a bit of money. If you're serious about it. Anyway, the learning process is half the fun of it, isn't it?'

A literary consultant will assess and give feedback on a writer's manuscript for a fee. Choose your literary consultant carefully. It would be very easy to take a writer's money even though their work really has no hope of ever getting published. Literary consultancies should, like an agent, be there to help you make money (i.e. sell your work) rather than just take your money. Writers' forums, word of mouth and agent referrals are a good way of finding a good literary agency.

The following have all been rated by agents and editors as offering reputable service:

- Cornerstones (www.cornerstones.co.uk)
- Hilary Johnson (www.hilaryjohnson.demon.co.uk)
- The Literary Consultancy (www.literaryconsultancy.co.uk)
- The Writer's Journey (www.juliamccutchen.com).

Helen Corner, Cornerstones Literary Consultancy

www.cornerstones.co.uk

'We only take on writers we feel we can work with. I can't imagine doing it any other way. Two reasons: one, writers are often at the creative writing stage, even if they are talented, and to receive feedback too early can be damaging. So we like to work with writers who are at self-edit stage. The second reason is that there are raw manuscripts out there. If we took on everything, we wouldn't keep our readers and it would end up being vanity editing. We have quite a strong policy about that.

'First port of call is for an author to contact us. We look at their first chapter and synopsis, and see what stage they're at.

We then either take them on or suggest an alternative route, perhaps a creative writing course or something like that.

'If, having looked at their material, we do want to take them on we then figure out the best service which might be a report, workshop or brainstorming session. For instance, we may recommend a general report if they're pretty much at a high standard already. Or, if we think they need more, we'll put their work through a more detailed editorial process.

'We are always hungry to see new talent and we ask our readers to flag up manuscripts with real potential. We have an internal grading system and if one of our editors gives a manuscript the thumbs up, we will let the author know that, following revision, we would like to consider submitting it to agents. Then my colleague, Kathryn Robinson, and I will look at the first 50 pages and if we like what we see call in the whole MS [manuscript]. If we love it, we'll then work with the author at no charge for however long it takes – assuming the author can follow our editorial direction (and the best writers take it one step beyond).

'If the MS is at a high standard already we can move quickly. One of our authors, Ava McCarthy, The Insider, we placed with an agent within a week, and the agent got a sizeable publishing deal two weeks later. Another author, Sarwat Chadda, The Devil's Kiss, we worked with for a year or so before we got him an agent and who then got a transatlantic publishing deal. When we work with authors with a view to passing them through to agents, we don't charge them for our time or contacts but we do receive a one-off 10-per-cent fee on the initial worldwide advance (so no ongoing royalties or subsidiary rights).

'Because we don't charge agents to take on our authors, they are generally open to looking at our authors' work, they give us a quick turnaround, and we often get more feedback than an author would if they submitted their own work. We sometimes end up working together – author, agent and us – which is an enjoyable process.

'I suppose you could call us an agents' agent, in terms of filtering and passing new talent to them that's already been shaped to a high standard. However, an important part of our job is to manage an author's expectations and they're primarily coming to us to learn how to shape and self-edit their MS – a vital writing skill that can be taught. But no one should come to us expecting to pay for a fast route to getting published.

'When I first set up, there was one other literary consultancy. Then, more started springing up: freelance consultants with a small number of readers, and some companies like ours, so yes, it is becoming a firmer, more established rung in the publishing industry. As far as I know we're the only consultancy to have a filter system but where we still provide feedback on the opening pages even if we don't take on an author. We're all about teaching authors the skills to edit their own work and have spent years dissecting the components of great writing; we run specialist workshops on how to self-edit and submit and our book, Write a Blockbuster and Get It Published (Hodder), is based on these.

'Authors should be wary of any company that seems like it's not a personalized service, or where pound signs speak louder than anything else, usually in the £1,000s. That's why word-of-mouth recommendation – via an agent, publisher, writer's forum or community or writing magazines – is a good indication of a reliable company; if in any doubt, contact the Society of Authors.

'A good literary consultancy is all about finding the right route for an author. It depends what stage they are at with their writing; whether it is even the right book to launch them. It can be hard to say to an author that the book they've been working on for years doesn't seem to be improving and the best solution is to put it to one side and start a new one. It's important to work out which book should launch an author especially with the unforgiving EPOS (electronic point of sale) system. If a first book doesn't sell that well, it can damage an author's career before it's even begun. No book is ever a waste of time, though, and every draft should take an author's writing to the next stage. It's a bitter-sweet moment when an author no longer needs us, but ultimately we're all striving for the same thing, which is publication and ongoing success.'

The first meeting with the agent

Sarah Davies, literary agent, The Greenhouse Literary Agency

www.greenhouseliterary.com

'Quite often, there is one agent who will just stand out for you because they want you from the start – it's like a match made

> *in heaven. I would say it has to be someone you feel
> comfortable with. You need someone for whom you have a
> respect, a mutual respect, and a liking; where you know from
> their reputation that they do good deals and that they work
> hard for their authors; that they're energetic and that they
> have the kind of profile that you feel comfortable with.*
>
> *'It's got to be somebody you like – a kind of chemistry – so
> that you will enjoy working with this individual for a long
> period of time; I think that's very important.'*

Let us assume that you have reached the stage where all your hard work has paid off and an agent that you have approached contacts you and asks for a meeting.

What questions should you ask an agent?

If an agent shows interest in representing you and wants to meet, don't get so excited or grateful that you forget to ask the agent some questions of your own. They will not be offended; again, it shows that you have thought things through and done your homework. This is a business relationship primarily and you want to make sure that the person handling the business of getting you into print knows what they are doing and offers the kind of service you expect:

- How long has the agent been in business?
- Is the agent a member of the Association of Authors' Agents (UK) / Association of Authors' Representatives (US)?
- Do they have specialists in foreign rights?
- Do they have specialists for movie and television rights?
- Will the agent handle your work personally?
- Do they do editorial work or are they specialists in contracts and negotiation? Or do they do both?
- How closely will the agent keep in touch with the author regarding work being done on their behalf?
- Is there a standard agent–author agreement?
- Will the agent consult with you on any and all offers?
- If you should part company, what is the policy for handling any unsold subsidiary rights?

The agent will be looking at you as a person. Agents and editors are no different from the rest of us; they want to work with people who are going to be nice to deal with. Is this author going to be able to cope when they get setbacks? How are they going to act when they get successful?

Some agents often encourage an author to meet another agent because they feel it is important that the author has chosen them because they feel they can work together. Some authors choose their agents because they feel a bit scared of them; believing that if they are tough with them, they will be tough with publishers. Others have been known to pick their agent because they wanted to be able to have regular face-to-face meetings and so went with agents that were based near where they lived.

Remember that the agent ultimately works *for* you; they act on your behalf. They are experts who know the business, will have contacts with editors and publishing houses and who can work with you on your book to turn it into something special. But they can also be guided by you. This first meeting is your opportunity to ask questions, find out what they can do for you, who their contacts are (they should have a strong list of editorial contacts), what strategy they propose for your work. If you feel that the agent shares your vision of your work, that they will champion your book for you, that is a good sign.

Camilla Goslett, literary agent, Curtis Brown

www.curtisbrown.co.uk

'If you get an offer and you've met the agent and you've got on with them, why not go with them? You don't know if your manuscript is still sitting on the other slush piles. You've got to go with a gut feeling but if you've got someone who is willing to work with you, has got the contacts and knows how to represent their authors, what are you waiting for? It's the authors who realize that they are very hot property with several agents keen to represent them who can sit back and wait.'

When you do find an agent, you will sign an author–agent agreement. This will set out:

- the commission the agent will charge for the different sales of rights
- the rights the agent will handle
- the money that will be charged (be wary of agents who charge for editorial services)
- how the agreement can be ended (there is usually a set period of notice).

Some agents will offer editorial feedback. Work with them. An agent, particularly for a first book, is an author's creative ally. If you get editorial feedback from your agent, do not dismiss it out of hand. You have the right, as the author, to reject any editorial suggestions or revisions but remember that the agent knows the marketplace. They have taken you on because they feel your work will sell; but that does not mean that your work is currently perfectly formed and ready to go. Many agents are former editors and understand what makes a book work; they can take something that has promise and help you turn it into something quite special.

The first contact with the editor

 ## Kate Parkin, publisher, Hodder
www.hodder.co.uk

'The author is very important because getting a book published is a long and quite intimate process. As an editor, you have to feel that you can work with an author; that they are going to be reasonable, helpful and supportive because there will be a lot of things they will be asked to do to support publication of their book. I think you also have to feel that the author has a very clear vision of what they're writing and for whom. It's an intensely collaborative process. It is all about trying to do the best, most positive job possible.'

When your agent is happy with the manuscript, they will submit your work to a commissioning editor at a publishing house. Some editors have the seniority and expertise to be able to get the whole publishing house team on their side and take on a book pretty much on their say so; while other more junior editors, with slightly less experience, may have to solicit support from their colleagues (in sales, marketing and publicity, and so on) before going into the acquisition meeting (editorial committee, publishing meeting – the name is slightly different depending on the publishing house). You can have as many as eight different readers at a publishing house considering a proposal.

Heather Holden Brown, Literary Agent, hhb Agency Ltd

hhbagency.com

'I wouldn't submit to publishers and editors that I'm not happy for the author to end up with. What you're talking about is the potential relationship the publishing house has with the author, the culture of the company, how they handle their backlist and the strength of their sales and marketing. It's a gut feeling too. I always like to take an author for a meeting in the offices of an editor/publisher because it's like going to someone's house. You get a nice feeling (or not) about them. It's the same; it's instinctive.'

It is at this point that the publishing house will look at the book's format, the market for the book, what the competition is, when the book could be published. There may be a reader's report to consider. Financial considerations will be looked at: such as the expected sales revenue, how much it will be to cost the book, what the hoped for profit margin will be if the book sells out.

There is a lot to be thought about. This is why it is important that you consider your book from a business point of view – that's what the publishing house will be doing when they are deciding whether to take you on or not. Your book may get rejected at this point – either an outright rejection or the editor may suggest changes before it is resubmitted.

Accepting a publishing house

Trevor Dolby, publisher, Preface Publishing, an imprint of Random House

www.prefacepublishing.co.uk

'When authors come in, I want them to be knowledgeable and ebullient; know how they want to present themselves; what it is that they've got to offer. Are they articulate? Do they fit the image that the book wants to portray (if it's a book about

grooming, for example, you don't want them looking like a badly tied parcel)? We took on a travel writer who knows more about the history of travel writing over the last 50 years than anyone I've ever met; he's read everything; he's got first editions of everything so he's steeped in that subject. And because he's so knowledgeable, there's probably another book in him. He talked articulately about where he felt his book fitted into that particular genre. So, for the editor, there's a confidence that you've got a real author.

'We're not looking for books; by and large, we want authors. I'm looking for people I want to be working with in ten years' time. I'm not suggesting that authors come to the meeting armed with another five ideas. What they need to do is convince me that they're serious about this business; that this is not just one good idea that they've stumbled in on. I still may commission one good idea, of course, but it's not guaranteed.'

If the book is accepted, the publisher will make an offer to the author and/or the agent if the author has one. While any author will no doubt be thrilled to be taken on by a publisher, it is important that they are happy with what the publisher is proposing.

The aim is for both parties to get a good deal. If you have an agent, they will do the negotiation for you. If you are dealing with the publisher directly, you should expect to discuss:

- the advance – how much is it?
- when it is paid
- the timescale for delivery of the manuscript
- the rights the publisher wants to retain
- whether the subsidiary rights are set against the advance you will be paid.

Let's look at these a bit more closely:

- **The advance:** the larger the advance, the longer it takes to start earning royalties but that may not necessarily be important to you. If you do not feel that the advance is reasonable, you can always ask if it can be increased.
- **Payment:** the advance will be paid in stages (signature of contract, delivery of manuscript, on publication). Some publishers prefer to divide the payments into quarters, with the final payment on publication of the paperback version. You can ask that payments are made up to publication, rather than afterwards.

- **Timescale:** you know your schedule and what is realistic. Publishers always want the manuscript as soon as possible; authors always want more time than they get. If you believe that the deadline is too tight, say so. It is better that you are honest rather than say 'yes' to an unrealistic timescale and risk missing the deadline which could, in a worst-case scenario, negate the contract altogether.
- **Rights:** author's agents try to hold on to as many rights as possible. The more the author holds, the more there is to sell elsewhere. Bear in mind that this is difficult to do on your own if you have no experience of selling rights; there are agents who specialize in this (see the various writers' yearbooks etc.).

As well as being happy with what you are being offered in terms of money and timescales, you should also consider whether the publishing house is right for you. The editor will explain to the author what the publishing house proposes to do with the book (further editorial work, publicity, publication date, etc.). As Heather Holden Brown points out, it has to *feel* right. Do you feel you could work with these people? Do you share the same expectations for the book?

When both parties are happy, the publisher issues the contract (see Chapter 4). On signature of the contract, the first part of the advance is paid. At this stage, the agent steps back and allows the author and editor to begin working together.

Trevor Dolby, publisher, Preface Publishing, an imprint of Random House

www.prefacepublishing.co.uk

'Publishers, like authors, want to work with people they like and who are easy to work with. If your first book was a success and you were a pleasure to work with and your second proposal is a good one, you'll get another deal. That doesn't mean that everybody is fawning over each other all the time; it means that you are straightforward, practical and communicative; you have good ideas and you do things when you say you'll do them. And it works the other way, too. If your editor was a pain in the a**e and now, only when the book is successful, are they all over you, you can make the decision not to work with them next time as well.'

Case study: Bryony Pearce

Angel's Fury (Egmont), *The Weight of Souls* (Strange Chemistry)

www.bryonypearce.co.uk

'At university, I did English Literature but I think analysing so many amazing authors just killed my ability to write myself. After I'd been working for a while in London, I was desperate to start writing but couldn't put pen to paper. So I did a short-story writing course with the National School of Journalism, feeling that I would have to write something then. I didn't do it with a view to getting my work published; I did the course because I so desperately wanted to do something that I loved again and would make me happy.

'I decided to expand one of the stories I wrote on the course into a novel (*The Windrunner's Daughter*). I certainly didn't have a particular audience or market in mind. It was more a case of I wrote the book, then looked at it and realized it would appeal to teenagers.

'I didn't use any friends or family to read what I'd written – that would be far too embarrassing! What I did do though is talk to another children's writer who lives near me called Nik Perring who wrote *I Met a Roman Last Night, What Did You Do*? He read the first two pages and he gave me some advice on writing a synopsis and covering letter.

'*The Windrunner's Daughter* was written over a few years; the main part of it while I was pregnant with my daughter, Maisie. I sent if off to publishers and literary agents and got rejected... a lot. I even had rejections from people who clearly hadn't read my work. They would reply referring to my "stories", "We don't want to take on your stories." It's a novel, it's not a collection of short stories. It was a bit demoralizing.

'Although I didn't set out to see my book in print, once I'd made my mind up that I wanted to be published I was determined to do it. Every time I got a rejection, I allowed myself a day to feel really, really despondent. Then I picked myself up and said, "Right, you've got to do a rewrite." And that's basically what I did. Gave myself a day, then looked at it, tried to see what was wrong with it and fixed it. I think you have to be so stubborn, so thick-skinned and persistent and willing to rewrite. The feedback I was getting was that the second half wasn't working, so I realized I had to delete it and write it again. The number of times I sat down at my computer and deleted chapter after chapter of *The Windrunner's Daughter*; I literally just deleted the whole half of the book a couple of times and rewrote it. Not just tweaks, a massive rewrite.

'The rejection I got from the literary agent Caroline Sheldon wasn't the standard "We hate your story; go away" letter. It said, "Sorry we are rejecting you but have you considered going to the literary consultancy Cornerstones to get a report?", which I did. Cornerstones said it had a lot of potential but it needed rewriting. So I rewrote and rewrote and rewrote.

'Helen Corner, at Cornerstones, then suggested that I enter the "Undiscovered Voices" competition, which is run by the Society of Children's Book Writers & Illustrators (SCBWI British Isles) to highlight debut fiction writers. So I did and I was one of the 12 winners. After winning, I received two offers from agents in quick succession and I chose to go with Sam Copeland at Rogers Coleridge & White. Having been in the position of getting rejection after rejection, to suddenly having two offers, I was completely over the moon. And then I thought "Oh no, now I've got to choose between these two amazing agents. And upset somebody. And I've got to make a rejection now!"

'*The Windrunner's Daughter* got rewritten so many times but it kept getting rejected; although Sam called them "fantastic rejections"! Eventually, while it was out with a set of publishers, I decided to write another book, *Angel's Fury*, which I did in about seven months while I was pregnant with Riley.

'I got rejections for this as well, but then two publishing houses said they were interested so I went down to London to meet them. I was eight months pregnant, on crutches and it was my birthday. The first meeting went well and I came out thinking that, if I didn't get an offer from them, I wouldn't understand why. At the second meeting later that afternoon, I was flagging and could barely keep my eyes open. Coming out from that meeting, I thought if they didn't make me an offer I would know exactly why!

'In the end, I didn't exactly get an offer from either publisher. The first meeting had been with the publishers Egmont, who said that there were lots of changes they wanted made. But, as I was eight months pregnant they didn't want to give me a contract and push me to deadlines that I wouldn't make. I said, "Tell me what are the changes that you want and if I do them would they be willing to look at the book again?" They said, "Yes, absolutely,' obviously expecting me to get back to them in three years' time. I actually had the telephone conversation with the editor about the rewrites while I was in labour. Then, I rewrote the book and got it back to them before Riley was three months old.

'Fantastically, Egmont then took me on. They sent me a lovely email with their offer, saying how pleased they were with the book. One of their comments was that I'd "handled the rewrites like an utter professional". I think that was one of the things that swung it in my favour. The fact that the editor now knows that I may have a brand-new screaming baby and be on crutches but I'm still going to turn round a book rewrite for her; she can rely on me to do it so I think that helped.

'It's been wonderful working with Egmont. Philippa Donovan, my editor, is lovely. We are very much on the same wave length and the changes that she has asked me to make have improved the book dramatically. So it's been a fantastic experience; partly because I'm learning a lot and partly because it's improving the book. Every time I make changes it is getting better so it's turning into something I can really be proud of. And Philippa is lovely. She's on the phone when I need her; she's there to talk me through the changes if I want that; she's completely happy to do that.

'It feels like a partnership between the two of us. I've provided the rough script and she's used the benefit of her expertise to show me how I can make it the best it can be. I'm using the benefit of my talent, I suppose, to provide something for her that I hope is going to sell well – and make her publishing house some money and therefore help her out. We're helping each other out really.

'The original offer from Egmont is for a one book deal but the publishers have said that they want first look at anything else I write. I am in the process of writing the next book and have shown the synopsis to Philippa. She likes it and I'm hoping that when she sees the rest of the book she'll like that, too.

'I will go back to *Windrunner's Daughter*. I still think there's something there because so many publishers asked to see it based on the first three chapters. Having had my second novel picked up and had the editorial comments come back on that book, I now know what's wrong with *Windrunner's Daughter* and I should be able to rewrite it properly.

'I have been learning a craft. I feel very strongly that this is important. Belief in yourself is, obviously, crucial but being willing to learn from the people in the industry is hugely important. You hear stories of authors who are so entrenched in their work that they refuse point blank to listen to anyone else; they won't make changes, they won't learn. That's so arrogant. Who has nothing to learn?

'What did I really want from this? It was a fulfilment of a lifetime dream; I'd always wanted to write. It has gone at my own pace and I've sold my book. You can't really ask more than that, can you? If I can get a photograph of someone in the street reading my book or me standing next to a display of my books in Waterstones, then that's all I really want from it. The money is a very welcome bonus but what I'd really rather have is a fan letter saying how much they liked my book.'

Focus points

- Expect rejection; every writer gets rejected – many times. The most successful writers get the most rejections because they are the most persistent. If you get a rejection, don't believe it. It is one person's opinion on that day. Use rejection to help you improve your manuscript.
- Be prepared to edit your work – which can often mean cutting out some of your favourite bits. Make every word count.
- The author–editor relationship is a mix of business and mutual respect and liking. You need to trust and get on with your editor.

Next step

You have written, rewritten and edited your work. You have been rejected but persisted. The next step in the publishing process is preparing your work for printing. Before we get to that stage, however, in the next chapter we will look at the legalities and practicalities of the publishing process which can affect you as a writer.

4

Legalities and practicalities

'No man but a blockhead ever wrote except for money.'
Samuel Johnson

Publishing and bookselling are no different from any other business and are affected by general legislation as well as regulations where consumer protection, trading standards, price fixing, copyright, obscenity and libel are concerned.

Sarah Davies, literary agent, The Greenhouse Literary Agency

www.greenhouseliterary.com

'Negotiation, and negotiating the contract in particular, is a huge part of what we do for an author. There really is no way an author on their own is going to be able to negotiate an optimum contract for themselves with a corporate publisher. Finance and being able to advise on tax, move money in a timely way to where it should be, advise people on tax forms (if you're a Brit and paid by an American house or vice versa) – these are all part of an agent's job, too.'

RIGHTS

As the author, you hold the rights to your work. When you agree to have your book published, you give a publishing house the exclusive licence or 'right' to make use of your work. Signing over all your rights to the publisher is unusual; it tends to happen with book packaging, when an author is commissioned to write for a flat fee. If the idea was not yours (it was the publisher/packager's) and you are happy with it, then that is absolutely fine.

You can also give copyright to the publisher while the contract is in place; this is called copyright assignment (see below).

The primary right is to publish the book itself; all other rights are secondary (or subsidiary) to the right to print. Agents generally want to hold on to as many of those secondary rights as possible, while the publisher wants to keep as many of those rights as they can. The contract (and the negotiations that lead up to the final contract) lays out who has what rights.

The secondary rights are attractive (and lucrative) to agents and publishers because nothing has to be physically produced when they are sold.

COPYRIGHT

Copyright exists as soon as you or anyone else records anything original to you on paper, film or disk; therefore, you don't have to actually physically register copyright. Neither do you have to put the copyright symbol on your manuscript (or sample chapters) when you submit to agents or publishers; you are automatically covered by the law.

Copyright protects authors, giving them legal ownership of their work. It establishes that an author's work is their own personal property. Because they own it, the author has the right to sell or license it to others.

If the copyright was assigned to the publisher, the author's name is next to the © on the title verso page (the page on the other side of the title page; the 'copyright page'); under an exclusive licence it is the publisher's name. Assigned copyright will revert to the author when the contract is terminated; the reasons for termination will be laid out in the contract (such as the book going out of print, which is what you would hope to have in a contract).

In the UK, Europe and the United States, copyright is protected during your lifetime and for 70 years after your death. So you could quote Queen Victoria and Benjamin Franklin but not Winston Churchill or J.D. Salinger without permission (agencies not only represent living authors but the estates of dead ones, too).

Copyright is your intellectual property, which means you can sell it outright but that means you then have no further claim on that work and, therefore, cannot make any money from it. In other words, your work no longer belongs to you. You cannot even rewrite it because that would count as adaptation. You may not be allowed to reuse characters from the original work. However, even if you do give up the copyright, you are still entitled to be attributed as the author of that work.

KEY POINTS REGARDING COPYRIGHT

- There is no copyright in ideas or in the title of a work (though you would obviously avoid calling your work something like *Harry Potter* or *The Da Vinci Code*).
- Copyright exists in the expression of ideas (i.e. when they are written down).
- Copyright can be held jointly.

- A work must be original in order to be covered by copyright.
- If you have created your work during working hours, as part of your terms and conditions as an employer, the copyright will belong to the employer.
- Copyright in translation belongs to the translator.
- Breach of copyright is still illegal even if no financial gain has taken place.

 Key idea

If you are putting your work online, it is worth putting a copyright notice on it. While laws vary from country to country, the copyright mark shows that you are claiming the rights to your work and that it is not available for everyone to use.

Under the Universal Copyright Convention (1952), all books should carry a copyright notice. You can find the information and logo on the title verso page. A new edition of a book has a new date in the copyright line. If you are self-publishing:

- make sure that the copyright symbol © is on the correct page
- put the year the book was first published
- put the name of the copyright holder
- look at the wording of the copyright statement in printed books and ensure you include it in your book if you are self-publishing (see Chapter 6)
- if you and a co-author are self-publishing a book, write and sign an agreement on how you both want the copyright to be shared. It is usually a 50/50 split. However, if one of you has put in less or more work than the other, you may wish the split to reflect this. Settle the issue now, rather than when the book is published.

In the United States, authors have to register their work as proof of ownership. The US Copyright Office is the authoritative source for information, procedures and searches, including texts of relevant laws (www.copyright.gov).

The Authors' Licensing and Collecting Society (ALCS) in the UK and the Authors Registry in the United States manage the collective rights for writers. They make sure that writers are compensated when their work is copied (e.g. photocopied). For more information on registering with these agencies, see Chapter 10.

Moral rights

Moral rights are covered in the UK by the 1988 Copyright, Designs and Patent Act. They include:

- **Paternity** – the author's right to be clearly identified as the person who created the work; same duration as copyright
- **Integrity** – the right for the author to prevent any distortion or mutilation of their work that could damage their reputation – it has the same duration as copyright
- **False attribution** – this prevents the author from being credited with something they didn't write; lasts for life plus 20 years.

The right of integrity is automatically granted but you have to assert your right of paternity in writing. You can assert your right of paternity by putting 'The moral right of the author has been asserted' on the title verso page, which contains the ISBN (International Standard Book Number), copyright information, year of publication, etc. Look at printed books to see examples of this.

Moral rights are separate from copyright. You can waive your moral rights but, if you do, you give up the right to have that work attributed to you. Your work can then be changed in any way; your permission does not have to be sought.

Contracts

Most UK publishers use *Clark's Publishing Agreements: A Book of Precedents* as a guide when drawing up contracts. Contracts will vary slightly from one publishing house to another but all should contain:

- the date of agreement
- the names and addresses of publisher and author

- the title (or working title) of the book
- the author's obligations
- the publisher's obligations
- detailed specification of rights assigned
- provision for revised editions
- specification of royalty
- specification of accounting periods
- warranties and indemnities
- termination and reversion of rights
- miscellaneous subclauses pertinent to particular agreement.

The contract will be between the licensor (the author who owns the rights) and the licensee (the publisher).

If you do not have an agent, you really should consider becoming a member of the Society of Authors (or the Authors Guild in the United States), which will check through the contract before you sign it for free. They also give advice on negotiating items that an author may want changing. See Chapter 10 for more information on the Society and the Guild. If you are a member of the Society (or Authors Guild), let your publisher know before it draws up the contract.

The Society and Writers' Guild of Great Britain have drawn up a Minimum Terms Agreement (MTA). This gives a basic code of conduct for publishers to adhere to when drawing up a contract. Not all publishers have signed up to it but many of the larger houses have.

Equally, the offer of a publishing contract makes you a much more attractive prospect for a literary agent so you could try approaching one who could negotiate better terms for you as Isabel Losada did (see Chapter 2).

 Key idea

All contracts are negotiable, no matter what the publisher tells you.

Let's look at some of the elements of a typical UK publishing contract in more detail:

- **Format:** this states whether it is hardback or paperback, the approximate UK retail price and an estimated first print run.
- **Rights granted:** this clause will show whether the contract assigns rights to the publisher or licenses them to publish an author's work (i.e. whether the author retains full copyright and the publisher buys the licence to publish the book). It will explain what rights are assigned to the publisher and which to the author/agent.

- **Copyright and moral rights:** see above – this clause states that the author owns the copyright. Many authors and their literary agents are now keeping their ebook rights so that they can publish in their own right.
- **Typescript and delivery of the work:** this covers details of the work including title and length. It states the agreed delivery date for the manuscript and also what the author has to provide in the nature of original artwork, photographs, illustrations, maps and so on (not relevant for all titles, of course). If the contract states that the book is a 60,000-word historical crime title, that is what you must deliver.
- **Proofs:** this clause deals with correction of proofs. As the licensor (the author of the work), you are entitled to see the proofs.
- **Printing and publication:** the publisher agrees to print and publish the book. It may include an agreement that the author be consulted over cover design, illustrations and so on. There should also be a commitment to publish the work in a set period of time (12 months, for example); the commitment to publish should not be subject to approval or acceptance of the manuscript.
- **Quotations and illustrations from other sources:** see 'Permissions' below. It is usually the responsibility of the author to get and (if necessary) pay for the permission. If a publisher has to do the research themselves, they may put the cost of the permissions against the author's royalty.
- **Warranty and indemnification:** you 'warrant' to the publisher that you have done certain things (like checking facts, clearing copyright, etc.). Publishing houses ask authors to indemnify themselves against the risk of libel, invasion of privacy and infringement of copyright. Publishers often insist on altering the text to remove anything that they think might be actionable; if you think that may be the case, you could add the proviso that you get final approval on the text. Some authors take out professional indemnity insurance to cover the risk.

Bryony Pearce, author

www.bryonypearce.co.uk

'When I was going down for my meetings with Egmont, my agent said, if they made an offer, I would get an advance. So I asked how much. "It will be small," he said. My friend Sarwat Chadda got a six-figure book deal for his first book. My agent

paled. That's when he realized what my yardstick was, so he had to beat my expectations down to the point that I would have been grateful for two chocolate bars and a hundred quid. So when I did get a bit more than that I was grateful!'

THE ADVANCE

Unlike a flat fee for a commission, this is an advance on royalties which are earned on book sales. One tends to read about the eye-popping large advances in the newspapers. They are the exception rather than the rule. They can be as little as £500 or go as high as six figures plus.

The advance is divided up and the author receives each part at a specific point in the delivery of the book: first amount on signature of contract; second amount on delivery of manuscript; third amount on publication (there might be a fourth amount if the book was originally a hardback and is subsequently published as a paperback). Advances are usually non-returnable unless you fail to deliver the manuscript.

If you have an agent, the advance is paid to them; they will take off their fee (usually 15 per cent) and then the rest is passed on to you. The agent will usually pay the amount owing to income tax as well.

ROYALTIES

Authors usually receive a percentage of sales of their book after the advance has been covered. Royalties can be based on:

- the cover price of a book; *or*
- the net sales revenue (i.e. the amount of money the publisher gets after trade discounts have been applied to the cost of the book).

For example, if the recommended retail price is £20 and the average trade discount is 50 per cent, the net sales revenue will be £10.

If the royalty is 10 per cent of the published price, the author would receive 10 per cent of £20 = £2 per copy sold.

If the royalty is 10 per cent of the net sales revenue, the author would receive 10 per cent of £10 = £1 per copy sold.

First-time authors often get quite a low royalty rate. Royalties paid to an author can increase with book sales. The publisher aims to cover their costs with the first print run; as sales continue to rise, the book is reprinted and the costs (and the losses) to the publisher go down; for example, a hardback royalty of 10 per cent on the first

2,500 copies may rise to 12.5 per cent on the next 2,500, then 15 per cent as the sales increase. Mass-market paperback sales have a royalty of 7.5 per cent; after 30,000 copies have been sold, that rises to 10 per cent (although fewer publishers are distinguishing between hardback and paperback nowadays). Export sales usually attract a lower royalty rate than home sales (publishers have often given a higher discount to the export market). There will also be a royalty paid on the highly discounted books (such as those sold in supermarkets, large bookstore chains, wholesalers), which is generally a lot lower than other royalty rates.

In some cases, the rise of ebooks is changing the way authors are paid. Some are being paid on a fee basis and, when royalties are paid on ebooks, they are higher than they are for print books.

You should keep royalty statements for tax purposes. Any royalties should be declared as income and not expenses.

PAYMENT DATE

This confirms when you will get paid. You should get some of the money when you deliver the manuscript. If you can, avoid having a clause which says you will be 'paid on publication'. If something untoward happens (the publisher goes out of business before the book is published), you will not get any money even though you have done the work.

> ## Key idea
>
> Make sure that you are offered a rising scale of royalty rate; if it is not in the contract, ask for it to be included. The publisher will have an idea of the break-even point (i.e. the point at which they stop making a loss and start to make a profit). That is where your royalty rate should increase.

AGENCY

If you are represented by an agent, this clause authorizes the publisher to pay any money to the agent on the author's behalf.

CHEAP EDITIONS AND REMAINDERS

This sets out the minimum time the book has to be available for sale before being remaindered. It states that the author will be told when books are to be remaindered and allowed to buy them at the cheaper rate.

REVERSION OF RIGHTS

This outlines what will happen if a publisher no longer actively exploits the rights to a book. Rights do not always automatically revert to the author. There should be a clause that terminates the contract if the book goes out of print or drops below an agreed level of sales.

SUBSIDIARY RIGHTS

The contract will likely include an agreement which allows a third party to produce your book in a different format – for example, translation rights, foreign English-language markets, large print, film rights, electronic rights, anthology rights, audio books, periodical rights (first serial – extracts printed in magazines/newspapers before publication; second serial – extracts printed after publication).

 Key idea

In 'Don't Get Diddled in the Digital Age' (ALCS Spring 2010 newsletter), Mark Le Fanu, General Secretary of the Society of Authors, wrote that the phrase 'digital rights' in a contract was too vague and that authors should make sure that every contract deals separately with all the different ways and contexts in which a book can be exploited.

As epublishing has developed, contract terms have had to change as well. Initially, ebooks were seen as just another format (like paperback or hardback). With digital works having a global reach, it was clear that subsidiary rights for digital needed to cover this.

Electronic rights cover the right to make use of the book in its digital format. As Mark Le Fanu has pointed out, clauses dealing with 'digital rights' can be vague. If you are concerned, it might be worth asking that the electronic rights clause be reviewed in the future. The publisher usually has the right to sell an electronic edition within two years of the first UK publication of the book.

Electronic rights can mean:
- making the book available online
- interactive (with audio or video)
- print on demand
- apps for mobile phones and tablets
- games/merchandise
- territorial rights.

A book printed and published in one country can be sold to any number of other publishers in other countries. English-speaking rights gives licence to publish an English edition of the book in a different English-speaking country. World rights means a publisher can distribute, or license the distribution, in any country in the world. Publishing houses and agents have well-established contacts around the world. It is more difficult for a self-publisher to do this.

It is difficult to regulate territorial rights in a digital world. There is a move towards global rights and having fewer territorial restrictions.

RESERVED RIGHTS

If any rights are not specifically granted to the publishing house in the contract, then they are owned by the author. More authors are retaining their digital rights, allowing them to publish their own work electronically.

COMPETING WORKS

This clause prevents the author from writing a similar (therefore competing) work for another publisher. Make sure that the definition of 'competing work' is very clear.

ACCOUNTS

If an author finds an error on the royalty statement, they have the right to get an independent auditor to look at the publishing company's accounts. In reality, this rarely happens; paying an accountant to pore over the accounts of a publishing house costs a lot of money. If there is an error in the statement, contact the royalty department and ask if it can be sorted out. Mistakes can happen so don't be confrontational.

AUTHOR'S COPIES

Sometimes referred to as presentation copies. This tells you how many free copies you can expect to receive. It is not usually a huge amount (possibly 10 copies); US publishers tend to be more generous than their UK counterparts.

OPTION ON NEXT WORK

This means that the author has to show the publisher part or all of their next work; it is more common with fiction. It does not mean that the publisher is obliged to take that next work. It is easy to be flattered by this but do not get tied into having to show *all* your future titles to this one publisher. If the clause is included, ask that it be restricted to one book, on terms that are mutually agreed (not on 'the same terms' as the current title) and have a time limit on enforcing this.

Avoid having a phrase that says you have to offer the publisher a whole manuscript; that means that you have to write the whole book before you can show it to them and get a decision on whether they want to go ahead or not. Suggest an outline and sample chapter as a better option for you.

NEGOTIATION

Discussions over advances and rights often begin before the contract is issued. If you do not have an agent, should you drive a hard bargain with the publisher? Or do you feel that you should just accept whatever they offer?

As Sarah Davies says at the beginning of this chapter, negotiating an optimum contract with a commercial publishing house is something agents do every day, not authors. However, if you do not have an agent and there are parts of the agreement that you feel strongly about (you would like a slightly larger advance or a lower-quantity threshold where the royalty increases), you can but ask. If a publisher wants you badly enough, they will probably be happy to agree to some terms but not all; perhaps they will agree to meet halfway.

If there is something you do not understand, just ask. The intention is not to confuse you or hide things but a contract is a legal document and the language is not always clear to a layperson.

 Carole Welch, publishing director, Sceptre

www.hodder.co.uk

'The recession has undoubtedly caused advances to come down, though exceptions remain – especially for debut authors who have a fresh slate and for authors whose books seem to be sure-fire winners. This isn't necessarily a bad thing for authors – instead of a book selling well but the publishers still perceiving it as a disappointment because it didn't earn its advance, if a book earns out a lower advance everyone should be happy – the author will earn royalties, the agent will earn commission on those royalties, and the publisher will have recouped their investment and feel confident about publishing the author's next book.'

If you would like a more detailed breakdown of what publishing contracts contain, read *Understanding Publishers' Contracts* by Michael Legat (Robert Hale) and *From Pitch to Publication* by Carole Blake (Macmillan).

Mo Smith, author of self-published *The Purple Spoon* and *The Lazy Cook's Family Favourites*

www.lazycookmosmith.co.uk

'*[A freelance agent for a publisher] was also responsible for setting up a contract with a major publisher. There would be a marketing and publicity campaign with a nationwide tour and an initial print run of 12,000 copies. However, a few days after that meeting, another major publishing house got in touch and said they would like to meet me. I was keen to follow this up and delayed the signing of the contract on offer. We had a good meeting; they appeared enthusiastic but eventually turned it down. In the meantime, the first editor suddenly left her job. The unsigned contract went on hold until a new editor was in place who then decided not to pursue it. I blame myself for not signing it at the time. It was a salutary lesson... a bird in hand and all that!*'

If you are self-publishing and choose to use experts, such as a designer or printer, use a basic contract to cover your agreement. It could just be a one-page written confirmation of what has been agreed between the two parties. This would cover:

- when the work should be finished/delivered
- payment
- who has copyright
- what work is required.

'BOILERPLATE' AGREEMENTS

A boilerplate agreement is a standard contract drawn up by a publishing house and a literary agency who have dealt with each other on a regular basis. It avoids having to go down the route of quibbling over standard clauses.

Other legal considerations

DIGITAL RIGHTS MANAGEMENT (DRM)

There is a worry that digital publishing will go the way of the music industry and be rife with illegal downloads. The publishers' fear of piracy meant that they use DRM in their epublications.

DRM enables rights owners (generally publishers) to embed code in an ebook so that it restricts the use of digital content for those who have bought the right to use it. It can also track usage and collect appropriate revenues. Basically, DRM lets you restrict whether files can be copied from one device to another.

The downside is that you may be prevented from reading an ebook that you have legally bought on other devices. Many self-publishing experts believe DRM is not worth having on an ebook. Mark Coker, founder of Smashwords (an ebook self-publishing and distribution platform), insists that any work sold on his site is DRM-free. He believes that piracy isn't the problem; anything that makes your work less available is. If you are being pirated, he argues, your work is desirable to others. The way to beat piracy is by convenience and price. DRM-free books, he believes, are more accessible.

DRM software has other problems; it can be broken into by hackers. It can also be simply sidestepped by the user scanning in a printed book and posting it for free on the Internet. The Society of Authors points out that 'DRM technology can interfere with software used by people with disabilities to make ebooks accessible (e.g. text-to-speech systems used by the visually impaired).'

If you are self-publishing your book electronically, you will be given the option to use DRM – or not – on your ebook files. The choice is up to you.

There is a difficulty in keeping track on any material that might have been posted illegally. It is proving something of a headache to publishing houses that have thousands of titles; it is helpful if authors (whether published or self-published) keep a lookout on the Internet for any pirate copies. If you find a pirate copy and you are published by a publishing house, contact them and they will take the appropriate action. Don't take the matter into your own hands if you have a publisher because it can complicate matters; the publisher can use the Publishers' Association anti-piracy portal.

If you are self-published and think that your copyright is being infringed, contact the website operator and ask them to remove it because it infringes your rights. Alternatively, contact the Internet Service Provider (ISP) and ask it to close down the website

LIBEL

A statement made in writing or in print which defames the character of an identifiable living person by holding them up to ridicule or contempt. Be careful with the names of characters and company names. Try to check that you haven't accidentally named a real-life person or business. If you think you may be writing something that could be libellous, get professional legal advice.

The Society of Authors has a guide to libel which is worth reading, and it can advise on insurers who offer libel insurance. The Society also has a professional indemnity insurance scheme for writers. The Alliance of Independent Authors can also give legal advice and feedback on contracts.

PERMISSIONS

If you wish to quote from another writer's work or use an illustration of some sort, you should get permission from the publisher of that work. There is often a cost involved.

You do not need to get permission if the quote is considered 'fair dealing' – where you can legitimately use published material 'for the purposes of criticism or review'. That means using a line or two to help you in making a point; however, you must acknowledge the source of the quotation.

The Society of Authors considers as fair dealing:

- use of a single extract of up to 400 words; *or*
- a series of extracts (of which none exceeds 300 words) up to a total of 800 words from a prose work; *or*
- extracts up to a total of 40 lines from a poem provided that this does not exceed a quarter of the poem.

The words must be quoted in the context of 'criticism or review' of the work quoted.

To seek permission for use of an extract from someone's work, you need to either contact the publisher of the first edition of the work – write to the Permissions Department at the publishing house. Alternatively, if you need to track down the rights holders, you could approach the Association of Authors' Agents or the Authors' Licensing and Collecting Society (ALCS) – contact details are in the Resources section at the end of this book.

Plagiarism

This is using work covered by copyright that is held by someone else, not getting permission for that use and passing it off as your own without crediting the original author. Plagiarism covers ideas as well as finished work. If you steal someone's work, you can be prosecuted under copyright infringement or sued in court for loss of earnings and reputation.

Proving that your work has been plagiarized can be difficult, unless great chunks of your work are reproduced. There are also cases when some authors have plagiarized works without knowing it.

To protect yourself against plagiarism, follow these guidelines:

- If you use other people's works in your book, get permission and/or keep a list of all the sources you use so that you credit them clearly.
- Use work that is out of copyright (although you must still credit the writer).
- Be careful about whom you share your ideas and work with.
- Open forums and blogs are easily accessible, so be careful what you write on them if you wish to use them in your work.
- If you think you may have unwittingly written something that sounds familiar, type it into a search engine and see if it throws anything up.

If you are worried about your own work being plagiarized, you could use Google alerts (www.google.com/alerts) to help you. You create alerts for your book by using several phrases (six or seven words long) from your book. You will be sent an email if one of those phrases is picked up.

Industry classifications

Books are classified with standard subject headings. Go to the Book Industry Communications (BIC) website (www.bic.org.uk), which runs the classification scheme for the UK book trade and other English-language markets, to find out what your book should be listed under. You will need this information if you are planning to publicize your book and send the information out to retailers and wholesalers.

Children's books have a whole separate marketing category (also found on the BIC website). You have to choose just one value from each of the five sections listed that cover different aspects of the book. The five sections cover:

- interest level (indicating the age range for which the book is intended)
- broad subject (e.g. poetry and song, early learning, fiction)
- type/format (e.g. activity book, printed book, annual, electronic)

- character (whether the book has an established children's character or not)
- tie-in (tied in to a film or television programme or not).

For example, a book labelled C1M79 is an ordinary printed poetry book for seven to nine-year-olds that has no established character and is not a tie-in book.

ISBN (International Standard Book Number)

There is no legal requirement to have an ISBN but, if you want to sell your book on Amazon, through another online retailer or via a bookshop, you need one. An ISBN is a product identification number that you will find on the back of most books and is required for booksellers and libraries. Originally 11 digits, the ISBN became 13 in 2007 due to the increase of new titles appearing. So, while some books may have similar titles (*Teach Yourself Spanish*, *Get Fit*, *Lose Weight* and so on), they will each have their own individual ISBN.

ISBNs cannot be bought singly. You have to buy them in batches; the minimum amount is ten. They are available from:
- isbn.nielsenbookdata.co.uk (UK and Ireland)
- isbn.org (US)
- bowker.com (US).

They cost around £112/$240 for ten ISBNs and take around ten days to be processed. You will get an information pack when you order your ISBNs which will outline your responsibilities as a publisher and the rules that pertain to the ISBN.

Note:
- You need to get an ISBN before you print your book.
- When filling out information for an ISBN, you will have to put down the book's title, format and length.
- You will also need to put down the publisher's name (either your name or the name you give your publishing company).

Key idea

Your contact details will be needed when you register for an ISBN. These will be used by wholesalers and bookshops to order books. If you are self-publishing, make sure that your contact details are kept updated.

Whoever registers the ISBN will receive all communications regarding that book. So, if you use a self-publishing company and they supply one of their ISBNs, the book trade will contact them and not you. This is absolutely fine if you do not want to handle sales and distribution yourself. If you have a publisher, you will receive an ISBN with your book. Each book is allocated one ISBN; each version of a book (hardback, paperback, ebook, etc.) will each need a separate ISBN.

It is not necessary to have an ISBN for an ebook if you are publishing through Kindle Direct Publishing or NOOK Press (respectively Amazon and Barnes & Noble's digital publishing companies). Sony and Apple do want ISBNs for their ebooks. Smashwords will provide an ISBN (for free) if you are publishing your ebook through them so they can distribute your book to other retailers; however, if you choose this option, Smashwords will be identified as the publisher of your book.

Barcode

The barcode incorporates the ISBN. The Bookland EAN is the most widely used barcode in the publishing industry because can be used worldwide. When you register for an ISBN, you can get information on EAN barcodes. You can get your barcode from the ISBN agency (for a bit more money) or you can go to a third-party provider who will create a barcode for you.

GS1 UK is a not-for-profit organization that offers a free service to convert an ISBN into a barcode. For more information, go to: www.gs1uk.org

The big book retailers and wholesalers will require print books to have an EAN barcode. The standard position for the barcode is the bottom right-hand corner of the back of a print book. You will receive your barcode in the form of a high-resolution graphic file.

Nielsen BookData (UK)

Nielsen BookData is the provider of book information to the book industry in the UK. Some chains, like Waterstones, will only take information from here. It is the responsibility of the publisher to make sure that Nielsen BookData has an accurate record for their titles and to provide updates when anything changes.

Nielsen BookData do not charge for a basic record (which includes a jacket image) but you can opt for a subscription-based enhanced service. The basic full record includes:

- ISBN
- author
- title
- subject classification (plus BIC code – see above)
- imprint and publisher
- UK availability (whether it is in print or not yet published)
- format (paperback, hardback)
- territorial rights statement (which must say that the book is for sale in the UK)
- UK publication date.

It takes around six weeks for new submissions to be put into the BookData system. If you want further information or to check whether your details are in the system, you can call the BookData Publisher help desk (t: 0845 450 0016) or email: pubhelp.book@ nielsen.com

Nielsen BookData has an online-editing service, called Pubweb, which you can access via the website (www.nielsenbookdata.co.uk).

Books in Print (US)

In the United States, when a book has an ISBN, it can be registered on Books In Print (at www.bowkerlink.com). Books in Print, like BookData, is the main directory that bookstores, online retailers and libraries use when looking for books for their customers. It is published in October each year.

Cataloguing-in-Publication

This is basic cataloguing data prepared before publication by the national library of the country where the book is being published – for example the British Library or the Library of Congress. It is usually found near the bottom of the copyright page.

A publisher has to send in information on a book at least four months in advance of publication, including the book's ISBN. It is a way of letting libraries know about new books. The CIP programme is free of charge to participating publishers.

Library book deposits

By law, all publishers (including self-publishers) must send one copy of every print book they publish in the UK to the Legal Deposit Office at the British Library within one month of publication. In the United States, you will have to send a copy to the Library of Congress (ebooks that have no printed edition do not have to be sent).

Publications are recorded on an online catalogue and are available for all users. Within the terms of the Legal Deposit Libraries Act 2003, 'publisher' is to be understood as anyone who issues or distributes publications to the public. Items published in the UK and in Ireland are liable for deposit, as are items originally published elsewhere but distributed in the UK and in Ireland.

In addition, in the UK and Ireland, the following five libraries should also receive a copy:
- The Bodleian Library, Oxford
- University Library, Cambridge
- National Library of Scotland, Edinburgh
- National Library of Wales, Aberystwyth
- The Library of Trinity College, Dublin.

You don't have to send five separate copies to five separate addresses. Send the five copies in one parcel to the libraries' agent, the Agent for Copyright Libraries (see Resources for contact details). Remember to include these books when you are calculating how many books to print off.

Public Lending Right (UK)

Public libraries are an important market to publishing houses, especially in fiction. They are also important to writers because it is possible to earn some money from the Public Lending Right (PLR).

The PLR is a publicly funded payment made to authors whose books are lent by public libraries. Each loan generates a tiny payment but which adds up to a considerable overall sum. If your book scores only a few loans, earning less than £1, no payment is made. The maximum payment an author can earn from the PLR is £6,600.

Payment is made once a year and is proportionate to the number of times a book is borrowed. It is recognized in 28 countries; currently, the United States is not one of those countries.

The PLR is something published authors are rarely told about, certainly not by their publishers. There is nothing sinister in that; it is just an oversight. As the author, it is your responsibility to register your published book yourself with the PLR Office. You can either download a form from their website (www.plr.uk.com) or send for a registration form. Currently PLR only covers print books, not audio or ebooks.

If you are an Amazon Prime member, you can borrow ebooks from the Kindle Owner's Lending Library. Independent authors who include their books in the Lending Library get paid each time their book is borrowed; payment is around $2 per borrow. Unlike PLR, the fund changes from month to month; it is shared out between all ebooks borrowed that month by Amazon Prime members.

Pseudonym

Otherwise known as a 'pen name', a pseudonym hides the real name of the author. It can be useful if you write in more than one genre and want to be distinguished between each one. Catherine Jones is a writer of romantic fiction; she also writes under the pseudonym of Annie Jones when collaborating with another author and as Kate Lace for Little Black Dress when writing funny, contemporary stories. Rosemary Laurey writes romantic fiction but she has two other alter egos: Madeleine Oh for her erotic novels and Georgia Evans for her fantasy books. It can be a useful tool to keep your various writing personas in place.

A pseudonym also comes in handy if, when you start writing, you find that there is another author with a name the same or similar to yours.

If you are considering a pseudonym:
- check whether anyone else has 'your' name
- make sure that your name reflects your readership (a young name for a youthful audience, for example)
- pick a name that will be placed near that of a best-selling author in bookshops and libraries.

Michael Ridpath had been a successful writer of financial thrillers. When he decided to change genre, he got his agent to send his submission out under a pseudonym because he wanted people to focus on the book rather than his (known) name.

If you choose a name that starts with a letter at the beginning or end of the alphabet, your books will appear at one end or the other of bookshelves. If you choose a name beginning with a letter from the middle of the alphabet, you will be placed in the middle shelves.

Word count

You will need to know how many words there are in your manuscript. Computers will give you a figure and your editor will do a count after the text has been edited. However, computers do not give the figures that the production department are interested in. A computer's word count includes headlines and subheads. When it comes to typesetting, these headings are in a different size than the main body text so will be counted separately to make sure that there is enough space for them.

One quick way of estimating your word count is to count each word on a sample page and multiply that number by the number of pages in your manuscript. As a rough guide, 250 is the average number of words on a double-spaced A4 page.

If your book is illustrated, add up the number of pages of illustrations (an approximate number is fine) and take that away from the total number of pages. Get the average number of words on one of the remaining pages and multiply as above.

Look at other books in your genre. Your manuscript should be around the same length, give or take 10 per cent.

Case study: Robert Forsyth, publisher, Chevron Publishing

www.chevronpublishing.co.uk

'I wrote my first book about a German fighter squadron in the Second World War. I've always been interested in military history and I enjoyed writing it. However, I hadn't really thought about publishing it at all. I was having a drink with a friend who asked me what I was going to do with it. He suggested we publish it. And that's how we started the company.

'So far, we've done over 150 titles. I've gone from writing a book, to writing books for other publishers, to publishing under my own imprint and now I'm involved in book packaging. Virtually all of what I do now is specialist, boys' toys kind of stuff: aircraft, weaponry, military and so on. We commission, edit, design and we do the repro. We tend not to get involved in print unless I'm doing a book myself; we generally leave that to our publishing client.

'Although we do specialize in a particular subject, what I'm describing applies to the packaging industry as a whole. Book packagers work for a range of publishing clients who come in all sorts of shapes and sizes; they can be general mainstream and they can be very specialist. The publishers need to sustain their book publishing lists and book packagers are an extra pair of eyes and ears in the market.

'For example, if a publisher determines that the 70th anniversary of the first flight of the Spitfire is coming up, they will get in touch with someone like me. We ask them about the kind of format they're looking at (hardback, softback, x number of pages, x number of illustrations; whether there's a budget for graphics, colour, maps…).Then the haggling starts which is when the publisher tells you how much they want to spend and we tell them what we can do for that budget.

'Book packaging and specialist publishing is subject driven, not author driven. There are, of course, in our specialist world, authors who are very highly regarded and people will buy their books. Generally, however, I as the reader have an interest in the Spitfire, for example, and that interest is going to fuel my purchasing decision, not who wrote it.

'We will know a small number of authors and experts whose name will be credible enough to appear on a book, whom we can approach and ask them whether they would be interested in the project. We'll tell the author how much we have got to pay them and how long they have got to write the book. Generally speaking, the writing period can be anything from six months to a year. At that point, if the author says, "Yes", contracts are issued.

'So the author becomes one element of the production process. However, that author may not have any photographs to go with the text. It is also unlikely that the author will know how to commission colour graphics, colour artwork and so on. The role of the packager (and the value of the packager to the publisher) is that we will go off and do that for them. So, the author, the photographs, the illustration, the editing process and then the design are all components of the ultimate product which we then put together.

'In this particular case, we would normally contract an author direct; in other words, it's a fixed fee with the author and it normally constitutes an advance on signing of contract; then, a second-stage payment on delivery of all materials to us (when we make sure that the author has actually done a book that we were expecting). We then deliver it to the publisher and the balance of fee is paid on publication; so it's a three-stage payment to the author. However, authors are all different. Some people work on the basis that they want as much money as they can get up front; others will say that they don't want any advance because, if they get the money first, they won't have an incentive to finish the book. They want to get paid when they deliver. As the commissioning editor with the packager, I have to work with each author separately.

'While the author is producing the copy, we will have sourced photographs, scanned them in and made sure they look good. In our particular line of work, our market demands quality, so we place a massive emphasis on it. So we work very closely with the author to maximize reproduction values; we commission any artwork that is going in the book.

'We then edit the book. I tell a lot of our authors that they just have to think of me as the person who has either bought the book on line or wandered into a bookshop and I've taken their book home and I'm reading it. If I don't understand something, the reader isn't going to understand something. So, if I query something in the text, don't take offence. A lot of authors bristle when an editor does this; they think editors have one mission in life and that is to surgically slash apart their manuscript. That is not an editor's role. Editors are there to fine-tune and make a work acceptable for what could be a global readership.

'Then we proofread. While that is being done, we start the design process. We issue a set of proofs to the author to make sure we've done a good job and he's happy with the book and we then send a set of proofs to the publisher to make sure they are happy. We then submit the book as a DVD or CD and deliver that to the publisher with our bill, they pay and the book is published.

'Sometimes, the publisher wants us to deliver a printed book, on a pallet. So we then get involved in print, which usually means sourcing it from countries such as China, the Far East or Poland. Normally, though, the publisher arranges their own printing. Very rarely do we get involved in sales or the marketing of the book; that's down to the publisher. We are a production company.

'In the scenario I've just described, the publisher buys the rights entirely. It is accepted publishing practice, if you like, that when a publisher says they've got an idea and commission someone to go away and produce that book, it "belongs" to them. To put it crudely, they are actually making you guns for hire; you go off and get your posse which includes your author, your designer, your illustrator and so on. You are working for a client. Some publishers are more generous than others; if they get massive interest from the States, they might give you a percentage of earnings of foreign rights. Unfortunately, that happens less and less now.

'The other path you can go down is that the fundamental process is exactly the same but it works the other way: the author comes to us. I then wear a different hat and look at the idea as an editor in a publishing house would.

'So, for example, an author I've never heard of comes to us and says he's got an idea for a book about subject x. I say that it sounds interesting and ask for an outline synopsis, idea of title and, very important for us, what the word count is, at least the word count of the narrative text; because we have to get an idea very quickly on the kind of size of book we will be working with: will it be a huge book or will it be a slim volume? Does it have photographs? Is it going to be illustrated? The first thing I try to do is get inside the author's head and work out what he wants us to produce. I then ask why should I want to buy this book? Some authors get a bit shirty about that. You really want to know what their motivation is for writing the book; what do they think the USP is.

'If I like it, I would then have further dialogue with the author, fine-tune a few points, maybe raise a couple of issues with him. For instance, I was talking to a military history author who wanted to do a book on one month in the Second World War. It was a pivotal month, there was a lot happening during that time and he wanted to cover events in Europe, the Eastern Front, Western Front, the home front and the Pacific. I felt he didn't need the Pacific in the book; I'd need the book in a year and that would have involved a huge amount of work on his behalf. We discussed it and, in the end, we decided that the book would be interesting and work just as well without that element in it. So there's this dialogue with the author, and the more you can get what you think is a good idea, the more likely you are to be able to sell it into a publisher.

'I then have to map out a book proposal, based on my conversation with the author, and I take it to a publisher. All publishers are different: some will come straight back and say that, yes, they like it; others will have various meetings (board meetings, appraisal meetings, sales and marketing meetings) before deciding whether to take the book or not. Sometimes, it can take a year to get a book commissioned. They sound out their US distributors, their European sales force; they are very prudent and check ideas out. Then they either come back and say "no" they don't want to do it – in which case you have to find another publisher or you give up the project– or they say "yes" and the book is commissioned and whole process that I described above kicks in.

'In this particular instance, the author gets a royalty because it's the author's idea. Again, we don't stray into the arena of sales and marketing; once the book is commissioned, our job is very much that of a production house. The publisher would sort out any author signings, talks, advertising, etc. Our job is done when we deliver the book as a DVD to the publisher.

'There is also third strand to book packaging – we generate ideas ourselves. For example, we did a series on vintage motor sport and the history of British racing green and Italian red and so on. We got it commissioned by a publisher; we went off and found the authors, the photographs and so on. That really is the whole packaging process and what I've outlined is the same whether it's a book about airplanes, horses or whatever.'

Focus points

- Copyright is protected during your lifetime and for 70 years after your death. It exists as soon as you or anyone else records anything original to you on paper, film or disk; therefore you don't have to actually physically register copyright. Assigned copyright reverts to the author when the contract is terminated.

- If you do not have an agent, consider becoming a member of the Society of Authors (or the Authors Guild in the United States), which will check through the contract before you sign it for free. Books are classified with standard subject headings. Go to the Book Industry Communications website (www.bic.org.uk) to find out how to classify your work.

Next step

Writing is a creative process and so is editing. Getting a book ready for publication can be a collaborative, intricate process. In the next chapter, we look at production: the production of your manuscript, how to prepare it for submission and how a publishing house turns that manuscript into a published book.

5

In production

'An editor should tell the author his writing is better than it is. Not a lot better, a little better.'
T.S. Eliot

Once a contract is signed with a publishing house, the editor will be working backwards from a proposed publishing date. They need to make sure that the author delivers the manuscript on time, that copy-editors, illustrators, designers, typesetters and printers are all ready for their input at a set time in order to meet that publishing date. Time is money, both for you as the writer and your editor, representing the publishing house.

Robert Forsyth, publisher, Chevron Publishing

www.chevronpublishing.co.uk

'If I commissioned a book as a packager and an author let me down, I would think very hard about using them again. The worst thing you can do is to be late. If you cause pain, you won't be used again.'

Trevor Dolby, publisher, Preface Publishing, an imprint of Random House

www.prefacepublishing.co.uk

'You need to understand your editor, what they are doing, what they need to do and the processes in their lives. Any aspiring writer should read Scott Berg's biography of Max Perkins. He was one of the great editors of the twentieth century who discovered and published many great authors, from Hemingway to Scott Fitzgerald. He changed the editor's role from the Edwardian era when manuscripts were pretty much delivered and published to the modern role of an editor which is much more of a working partnership between author and editor. For sheer enjoyment, aspiring authors should also read among much else Diana Athill's Stet.'

Preparing your manuscript

If your manuscript looks professional, you will appear professional. Anything that makes life easier for editors, typesetters and others will be appreciated.

- Don't send your only copy.
- Usually you send an electronic copy these days. However, if hard copy is needed, follow the advice given in Chapter 2 in the section on submissions.
- If it is in hard copy, editors want to see well-presented manuscripts – definitely not handwritten ones.

- Number pages straight through from beginning to end; don't start each chapter with page 1. Imagine what would happen if someone were to drop the lot on the floor; the reader wants to reassemble them as quickly as possible, not try to guess in which part of the manuscript the various page 1s belong.
- If you want acknowledgements, list of contents, dedication, other books you have published, either leave unnumbered or use lower-case roman numerals (i, ii, iii, etc.).
- You need at least a 4-centimetre (1½-inch) margin on the left-hand side so that any editorial comments and typesetting instructions can be written down (although most manuscripts are edited on screen nowadays).
- Create a title/cover page, showing the title and your name (or pen name). Add your name and address at the bottom right-hand corner and also include it on the first and last page of your manuscript.
- If the instructions are clear, there are fewer misunderstandings and mistakes. This will mean that the work can be processed quickly and accurately, which in turn keeps costs down and maintains quality.

If you have photographs or illustrations, put an identifying mark on the back of each illustration and a corresponding one where it is meant to be in the manuscript. Put the list of illustrations, with captions, on a piece of paper.

Meeting deadlines

A date for delivery of the manuscript will have been agreed on signature of contract. When you negotiate this date, always give yourself at least three weeks longer than you think you will need – just in case.

Keep your editor informed of how you are progressing. If you look like you will be late, let your editor know *as soon as possible*. Everything has been geared up to a particular publication date and missing that can have serious repercussions for both the author and the publishing house. If they know there is going to be a delay, they *may* be able to delay the publication date. At the very least, the production team, printer and sales force will need to reschedule.

When the commissioning editor, copy-editor and author are happy with the marked-up typescript, it is sent to the production department for design and typesetting. Junior editors will work with the production department to make sure that the book is progressing as planned.

What happens when the manuscript arrives at the publishing house?

 ## Sue Fletcher, publisher, Hodder & Stoughton

www.hodder.co.uk

'The editor has a very important role – as an advocate for the author within the publishing house. Maybe that's something that has changed over the years. People's image of an editor, going back to Maxell Perkins and Scott Fitzgerald, is of a rather erudite person with fantastically good grammar, and a comprehensive general knowledge who is going to hone your prose into a thing of beauty. That is still part of it nowadays. But on the commercial fiction side, which is where my expertise lies, while that is important it's not actually the main part of the job. In some cases, we use freelance editors to tidy up the manuscript rather than somebody like me doing it. My job is to be an advocate for the book within the company. So that everyone in the company takes it seriously, understands its potential and understands what we expect of it. I'm a sort of cheerleader for my authors and for their books as well as the person who says "I think this character is really awful and the book will be better without her."'

Your manuscript receives a structural edit; in other words, the book is looked at as a whole (for fiction: narrative pacing, characterization, general style; for non-fiction: illustrations, appendices, bibliography, references). It will be checked for length and quality.

The copy-editor is often a freelance employed by the publishing house. The copy-editor may also be responsible for the structural edit. For the copy-edit, they check the manuscript line by line, word by word. The process is designed to catch all errors and inconsistencies in text, facts, spelling, punctuation and sense. They will also be looking for any comments that could potentially be libellous. Mostly this is now done on screen, but sometimes is still done on the typescript. Any queries are put on to a marked-up manuscript, which is sent to the author to be checked. The author is then asked to answer any queries that may have arisen. If the publisher has a particular house style (preferred spellings etc.) that they like to see in their books, the changes will have been made at this stage.

Some of the points will be out-and-out errors; others will be suggestions from the copy-editor. Apart from the obvious mistakes (someone has green eyes in Chapter 3 and hazel in Chapter 5), you do not have to agree to all the suggested changes. You will have to go through the marked-up manuscript, make any changes (or not, if you don't agree with them) and send the manuscript back to the editor.

Doug Young: publishing director, Sport and Entertainment, Transworld

www.transworldbooks.co.uk

'Be open to the idea that the publisher might want that book to be arranged or targeted in a slightly different way. The focus that you have as a writer, the kind of thing that's driving you passionately, may be key as far as you're concerned. But from a commercial point of view, a publisher might suggest you take an entirely different route but to the same end. Now you may choose not to believe them or take their advice but it's just as well to be aware that some people might see your subject differently.'

As an author, you may need encouragement, praise or a whip cracked. It will depend on your temperament and the relationship you have with your editor. Most editors are very good at reading what kind of people their authors are and dealing with them accordingly. Remember, though, that your editor is not working exclusively with you; they will have other authors who demand their attention.

Feedback

Key idea

As far as some authors are concerned 'feedback = criticism'. Don't be too oversensitive or stubborn about criticism. If you are flexible and accommodating, the editor will want to work with you again and it can be a pleasant experience for both of you.

Give your editor the courtesy of listening to their professional editorial feedback. You don't have to make the changes if you don't want to. Editors will often dovetail their comments with feedback from the copy-editors so that the author gets only one set of comments. It is in the interests of the publishing house that the author is happy with what gets sent off to typesetting.

 ## Trevor Dolby, publisher, Preface Publishing, an imprint of Random House

www.prefacepublishing.co.uk

'Working with your editor is all about straightforward collaboration. Making sure you have a dialogue with them. It's asking the right questions and remaining in contact with each other; for example, phoning up your editor and telling them when you've got a really thorny problem that you're not sure how to get out of, can they help? All authors work differently but I don't think writers should just deliver their manuscript on time with a nice email, Word file attached, saying, "I hope you like it; give me a ring when you've read it." Simply don't do that – collaborate with your editor.

'Any editor worth their salt will want to work with an author, particularly a first-time author. The more you collaborate as the book is produced, the better it will be. I'm not suggesting sending one page in at a time. I'm suggesting that you send in, very early on, a couple of chapters and get a critique from your editor because they don't want to get to the end of the book and find they've got something they're not expecting. An editor will be really grateful for that because it makes their life easier; it gives them the necessary knowledge they need and makes them feel secure.

'It is extremely rare that the manuscript will get rejected in its entirety. If this happens, it is important to establish exactly why it has not made the grade. Get the comments in writing, and then find out what the editor would like you to do; ideally, you want the opportunity to rewrite it.'

If they do not want a rewrite, you can either try and insist that it gets published or (if the idea was yours in the first place) take it away and get it published (or self-published) elsewhere. However, you should be able to avoid anything like this taking place by, as Trevor Dolby suggests, collaborating with your editor.

Carole Welch, publishing director, Sceptre

www.hodder.co.uk

'It's true that editors have to balance looking after an author and representing their publishing house, but it doesn't often feel as though there's a conflict between the two because we're all after the same end, which is to publish their book as successfully as possible. Of course, sometimes an author might feel their book is not, for example, getting as much of a marketing push as another and that's something the editor has to explain. Sometimes time is a factor: for example, an author might want their book cover to be changed or a quote added, but to do so would delay the book's production. This is where agents can be very useful arbiters, explaining to the author the mechanics of the business and reassuring them that their publisher isn't just trying to be awkward.

'Prima donnas aren't fun to work with. I consider myself fortunate because I don't have any authors like that. I have to say that, on the whole, I get the impression that there are more prima donnas in commercial genres, perhaps because they are often more financially successful than literary novelists so feel more able to call the shots. But then there are plenty of extremely successful commercial writers who are not like that at all – and some extremely successful literary novelists too.

'Obviously, it's like any normal relationship; you don't want someone to be a complete pest but, on the other hand, authors are going to be interested and want to know what's going on... and they should know what's going on. It's up to the editor to keep them informed.'

The **front matter** (or prelims) and **end matter** of a book – the first few and last few pages of the book – will usually be done by the publishers. The font matter includes:

- the half-title page
- the title page
- the copyright page, including ISBN and Cataloguing in Publication (CIP) data

- the contents
- the acknowledgements
- lists of illustrations, figures, maps, etc.

The end matter (usually reserved for non-fiction) includes:

- any appendices
- the index.

Key idea

Iris Murdoch refused to be edited. That is not to be recommended for most authors. The editor is, at this point, thinking primarily of the reader, rather than the writer. If the editor is suggesting making changes, it is because he or she thinks it will improve the reading experience for the person who buys the book.

Proofs

The author returns the amended marked-up manuscript; it is often sent back again for a final check in its revised form before going to the proof stage. The first proof is seen by the author and a proofreader (often another freelancer). At this stage, it is important to check for any typographical errors that may have crept in during the typesetting process. Editorial changes should have been done during the manuscript stage. Anything that the author wants to revise that is in excess of 10–15 per cent of the typesetting cost, they will be expected to pay.

When the proofs come back, a junior editor will collate them and mark them up using standard symbols, on a master copy. As an author, you will not see this master copy or need to understand the special symbols.

This second proof is then checked against the first proof to make sure that all the amendments have been made. The index is usually compiled at this stage. This set of proofs is returned to the production department to be made into final proofs. Everything is checked and is then ready for print.

Camilla Goslett, Literary Agent, Curtis Brown

www.curtisbrown.co.uk

'I think it's really important that, once you've done a deal as an agent, you step back slightly; in other words, you shouldn't

interfere too much with the editor and the writer and their relationship. Yet you always need to be there for your author. The editor will phone and update you and tell you what's going on. You'll always be a part of it; at some stages more than others. The editor is the person who has bought the book and they did so because they are enthusiastic about it.'

Design

Think about what makes you pick up a book when you are in a library or bookstore – very often, it is purely because you like the look of the cover design. Work on the cover design begins months in advance of the publishing date. Hardback jackets and paperback covers are used as the main selling tool. Most buying decisions are made by trade buyers even before a book is printed – and often all they have is the cover to go on.

If you are with a publishing house, you can make comments or suggestions on the book cover (as early on in the process as possible), but the final decision will lie with the publisher. They know what works in the market so it is not helpful to stubbornly insist that they use a picture that your five-year-old son painted.

We will look at designing your own self-published book in Chapter 6.

Todd Armstrong, senior acquisitions editor, Communications and Media Studies, SAGE Publications

www.sagepub.com

'I always want to see the first draft within 18 months of signing the contract because we can realistically work back from that. In US educational publishing, books usually have 15 chapters because there are 15 weeks in a semester; as a student, you will do one chapter a week on your course. This gives my author a chapter a month to write. A chapter will be 30 manuscript pages and that's a manuscript page a day. As I tell my authors, if they break things down to smaller parts it becomes more manageable.

'When I was the history editor at Simon & Schuster, I found some authors would start revising their textbooks and then suddenly want to add on a chapter to their book on modern American history to reflect recent events. I'd have to point out that, despite all those developments, professors would not be given an extra week to teach it.

'I really don't want the books to be longer than 256 pages, which will be roughly 100,000 words. This is for a couple of reasons. Unless it's for an introductory course, the tutor will probably use more than one book for the course; so they need to be able to get through all the material in the given time. If my author's book is too long, it just won't be able to fit into an academic course's timescale. The other thing is the cost factor. Paper is the most expensive component of a book. Remember, the publisher incurs that cost before they sell any copies of the book. And they incur that cost whether that books sells right away or sits in the warehouse for three years. So length of book is very important.'

Production

The production department handles all aspects of book production including text design. The production processes are:

- typesetting
- printing
- binding
- packing and distribution.

TYPESETTING

The typescript usually goes to an external typesetter to be made into page proofs. They process the text, either by rekeying it or by taking computer disks supplied by the writer, inputting any editorial changes from the marked-up hard copy and then producing the typeset pages. They tend to use applications such as QuarkXPress or Adobe InDesign. Once laid out, they will supply paper proofs or PDF files for checking by the publisher and author.

PRINTING

Traditionally, printing was done as offset lithography; printers use offset metal plates treated so that certain areas attract the ink and repel water; while other areas attract water and repels ink. Litho is still used for large print runs.

Digital printing has become more popular than offset lithography and is used for short runs and print on demand. Wholesalers can now print off books using digital files supplied by a publisher.

The size of the print run is dictated by the market. Retailers are not keen to subscribe to a book by an unknown author up front; they want to see how it performs before they put in a huge order. So, they will order a few copies (if you are lucky) and will then wait to see what happens. This affects publishers (and self-publishers) who will print fewer copies on the first print run; they do not want to be left with a huge amount of unsold books.

Binding can be (described in more detail in Chapter 6):

- perfect binding
- slotted/burst binding
- wire stitching
- sewn limp.

PACKING AND DISTRIBUTION

The books are packed in quantity by the printer, shrink-wrapped and either parcelled up in boxes or on pallets. They are then sent to a specified warehouse, either belonging to the publisher where they are then sent on to the main retailers and wholesalers, or directly to the customers (retailers/wholesalers).

Sales

We will look at the process of selling books in Chapter 9 but it is worth mentioning the sales process at this stage. The sales department is an integral part of the publishing team. They are responsible for getting books into bookshops so that people can buy them, which in turn earns you money. Sales representatives ('reps') go to bookshops selling the up-and-coming titles; they operate several months in advance of publication.

There are also freelance sales reps who will take a percentage of the orders they take plus any reorders from the same shop. They will not always take on one book from a (self-)publisher but if you contact them and convince them that your book is saleable, you may persuade them to take you on. With these pre-orders, the publishing house has an idea of how big the first print run should be.

Key idea

It is unlikely that you will get to meet members of the sales team unless you are one of the publisher's major authors; then you may get to go to the annual sales conference.

Whether you meet them or not, remember that they have a huge role in helping to make your book a success. You can help them by delivering a good book and doing as much as you can to promote yourself and your book.

Part of the selling process also comes from the rights department, which sells the publishing rights to other publishers (in other countries) and/or serializations in newspapers and magazines.

What happens if your editor moves on

It is not uncommon for editors to move to different publishing houses. It can be upsetting for an author if their editor leaves in the middle of a project. However, the contract is with the publishing house, not with the editor. You will have to finish your current book with that house. If, when you have finished and your contract allows it, you can always take your next proposal to that editor (if you enjoyed working with them).

If it happens to you, remember that the publishing house has committed to publish your book so it is in their interest to make sure it reaches publication. If you are concerned that you might find yourself in this situation, you could always ask who would take over in such a scenario at your first meeting with the editor – and then ask to meet them.

Case study: Annie Ashworth & Meg Sanders

Authors who write together as 'Annie Sanders'

Fiction: *Goodbye Jimmy Choo, Warnings of Gales, The Xmas Factor, Busy Woman Seeks Wife, Gap Year for Grown-ups, Getting Mad Getting Even, Famous Last Words, Instructions for Bringing up Scarlett* (all Orion)

Non-fiction: *Trade Secrets*, *Trade Secrets Christmas*, *Trade Secrets Parenting*, *How to Beat the System* (all Orion), *Fat Club* (Granada Media), *The Chain*, *The Madness of Modern Families* (Hodder & Stoughton)

www.anniesanders.co.uk

MS 'We only got an agent when we started writing novels. Prior to that we were writing non-fiction and we managed pretty well without an agent, I think; although looking back, there were probably things that would have gone better if we had had an agent.'

AA 'I agree; we were so naive. We were just glad to get the work. When it came to finding an agent, we spoke to people in publishing, asking if they recommended anyone because the most important thing is to get an agent who specializes in your genre.'

MS 'If you don't have contacts in publishing, find a writer whose work you admire, look in their acknowledgements and see who their agent is. And, of course, the *Writer's Handbook* is invaluable.'

AA 'We targeted three or four agents. We had a very positive response from one but the agent we have now stepped in within 24 hours of receiving our manuscript. It takes a very brave author to say "Hang on a minute, I'll wait and see if anyone else comes along!"'

MS 'Also, she was so decisive about our book, whereas others weren't so sure. They had been suggesting we changed certain things… Stuff that we didn't necessarily feel comfortable with changing. It's good to have an agent that shares your vision; I don't think we'd have done as well with the other one.'

AA 'So we signed with her. Ironically, just a month before that, she'd had lunch with the editor who eventually published us who said she was looking for a book just like the one we wrote. So it was absolutely 100 per cent the right place and the right time. We were really lucky in that respect.

'We sent in three chapters and a synopsis to the agent and we then had to write the whole of the book before she'd submit it. So we did that in three weeks.'

MS 'It was crazy, I remember, we were working until three or four in the morning!

'The relationship we have with our agent is the one that we want. I think there are different types of agent who give different types of support. Some agents hold your hand, read your manuscripts, suggest ideas for books and are very editorial. Whereas our agent is much more contract oriented; she's a Rottweiler in that respect.'

AA 'She comes from a rights background, not an editing one, and that could be a consideration for someone looking for an agent. Most authors, I think, submit to their agent first and then the publisher. We submit to the publisher and c.c. the agent in; her interest and skill lies in the more commercial side of things. A good agent should check that you're going to deliver on time and should be on your side.'

MS 'We have each other to talk to about the book so we don't need that tremendous editorial support that some people do. They say writing is a very lonely business; well, it's not when you're writing as a pair because we can talk to each other all the time about it. We know that we are just as interested in the book as each other and we understand it in as much detail. So that's one huge advantage of working together and perhaps makes us slightly less in need of moral support.'

AA 'Yes, I've been to author events where the agent has come with the author and that's something that would never happen with us… because it doesn't need to happen.'

MS 'I think there are many different relationships between writers and editors as there are between writers and agents. But some editors are much more hands on than others.'

AA 'In our case, that "third eye" of the editor is so useful. Because they know the market, they know you, your strengths and weaknesses. When we submit a manuscript the editor will come back and say, "It's really strong there but I think you should build it up here…" It's a bit like a teacher handing back your homework. And they're usually right. But there have been a couple of times when we have disagreed with her suggestions. There was one whole character in a book that we fought to keep and I'm glad we did. I thought she was valuable. And if your editor respects you, she should accept that. It's a bit of give and take.'

MS 'Almost invariably, when you get big changes suggested, you think, "No, I can't do that! That can't happen." But then you just have to back off and let the idea of change percolate through your subconscious – and often the changes make sense. It's just that you have a concept of your story as being all in one and you can't see how to start pulling it apart without it falling to pieces.'

AA 'Yes, that is the danger. It's like a knitted sweater; if you unravel too much, the whole thing falls apart.'

MS 'I don't know if the editorial hand is heavier nowadays than it used to be. But I know there was a book that was published in the States which did extremely well. I read the first one and loved it. A sequel came out and it was just dire. Apparently, in between times, the author and the agent had fallen out and there's a suspicion that the agent had had a big hand in rewriting the first one.'

AA 'William Golding's *Lord of the Flies* was unpublishable when it first came in and was heavily edited so writers mustn't think that what they deliver is impossible to salvage… because a good idea is salvageable.'

MS 'Do you know what is so great about having an editor? You get very close to your manuscript and it's difficult to step back and see the overall structure. Maybe that's an advantage of submitting a complete manuscript rather than doing it in bits and pieces. The reworking might be more but the editor gets a really fresh look and is able to see that big picture. A good editor will pick out what's working in a manuscript.'

AA 'An awful lot of authors will submit their first chapter to their editor just to say "This is the route I'm taking, this is the tone." Really well-known authors. We don't do that; we just write the whole thing and send it off and wait for the feedback. Maybe it works for some people to have the reassurance.'

MS 'I think an awful lot of people don't do what we do. I think we're unusual because there's two of us.'

AA 'Yes, they do leave us alone!'

MS 'In fact, when we were signed originally the editor who took us on said she overcame a 25-year prejudice against working with joint authors. And that's why our publishers only wanted to give us one name.'

AA 'If you haven't got a publisher, you've got all the time in the world with your first novel. But if you're on a two book contract, like we are, one book a year, there are deadlines to hit.'

MS 'Everything works back from publication date and it's very mechanistic at that point. Forget art!'

AA 'You can be terribly self-indulgent when you're writing but you've got to remember that you are writing for someone else to read it. You have to write for the market. Most of us read in bed; don't give me 24 characters whose names begin with "C" in the first chapter, I can't be bothered. I don't want to read books where I have to work hard.'

MS 'Reading is also very important for a writer. Although I must say I can't really read while we're writing – at least not anything in our genre. It's like washing a red sock in with your whites; you can't prevent it seeping into your writing and I think that's to be avoided at all costs. I'll read detective stories or something when we're writing but I can't read another women's commercial fiction book because I'll get it too mixed up with my own ideas.'

AA 'Unless you are very successful, there's always this sense that you have to be eternally grateful for being published. People tell you all the time how lucky we are and Meg will turn back and say, "Luck's only part of it actually!" You do have to be able to produce the goods.

'Compared to what most people do for a living, you get pretty short shrift if you whinge about it. I'm surrounded by people who think it's all a waste of time and/or a very easy way to make money. Although if you are making money out of it, it's a very nice way of doing it.'

MS 'Somebody said they loved writing because they got to meet such interesting people. The people that they had created in other words. So you can do that as a writer, enter a world that you want to be in, with people you like to spend time with. That's very nice indeed... and you can do it in your pyjamas.'

Focus points

- Presentation of the manuscript is important: pages should be numbered, margins should be at least 4 centimetres (1½ inches), so notes can be written by the editor; use double spacing throughout. Photographs or illustrations should have an identifying mark on the back and a note in the manuscript so that the editor/typesetter knows where they should go. They should not be stuck into the hard copy of the manuscript.
- A manuscript will be looked at for style, pacing, characterization and length. This is the structural editing process. Editorial feedback is designed to improve the book; the editor looks at the manuscript with the reader in mind.
- The proof should be checked carefully; mistakes are expensive to rectify once the manuscript goes to the second proof stage. A copy-editor will check through for inconsistencies and errors.

Next step

That's how it's done in traditional publishing houses. Now we'll look at what to do if you want to self-publish. We look at how you should identify your market, prepare your book for publication and the various routes there are to self-publishing.

6

Self-publishing

'If you are in difficulties with a book, try the element of surprise, attack it at an hour when it isn't expecting it.'
H.G. Wells

Self-publishing used to have a poor reputation; it was seen as the last-ditch attempt of authors who couldn't get published anywhere else. Production values were poor and retailers never used to take them on.

All that has changed and self-publishing has come of age. Personal computers allow writers not only to create the written text more easily but also to design and produce the books themselves. Affordable print on demand (POD) and ebook publication have been a gift to writers wanting to self-publish. Publishers and retailers take self-publishing more seriously. As for the book-buying public, if the quality of the book (both in content and production) can rival that of a traditionally published book, the self-publisher can market their title with confidence.

There is a great deal more advice on self-publishing given in the second part of this book.

One of the advantages of self-publishing is that you can go at your own speed. Once you have decided you want to get your book published, there is no time spent hawking it round agents or traditional publishing houses, hoping someone will pick it up. You just get on and do it yourself.

 ## Mo Smith, author

www.lazycookmosmith.co.uk

'*Everything changed when my husband suddenly had to have a life-threatening operation and I became his carer. Shortage of time and energy caused me to rethink my style of cooking, producing healthy meals very quickly and with these newly created recipes I called myself "The Lazy Cook". I was wondering how to promote this new range of recipes when a friend said, "Why don't you publish your own book? If you had a hundred printed everyone in the village would buy one – make it your Millennium project?"*'

'*All I had at that time was a portable typewriter on the kitchen table but I set to and wrote* Enter the New Millennium with Lazy Cook Mo Smith. *My enthusiasm for this new book was such that I didn't have just a hundred copies printed but a thousand! I collected them from my local printer at the beginning of November, leaving me just a few weeks to sell them all, which I did.*'

'*Encouraged by the success of my first attempt at self-publishing and still having many recipes to promote I asked myself, "Why not do another book and aim for sales in major bookshops and supermarkets?" This meant that it would have to be perfect bound, with a barcode and an ISBN. For the title of this second book I chose* Lazy Cook in the Kitchen: Mouth-watering Recipes for the Time-pressured Cook. *I opened a Lazy Cook bank account to make it more businesslike and on advice I patented my "Lazy Cook" title including the hammock logo. A neighbour put me in touch with a designer who suggested a cover. For the barcode I looked in* the Yellow Pages *and found a company which was helpful and inexpensive. An ISBN was more of a problem, a friend offered to supply one but that meant I would then have to put his name alongside "Published by". Proud of my attempts at self-publishing I felt unable to accept his offer. Again I turned to* Yellow Pages *and looked for a large printing company and asked, "Can you supply me with an ISBN?" The reply came, "No,*

> *but I know a man who can" – problem solved. Choosing the recipes and planning the layout of the book was interesting; typing the recipes was a longwinded chore and remains so.*
>
> *'Two important decisions remained – the price of the book, I decided on £5.50 per copy with a percentage from each sale to be given to charity, and a first print run of 5,000 copies. My husband pointed out that 5,000 books weighed quite a lot and that we couldn't keep them in the house. I hadn't thought about storage. On my next visit I mentioned this to my printer who replied, "I'll store them for you."'*

It can be quite daunting. Suddenly, you are no longer a writer but a publisher, editor, agent, salesman, marketing and publicity specialist all rolled into one. What you do not have is the support and assistance of someone (an editor or agent) who knows the publishing world and can guide you step by step. On the plus side, you are in charge of how your book gets into print; you control the decisions, the timing and you can produce a printed book exactly the way you envisioned it.

You also control and decide what you want to do with your book. It may be that you just want to have a copy of your book on your shelf, maybe you want to give a few copies to friends and family members, sell to a niche market or you are determined to sell as many copies as you can and make a profit.

If it is the latter two, you need to have a realistic idea of potential sales; plan your distribution and be proactive when it comes to researching your market. You also need to compete with traditionally published books; that means that your production values have to aim to match the technical standards of book production that the publishing houses do (error free, well produced, edited). If you don't like the thought of marketing and selling your book, then self-publishing is probably not for you.

Kate Parkin, publisher, Hodder

www.hodder.co.uk

'I think the most important thing for an author is that they have something they want to say, either in fiction or non-fiction. Writing a book represents a colossal effort. Anyone who can sit down and spend that length of time in their own head, feeding on their own resources is to be admired.'

Self-publishing is not a new phenomena. Best-selling authors include:

- Rudyard Kipling
- Edgar Allen Poe
- Ezra Pound
- Upton Sinclair
- Walt Whitman
- Mark Twain.

 Key idea

Self-publishing can help you to develop your writing. You can get a book out of your system before moving on to your next project.

Considering self-publishing

If you are serious about self-publishing, you should ask:

- Whom are you writing for? What is the target market?
- What genre is it?
- Where would you put the book on a bookshelf?
- What is special/different/unique about the book?
- Why would anyone buy it rather than another title?
- How will it be marketed?

These are essentially the same questions that a publisher will ask of any book that comes to them.

A self-published book must have your name appear as the 'publisher' on the copyright page of the book; this can be your own name or you can give yourself a publishing house name. The book's ISBN must also be registered to you, as the publisher, by the ISBN agency. Copies of that book are then yours to do with as you wish. You must include the standard statement about copyright on the inside page:

> All rights reserved. No part of this book can be reproduced, stored in or introduced into a retrieval system, or transmitted, in any form, or by any means (electronic, mechanical, photocopying, recording or otherwise) without the prior written permission of the publisher.

This means that you own the rights (television, film, translation, etc.) and these rights cannot be exploited unless you give permission.

As your own publisher, you need to get the design and presentation of your book right. You need to consider:

- size
- length
- format

- usability
- fitness for purpose
- quality
- accuracy of content
- the look (the design) both internally and externally.

Set a budget and a price

This is for print books; we will look at the pricing of ebooks in the next chapter. How much you spend is entirely up to you but you should put aside a set amount of money before you start. You will not be able to set a budget and price the book in one session. You will have to collate the information and readjust figures as you progress until you are happy with the costings. Costs for producing your own book can start from as little as a few pounds/dollars to a few thousand.

Pricing the book is related to the cost. While it is worth going round bookshops and looking at online retailers to see what other publishers are charging for their books, remember that as a first-time author you do not have a track record with the buying public. They are not waiting for your book with bated breath. So don't price the book so high that you put them off.

Look at the type of book you are intending to produce and see how similar titles are priced and produced. This will give you an idea of what the market expectations are: some books will work if they are cheap and cheerful, while others will be expected to have higher production values and therefore will command a higher price.

You will also have to bear in mind that booksellers demand a discount off the retail price of a book (we look at discounting in more detail in Chapter 9). For now, remember to factor discounts into your costings.

> ## Key idea
>
>
> Pitfalls to look out for are underestimating your costs, overestimating demand and under-pricing your product.

The total production cost for your book will be made up of fixed costs and variable costs.

Fixed costs will not change no matter how many books you have printed. They may include:

- payments to freelancers (e.g. illustrator, designer, indexer)
- ISBN registration
- permission fees (if using other material – e.g. image for book cover)
- legal fees (if you have to check through for libel).

Variable costs will depend on how many books you have printed. They can include the cost of:

- printing
- paper
- binding
- storage
- delivery/distribution/postage.

Other variable costs include:

- advertising (including flyers, bookmarks, AI sheets)
- publicity and promotion
- website design and maintenance.

Unit cost – this is the average cost of producing each copy. You calculate this by dividing your total costs (fixed and variable) by how many books you have had printed (or are thinking of getting printed). The more you have printed, the lower the unit cost, though the total cost, of course, will still increase.

Remember that your potential customer will not be worried about whether you have printed enough books or what your costs were to get the book out. They will consider whether they are prepared to pay that amount for your book. Trying to keep the variable costs low by opting for cheap paper, for example, could put buyers off.

NET SALES REVENUE

This is the amount of money a publisher (or self-publisher) will receive after the trade discounts have been taken off. For example, if a book has a recommended retail price of £20, it may be sold to a bookseller by the publisher with a 50-per-cent discount. In other words, the bookseller pays the publisher £10 for the book. £10 is the net sales revenue for one copy.

TOTAL REVENUE

To work out the total revenue of a book, you have to make a sales forecast. This involves setting a price for your book so that it is competitive within the market.

- If you price a book too highly, you won't sell many copies and your total revenue will be low.
- If your book is under-priced, you miss the opportunity to maximize your income for that title.

If your book doesn't sell well but you priced it high enough, you may still retain some profit. Too low a price and a garage full of books that nobody is buying, you will be out of pocket. The overall cost of your books should be divided by the number you sell, not the number you print. Work out the break-even number you need to sell.

Being a publisher

There are various ways to go about it: you can do it all yourself (layout, design) and take it to a local printer; or you can go to a company which will produce and publish your book for you; or you can use a website company which allows you to download software, lay out your book and then, for a price, will produce and print it for you.

Orna Ross, founder and director, Alliance of Independent Authors

www.allianceindependentauthors.org

'If you want to become a writer who actually has something worth saying, that readers want to read, and where you have influence through your words, you have to get to a point in your own creative self-development where you actually know that you're good. And that can take years. A lot of writers need validation from somebody else, be that an agent or publisher. For such writers, author publishing may not be a good option.'

Using experts

Buying in external services is something all publishing houses do. As a self-publisher, you will do the same. Some of the roles you can take on yourself or you may choose to bring in professionals at each stage. If you do choose to use the professional services of someone, get as many competitive quotes as you can.

EDITORS AND PROOFREADERS

Using a professional editor or proofreader will bring a fresh set of eyes to your work. Costs will vary but the UK's Society for Editors and Proofreaders has suggested minimum hourly rates that will give you an idea of what to expect. The National Union of Journalists has a freelance fees guide as well as prices for design, translation and so on.

Many editors and proofreaders will work in a particular area in which they have specialist knowledge, so, if your book is aimed at professionals or academics in a certain subject area, make sure that you get an editor or proofreader who has the same speciality.

When sending out your typescript or proofs to a copy-editor and/or proofreader, you need to let them know the following:

- what you will you be sending them
- whether there are illustrations or photographs (and, if so, whether permission has been sought and agreed)
- whether there is any outstanding material to come
- what you want the copy-editor to do: the minimum, restructuring and/or rewriting
- what you want the proofreader to do: read against copy (against the marked-up typescript, for example) or blind (just the proof itself)
- who the target audience is
- what the deadline is for delivery
- the agreed payment/fees – the hourly rate, page rate or lump sum.

USING FRIENDS

Halfway between using a professional editor/proofreader and doing it yourself is asking a friend or acquaintance to look at your work. It should be someone you trust and you must be very specific about what you are asking them to do. We looked at this in Chapter 3. Ask them:

- Where do they think it is good?
- Where do they think it is bad?
- Where do they think it is slow?

BEING YOUR OWN EDITOR

A self-publisher needs to build in quality control at every step. You will be judged against 'professionally' published books.

Key idea

Most writers believe their work is ready to be sent out when they finish the first draft. It almost never is. Don't send your first draft for feedback or to go to print. Revise it and make it the best you can before you go to print.

As your own copy-editor, you will need to go over the text with a fine-tooth comb to check for any mistakes or confusions. You need your manuscript to be:

- **consistent** – so check spellings, hyphens, capitalization, quotation marks, speech marks, parentheses, etc.
- **clear** – have you made any misleading or contradictory statements? Is there repetition? Will your text be understood by its readership? For example, if you are a US writer aiming at a British audience, have you allowed for cultural or linguistic differences?

For guidance, use *The Oxford Style Manual* (in the UK) or *The Chicago Manual of Style* (in the United States). They are used by publishing houses and offer guidance on words and how to use them.

As the copy-editor, you will also need to check for any legal issues regarding copyright, libel, obscenity and so on.

PREPARING AN INDEX

Most non-fiction books come with an index. Traditionally, if your book was with a publishing house, it was the responsibility of the author to provide the index; nowadays, it is more commonly outsourced to a professional indexer.

An index has been described as a road map, guiding readers to where they want to go. It is a skilled art. As well as analysing text, indexers need to be able to represent concepts using a few words, create cross-referencing and utilize entries, subentries and even sub-subentries. If you are producing a book that needs an index, I would recommend that you consider using someone who has experience as a professional indexer.

The Society of Indexers (or the American Society for Indexing – contact details are in Resources) will have a list of members as well as recommended price to charge to give you an idea of costs. There is also advice on websites on how to commission an index.

Design

The 'design' of a book is made up of many elements:

- size
- cover design, front and back, including the blurb
- layout (inside the book)
- font and typeface
- illustrations.

A well-designed book is a pleasure to read; get the look, the design and the feel right and people are more likely to pick up and buy your book.

Look at books to see what you think works and what you like; you should consider the following:

SIZE

Books come in a range of sizes. The standard book formats (the following are approximate measurements) are:

Paperback/ classic hardback	Demy octavo (C format)	216 × 138mm	Royal octavo (C format)	234 × 153mm
Paperback/ mass market	A format	178 × 110mm	B format	198 × 129mm

Look at other books in your genre to see the sort of shapes and sizes used. Novels are usually in an A or B-format paperback. Again, look through a bookshop and see how size gives an indication of the type of paperback it is: literary or mass-market. There is a wider choice in size for non-fiction books.

Make sure that your book can be stacked on a shelf comfortably. Is it easy to hold and read? If you are planning to post your books out yourself, does it fit comfortably into a standard padded envelope?

Other book sizes are:

A4	297 × 210mm
Demy quarto	276 × 219mm (often hardback format)
Pinched crown quarto up to	248 × 175mm
A5	210 × 148mm

The size will dictate the width of the spine. In the UK, the dimensions are given with the head to tail (top to bottom) measurement first; while in the United States and Europe, the width measurement comes first.

> ## Alex Milne-White, Hungerford Bookshop, Independent Bookshop of the Year 2009 (British Book Industry Awards)
>
>
>
> www.hungerfordbooks.co.uk
>
> *'Authors should always make sure that their book has a spine with writing on it. Obviously, when we first have a new title, we have it face up on a table but after a while it's going to end spine-up on a shelf and if you can't see the book it will be lost for ever.'*

The cover will need to have some kind of protection. Hardbacks often have dust jackets; paperbacks are usually laminated. If you want your book to be seen on a bookshelf (in a shop or a library), as Alex Milne-White suggests, it needs to have 'perfect binding'. This means it will have a spine that shows the title, author and publisher; this helps sales. It is more expensive than other forms of binding but books with perfect binding tend to last longer.

People take about eight seconds looking at a book deciding whether to buy it or not. A catchy title and a well-designed cover sell the book because it makes someone pick it up; once they have got it in their hand, they will read the blurb on the back and maybe the first page.

The design department in a publishing house will aim to produce a cover that is striking enough to be picked up by someone browsing as well as clear enough to be reproduced in catalogues and online. If you can, take a leaf out of the publishing houses' book and get your design well in advance of publication. Publishers will use the cover design to promote and sell the book.

If you are unsure about your skills as a designer, consider getting help from a design professional. When thinking about the cover design and if you are briefing a designer, you should consider the following:

- What your budget is for designing the cover.
- How many colours? Printers will quote on full colour, three, two or one colour (white, in this instance, does not count as a colour; therefore, black and white is a one-colour print process,

while red, black and white would be a two-colour process). Full colour is more expensive to print than using three.

- The design should be aimed at attracting the readership you have identified for your book – should it be contemporary, quirky, traditional?
- You need to make sure that the title and author's name are presented clearly.
- While you may not have your self-published book in a sales catalogue, you should plan to have a thumbnail image of the cover on your website and, with any luck, on retail sites such as Amazon. So the design needs to work in those circumstances as well.
- Try to work out a clear idea of what you want from the design before you brief a designer; if they produce a draft design and you don't like it and want something completely different, it will cost you money every time the designer has to go back to the drawing board.

Look at other books in your genre to get some ideas. Find out what you think is effective and works well and what elements you do not like.

COVER DESIGN – BACK

The back cover is usually the place for the **blurb** (the marketing copy that tells potential readers what's inside). In the 1990s Penguin and Orion conducted research into a book's blurb which revealed that it was a key factor in a person deciding whether to buy a book or not.

In fact, the Book Marketing Society (BMS) now has an award for 'Best Blurb of the Year' to recognize the work of those who write the all-important cover copy. As the BMS says, this is perhaps the most underrated discipline in the publishing industry but one that is so important.

So what makes a good blurb?

- People are prepared to spend only a short amount of time when reading a blurb, so make it short – no more than 120 words.
- It needs to be relevant, have impact and intrigue the reader.
- Sell the atmosphere rather than tell the story.
- Consider using a review quote (but don't make them up!).
- Bullet points can help get across the key benefits of a book, especially a non-fiction book.
- Fiction blurbs can afford to be a bit more emotional.
- Short, punchy sentences can be really effective when you are writing your blurb.

In addition to the blurb, the back cover also needs to feature:

- an ISBN and a barcode
- the price and publisher information (next to the barcode)
- any reviewer's comments
- information on you as the author (useful if your book is non-fiction).

A photograph of you, the author, is not necessary but it can help with marketing the book. The photograph needs to be good quality, so consider getting one done professionally (you can always use it in your marketing and on your website).

LAYOUT

Katherine T. Owen, self-published author of *It's OK to Believe*

'When designing the layout of your book, look at the books you've already got. Look at the order of the title page, the copyright page, the preface, the acknowledgements and the contents. Do you want footnotes or endnotes? Do you have an appendix? Make sure that you have included everything a professional book would have. Note that the copyright page is usually centred.'

A page layout usually consists of two facing pages, based on a grid, within which you place the text and any illustrations. The structure should be clear and consistent, so that the reader finds navigating their way around the book easy and uncomplicated.

As we have seen, the front matter is the first few pages right at the start of a book before the actual text begins. You do not have to have a set number of front matter pages but you must include a right-hand title page and a left-hand copyright page.

Right-hand pages are known as recto. Left-hand pages are known as verso. The title page will be recto (right); it is required and should include:

- the full title
- the author's name
- the publisher's imprint (your name or your publishing/imprint name).

The title verso, or copyright page, follows. This too is required and should include:

- the copyright information
- the year of publication
- ISBN
- the assertion of moral rights
- if the book is a work of fiction, a disclaimer saying that it is a work of fiction
- the publisher's address
- the country of manufacture (where it was bound and printed).

Other front matter pages are optional and could include:

- a list of contents
- acknowledgements (recto)
- a list of other books by the same author (verso)
- a dedication (recto)
- a preface and/or foreword (recto).

If you want to paginate the preliminary pages, you should use lower-case roman numerals (i, ii, iii, etc.). When you start the book properly (on a recto) and reach the introduction or opening chapter, switch to arabic numerals (1, 2, 3, etc.).

The pages at the end of a book (the back matter) are used for appendices, index, bibliography or notes. You could also use them to advertise your website or other books that you have published. Some self-published authors use the last inside page of the book as an order sheet which can be cut out or photocopied to order more books. It is common marketing practice to have the opening pages of the author's next book here as well.

FONTS AND TYPEFACES

The following are some of the most commonly used fonts and all are in 11-point size:

- Arial is a sans serif font.
- Times New Roman is a serif font
- Garamond takes up a bit more room than other fonts.
- Palatino takes up less space.

You can experiment with fonts; most computers now have a dazzling array but the aim should be clarity, ease and comfort when reading. Avoid quirky, hard-to-read fonts. Study published books to check the style. Even though you are self-publishing, your book will be judged against the standards of 'professionally' produced books; mimic their style. Pay particular attention to:

- quotation marks for speech – typically, single in the UK; double in the United States
- justified text
- indents at the beginning of paragraphs
- hyphenation at the end of lines (see the *Oxford Style Manual / Chicago Manual of Style* for advice on when and how you should words).

WIDOWS AND ORPHANS

A widow is the last line of a paragraph at the top of a page. An orphan is a one-word line at the end of a paragraph. Good typesetting will make sure there are no widows or orphans in the text. When you proofread your typeset work, look out for them and amend any you find (often by adding or cutting words).

DROPPED CAPS

Dropped capitals are used as a decorative flourish at the beginning of a chapter. This is not a requirement but it can look stylish for some types of books. This allows you to drop the capital letter over a number of lines of text.

ILLUSTRATIONS

Obviously, illustrations and photographs are not necessary for all genres but they can add value (to a cookery book, for example). There will be a cost to reproduce the photos and illustrations (as there will be if you work with an illustrator or photographer to produce new artworks for your book), so you need to work out whether that extra cost will contribute to selling more copies; in other words, do they add value? You also need to consider:

- Do you need permission to reproduce them? If so, you may have to pay for that permission.
- Can you reproduce them in sufficient quality?

The cost of getting permissions will depend on what size you will use; a quarter-page image will be cheaper than a half-page image, and a front cover will cost more than one in the body of the text.

You can source illustrations and photos from the Picture Research Association; they have a list of photo libraries and freelance picture researchers. If you want to use an illustrator, contact the Association of Illustrators for a list of members and to get an idea of costs. One way of avoiding having to get permission would be to take the photographs yourself.

Binding

Hardback and paperback books are bound differently; hardback binding is more expensive. The two most common forms of binding are:

- **perfect binding:** the spine of the folded section is trimmed off, glue is added and the cover is put on
- **slotted/burst binding:** this is the same as perfect but here grooves are cut into the spine.

Print run

Booksellers want to see how a title performs before they put in a large order. They tend to order a few copies (if you are lucky) and then wait and see how they sell. As a result, publishing houses now print fewer copies on the first print run because they do not want to be left with a huge amount of unsold books.

As a self-publisher, you should think about the numbers you want to print for the first run:

- Print too few and you could run the risk of losing sales while waiting for reprints if the book proves to be popular.
- Print too many and you could have problems and costs regarding storage.

Remember that you will want to send some books out as review copies (publishing houses send around 30–50 but that would not be practical for a self-publisher) and keep some for gifts and as a record of your achievement. Some may be incorrectly bound and a few might get damaged in transit, so you will need to build these in when considering your print run.

PRINTING

Find a local printer who is used to book production and who is willing to help you through the process; not all printers have the correct machinery or expertise for book printing. Ask to see examples of books that they have produced before. Check whether they will do short print runs or have a minimum print run. You do not have to go with the first printer you contact; they are used to giving quotes for jobs, so ask for a few to compare and contrast.

For your meeting with the printer, take along some examples of books that you like and would consider having as your final production copy. The printer will be able to tell you how much each version would cost and what is the best option for you. They will also be able to help you choose the right weight of paper for your book. If they don't do the kind of binding you want, or only do very large print runs and you just want a few hundred books, ask them to recommend another printer.

Paper comes in 'weights'; the pages of most paperback books are printed on paper that weighs from 60gsm to 100gsm (gsm stands for 'grams per square metre'). The lighter the paper, the flimsier and cheaper it feels. Heavier paper, obviously, weighs more; while this makes the book feel more expensive, it costs more and should be a consideration if you are going to be posting your book.

The cover of a book, called a 'coverboard', is coated on one side only and usually weighs around 220gsm to 240gsm.

Ask for paper samples (both pages and cover) and see which ones you like the feel of and always get a written quote.

Think about where you will store your books once they have been printed. Your printer may be prepared to store your books for you if you do not have the space yourself. You will be responsible for distributing them as well. Some printers offer print on demand (POD) and have links to wholesalers and distributors like Gardners (see Chapter 9 for more information on distributors).

Before the book goes to print, you should see a set of proofs and 'sign them off'; that means, you have said that you are happy with the proofs and that the book is ready for printing. If you miss any errors, then that is your responsibility. If, when your books are printed, there is a fault and it is found that the printer is to blame, you can get the books reprinted for free.

Typesetting

Some printers offer typesetting as part of their service. Otherwise, you could typeset it yourself or you could use a professional typesetter.

There are publishing consultancies, such as Amolibros (www.amolibros.co.uk), that offer services such as typesetting and have a list of contacts for printing, design and websites. The Alliance of Independent Authors (ALLi) is a good source for author services (see Resources).

Typesetting your book allows you to work out the number of pages you will end up with. POD uses single sheets of paper in the production process so that is very straightforward. Conventional printing uses large sheets of paper which make up 32 pages; these are folded and trimmed into 32-page sections. A paperback is therefore made up of any number of 32-page sections. Each 32-page section increases the print cost.

Having laid out your text, for example, you find that your total number of pages is 180. You can either opt for another 32-page section (which would give you 192 pages) or do a bit of judicious editing and get the pages down to 160. Editing does not mean cutting out text; you can reduce the point size, cut down the front matter pages or change the margins, the leading or the tracking.

Vanity publishing

As we are looking at using 'specialists' to help you produce your book, this is a good point to consider vanity publishing. Vanity publishing has a bad name. The 'vanity' bit comes from the effusive reports sent by many of these firms, praising the work of the authors for their wonderful manuscripts (regardless of whether those manuscripts have merit or not). Not surprisingly, firms offering this service do not call themselves 'vanity publishers'; they use terms like 'subsidy', 'self-publishing', 'joint venture', 'shared responsibility' or 'co-operative publishing'.

If you sign up with a vanity publisher, you will be asked to grant them exclusive licence to exploit your work. What you are paying for is the actual publication of the book. An unreliable and dishonest vanity publisher will print as few books as possible.

In most cases, the vanity publisher advertises for writers ('Authors wanted') and charges them a lot of money (often thousands of pounds – up to £10,000 in some cases) to print a number of books. The vanity publisher takes the money from the author so has no need to sell any books to make money. Royalties may be promised but are seldom paid. The author pays a vanity publisher to print their book but they do not own the books; they are the property of the publisher. Vanity publishers sometimes claim to have a special relationship with some booksellers, implying that they will get your books stocked there. That is unlikely. Production values are not always very good.

Read the fine print of the agreement; a clause which says the publisher will print 'up to 1,000 copies' or send out 'up to 20 fliers to reviewers' doesn't really mean anything; they could technically just send out one copy. Be wary, too, of references to storing and warehousing; subsidy publishers tend to use print on demand.

However, not all subsidy publishing involves being ripped off and exploited. Many print-on-demand firms are subsidy printers. The publisher provides a service (laying out and producing copies of a book) for a reasonable price. A good subsidy publisher will:

- explain the services on offer
- allow you to retain all the rights to your work
- tell you that you can order more copies after the first run
- allow you to have your own imprint/publishing house name on the book
- not promise to get great press coverage
- not tell you how brilliantly written your book is
- not promise that your book will make money
- happily send you examples of other books they have produced for clients
- allow you to terminate the relationship at any time and with no penalty.

The Society of Authors and the Alliance of Independent Authors provide useful advice on vanity publishing and self-publishing.

Print on demand (POD)

Print on demand means, quite simply, printing a book (and it can be just one book) only when an order is placed; it is not another term for 'self-publishing' nor is it a form of vanity publishing. Storing and distributing books is an expensive part of the publishing process, so being able to order books as and when you need them (often in very small quantities) is an attractive prospect for some authors. Many of the big publishing houses use POD for some of their backlist. Print on demand is a form of digital printing, as opposed to lithographic, which makes it a cheaper option for shorter print runs.

This also means that practically any book can be bought even if the publisher does not hold any stock. If the book is listed on Amazon or in a retailer's catalogue, when an order comes in, it will be sent on to a POD printer (as long as that printer has EDI – electronic data interchange) which holds the digital file for the book and they will then produce and print one copy to meet that order on your behalf.

USING A COMPANY TO SELF-PUBLISH

There are many companies that offer POD to self-publishing authors. They are a form of subsidy publishing in that an author pays some money to get their book into print. Lulu, Pen Press,

CreateSpace, Blurb and many others offer POD self-publishing in various formats. In many cases, they are also epublishers (there's more about epublishing in Chapter 7).

POD packages will be slightly different with each company. An advantage of using a self-publishing company like Matador, Xlibris or Pen Press is that the books can be ordered on Amazon and via other bookshop sites so you do not have to be part of the distribution process. Anyone visiting that company's site will also be able to buy your book.

Companies like Lulu will keep accounts for you and organize the production of print on demand. Profits are paid into a bank or PayPal account. You set the selling price and the epublisher will tell you how much each will cost to print. After printing costs are deducted, you receive an agreed percentage of the profits.

HOW TO CHOOSE A POD PUBLISHER/PRINTER

- There are a lot of companies advertising POD with some services as an added extra (such as marketing, getting ISBNs). Get all the details and compare and contrast; what do they offer and what do you need? Ask to talk to some of the writers who have used their services.
- Read writers' magazines and forums and see which companies are getting the good (or bad) press.
- Ask to see some samples; there should be guarantees about the quality of paper and the binding.
- Ask for contact details of authors who have used their services more than once; you want to make sure the company is well established and reliable. Were they happy with royalties and contracts? Were there any unexpected costs or loss of rights. What was the quality of the product?
- Ask how quickly orders will be met.
- Find out how you can terminate the publishing agreement if you change your mind (the Society of Authors / Authors Guild / ALLi will check through contracts before signing); a non-exclusive contract with no yearly commitment is best.
- Check ISBNs are included if you want them provided.
- Ask whether they will let you use your own ISBN and imprint name; not all POD companies are flexible in this way so that can be one way of narrowing down your choice.
- Check the licence and what you are granting to the POD publisher – what authority does the service have over your work? You want to be able to keep the rights to your book.

- Make sure that nothing is being licensed to a third party without your agreement.
- Where is the book being distributed or sold?
- Is the service exclusive or non-exclusive? In other words, can you sell your book elsewhere while using their service? There are two exceptions to this relating to ebooks (see Chapter 7).
- Go to the service provider's website. Are they promoting books or services? This is especially important if you are opting for a service which will sell your books for you. In this case, a website should display books clearly; there should be buying links on the website; biographies of writers; external links to other book industry organizations; a social media profile (such as Twitter or Facebook) and proof of membership of reputable industry organizations (such as ALLi).

Key idea

Do not go with a company that requires 'grant of rights' – you are signing away your exclusive rights to publish, reproduce and distribute your work for the full term of copyright (i.e. your lifetime plus 70 years).

Websites such as Lulu and Blurb offer free software so you can lay out your book yourself. Only when you order a printed copy (or copies) do you pay. You upload your manuscript and photos, use the formatting tools to choose the size, binding, cover, page layout and so on. You can play around with the format until you are happy with the finished product. As John Richardson explains in the case study at the end of this chapter, the costs are so reasonable that it is worth getting one copy printed, just to see if you are happy with the finished product; if not, you can go back, play around with the formatting some more until you are happy. The other advantage of using POD is that printing can be done very quickly. You can have your book in your hand in a matter of weeks.

Marketing and promotion

As a self-publisher, your success in selling your book lies with how motivated you are and whether you have the time and desire to market your 'product' (i.e. your book).

Every book needs the marketing efforts of its author behind it; more so when it has been self-published. You do not have the muscle and know-how of a publisher's publicity and marketing department behind you; you do not have their budget (although marketing budgets are not very big unless you have a proven track record of success). Although some self-publishing POD companies offer marketing (usually at an extra cost), it cannot really match the efforts of a committed author.

 ## Katherine T. Owen, self-published author of *It's OK to Believe*

'Self-publishing can be a route to getting taken on by a mainstream publisher. If you sell a few hundred books, you've shown that you have got a market. It's telling the publishers something about your motivation and your profile; that you're prepared to put time in on marketing.'

Self-publishing can be a way of proving yourself to a publisher before they take you on. If you have a finished product that is successful, this is an attractive prospect to a publisher. A traditionally published mass-market book, even if it sells poorly, should sell between 5,000 and 10,000 copies. If you can start to match those figures, you may just find agents and publishers sitting up and taking notice.

What you do have, though, is the self-belief that the book was worth printing in the first place. You know the story behind how it was written and what it is about better than anybody. You know the audience a lot better than a publicity professional does. Unlike the professional publicity people, you do not have to promote anyone else's book but your own.

Other information

The Arts Council of England supports a website for new writers, helping them to develop their writing: www.youwriteon.com. Members upload opening chapters or short stories and the YouWriteOn system randomly assigns these to another member to review. You then review another member's story excerpt – assigned to you at random – each time you want to receive a new review back in return. After five reviews a story enters the chart system and the highest-rated writers receive free feedback each month from editors working at the leading publishers Orion and Random House.

Booktrust (www.booktrust.org.uk) is an independent educational charity that aims to bring books and people together. The website has useful information, including a fact sheet for authors looking for a publisher or authors who are thinking of self-publishing.

Case study: John Richardson, self-published poet

'A lot of the great poets have self-published; William Blake, for example, produced and published almost all his work himself. It was a recognized way of publishing poetry. So now that self-publishing is becoming popular again, it's gone full circle.

'The self-publishing route I have taken is easy; you don't have to be that technically literate and people pick it up readily. There are several sites on the Internet [such as Lulu, Blurb] that offer free, downloadable, book-layout software which you use to create your own books. You compose your pages and you can build a book in about an hour. You then upload your document to the web server and the company turns them into books; I've used Blurb for my poetry. I have an artist friend who put a lot of photographs in her self-published book which worked well. The hardback ones, in particular, are lovely.

'It does have some drawbacks; it's not as sophisticated as Word. I did a paperback version successfully and thought it would also work as a hardback but when it came out in hardback the text had run to one side. But this is a minor problem and I can send it back to have it done again. You can literally move a word one space and it can throw the whole book out because it can shift text around and the formatting can bleed from one page to another. So if you change something at the bottom of one page, you have to check all the following pages, which probably means it isn't ideal for novels. Also it doesn't do automatic indexing. But for something like poetry it is perfect because, with poems, you usually do a page at a time.

'Colour can be a problem, too. With a traditional printer, they colour-match what they print carefully. When you're doing it from a computer screen yourself, it isn't always quite the colour that it appears on the printed version. And, if you're very particular, like an artist, that's going to be important for you. For other self-published writers, it's unlikely to matter to them.

'There is an element of toing and froing, of experimentation, to check that the final reproduction is right; one book I did had a photo on the front which was a bit too dark at first. So my advice is to have one book printed, to see how it looks, before you decide to do an actual print run of several copies. That is the other thing that makes this so practical – the cost. I've done one book for £2.95. It can cost very little to produce a book. For example, I had a budget of £300 to produce a book for one of our poetry societies. I got 76 copies, plus postage, for something like £275. There are about half a dozen formats to choose from so the size of the book is physically limited by those formats. There's a price calculator to help you work out the cost, and if you buy more than ten books, a discount kicks in.

'I'm not interested in making a living; all I want to do is cover my costs. With my first book, I set myself a budget of £100, worked out how much it would cost and then said to myself, "Right, I've got to sell at least 18 of these to cover my costs" and I did that easily. For me, this is a hobby. So putting in £100 on my hobby is fine.

'I did choose to do one book in a seven-inch square format. It took me about four days to get it laid out but I'd made the mistake of doing the design before checking how much it was going to cost. When I did that, I realized that the book would work out at £10 a copy. I couldn't do it that way on the budget I had, so I went back, found another design, checked the price and laid it out again.

'From bitter experience, I've learned that you should get feedback from other people. I strongly recommend that. I thought my first book was perfect when I put it together. I sent it to friends, and one of whom told me that the poems were in the wrong order. I replied they didn't need to be in any order; they were just separate poems but she insisted that there was an order. And she had a point, I realized. I didn't think it mattered but in fact it does. I've read a lot of poetry books since then and, if you look, you can see that there is a structure to them.

'There is a great deal in terms of putting a book together. Simply choosing the right cover, getting the right image, the right type font and all the rest of it, how to lay it out… I had a commission from a friend to produce one book, a book of love poems. I gave it to a friend who was an artist and she pointed out that I couldn't publish it with the design I had chosen because it was too stark; it was bright white shiny paper and black text. So she suggested toning it down, making it less shiny and using grey instead of black which softened it, making it much more appropriate for love poems. It would never have occurred to me to do it that way.

'I wanted to use a copy of a William Blake painting on the front of one of my books and I thought there wouldn't be a copyright problem because Blake was dead. I found the painting, which is in the Birmingham Art Gallery, and thought I'd just better check it would be OK. Could I use it? No, they said, you've got to pay us. Even though it's on the wall of a public art gallery and the image is all over the Internet, the photographic copyright is owned by the gallery and that's what I'd be using. I was able to use it in the end because I did pay them some money, but if I hadn't, I could have been sued. And people do come after you now because it's very easy to search on the Internet to see whether you've infringed copyright. The best advice is take a picture yourself; then it's yours. Or get official permission from the owner.

'I hadn't realized at first that every book has an inside cover, with the name, the publisher, the title on it. You have to have a page with the ISBN, references, copyright and so on. Even something simple like where to put the name of the poet in an anthology of poems has to be considered. I put the names on the bottom left because some poems extend over more than one page. So you know if a person's name is at the bottom, you've come to the end of the poem. It's not a right or wrong; it's just my decision to have it laid out that way but it has to be consistent.

'The one thing I've learned, particularly about self-publishing poetry, is that the words are important. With poetry, you have to be conscious of the odd word hanging off the end of a line which looks wrong. Whatever else you do, you have to facilitate the reader reading the book and finding the poems. So everything you do has to be aimed at that; the font has to be clear, the title has to be clear; you give indications of where poems begin and end, particularly if there are different people's poems in the book. As long as when a person opens the book, they don't get any unexpected surprises, like a sudden change of font. The easiest thing to do is to go and read other poetry books and see how they are done. They are the professional people; they know how it works and what doesn't. I think this is particularly important with poetry.

'A big poetry book sells in the thousands; contrast that with a successful novel that sells in hundreds of thousands. I know I can sell 20 books a year, that's no problem. I do readings; that's where the market is for self-published poets. All I'm interested in is selling one or two books after a reading. That's the easy way to test the market. You can also test the poems in your poetry group. Sometimes, I publish work that I like and I'm not too bothered whether other people like it or not because I have the freedom to do that.

'It definitely does something when you have a book in your hand. There's a world of difference between an electronic book and a physical book – a book you can put in your pocket. There's something almost organic about having the words on the paper and they're your words; it does something to your spirit.

'I never considered trying to get taken on by a publishing house. The route for that, while it is practicable, is a long one for a poet. You've got to establish a track record, which means being published in magazines for several years; ideally, you've got to win a reasonably prestigious competition; you have to do readings; in other words, you need a "poetry presence". When you do, you could start to approach publishers. And it would probably be a small printing press that might take you on and they'd probably only print several hundred of you books. If you sell a thousand poetry books, you're in the top league! I can publish 50 and it costs me less than £200, so why should I bother trying to get a publishing house to take my books? I'm not interested in trying to be in the top flight; I just want my books on my shelf and for friends to be able to have copies of my books.'

Focus points

- Self-publishing allows you to be in control: you can make all the decisions and you control the pace of the project. Self-publishers must be publisher, editor, agent, salesperson and publicist if they want to sell their books.
- Vanity publishers should be approached with caution; they charge a lot of money and can make promises that they do not keep.
- When you are producing your book, you will be judged against the quality and production values of professionally published books.

Next step

An important part of the self-publishing revolution has been ebooks and epublishing. In fact, when many people talk about 'self-publishing', they mean digital self-publishing. It is estimated that ebooks now account for around 25 per cent of the market. In the next chapter, we look at epublishing in detail and how you can publish your work as an ebook.

7

Ebooks and epublishing

'This paperback is very interesting, but I find it will never replace a hardcover book – it makes a very poor doorstop.'
Alfred Hitchcock

Epublishing has been around for longer than you might think. It began in 1971 with Project Gutenberg (www.gutenberg.org), now the oldest digital library of electronic books. In 1986 Franklin Electronic Publishers produced the first commercially available handheld reader. One of the first examples of a successful transition to epublishing was science journals. Scientists and academics were quicker than most to circulate their work within their community in a digital fashion.

But then things really began to take off and the market for ebooks grew considerably. In 2007 Amazon launched the Kindle e-reader in the United States, which rapidly became a mass consumer item. More devices became available (such as Apple's iPad) which helped drive the developing ebook market. In 2013 the ebook market was worth £17.6 million and sales of ebooks in the UK accounted for around 19 per cent of all books sold. For books on romance, science fiction and fantasy, that figure was nearer 25–30 per cent.

Now, all traditional publishers have been adding to their ebook list and more titles, both fiction and non-fiction, are becoming available. Some trade publishers have even created specific digital imprints, such as Random House (with Hydra, Alibi and Flirt). Books that were once out of print are coming back into circulation and, thanks to Project Gutenberg, you can download a huge number of out-of-copyright ebooks for free.

But it is the self-published authors who have really embraced epublishing and there are already numerous success stories. In 2010 US writer Amanda Hocking wanted to make $200 to go to a Jim Hensen exhibition in Chicago so began uploading her paranormal romance stories online. A year later, she had sold more than one million copies of nine novels, reputedly earning $2 million in the process. British writer Stephen Leather was already a successful thriller writer published by Hodder & Stoughton. He brought out three electronic versions of his unpublished work and was soon selling about 2,000 ebooks a month. John Locke was the first self-published author to sell a million Kindle ebooks. He was signed up by Simon & Schuster to print his physical books, but Locke kept control of his ebook publishing.

How to epublish

 Trevor Dolby, publisher, Preface Publishing, an imprint of Random House

www.prefacepublishing.co.uk

'The changing face of the book marketplace occupies publisher's minds greatly… I don't think an author should worry about this. If anybody knew what we knew, no books would get published!'

Whether you aspire to reach the bestseller list or just want to bypass the traditional publishing route, epublishing is now a popular choice for writers. You can either use an epublisher to produce your book or you can do it yourself.

Todd Armstrong, senior acquisitions editor, Communications and Media Studies, SAGE Publications

www.sagepub.com

'There are a lot of different platforms out there (Cybook, Sony Reader, NOOK, Kindle and so on); you can read on a variety of devices. My iPhone can hook into my Amazon account and I can download ebooks on to that. Project Gutenberg is great, too; I can read all the works of Shakespeare for free by downloading them on to my phone. I am really surprised at how I like the e-readers. Why buy a book for $25 when I can get it for $9.99? And read it on my phone, in the cinema while I'm waiting for the movie to start. I thought I would miss the tactile feeling of turning the pages but I don't.'

Ebooks can be downloaded and read on a PC, ebook readers (e.g. Amazon's Kindle, Sony's Reader, Barnes & Noble's NOOK), tablets or mobile phones or even printed off and read as hard copy. Some ebooks are tied to a specific e-reader, like the Kindle; while others can be read on various devices.

Key idea

Most writers will start the epublishing process with their text as a Word document (either .doc or .docx) file with any images or tables supplied in appropriate file formats (such as a TIFF, JPEG or EPS). This will then be converted into the suitable ebook software.

One popular ebook formatting system is ePub (which has an .epub file extension). This is a free and open industry standard for ebooks, designed for reflowable content ('reflowable' means text that can be optimized for different e-readers). It can be used with complex layouts, rich media and interactivity. It is used for a wide range of digital content which includes books and magazines. It is the most popular ebook format used for Apple, NOOK, Sony, Kobo; Kindle now also takes ePub as well as its own Mobi format and Smashwords also takes ePub files.

Preparing your manuscript

Any computer software jargon can be off-putting, especially if you don't consider yourself to be a technical expert; however, self-publishing your ebook is fairly straightforward. The digital equivalent of typesetting is formatting. Different ereading devices use different software for their ebooks. Formatting ensures that your book will display correctly on different screens and that it flows properly however the reader chooses to view the text (landscape or portrait; large print or small).

You can prepare your manuscript yourself or use a conversion house to do it for you. Most ALLi members, for example, use Scrivener to create epublications, .mobis, .pdfs and .docs. Other options are Jutoh and Calibre.

The main ebook publishers, such as Amazon's Kindle Direct Publishing (KDP), Kobo Writing Life and Smashwords, have clear guidelines on how to prepare and format your document prior to publishing.

Don't worry about formatting (such as italics or bullet points) when you are preparing the first draft for conversion. Proofread the document, add any pictures (such as photos, tables, video, weblinks, PDFs) and, once you are happy with it, you can then start formatting.

Here are some basic tips:

- You don't need page numbering; each format has its own inbuilt numbering system.
- Put chapter titles in capitals.
- Don't use large fonts (12 point is fine for the main text; 14 point for headings and titles).
- Avoid tabs and indents.
- Don't use bullet points: use a dash instead (epublishers don't always recognize a bullet point because it is in a special font).
- Avoid fancy fonts (Kindle, NOOK Press, etc. don't like them), so the document may not upload correctly or get rejected. Use something basic like Times New Roman, Arial or Helvetica.
- Use a return to create a space between paragraphs or pages; use no more than four.
- Avoid using headers and footers.

Amazon dominates the ebook market, both in sales and in publishing; it is followed by Barnes & Noble, Apple and Kobo, in that order. It is easy to set up your ebook for free and only 'pay' (i.e. give a percentage of the sale price) when your book sells.

You will need to set up an account with one of the publishing platforms listed below. They all have slightly different sign-ups but, in the main, they will require you to:

- set up an account with them
- add your bank details so you can be paid
- describe your book (do two versions: a short description, around 75 words and a long one, 4,000 words maximum); this is your blurb – make it engaging (see Chapter 6 on writing blurb copy)
- add the publisher's details (you can create your own if you are doing it yourself)
- add the author's details
- add in a copyright page
- choose the categories the book fits into
- verify your publishing rights
- add in keywords (see below for more details on this)
- upload the book file
- upload the book cover
- enter your pricing details
- indicate whether you want DRM (see Chapter 4 for more details).

You are usually able to preview your book before it is published. The beauty of an ebook is that you can go back and change things (layout, words, etc.) as many times as you want.

Orna Ross, founder and director, Alliance of Independent Authors

www.allianceindependentauthors.org

'Our Canadian writers are very interesting in that Kobo is a Canadian-based organization and so is Wattpad, which is driving bestsellers in some of the newer territories. Anywhere where a technology platform meets the writer becomes very vibrant, like the United States when Amazon first started it all.'

Platforms and other services

AMAZON – KINDLE DIRECT PUBLISHING (KDP)

Amazon dominates the bookselling market and KDP is the most popular epublishing format for writers. In many instances, when an author talks about self-publishing an ebook, they are talking about KDP. It is straightforward and clear and offers good royalty rates to the largest audience. Latest figures show that 79 per cent of people who have downloaded, accessed or shared ebooks in the UK did so using Amazon's Kindle platform (source: Ofcom survey into consumers' digital consumption, 2013).

KDP pays a royalty rate of 70 per cent from sales of ebooks priced at £1.49 and above or 30 per cent for books priced between 70p and £1.49. Remember that the 70-per-cent royalty rate incurs a delivery charge. You can set different prices for different countries or set all prices to match the US/UK price. There is no charge for uploading your manuscript.

Amazon will take 30 per cent of your royalties for tax reasons unless you send them a W-8BEN form and an Individual Taxpayer Identification Number (ITIN), which you can get from the US Internal Revenue Service (US embassies will have information on this or you can download forms from the Internal Revenue Service: http://www.irs.gov/forms-&pubs). The Society of Authors has information on this as well.

If you enrol in the optional KDP Select programme, your book becomes available to borrow from the Kindle Owners' Lending Library; every time your book is borrowed, you get a fee (paid from the KDP Select Global Fund). This varies each month but can be around two to three dollars for each loan. Plus you earn 70-per-cent royalties from sales to customers in Brazil, India, Mexico and Japan. You can also take advantage of two marketing tools: Kindle Countdown Deals (limited-time promotional discounting for your book) or Free Book Promotion (where readers worldwide can get your book for free for a time), which is a handy way of pushing your book up the charts.

 Key idea

In return for being part of the KDP Select programme, there is an exclusivity clause. You cannot offer your book for sale anywhere else; the initial enrolment in KDP lasts 90 days. Your book will be automatically re-enrolled once the 90 days are up, so if you want to publish your books on another platform, you will have to cancel your enrolment before the 90 days is up.

APPLE

You can publish through Apple (i.e. upload a file yourself) but you will need a Mac computer. If you want to sell your ebook via the

Apple iBookstore, it is easier to publish through Smashwords (see below). You will need an ISBN (which Smashwords will give you for free if you publish through them).

For non-American writers, getting your book published with Apple can be rather convoluted. If you live outside the United States, you will need a foreigner's ITIN (Individual Taxpayer Identification Number) – see above. Getting an ITIN isn't straightforward and can take some time. The Society of Authors has guidance notes on how to get an ITIN.

Apple's iBook Author app is aimed at writers who want to build textbooks but it is a useful tool for anyone who wants to publish an enhanced ebook.

BARNES & NOBLE – NOOK PRESS

Amazon has the Kindle, Barnes & Noble has the NOOK, the second most popular e-reader in the United States. Formerly PubIt!, Barnes & Nobles' self-publishing arm is now called NOOK Press. It allows US writers to write, edit and format their ebook in one place (you need a valid US bank account, US credit card and US tax ID to sign up to it).

It is non-exclusive (authors and publishers can sell the ebook elsewhere). Barnes & Noble will take a percentage of the list price when the book sells. Titles can start at $0.99. NOOK Press titles priced between $2.99 and $9.99 get 65 per cent of the list price. Titles priced at $2.49 or less or more than $10 get 40 per cent of the list price.

International writers can get on to Barnes & Noble via Smashwords (see below), but they will receive reduced royalty rates and lower visibility online as display preference is given to NOOK Press authors.

When you set up an account, you can upload, write, edit and publish directly into the NOOK Press format. It offers detailed sales and usage data on books. You start by uploading a Word document.

KOBO WRITING LIFE

Kobo (an anagram of 'book') makes its own e-reader and it's an ebook retailer, similar to Amazon's KDP. Writing Life is a platform that allows writers to self-publish directly through Kobo. You need to start with a Word, Open Office or Mobi file, which you upload directly to Kobo where it will be converted into ePub. Your book is then available to Kobo customers worldwide who can buy your book directly on to their e-readers.

Kobo sells directly but also has partnerships with organizations around the world (such as Chapters/Indigo in Canada, Angus & Robertson in Australia, WHSmith in the UK and Whitcoulls in New Zealand).

You don't need an ISBN but Kobo recommends it; publishers in Canada can get ISBNs free from 'Library and Archives Canada'. Kobo doesn't require exclusivity; you are free to distribute your ebook elsewhere.

It is free to upload to Kobo and authors get 70 per cent of the royalty rate on books priced between $1.99 and $12.99; the royalty rate is 45 per cent for books outside this price range. Authors can also 'sell' their book for free with no penalty or hidden costs.

SMASHWORDS

Smashwords will format ebooks and act as a distributor of ebooks. It doesn't sell huge amounts of ebooks itself but it is the authorized ebook distributor for the major online ebook retailers (iBookstore, Barnes & Noble, Kobo, Sony, Diesel, Flipkart, Baker & Taylor and Page Foundry). This is the easiest way to get your book into the iBookstore. It is the only way to get your ebook on to Sony and Diesel and the only way for non-US authors to get their ebooks on to Barnes & Noble. It does not distribute to Kindle; however, it will produce your book in a Mobi format which allows purchasers to read an ebook on their Kindle.

Smashwords accepts Word or ePub files and automatically converts them to suitable software for a variety of devices. You only need to load one master document. It uses its proprietorial 'Meatgrinder' method which converts the Word document into multiple formats. Smashwords suggests you format your document using its comprehensive style guide before uploading your file. You can preview your book before publishing and it is easy to update your document after it has been published.

Creating an ebook is free; Smashwords takes a percentage of each sale (usually 15–20 per cent) before forwarding the author's royalties to PayPal. You set the price and readers can buy the book from Smashwords directly or from other ebook retailers. You will need an ISBN for Smashwords, which you can either purchase yourself or Smashwords will give you one for free. You can also generate promotional coupons, which is useful for marketing.

SONY, DIESEL AND GOOGLE

The only way to publish via these platforms is through Smashwords.

LULU

Upload your manuscript in Word file and Lulu will convert, place and distribute your book to e-retailers like Amazon and Barnes & Noble. It receives 10 per cent of each book sale.

BOOKBABY

Supply an ePub file and BookBaby will distribute your book to e-retailers such as Amazon, Apple add Barnes & Noble. It charges a one-off fee based on three different service level options and pays 100-per-cent royalties. The standard set up is $99 plus an annual fee of around $19. If you are selling a healthy number of books a month, you would cover your set up fee and make a profit.

Helen Corner, Cornerstones Literary Consultancy

www.cornerstones.co.uk

'Why does an author need an agent or publisher these days? Why does an agent need a publisher? And does a publisher even need a bookshop? An author can go online and self-publish and potentially accrue better royalties with faster returns. And, the book goes straight to the consumer. There are huge possibilities for writers. Up until now, Internet publishing, POD, was a new industry. It was considered the poor man's choice, the "you've not made it as an author" option where the quality of the product wasn't guaranteed. But some writers are doing it because it makes money sense, especially if they've got a niche market. I say why not? It could even be seen as a savvy decision. As long as they market and edit professionally and aim to at least cover their costs.'

Epublishers

There are dedicated online publishers who take on authors' works in much the same way a traditional publishing house would and produce their work as ebooks. In other words, they pay to license your book. Their submission guidelines tend to be similar to traditional publishers (see Chapter 2).

Do not send your manuscript unless asked to do so and follow the submission guidelines – unsurprisingly, these will be electronic submissions. Epublishers tend not to pay advances but do often pay much higher royalties than traditional publishers. When your book starts to sell, you will receive royalties on those sales. Royalty rates vary from epublisher to epublisher, so do check what their rates are.

A word of caution: epublishing is popular with vanity publishers. Be careful about agreeing to pay an epublisher for services. Even if no money has changed hands, some epublishers make their money from taking advertising on their websites or by buying the rights to an author's work. Not all epublishers are suspect, but do some homework before you sign up. Ask yourself if the epublisher's website is the right place to sell your work.

If you are considering using an epublisher, do check out what they offer carefully:

- Ask what other authors and titles they produce.
- Do they have quality standards? Or can anyone place a book on their website, regardless of style, content matter and quality?
- How do they make money? Is it by advertising or by commissioning authors?
- How long have they been operating?
- Look at their contract and terms and conditions
- Is their site secure?

 Key idea

> If you do decide to go with an epublisher, only sign over English ebook rights; retain all the other rights, especially all electronic rights. And make sure that you can end the contract within a reasonable period of time (two years, for example).

Subsidy epublishers

We established in the previous chapter that subsidy publishers will publish your book for you on demand. They offer a range of services (editing, marketing, etc.) for which you pay an additional fee. You can either buy your books yourself from these companies (as discussed in Chapter 6); or they are available to buy by anyone browsing the site.

> ## Key idea
>
> Ebooks, unlike print books, are currently subject to VAT in Europe.

Cover image

Like a print book, an ebook will need a 'front cover' image. Most of the ebook publishing sites take JPEG or TIFF files. Unlike a print book, your ebook will not need a back cover or spine. Your cover will need to look good in both colour and black and white.

Often, the cover is being viewed as a thumbnail so you need to make sure that the words are bold and readable (avoid mixing fonts). You can use good stock images from the photo agencies (such as shutterstock.com, istockphoto.com, dreamstime.com or BigStockPhoto.com).

Stock photos come in set sizes: xsmall, small, medium, large, XL and XXL. You won't need a high-quality photo for the Internet. The size that works for both Kindle and Smashwords, for example, is 1600 x 2560 at 72 dpi.

Keywords and tags

Search engines look at keywords, tags and phrases to index the website or page. As the epublishing world is digital, it makes sense to use them to help promote your work as widely as possible.

Write out a list of words that you associate with your book (e.g. 'historical', 'romance', 'American Civil War'), then rank them in order of importance. Some epublishers allow you to list an unlimited number of keywords; others restrict you to three to five. Listing them by importance means you ensure that your top three words will be included. Tags (or metadata) are similar to keywords and help describe something so it can be found again by searching. For example, you'll find tags on each page of a book's description on Amazon.

The metadata (your book's description) will help you stand out from the competition. Readers will typically make their choices on ebooks in the same way they do for print: on the look of the cover and the book's description.

Analytics

If you are published by a traditional publishing house, you will get a twice-yearly royalty statement. If you are publishing using an online e-retailer, you can take advantage of real-time (or almost real-time) sales results.

There is more to this than having fun just hitting the refresh button to see how many books you might have sold on Amazon. Real- or near-time statistics give you useful feedback on any promotions you might be running (such as changing the price, an article appearing in a newspaper or magazine, a talk you gave at a book club…); you can see what works well and what doesn't.

Dashboards

This is not the control panel of a car but a way of viewing data associated with your account. In order words, you can see how your sales are doing, where people are buying your books, track any promotional activities to see whether there is a spike in sales. You can choose how you track sales (by region; by book; by date) and keep an eye on earnings.

Pricing

The American writer Boyd Morrison began selling his first book via Amazon's Kindle, priced at $0.99 and making his work available for free on his website. After three months, following a big push on the message boards of Kindleboard, MobileRead and Amazon (online forums), he had sold over 7,500 books. Kerry Wilkinson sold his first ebook, *Locked In*, for 98p in the Kindle store (earning him 34.4p royalty at Amazon's 35-per-cent royalty rate). Within three months of being released, the book was a UK number-one bestseller.

We look at setting the price of your book in more detail in Chapter 9. However, it's worth touching on here. There is concern in the publishing industry that digital or electronic means 'a lot cheaper'; after all, as far as the consumer is concerned, if you buy house insurance online, you usually get a discount. Ebooks do not have to be printed on paper, stored in a warehouse or distributed. So, to the potential buyer, they are obviously not as expensive in that sense. Yet, the author's creative input was just the same as if it were a paper book and that creativity needs to be rewarded (financially).

Nevertheless, ebooks tend to sell for less than print books. Look at your competitors and see what they are charging. You will also be guided by the royalty rates that some of the epublishers charge which will have an effect on the final price of your book. Ebook prices are not set in stone; you can change the price of your book when you want and you could even consider offering it for free for a period as a marketing ploy.

Amanda Hocking priced the first book in her series at $0.99, using it as bait to hook readers in; subsequent books in the series were $2.99. Low prices are attractive for impulse buys but you would need to sell a lot to see any significant profit.

If you want to sell your ebook yourself, via your website for example, you could put your book on a CD and post it to the buyer or, if you want to offer it as a downloadable file, you have to try to ensure that it is not downloaded by one person and who then shares it with all and sundry for free. You need to use software that has security features that prevent buyers from sharing your book; software like the latest professional version of Adobe Acrobat.

If you are offering downloads, use an application like www.e-junkie.com, which provides you with a shopping cart and buy now button. Depending on how much material you upload, it can cost as little as $5 a month. For example, when a buyer clicks on the PayPal 'Buy it now' button and pays for the goods, PayPal notifies the application provider which sends an email to the customer with the download.

The future?

One of the many pluses to come out of digital publishing is the creative freedom it gives writers, leading to new (and old) literary forms being developed. The short-story form, for example, has been given new life by epublishing. Kindle Singles and Workman Shorts are popular with readers. Hellel's short political essay 'Indignez-vous!' was a global bestseller in 2010–11. Ebooks allow a story to be as long as it needs to be.

Advances in ebook technology have added to the reading experience. In 2001 Faber produced a digital version of T.S. Eliot's *The Waste Land*. With its interactive notes, a filmed performance and audio readings of the poem, this digitally enhanced text proved a hit with the public. The iPad app covered its costs in just six weeks.

Heavily illustrated books have proved more difficult to produce in a digital format (cookery books, for example, are still popular as print books) because it is difficult to replicate the original layout when text and images can be changed so easily for the reader. However, as technology develops and richer graphic content is added, this will surely change in the future.

Ebooks can be so much more than printed static text. You could consider making your book interactive by using:

- **hyperlinks:** these enhance your readers' experience by linking to other websites or maps
- **pictures:** use a medium- or low-quality setting (high quality makes the final ebook file too large)
- **videos:** each YouTube clip has an 'embed video function' – remember to keep the file size low, though
- **audio:** speak your words as well as write them – use an MP3 format (again, this will increase the book's total file size)
- **augmented reality apps** – allowing you to animate pictures.

While e-readers have yet to become affordable in some countries, the ebook market is already beginning to grow in Brazil, Russia, China, India and Latin America. As more ebook readers and tablets become available, the global market can only expand.

Case study: Orna Ross

After the Rising, Before the Fall, Blue Mercy Poems: Ten Thoughts about Love, Go Creative! Go Creative! It's Your Native State, F-R-E-E-Writing: How to Do It & Why You Should, Inspiration Meditation

www.ornaross.com

'What used to happen with writing was unique in the creative arts. You had such a small number of titles available to readers. They were chosen by people who worked in publishing, a fairly small group who tended to be white, well-educated Oxbridge types in the UK or Ivy League in the United States. It was a very particular type of person who was choosing what everybody was reading. You didn't know if what was being put out there was representative of what readers actually wanted to read.

'What we're seeing now is a significant band of authors who are well able to do it all themselves, with the help of a small team: they know how to pitch their writing to a readership, put a beautiful cover on it, have it editorially enhanced. In short, put out a product that is as good as, and, in some cases, perhaps better than, what is produced by Manhattan or London publishing houses. So everybody has had to sit up and take notice of that. The power dynamic is shifting and that changes the status of all writers, not just those who choose this pathway to publication.'

'Authors are now building their own audiences, their own readership online, and so when they sit down in a negotiation with a trade publisher – if one wants to take them on board and if the author does want that kind of support – well, they can have a very different conversation to the old one, which was pretty much: "Here's a contract, sign it and be grateful."

'It's becoming a cliché to call it [the rise of author publishing] a revolution but it *is* a revolution. Now, one human imagination can whisper directly to another, without anybody coming between them. Books are the most intimate art form, one human imagination whispering directly to another. What [author publishing] does is just make that relationship even closer, without anybody coming in between... I think we're only beginning to see what that means. More writers, both those who have trade published and those who have not, are seeing the potential and we're only at the very beginning of what I believe is a completely seismic shift.

'I suppose the biggest challenge for author publishers is that it is a lot of work with a lot of different activities. There's a huge learning curve at the beginning because you have to understand about all the different kinds of software that you need to deal with and the different dashboards that you're going to put your books up on. You have to make decisions about whether you're going to DIY it or which services you're going to use and how you're going to use them; will you hook up directly with distributors or will you go through Smashwords? You've got to decide whether you have what it takes visually to commission a designer, how do you handle an editorial team, do you use beta readers to read your work or professionals? Where are you going to find the money to invest in what is necessary in order to make a good book? Ask yourself how much is it going to cost me, how many books do I think am I going to sell... You're basically starting a small business in a climate where everything is new and changing rapidly. So those are the challenges and that's why I don't think this is the route for every writer.

'It takes a bit of time. You will make mistakes. It is, in and of itself, a creative process and has all the discomfort that goes with that. Some writers feel "Oh, it's too hard; I'll never get there" and they give up. Having said that, when you've done it once, it's so much easier the second time. And by the third time all those things that were so challenging at the start have actually become quite routine and you're back with the challenge of "me and my writing" which is always the biggest challenge anyway.

'It is a big learning curve and it's a fast-changing area. A lot of writers are people who live quiet, introverted lives and need that in order to do the work. Can you marry that with what's necessary to actually publish well? Publishing and writing are two quite distinctive paths calling for different skills; can you encompass both in one person? I think every writer should try [author publishing] at least once because I've come across people who've thought "This isn't for me," and are very reluctant. They just want to put publish their backlist, for instance, and are tempted only by the money and nothing else. Then they take to author publishing like a duck to water.

'I first published my own work as an experiment because everybody was talking about it. I didn't expect to have the reaction I had and I didn't expect it to be so amazing, to tell you the truth. I'm not terribly technologically minded; people think I am but I'm not at all. I use technology only where it's useful; I have no interest in gadgetry. I didn't know if I would be defeated by the technology so I did a poetry book thinking, "Well, this is fine because nobody will read it anyway." I just put ten poems together and that was my first effort. It was short and easy.'

'I also teach a meditation practice to foster creativity, called "Inspiration Meditation", and my group were asking me for a book about the method. I thought, you know what, rather than just doing a pdf to hand out or post off to people, I'll do it as an ebook and then they can download it on Amazon. So that's what I did as my first efforts back in 2011 – poetry book and a meditation book – on the basis that, if I made a mess of it, the only people who would have read them would be kind.

'But other readers actually bought them! Books about a meditation method, books about poetry! Not huge numbers, of course, but strangers had found and purchased these less-than-mainstream books. This was astonishing to me. The ease of it instantly struck me and I began to think, this really is huge; this has enormous potential. What might my novels do, books that already had proven sales? Within a few weeks, I was writing to Penguin, reclaiming my rights. Soon after I published them, the novels were hitting the top of their category bestseller lists on Amazon, but even more pleasing was the creative control I regained. I hadn't loved the way the publishers treated my books. Being able to give them the titles and covers and treatment I had originally envisaged for them was wonderful. I haven't looked back since and I never will. I love the creative freedom most of all; but the whole process suits me, the kind of writer that I am, so very well.'

Focus points

- Giving your reader a choice of format, ebook as well as paperback, helps to drive sales.
- Ebooks can encourage people who might not have bought a paper book to look at your work.
- Epublishers do not always pay advances but their royalty rate can be higher than traditional publishing houses.

Next step

The book is finished. It has been typeset, proofread, printed or uploaded. Copies of your book are ready to be sold. However, if you want people to buy and read it, you have to let them know about it.

In the next chapter, we will look at how you promote your book. In the past, the writer was an almost anonymous, shadowy figure. Now, it's as much about the writer as the book.

8

Promotion and publicity

'Without publicity, there can be no public support.'
Benjamin Disraeli

Nowadays, the writer is an integral part of the package and they must do more of the work of publicity than writers in the past would ever have done. A successful writer becomes a brand on which promotional expenditure can be based.

You are unlikely to have a reputation that will sell your book for you. You need to market yourself as well as your book; the writing alone is not enough. Shy authors do not sell as many books. The reward is that the more you promote your book, the more copies you will sell.

Suzi Williamson, Publicity, A & C Black

www.acblack.com

'If a book is on quite a broad topic or it is a general fiction book, how are people going to distinguish between your book and all the others out there? It can be the author that makes the difference. In radio, even TV, they want the personality. You wouldn't get an author on the radio who couldn't talk passionately about their book or subject area. You want someone who is interesting, who will respond, who will come back with interesting angles and ideas – showing the personality behind the book.'

 ## Mo Smith, author

www.lazycookmosmith.co.uk

'I had no experience of marketing but I began by cold-calling local shops, both independent and national chains. I never telephoned first because I didn't want to give the buyer or manager the opportunity to say "No thank you" before they'd seen the book. I was offered a book signing at my local WHSmith. I approached Ottakar's [a former bookshop chain] in Cirencester. The manager was so enthusiastic about my books and always displayed them front facing on a stand of their own. But if you really want to get anywhere, if you're really serious about your book, you need to promote it beyond your local area. That's when you start to write to national newspapers and magazines. When I look back at my letters from that time, I do laugh. Some of them are two pages long! My daughter intervened: "You've got to email them, then follow it up with a phone call and actually speak to them." I found it really hard getting to speak to the right person; tracking down the correct phone number was an art in itself and you could immediately tell from the tone of their voice whether they were interested or not. The reply I mostly received was, "We only feature celebrities." My local Waitrose directed me to their head office. After many phone calls, the buyer said she would take my book. I couldn't believe it! It wasn't just my local store; it was countrywide.'

Maeve Binchy is a recognizable brand, even if most people would be hard pressed to name all the books she has written. Mo Smith chose her brand, the Lazy Cook, early on in her writing career and has maintained it throughout. When you are not writing, you need to think of yourself as the 'product'.

Consider the following:

- What do you want your brand to say about you?
- Decide whether you want to brand yourself as a writer in a particular genre or keep the branding as broad as possible.
- You could confuse people if you start as a poet, write a romantic fiction novel and then turn your hand to literary fiction; a pseudonym could come in useful.
- Will your website represent your brand?
- A uniform style should be reflected across your website and in your stationery (AI sheets, flyers, business cards, letter-headed paper).
- Enhance the brand; become an expert in your field; give talks and workshops.

In-house marketing and publicity

The publishing house **marketing department** is responsible for:

- originating all sales material (catalogues, 'blads' – book layout and design, samplers, etc.) which the sales team will use
- working with the sales team and big bookshops/supermarkets on special promotions
- preparing advertising for trade (post-published press advertising, along with reviews, other publicity)
- organizing companies sales conference where the new season's publishing is presented to sales reps and overseas agents.

The publishing house **publicity department**

- works with media on 'free' publicity (reviews, features, author interviews, bookshop readings and signings, festival appearances, book tours, radio/television interviews).

Each author/book gets a publicity campaign that plays to the book's or author's strengths.

The timescale for planning book publicity is different depending on the type of book. For a lead fiction title from one of the major publishing houses, they might be planning 18 months to two years in advance of publication; particularly if it is for a bestselling author. For general fiction, a medium-sized publishing house would generally plan marketing and PR around 12 months in advance and they would start to firm up their plans maybe six months in advance of publication. That would include making sure that journalists and researchers are aware of the book and have features or interviews in their schedule.

In the traditional world of publishing, a new print book usually only has a short time, maybe two to three weeks, to start selling. If that does not happen, retailers will send copies back to the publisher to get their refund and the publisher will not print any further copies. For ebooks, the timescale is slightly different. There is no worry about unsold stock cluttering up bookshelves. Ebooks develop over time, so there isn't the same urgency to build sales and an audience as there is with a print book.

Even if your book has been picked up by a publishing house, it does not follow that the publicity department will put its muscle – and its money – behind your book to promote it. Best-selling authors will get that level of interest and finance because there is more of a guarantee that the money will be recouped. It is a fact that publishers spend money on books that are going to do well. But you can help by working hard at your own publicity – whether it is supporting the publicity department or being your own PR agent.

What makes you interesting?

 Trevor Dolby, publisher, Preface Publishing, an imprint of Random House

www.prefacepublishing.co.uk

'The days of authors sitting at their desks, waiting for calls from their publisher's publicity department are long gone. Once the book has been commissioned, I will bring an author in and ask them to keep a note of everything that occurs to them while they're writing the book in terms of where they can sell it; people they can tap into, contacts they know, just write them down. So when we come to the point, three to five months before publication, the author can come back to us with a list of things we might be able to use to help us sell the book. And I expect them to come along with stacks of ideas; three quarters of which we hope we've already thought of and a quarter which will be fantastic new ideas.'

If you are with a publishing house, you will be asked to fill in an author's questionnaire or publicity form. Remember that publicity people do not know the detail; you do as the author of the book.

An author publicity questionnaire could ask you for/about the following:

- a brief biographical sketch – include anything relevant to the writing of the book or that is newsworthy
- whether there are any competing titles – if so, how does your book differ from them?
- whether there are any academic or professional courses that could use your book
- whether there are professional bodies, organizations or clubs which you belong that could be useful in promoting sales of your book
- whether you would be prepared to visit schools, libraries – will you be attending any events to promote your book?
- whether you would be prepared to give media interviews – if so, are you happy for your contact details to be passed to the press?
- whether you have any press contacts
- whether there are any journalists you think should be approached about your book
- whether you have your own website – are there any websites that would link to yours?

The form may ask you for your date of birth; this is needed for eligibility if your book is being put forward for an award.

If you are doing your own publicity (or having to fill out a publisher's publicity form and need a bit of help to formulate your answers), ask yourself the following:

- What is your USP (unique selling point)?
- What would make you stand out to the press?
- Why would a journalist want to write about you?
- Are you prepared to answer questions about yourself as well as your book?

Even if you have been picked up by a publishing house, it is still worth driving your own publicity. It proves to your agent and publisher that you are making an effort to be read by others.

Promotional material

Publicists for traditional publishers produce an AI (advance information – also known as an 'advance notice' or 'forthcoming title') sheet, to show the booksellers what the book is about. It is produced about six to nine months ahead of publication. It contains:

- a picture of the jacket
- a description including hardback or paperback
- the number of pages
- format
- classification details
- blurb/summary
- ISBN
- price
- information on the author
- any publicity/promotion
- sales of author's last title
- contact details.

If you are a self-publisher, there is no reason why you should not produce your own AI and send them to booksellers, wholesalers and library suppliers. You can have an order form at the bottom or on the back. An A5 sheet of paper will be perfectly adequate for this.

When publishers print books, they have a certain number of free copies that they can give out that have been built into the overall budget at the very beginning. If you are self-publishing, you will have to be careful how many books you choose to give away as review copies. Those are books you have paid for and will not get the money back on them if you give them away. There is also no guarantee that a book reviewer will feature your book even if you do send them a copy.

The book itself is a form of promotional material. Many authors supplement their free copies given on publication with ones bought from the publisher at a reduced rate. These can be given away (to friends, colleagues, interested parties) as you see fit. Mills & Boon were quick to spot a potential market when the Berlin Wall came down in 1989; the publisher had members of staff handing out 750,000 free copies of their romances to people in the street. While you probably don't want to operate on the scale that Mills & Boon did, free copies can help promote you and your book. They work especially well for authors who write book series; give the first one away and, if readers like it, they are more likely to buy the second book in the series.

 Key idea

Before you send out a review book or give one as a gift, check through for any errors (pages not trimmed properly, binding inadequate). Mistakes do happen but you should be the one to discover them, not a potential reviewer.

If you are working with a publisher, ask them for leaflets or flyers of your book so you can leave them in relevant places (bookshops, libraries or, if it's on a particular subject, somewhere relevant; for example, in a gym or leisure centre for a healthy eating book). The publicity department should also be able to supply you with a .jpeg file of the cover of your book that you can use on your website and own publicity material.

Here are some other promotional ideas:

- Use your book cover image for promotional material. It helps fix the image of the book in a potential buyer's mind.

- Bookmarks are relatively cheap to produce, useful and don't cost the earth to mail out. If you do use them when you send out your books, don't put them inside the book where they could get missed.

- You could use other items (T-shirts, mugs, stickers, badges, posters) as promotional items.

- With an ebook, use the 'Look inside' feature wisely. This shows the first 10 per cent of a book, so make sure that the front matter is different from a traditionally printed book. You want the cover, then the blurb, a table of contents, your preface/foreword (if the book is non-fiction) and then Chapter 1. Acknowledgements can go at the back, along with the first chapter of your next book.

Publicity in the media

Suzi Williamson, Publicity, A & C Black

www.acblack.com

'Self-published authors can often achieve good PR; if a publicist contacts a journalist, they know immediately that you've got a book to plug and can very quickly say "no". Authors can get a better response than we would get, because they are the authority and have passion for their subject. Don't be afraid of approaching journalists yourself. Think of all those pieces in the national press with author interviews, background stories and profiles; there will be a short byline at the end of the piece with details about the book. The book gets a mention but the journalists are often interested in the author.'

Read newspapers, look at television programmes, listen to the radio; make a note of where books are mentioned and work out where you could promote yourself – national prime-time morning radio programme or local radio station afternoon programme? Style magazine or business newspaper?

As Trevor Dolby suggests, it is worth keeping a list of potential contacts as you work on your manuscript. It could be a local newspaper journalist, a radio producer or a magazine editor. As with approaching agents and editors, make sure you have the right person and that you spell their name correctly.

You can buy media lists from publicity companies that show relevant media in newspapers, magazines, television, radio, online publications and blogs. These will help you target your key audiences. Companies such as Handle Your Own PR (www.handleyourownpr.com and www.handleyourownpr.co.uk) or Smith Publicity (www.smithpublicity.com) sell media lists. Alternatively, you could send a press release to a distributing service (for example, PRWeb or PR Newswire (www.prweb.com / www.prnewswire.co.uk). Lists and contacts are invariably international so you can target relevant countries.

Pulling together your own author questionnaire will help formulate some ideas for your self-promotion. It can also provide information for your press release.

The media is interested in the author, rather than the book itself, so you need to take this slant when producing your press release. What makes you special? What makes you stand out to the press? Consider the following:

- Local reporters are always interested in local published authors
- If your story or subject can be linked to a place, the local media in that area should be contacted.
- There are several publications for the over-50s; contact them if you are a 'mature' writer.
- Consider your gender – can you tie into publications aimed specifically at men or women?

Other ways to promote yourself:

- Enter writing competitions; if you become a finalist or, even better, win, you are newsworthy.
- Write a regular column in a local newspaper or magazine.
- Offer to write reviews for newspapers/magazines.
- Add yourself to Wikipedia.

Newspapers and magazines

Katherine T. Owen, self-published author of *It's OK to Believe*

'Marketing yourself is a big job. I would love a publisher to do that for me. But when I discovered that you really have to do it yourself anyway, it made me look at self-publishing as an option. It's going to be you building up your profile and looking for and doing interviews; the publishers are not going to do it all for you. Some publishers now even want evidence that you will do this work before they take you on.'

It is a sad fact that traditional book reviews in newspapers and magazines are becoming scarce but there are still some publications that print them. Traditionally, they have only dealt with print books. The role of the literary editor in the book pages of a newspaper or magazine is not to sell books. Their function is to entertain and be informative.

Getting publicity here depends on the lead times of magazines and newspapers; some monthly publications have quite lengthy lead times and they would want to plan their seasonal and major features or interviews six to nine months in advance so you have to get the information to them then.

Publicizing a book can be quite time critical, particularly with the news media or newsy magazines. They won't touch it if it's been around for the last six weeks. That's the same with the monthly magazines. You need to plan ahead. If your book links in with the Christmas market, it would be sensible to start thinking about approaching some publications in April. For the specialist market, publications don't mind waiting and reviewing a book after publication. Journals, for example, may only come out every three or six months so would happily review a book 18 months after publication (certainly if it was an important title).

Journalists and broadcasters generally prefer to be approached initially by email (a short email with two or three paragraphs; get to the point straight away and explain why your story would be suitable for their publication or programme). Don't just send an email to a group of people at the same time; they want to feel that careful thought has gone into the approach and that your pitch is relevant. If you say that you feel your story is perfect for a particular section or page or on a particular date, you imply you know what their publication is all about.

If your work is in a specialist area, subscribe to magazines that cover those subjects. They will often review books and interview authors. If you think that they will be interested in you and your work, get in touch with them.

Pass on the details of your local or specialist press to your publicist (if you are working with a publisher) and ask them to send out review books for you or do it yourself if you are self-publishing.

The Writers' & Artists' Yearbook, *The Writer's Handbook* and *Writer's Market* all have a list of national, regional and local newspapers as well as weekly and monthly magazines.

If you do get (good) reviews:

- keep copies
- post them on your website
- ask whether you can post the review on Amazon
- send copies of the review to bookshops and libraries.

 Key idea

Offering your book as a prize in a competition or as part of a readers' offer in a magazine or newspaper is a good way of getting your book cover in front of people and is a lot cheaper than having an advert.

 Suzi Williamson, Publicity, A & C Black

www.acblack.com

'Books that are on a niche, specialist topic often stand out on their own. You don't need to be able to talk to the media if you've published on a specialist or newsworthy topic, such as climate change or politics, birdwatching or crafts, because readers in your specialist area, or in the press, will be talking about it anyway; the content of the book is what is important here. But I think if you've written a fiction book, for example, it's more about knowing your market. So go along to literary *events and listen to interviews with authors; make sure you read articles. Media training can be useful, but you don't need to pay for media training to become media savvy; it's about being aware of what's going on and how other people respond and get news for their books. It's all about common sense really. Where could you see your book being featured? In which paper or magazine? It also might be a good idea to role-play questions and answers with a friend before any interview, making sure that you're well prepared for any difficult topics.'*

Television and radio

Relatively obscure and unknown books and authors have enjoyed success after being featured on TV programmes or segments like 'Oprah's Book Club', 'Richard & Judy's Book Club' and *The TV Book Club*. *The Bookseller* looked at the effect 'Richard & Judy's Book Club' had and estimated that, in the six years the Club was running, over 30.8 million copies of the hundred books featured were sold.

Getting a title on to a show like this is not easy and, rather like the initial submission process, a book is up against stiff competition. The odds are against a book getting through. However, nothing ventured, nothing gained. By all means, send out a review copy but more in hope than certainty.

A list of regional and national television and radio stations can be found in *The Writers' & Artists' Yearbook* and *The Writer's Handbook*.

Annie Ashworth & Meg Sanders

www.anniesanders.co.uk

AA *'We're not very good at self-publicity; it's not in our nature. I would rather die than go out and say "Hello, here I am." The author, Jill Fraser, talks to Women's Institutes three a week sometimes, which is fantastic.'*

MS *'We should do that.'*

AA *'I know we should. It helps to have someone with you. I was in a bookshop in a motorway service station which had copies of our books on display. My partner went in and said, "This is the author, do you want her to sign them?" So I signed six and that's six sold. I wouldn't have done it on my own though; I would have walked straight past.'*

MS 'I think you have to be really brazen at times. The more you do the better you become. You have to be more proactive than you would probably feel comfortable being.'

AA 'My absolute is that you have got to keep your dignity and credibility. There are areas I won't discuss or write about just to flog books; why should I? It's my private life and I think Meg feels the same way.'

MS 'I think it's a very, very short-term gain. You might shift some more books [if you do reveal things about your private life] but the damage that it could do to your relationships is much more lasting.'

The Internet

Book reviews may be few and far between in newspapers and on television or the radio, but online reviewing has never been more popular. Research has found that the web is currently the most popular source for finding out about the latest books, followed by browsing in shops.

A website and/or a blog help define your identity and give you a presence on the Internet. And if you are a rather shy person, who shudders at the thought of knocking on doors to raise awareness of your book, websites and email can help with promotion.

Never buy reviews. There is nothing wrong with asking someone to review your book but then stand by what they say – even if it isn't that flattering. And never create fake reviews of your books by pretending to be someone else.

AMAZON

Once your book is listed on Amazon, you can join Amazon's Author Central, a free service which allows you to promote yourself and your books to users of the website. You can have a photo, biography, upload missing book cover images, blog with readers, list all your books and give notice about any talks or signings you may be doing. You can add your books to programmes like 'Search Inside the Book' and Kindle so that they are available for customers to buy (only the book's rights holder can add the book to 'Search Inside'). For more information visit https://authorcentral.amazon.com

If you feel particularly confident, you could post a video book trailer on your Amazon author page (as well as on YouTube), introducing yourself and your book. Amazon uses short author videos of authors talking about their books. Professor Stanley Wells did a three-minute video piece, off the cuff, for his book *Shakespeare, Sex and Love* (Oxford University Press) as pre-publicity.

Amazon allows authors to have one video at a time on their author page. They ask that the video focus on specific features of the book and your experiences as a writer.

Instructions on how to upload the video can be found on Amazon's Author Central page.

KDP Select is a programme run by Amazon for independent publishers and self-published authors. The downside is that when you sign up to it, you cannot publish on any other website for 90 days. The upside is that while you are in the programme, your books can be enrolled on the Kindle Owners Library which allows Amazon Prime members to 'borrow' books for free; authors whose books are borrowed get a share in a monthly fund. People who borrow books tell their friends about what they're reading and are potential purchasers of the future. KDP Select also offers its authors several promotional tools, such as offering books free to readers for up to five days. Offering your book for free is a good way of increasing its visibility. Authors have noticed that when their book is 'free' on Amazon, sales of their other books increase.

Many authors check their sales rankings on Amazon regularly. No one is exactly sure how the calculations are made, but any book that is sold on Amazon gets a ranking: from 1 to the millions. Fiction is a tough genre to get high rankings in; it is easier if your book belongs to a more niche genre (gardening, cooking, military history, etc.). If you get it into Amazon's top 100, you have a bestseller on your hands.

Average ranking on Amazon – what it means	
2,000,000+	one consignment copy has been sold
1,000,000+	around 50 copies of the book have been sold
100,000+	up to 200 copies sold
10,000+	anything from 1 to 50 copies sold a week
1,000+	10–100 copies sold a week
100+	between 1 and 100 copies sold a day
10+	100–500 copies of the book sold a day
Under 10	around 500 copies sold each day

Here are some extra tips when trying to boost your sales via Amazon:

- Get your friends and family to buy your book from Amazon on the same day. A spike of sales affects the sales rankings; Amazon re-ranks books every hour so a big sale in one hour can have an effect.
- If you can keep your ranking in the top 10,000 (a couple of sales a day) that is considered to be a solid commercially viable book.
- Seasonal timing can affect ranking – that is, where your book is popular at a certain time of the year.
- Get friends to rate your book – one that receives five-star reviews that are rated helpful by others will be promoted by Amazon; it is programmed to recommend books that have positive activity.

YOUR OWN WEBSITE

Maria McCarthy, author

www.mariamccarthy.co.uk

'One of the most important things you can do for yourself as a writer is to get yourself a website. Definitely, everybody should have a website – because if journalists want to get in touch with you, it's so much easier if they can just Google you and have your website pop up. I did – it cost me £300 and has been worth every penny. A website helps to raise awareness of yourself and your book and act as a point of contact.'

All the authors interviewed for this book would not be without their websites. For them, it is a way of promoting their work and having a point of contact with their readership. Author Christopher Fowler left signed, customized first editions of his books in locations in London. He posted clues to their whereabouts in his blog on his website. One of the first books was left in a pub in Kentish Town; Fowler put the clue up on Sunday morning at 8 a.m. At 8.10 a.m., the pub landlord phoned him, complaining that there was a queue of people outside demanding to be let in.

A website does not have to be complicated; in fact, the simpler the better because, if it is too complicated, it takes too long to load. The aim is to show your work and, ultimately, sell your books. Make sure that the style and feel of your website fits your image and brand.

Here are some key tips:

- Have a photograph of yourself and of the cover of your book(s).
- If you have a strapline, use that as your domain name; otherwise, just use your writing name.
- Useful links should be just that – useful – and relevant; don't include your favourite shopping sites. Give some thought to the links and your website could become a useful resource for other authors.
- Have a page for reviews.
- Advertise any talks or appearances you are giving.
- Use Google keywords to see what people are searching for. What words and phrases are people typing in to search engines? Make a list and use them in your website (or when you are planning the contents of your book).
- Use AdWords. Set a budget (a set amount each month), choose key words that you feel people would type in and drive traffic to your website this way.
- Set up a link to Facebook, Twitter, etc. on your website so visitors can access more information on you.
- Check whether your work is being discussed anywhere on the web and join in the discussions. Point people to your website.
- Reward people who go to your website; run a competition and have your book as a prize.
- Link in with local companies and offer your book as part of a sponsorship deal; for example, if someone buys your book on getting fit and running a marathon, they get a percentage off a purchase from a local sports shop.
- Put a website link on any promotional material you send out; ask whether they would like regular updates about your book/appearances/blog. Note: make sure that you say that you are keeping your contacts list confidential and not sharing it with others or handing it on to a listing agency.
- Create a reading group guide for your book. List points of discussion or questions that a group would find useful. Put them at the back of your book and online.

A website shows that you are prepared to engage with your readership and push sales of your books. That is something a publisher likes to see.

If you have a publisher and are planning to have a website built, ask whether they will supply images, logos and reciprocal links. The Society of Authors and ALLi have a list of website designers recommended by members.

Key idea

If you are writing for children or young adults, a website is doubly important. These are the readers who are online a lot of the time. If they want to find out more about you, they will go looking for your website, rather than go to the library.

Blogging

 Doug Young, publishing director, Sport and Entertainment, Transworld

www.transworldbooks.co.uk

'I think self-marketing is becoming increasingly important for authors. Having your own website, a blog, a presence, they're all grist to the publicity/marketing mill. Given that the print media are increasingly hard to get any presence in because there are fewer journalists, fewer book reviewers and fewer everything. The more authors can grab that particular bull by the horns and start to get their name out there by any means, the better. We always like it if an author comes along with dedicated website followers – that's an automatic plus from a book marketing point of view.'

Blog – the word comes from web-log. It's a kind of online diary that you add 'posts' to. Blogs can be topical, personal, or about the craft of writing. The advantage of blogging is that it is free and requires very little technical proficiency. But, if you are embarking on a blog, you need to keep them updated… and well written.

A blog doesn't necessarily lead to a book deal; editors are not glued to their computer screens searching for the next big thing in blogging. Blogs are like books – they are successful if people want to read them. However, some 'blooks' (books based on a blog or website) can do well:

- *Julie & Julia* won the inaugural Blooker Prize awarded to blogs that had been turned into books. Written by Julie Powell, it was turned into a book by Little, Brown and Company and a film starring Meryl Streep by Nora Ephron.

- The website 'One Red Paperclip' was created by Kyle MacDonald, a Canadian blogger who bartered his way from a single red paperclip to a house in a series of online trades over the course of a year. *One Red Paperclip: How a Small Piece of Stationery Turned into a Great Big Adventure* became a book, published by Ebury Press.
- *The Intimate Adventures of a London Call Girl* by Belle de Jour sold over 250,000 copies and was made into a successful television series.

These are exceptions to the rule; there is no guarantee that book buyers, or more to the point, literary agents and publishers, will read the blog and be inspired to publish it in book form. So don't feel you have to have one if you are an aspiring author. However, the discipline of writing a blog regularly can help improve your writing. Here are a few pointers:

- Check out other bloggers who write on similar subject (as you did when you were writing your book).
- Participate in other blogs; comments you leave can link back to your site which can lead to more people visiting it.
- Technorati (www.technorati.com) is an Internet search engine for searching blogs. Each blog is given a rating; the higher the number the better. You can use it to find out the influence of blogs that relate to your book or subject area by putting key words into its search engine.
- There are several websites that offer web or blog templates for free (e.g. blogger.com, blogspot.com or wordpress.com).
- Amazon allows you to blog through your Author Central account; each posting gets 'attached' to all the books you have published and featured on Amazon; the more books you have, therefore, the more exposure you get when you blog here.
- If you are blogging, give as much attention to the quality of your writing as you would your book.
- Don't share written work that you value on a blog; keep it for your book.
- Ration the amount of time you spend blogging; it might be a better use of your time if you actually worked on a book rather than a blog.

There are various websites that can help you to find people to read and blog about books, including:

- **BookReviewBlogs.com**: a network of blog directories called Blog Nation

- **NetGalley:** publishers pay to put electronic 'galleys' (a proof) of books to professional readers such as journalists, bloggers and booksellers to read on a variety of electronic devices
- **Ereader News Today:** this offers 'tips, tricks and bargain books for your Kindle'.

Key idea

Go on a 'blog tour'. You make an appearance on someone's blog in the same way an author would visit bookshops on a book tour. You could do numerous posts a day without leaving home. And it's free.

Blogs and tweets are only relevant if your target market of readers are bloggers and tweeters as well. They will not work for everyone.

Sarah Davies, literary agent, The Greenhouse Literary Agency

www.greenhouseliterary.com

'Our website is the hub of our business. We post interviews with our authors and we now have a YouTube channel where we post video clips of our authors so that anyone from foreign publishers and scouts to ordinary people can drop in and see our authors in action. I am also very interested in building a sense of community among our authors in various ways.'

'A lot of authors don't know where to start when it comes to having a website; some are very web savvy and others not. Personally, I think there's a bit too much emphasis on social networks but anything that helps to build a fan base is a good thing. I have a long-term dream that we could provide more structured information to help writers in terms of their self-promotion. We do what we can to help promote our writers – and this is something I'd like to enhance in the future – but, by and large, marketing and promotion is still mainly the province of the publisher.'

SOCIAL NETWORKING SITES

One advantage of using social networking sites is that they are global so you could be attracting a worldwide audience and network with like-minded people (either readers, other authors, or both).

And writers are not the only ones who have spotted the potential. Random House, for example, launched a Facebook application, called 'Random Reads' which allows a user to read extracts from over 7,000 Random House books and share them on their Facebook profile. Lulu has We Read – a social book club linked to Facebook, MySpace, bebo and others.

A cheap and easy way to promote your book via social networking sites is to set up a Twitter feed in one of your character's names. Or write micro-fiction. Philippa Gregory tweeted a serialization of her novel *The White Queen* for Simon & Schuster as did R.N. Morris for his crime novel *A Gentle Axe* (Faber). Stephen King's book, *Under the Dome* (Hodder) was promoted with a Twitter campaign and Internet marketing that used 5,000 bits of text hidden in websites which could be found following a set of clues. Even publishers have been getting in on the act with Penguin, HarperCollins, Faber, Profile and Random House all tweeting regularly. When Stephen Fry commented on *Sum: Forty Tales from the Afterlives* by Canongate author David Eagleman, it shot up the Amazon book charts by 250,000 per cent.

There are specific social networks aimed at readers and writers such as:

- Goodreads.com – created to 'help people find and share the books they love'. As you rate books, Goodreads learns your literary tastes and recomends books to you. Authors can use the 'Goodreads Author Program', which gives you a profile page where you can blog, publicize events, create quizzes about your book, have discussion groups and so on.
- NothingBinding.com – for writers and readers. Share your work and your reading.
- Shelfari.com – owned by Amazon, this is a social cataloguing website for books. You build virtual bookshelves of books you own, are reading or want to read.
- Google+ – allows you to join an existing community or create one of your own.

Social networking sites should not be the main plank in your publicity and marketing strategy. There have been several successful campaigns but, while they seem to work best if you want to connect to a particular group or community, book buyers are currently not turning to Facebook and Twitter for suggestions on what to read and buy. Indeed, this approach would not suit every book. Over half of children and young adults in the UK have a profile on a social networking site; for adult users of the Internet that figure drops to over a fifth. This is important if you currently want to connect with an older audience. Promoting a book on Twitter that is aimed at a more mature readership may not be the best way to target your audience.

Key idea

Make sure that you have a line under the signature of your outgoing emails that gives the name of your latest book or where you will be appearing to promote your book. Make sure that you keep it up to date.

If you embrace the social networking sites as a way to publicize yourself and your work, don't waste all your writing time. There are ways of updating all your sites in one go, for free, using websites such as www.8hands.com, www.hootsuite.com or http://ping.fm

Publicity in bookshops

The books that you see in the windows of the large book chains are not there because of their artistic merit. They are there because the publishing house paid for them to be there. Retailers charge publishers for including their titles in special promotions or placing them at the front of the store.

If you are being promoted by a publishing house, you might be one of the lucky authors who gets this kind of money put behind their book. For the majority, though, their best bet will be targeting independent and local bookshops and offering to do events in their shop as a local author.

Alex Milne-White, proprietor, Hungerford Bookshop

www.hungerfordbooks.co.uk

'We're very happy for authors to suggest doing a launch or a signing. If it's someone who isn't very well known, we explain to them then and there that in order for it to work, they will

have to do a lot of the pushing, the marketing, themselves and to make sure they have people they can bring along to it. Obviously, we have a mailing list and we let people on it know about events; we also advertise what we're doing. However, an unknown author won't pull people in off the street on the strength of their name so if they can bring along a crowd, then that's great.

'You don't have to pay the bookshop for this. Any money we make out of the event is from sales of the book. We'll sell tickets because if you don't, you never know how many people are coming or people will say they'll come and then don't bother to turn up. If they buy a ticket, they will usually make the effort to attend. And if someone buys a ticket, we tend to then give them back the money off the price of a book bought on the night.

'Even if you are an author published by a publishing house, I would still encourage you to approach your local bookshop yourself and not expect the publicity department to do it for you. A lot of the best events we've had are from authors actually coming into the shop, rather than us going through their publicist. For instance, my wife tried to get Julian Fellowes [novelist: Snobs Past Imperfect, Phoenix; *screenwriter and creator of* Downton Abbey], *for a signing but found it hard work to get a response from the publicist. And then, one day, Julian Fellowes just popped into the shop and we asked him whether he'd like to do an event. "I'd love to do an event," he replied, "It's just the right sort of town for me." And we had a very successful evening. Sometimes, it seems that publicists' jobs are to actually deflect attention away from their authors rather than organize events for them.'*

In order to survive nowadays, independent bookshops need to keep in tune with what their customers want. They have to be proactive and creative. Events are a popular way of giving customers something extra, bringing people into the bookshop. They also benefit authors, too.

Even authors who sell a respectable amount of books do not automatically get a book launch by their publishers. However, whether you self-publish or have a publisher, there is nothing to stop you organizing one yourself. You could ask your publisher for a contribution to the launch but it is not guaranteed that you will get anything. You are not restricted to holding the launch in a bookshop; that has just been a traditional venue in the past. Whether you have linked up with a bookshop (independent or part of a chain) or have decided to do your own launch, you need to offer:

- **A pleasant venue:** it could be a bookshop, somewhere relevant to the subject of your book, a café, an art gallery, a museum or a library. If you are paying for the launch, don't go anywhere too expensive. Cheap or free would be better. The advantage of holding the event in a public place is that you might be able to draw in passers-by; a low turnout in a private room offers no opportunities to increase the numbers.

- **A suitable time:** generally, launches take place in the early evening but you do not have to stick to that time. If, for example, your book has a strong business theme, you could consider having a breakfast launch; alternatively, you could have a launch after lunch. Avoid Friday and Saturday evenings.

- **Drinks:** you need a reasonable amount but you are not running a bar. Someone needs to be in charge of filling glasses.

- **Food:** not always necessary (unless you are launching a cookery book) but nice to have a few bits and pieces to nibble. A few biscuits with cheese goes well with wine.

- **Readings:** the author should consider reading some short passages from their book; don't go on too long.

- **Selling and signing:** give people the opportunity to buy the book and make sure you sign it.

- **Attendees:** make sure your friends and family attend, even if they are not going to buy your book; you need to create a good atmosphere and, for that, you need people. Send out invitations to make sure that they know when and where it is. Family and friends will form the bulk of the audience; you also need influential people to attend. Invite local journalists, radio presenters, bookshop managers, even your solicitor, bank manager and accountant. The more people you can get talking about your book, the better,

MORE TIPS FOR BOOK LAUNCHES OR EVENTS

- Avoid using locations outdoors unless you can guarantee that the weather is going to be good.

- Make sure that you publicize your event in advance. The invitations should go out in good time and you should have posters up to advertise the event (in the window of the venue, in the local bookshop, school, library, etc.).

- As the event gets nearer, contact your key people to ensure that they will turn up. You should also leave enough time to get a few extra people if you think numbers are looking low.

On the day:

- Arrive early and make sure the room is set up for the event.
- Get a table ready where you can sign books.
- Prepare the food and drink.
- Check that you have enough change if you are planning to sell your book.
- Make sure that the toilets are presentable and usable.
- Have bin bags so you can clear up.

Afterwards:

- Write a 'thank you' note to the manager of the venue
- If you wish to claim your expenses as tax-deductible, be careful about labelling them as 'party'. Expenditure on 'entertainment' is not allowed. However, a book launch is part of the promotion and selling of books.

Key idea

If you are going to be signing books, prepare three or four key phrases which you can use to write in the book rather than just writing your name. It looks like you've made more of an effort, which will be appreciated by the person buying your book.

If readers have electronic versions of your book, you can still 'autograph' it for them. You will need to sign up to authorgraph.com, which allows you to produce a personal, digital inscription for an ebook.

Amy Vinchesi, editor, Watson-Guptill, an imprint of Random House

www.randomhouse.com

'What is more important: the author or the book? It totally depends on the type of book. It's great if the author is known and has an existing platform on which to help promote and publicize the book. Obviously this is a big factor with fiction, where fans will always buy a favourite author's new release. But if the book is poor, that doesn't help anyone. Plenty of first-time authors have hit huge success because their books tapped

into a current trend or timely topic in a captivating way. With
publicity budgets what they are (shrinking), more and more
responsibility is given to the author to get his/her book out
there and seen/heard, which is why an existing platform helps.'

Literary festivals

There are growing numbers of regular literary festivals which
need an endless supply of authors. They bring readers and writers
together and create a wonderful creative buzz. If you get the chance
to appear at a literary festival, consider the following:

- Research the festival before you get there. Find out who else
  is appearing and what they will be talking about. If you can,
  attend one or two other events to get the feel for the festival and
  the sort of questions people are asking.
- If it is taking place in a town or village that you don't know
  very well, do some research the place which you can then relate
  to your talk.
- What format will your event take? Is it a small, cosy chat with an
  interviewer or are you expected to stand up in front of hundreds
  and give a talk?
- Don't be offended if people don't buy your book after your talk;
  think of it as an investment in future sales.
- Remember that people will be observing you when you are
  giving your talk and when you are chatting with people, so
  make sure you act as if you are delighted to be there.

It is always worth approaching the organizers of literary festivals
directly and asking them whether they would like you to appear.
This probably works best at some of the smaller festivals and
especially ones that are local to you; they like to promote local
authors. You could consider doing a double act with another writer.

Some festivals pay authors to speak but it is not a given and, even if
they do, it is not a huge amount of money. Be grateful if they offer to
pay travel expenses.

The advantage of literary festivals is that people are attending
because they want to and, if they've signed up to your talk, because
they want to hear you speak. Volunteer to help out at your local
literary festival. You will learn an awful lot about what makes a
successful event and you will build up goodwill with the organizers
who may look more kindly on you as a prospective speaker because
of your help.

For more information on festivals around the UK, go to the British Arts Festivals Association website (www.artsfestivals.co.uk).

Launch parties, book signings, literary festivals, conferences, panel discussions… these events are all about seeing you and your book. There may only be 20 or 30 people at an event but they can pass the word to friends about your book.

Remember that events like these are not purely for you to stand up and exhort listeners to buy your book. Look at how chat shows on television deal with authors who have books to plug; there is a brief mention but then the author is there to entertain. If they do that well enough, listeners are more likely to go out and buy their book.

John Richardson, self-published poet

'I'm thinking of putting a DVD in one of my poetry books. Bloodaxe Books did it; they recorded poets reading their work. I've got a computer at home, a camera; I could burn off a DVD, put it in a pocket in the back of the book. It would be easy. Listening to a poet is fascinating. There's a transformative process; the written word read is different from the spoken word and a good reader can bring a bad poem to life and a bad reader can kill a good poem. It's one way of publishing. Have you noticed on Amazon, when they sell books, there's often a little video to go along with it? I bought a Chinese cookery book for my son for Christmas. And I was quite surprised to see the little video on Amazon of the author, promoting her book. It's an example of the author selling it.'

Giving readings and talks

Offer to give readings at bookshops, libraries, schools and colleges. Visits to libraries, schools and colleges are particularly important for children's authors. If you are with a publishing house, they will support you at these events – either by sending out books for you to sell at the event or even (sometimes) providing drinks and so on.

If you give a reading, make sure that you collect the names and email addresses of the people who attended the event. You should be planning to build a list of people who are interested in you and your work; these are the people who will potentially be buying your books.

Leave fliers on seats, giving information on your website and also saying that, if people would like updates on your books, any other readings and so on, to leave their contact details. Offering an incentive, like an author newsletter, a chapter from your forthcoming book or a competition with a prize, is even better.

Data protection rules state that you must give people the opportunity to refuse the option of further information from you – that is, 'If you do not wish to receive further information from John Author, please tick the box.'

Organizations, such as the Rotary Club, the local Chamber of Commerce, the Women's Institute and so on are always looking for interesting and entertaining speakers. You will not get paid for your talk (although you may get travel expenses). It is an opportunity to spread the word about your book and you can always take along copies to sell and sign afterwards.

Whether talking to adults or to children, it is worthwhile finding out about your audience before you give your talk. You should ask:

- How many people will be attending?
- What kind of space will it be (a theatre, a meeting room)?
- Who will be introducing you? (Offer to give them some information or have a quick chat over the phone. Remember to get them to say that your book is for sale after the talk.)
- How long do they want you to talk for?
- Will there be a microphone? Will there be somebody there who knows what to do if it is not working?

When giving readings or talks to children, think about the size of the group you are happy to talk to and how many sessions you will do in a day. Think about the form your talk will take; will the children be interacting with you, or do you prefer to read to them and then answer their questions?

If you have a website, you can advertise your willingness to give talks and encourage schools and libraries to contact you to fix up a visit. Alternatively, there are several websites and publications that that list authors who are willing to undertake visits; some may charge a fee:

www.literacytrust.org.uk

www.scottishbooktrust.com

www.ncll.org.uk

www.nawe.co.uk

www.classactagency.co.uk.

Public libraries and School Library Services also have lists of visiting authors, as do organizations such the Arts Council.

Some schools and local authorities are insisting that individuals/groups that visit schools and libraries have some form of public liability insurance. The Society of Authors has details on this, as does the Arts Council.

Some places also request vetting and clearance from the Criminal Records Bureau. If you have not got clearance, consider getting it. Until you do, make sure that you are always accompanied by a teacher or librarian; partly to cover yourself and partly so you do not end up having to act as a substitute teacher keeping order!

You can also give talks and readings online, either as a podcast, a video posted on YouTube or using an online audio distribution platform like SoundCloud.com

A final word

Suzi Williamson, Publicity, A & C Black

www.acblack.com

'There is only a limited amount of work an editor can do on a book; at some point, they have to get it published and earning money. It's the same with publicity. You might think that you should be going on a world tour and being interviewed on Oprah but you have to be realistic about the amount of time a publicist can spend on your book. Publicists will grade your book and allocate time to it depending on their expectations of sales and PR opportunities; and they may be working on many books each month, so it's useful to be aware that they can't always drop everything to work on a last-minute idea.

'From September to December, it's the run-up to Christmas. September is the month when the most books are published, closely followed by October because that's when people want to get them out for the Christmas market. This means it's a difficult time to get press coverage for books, unless you are a famous author or celebrity. January is a good time for certain types of books – for example those relating to sports, *diet, New Year's resolutions and so on. Mother's Day is good for books for women; Father's Day for men. If it's books for schools, we publish them from April to August so they're ready for the new term. So it's just thinking about those seasonal opportunities which can help publicize your book.'*

Marketing and publicity are not something that should only happen a month after publication. It is an ongoing process if you want to continue to sell your book. Writing is a solitary process, getting your manuscript accepted demands persistence, promoting your book is neither – you have to be able to sell it. Someone said writing was a quiet business but promoting a book was a loud business.

Case study: Angela Waller

The Snows of Yorkshire, Before There Were Trolley Dollies

www.angelawaller.co.uk

'I had the first book, *The Snows of Yorkshire*, rattling around my head for about 25 years. Places I went, I would see things, a piece of furniture, a chair, or I'd hear a story about someone... they all slotted in to this story. I had never told anyone, except my husband, that I wanted to write it because the world's full of people saying "I could write a novel" until something tripped me up at a dinner party one evening. The host came over and said, "So what's this about a book?" I replied that it was just an idea I'd had about a family saga, covering 600 years but divided into five parts so you get the interesting bits and don't have to slog through the dreary bits. He was a retired professor of English Literature and said, "You should do it." So the next day, I sat down and started. And I wrote every day until I'd done 110,000 words, knowing I was going to edit bits out.

'I started writing magazine articles in my 60s when we moved back to England, having lived abroad for many years. Doing the articles has helped my writing because I have learned the discipline of moving things along, of editing my work. No matter how much I might think "That's a really lovely phrase", if I've only got 1500 words to play with I may have to cut it out.

Despite the fact that the *Writers' and Artists' Yearbook* tells you that every literary agent receives an average of 19 unsolicited manuscripts every day, I went through the list and cut out the ones who handled only crime or children's fiction and so on, and looked for the agencies that dealt in women's fiction, family fiction or history. I think I'd only tried about seven or eight agencies but the same big envelopes came dropping back through the letter box, along with a polite note saying "No, thank you. We wish you luck" and so on. It's no good telling yourself that Frederick Forsyth had his first book, *The Day of the Jackal*, returned by 18 agents and was only accepted by the nineteenth. You pick up this big brown envelope and you think, "I don't give a damn about Frederick Forsyth; this is me being rejected again."

'Then a cousin of mine, whom I trusted, said she knew someone who had self-published his book using a company called Pen Press [penpress.co.uk]. So I made contact with them. I didn't have a budget in mind at first; in the end, I paid £3,300 in total. That is £1,100 up front and then the rest at designated stages. You can opt for different "packages", from just having five books printed to a full partnership package. I sent them my book's synopsis and the first few chapters. They then wanted to see the whole manuscript. After that, they said they'd like to go the full partnership route with me because they liked the book so much.

'For this, a reader went through my manuscript and came up with suggestions on parts that should be edited. I didn't like taking out some of my favourite bits but it did help it move the story along. So I sent the amended, edited manuscript back to them. I then got a proof copy which I was told to read very, very carefully because any mistakes that were missed at that stage would be expensive to change afterwards.

'I had an idea of what I wanted on the cover. The publishers came back with a layout but it wasn't quite what I wanted, the house wasn't right, so my husband and I found a picture of a house which he doctored up on the computer and we used that. I had final approval of the cover design. From there, they went to print and I think the first print run was 300 copies.

'I was given 20 copies which I sent out as review copies and Pen also sent out review copies. The full partnership package includes marketing the book and they obtained several magazine reviews and I got some more, including one in *Saga* magazine. Pen also arranged an interview on a local BBC radio programme. I took the bit between my teeth and contacted other local radio stations. Only one got back to me but they've had me on three times. When my second book came out, I contacted them all again and I was asked back and did additional radio interviews. You have to be pushy. Perhaps "proactive" is a better word! Well, you don't have to be pushy but you're not going to sell as many books if you don't try to do all you can to promote it.

'You have to promote the book yourself. Nobody will know about it unless you do. There's no magic publicity fairy going round at night leaving notes on people's pillows, saying "Buy *The Snows of* Yorkshire because Angela Waller wrote it." Marketing and networking are very important for self-published authors. Nothing ventured, nothing gained. I contacted a couple of authors about whom I'd written articles, reminding them who I was and offering to send a copy of the book. Rosalind Laker (the romantic novelist) agreed to read the book and said she'd give me her honest opinion. Two weeks later she rang and said she loved it; would I like a comment from her that I could use on reprints? And so that was quoted on the cover.

Pen Press sent me and about ten other authors on a one-day marketing seminar which was quite useful. They teach you that, if you ever get hold of a features editor or someone who reviews books, first of all flatter them. Tell them you know how busy they are and get their email address so you can tell them about the book there. Practise explaining what your book is about. I've got it down to under 15 seconds. If they're interested, they'll ask you more. What they'll probably do is ask you to send them a copy of the book and get off the phone! You have to practise so you can get across the bits you need to say.

'It doesn't matter how old you are, it's never too late which is what I said to the people at *Saga* magazine. I wrote to them: "Your readership is 50-plus. I've just had my first novel published at the age of 76; would it be of any interest for a small article?" The Features Editor said they didn't think it would interest their readers but if I would like to send a review copy they'd pass it on to the person who reviews the books. I was thrilled and started to thank him profusely but he stopped me and pointed out that the book reviewer receives hundreds of review copies every month and will only review three or four. I sent it off nevertheless. About three months later, the magazine arrived and there, on page 17, was a photograph of the book and a review! I was thrilled.

'The publishers put the book on Amazon. A friend, who lives in Thailand, bought it on another website. I've no idea how it got there but I wrote to them, explaining that my book had been bought through their website and people had been very pleased with the service and I was happy to recommend them. That establishes a little friendly link. So when the next book came out, I contacted them again and asked if they'd carry this book as well and they do, as they consider it is "social history".

'When I lived in America, I went to a couple of British-American clubs which are all over America. So I went on Google, found out where there were branches and sent out 40-odd emails. I told the truth which is that I wrote the book because I love England and have a love of English history. I suggested that any of their members who were feeling a little bit homesick for England might enjoy reading it and it could be bought on Amazon. That resulted in quite a few sales in America.

'When my first book was about to come out, I went to my local branch of Waterstones in Chichester and asked to see the manager. I hadn't got a copy of the book yet but said it was coming out shortly, gave my 15-second description and asked if they would consider having me in the store to do a book signing. "Yes," she said. I then asked if they thought any of the Waterstones branches in Yorkshire would be interested and I went to Leeds, Hull and Sheffield three weekends in a row (wondering why I hadn't set the book closer to home!). After the book signing in Leeds, the manager came up and asked me how I thought it had gone. I told her I wasn't too impressed because we'd only sold 13 copies. "Well, you outsold Michael Parkinson when he did a book signing here." Now that made me feel better; I outsold Parkie! You only have to ask a bookshop. It's in their interests to promote and sell books. The library also asked me to go and talk to a reading group; they ended up ordering six copies for the library which is very good.

'I also do a lot of talks about being an air hostess in the 1950s and 1960s, which is how my second book came about. The publishers said, "Look, this talk is so popular, why not make it into a book?" I wasn't keen at first because I thought it would be too short but my husband said, "We've been married over 40 years and I'm still listening to your airline stories so why not give it a go?" So, I did, self-publishing again, using the same company as before.

'I contacted WHSmith's sales and marketing people, told them about the book and sent them a review copy. I felt the ideal place to launch it would be at an airport and I suggested doing a book signing for them there. They got back to me, saying it would be too difficult to arrange from a security point of view, which was disappointing. Then Pen, the publishers, got involved and WHSmith ordered 250 copies and put them in their airport bookshops, which was very nice.

'If you're going to self-publish, think about the subject matter of your book and contact every magazine that might possibly review your book. For the air hostess book, I contacted publications like *Aviation Weekly* and several other serious aviation magazines and they reviewed my book. The Royal Aeronautical Society also reviewed it. You can get details of all magazines from the *Writers' and Artists' Yearbook*.

'I was at a party where someone asked me what my second book was about and I replied, "Oh, it's all about what went on when I was flying." A retired BOAC captain was standing opposite me and I saw his jaw drop, and he asked, "Not all about what went on?" I just beamed at him and said, "You'll have to read it when it comes out, won't you?" whereupon he asked for a free copy. It's a common misconception that authors get their books free; they don't. I was given just 20. I do buy copies of my book so I can send them out. If I buy a hundred myself, I get a percentage off the full price.

'To help promote your book, consider giving talks to the Women's Institute or similar groups. You have to do an audition for the WI which they hold once a year. I went along thinking I was a bit old for this caper but they had about 200 people from all the West Sussex WI groups there as an audience. There were seven or eight speakers; you were given 20 minutes to speak and five minutes for questions. The WI has a directory for each local area and it is a great coup to get into it. The directories have the address and contact details of speakers, information on what they charge for mileage, their fee and so on. For anyone who has self-published a book who wants, likes or is able to give talks, this is a good audience.

'When I give a talk, I get there early and put one of my bookmarks (which has details about my books on them) on every seat. Bookmarks are very, very useful sales tools. If I chat to people in the supermarket queue, I'll mention my books and I'll hand them a bookmark. Never go anywhere without a copy of your book and bookmarks.

'There are also lots of free magazines, parish magazines, anything like that in your area so get a picture of you and your book and get a write-up in there. They may not have the biggest circulation compared to national magazines but they do have a readership. Out of one little magazine, with a circulation of 3,000, I've sold 16 books which isn't going to make my fortune but it is nice to think "There's another cheque being paid into the bank." And anyone you talk to, anyone who reads your book, is potentially going to talk to someone else about it.

'Maeve Binchy said that in publishing promotion is as important as the prose. And recently, someone sent me a little paragraph about John Grisham, who said that when his first book was published, he discovered it's a lot harder to sell a book than it is to write one. And I thought, "Ain't that true?!"'

Focus points

- Fill in your author questionnaire; if you don't, it is hard for the publisher to get you any publicity or support you. Be prepared to do some of your own legwork; the publicist is not your PA.
- Think about your USP, your hook or angle. How can you comment or contribute to an article, a discussion or blog which can promote you and your book?
- If you are blogging, give as much attention to the quality of your writing as you would to your book. Check whether your work is being discussed anywhere on the web and join in the discussions. Point people to your website.

Next step

Writing a great book and then spreading the word about it is vital to raise your book's profile. If people know about it, they are more likely to want to buy it. In the next chapter, we look at how to sell your book, both in print and digital.

9

Selling the book

'If you want to get rich from writing, write the sort of thing that's read by persons who move their lips when they're reading to themselves.'
Don Marquis, author and journalist

At the beginning of this book, we looked at how the publishing industry had changed dramatically over the years. Just as the publishing world changed, so did the booksellers. Those changes have had a major impact on how books are sold.

From small independent booksellers, university bookstores and independently owned chains, such as WHSmiths, the high street began to acquire new players. Barnes & Noble, in the States, expanded in the 1970s and 1980s; in the UK, Waterstones and Dillons appeared, offering a huge choice of titles. As the chains grew, so did the discounting. In 1975 Barnes & Noble was the first bookseller in America to offer *New York Times* bestsellers with a 40-per-cent discount off the publishers' list price. Waterstones was one of the first to do likewise in the UK.

Discounting is the percentage margin between the retail price of a book and the price that it is bought for from the publisher. Book retailers pushed for higher discounts, the right to return unsold books and longer credit periods. Since the chains were providing professional bookselling, well-stocked shops of the publishers' titles that were proving popular with consumers, the publishers agreed. The book wholesalers, who supplied the independent bookshops, also demanded a discount from the publishers to match that of the discounts the chains had won. In the 1990s the supermarkets began to add books to their stock list, especially the bestsellers, at extremely competitive prices, and now one in five books bought in the UK come from supermarkets. Alongside these sellers are the online retailers, with Amazon being the most successful; it is the largest bookseller in both the UK and the United States.

The discount approach is very much part of ebook retailing. The perception, certainly from people purchasing ebooks, is that they should be cheaper than print.

Out of every five books sold, it is estimated that one will make a profit, two will lose money and two will break even. Around 20 per cent of books will earn out their advance. The bookselling market is highly competitive.

 ## Annie Ashworth & Meg Sanders

www.anniesanders.co.uk

AA *'We had a gripe one day, didn't we, and we were reminded very smartly how much money they were spending on our behalf. Publishers have to pay to get you in a good position in Waterstones, they pay to get you in a good position in supermarkets… they have got money to pay out on top of everything. You have got to be realistic; it's like any business. They're selling a product and your creation is suddenly that product, like a tin of baked beans. As "Annie Sanders" we are now a product; they are making us into a brand and you have to go with it. It's the nature of the beast. Let's face it: people buy Maeve Binchy now without reading the blurb. People buy what they know.'*

MS *'We once had an idea for a radically different book and the response from the publishers was 'No, we don't want that' because once you've become a successful, saleable product* *they don't want you to change. There are some well established writers who write very different books. Susan Hill, for example, has written non-fiction, ghost stories, crime; Robert Harris has gone from writing books like* Enigma *to books on ancient Rome that have done fantastically well. Generally, though, once you're known for writing one type of genre, publishers are very uncomfortable with you changing.'*

Publishing a book does not automatically mean that it is stocked by a retailer. Some of the biggest publishers negotiate long and hard with the booksellers, having to agree to substantial discounts, just to get their books on the shelves. On some of the bestselling trade books, it is not unusual for the big retailers to get a 70-per-cent discount off the price of a book; that is in addition to what a publisher has to pay to promote the book (for example, paying for it to be at the front of the shop). Even small and self-publishers will be expected to give a discount off their books. In that respect, they are no different from a traditional large publishing house.

Authors never like the idea of discounting their books but, if you are dealing with retailers and wholesalers (we will look at wholesalers in more detail later on in the chapter), you will have to offer a discount. Most wholesalers expect between 55 and 70 per cent, which is fairly standard for any new publisher. At that level of discount, a wholesaler such as Gardners can give all their customers their normal trade terms. If they get less than that, they will cap the discount to the customers. The more the publisher gives (in discount terms), the more the wholesaler can pass on to their customers and, therefore, the more attractive the offer is.

So, if you only give 20-per-cent discount, the wholesaler (who works roughly on a 15-per-cent margin) is going to give their customers 5-per-cent discount. If a bookseller looks on their system and sees that they are not going to make much, if any, money on the book sale, they will not bother to stock it. It is in the publisher's interests to give the best discount they can.

If you (as a self-published author) do any direct business, you can charge what you like for your book (via your website, for example). Offset what you are having to give the wholesaler for a small number of orders against the direct orders where you are going to get your full money. And maybe you will have to do it as a loss leader if you want to get across the door of Waterstones or somewhere similar. Think where else you could get your full money.

Sales

If you decide to sell and distribute your books yourself, you will need to handle all the orders. This will involve generating invoices, sending the books to the customer and dealing with any returns. If you use a distributor, you will have to pay them a fee for their services.

You will have to make sure that books are packaged so that they do not get damaged and you will have to remember to add the postage costs into your overall budget (don't expect trade customers to pay carriage costs). If there are returns, you will need to issue credit notes or refunds.

The advantage of selling your own books is that you set your own rules. If you use a wholesaler or bookshop, you have to abide by theirs.

Returns policy

Wholesalers and most retailers will take your book on a 'sale or return' basis; in other words, if they do not sell your book, they can return it to you. This will be part of your agreement.

If you are selling to members of the public, offer a refund or to replace the book. Don't quibble with them and put them off buying from you again.

Getting paid

If you are selling books yourself, you can either accept payment by cheque or credit card or, if selling online, you can use PayPal.

If you want to accept credit card payments, you should shop around and find out what the costs of accepting card payments will be. You will be charged differently for credit card and debit card transactions (credit card and charge card charges can be anything from 2 per cent to 6 per cent of the value of each sale). There will also be a monthly fee if you rent the card terminal. Talk to your bank to find out the costs. It may work out that the amount of use would not cover your costs.

If you are starting out selling online, using a service like PayPal probably makes more sense. PayPal gets you a free shopping cart on your website. It accepts secure payment by credit card. You pay a set amount per transaction (currently 20p), plus a percentage of the cost of the transaction (between 1.4 and 3.4 per cent). Go to www.paypal.com for more information.

Keeping records

If you are selling your books, you must keep accurate records so that you know when orders came in, how many books were ordered, what the payment was, when the books were sent out and if there were any returns. This system should apply to all sales: wholesalers, bookshops, members of the public. Update this system regularly.

Draw up some order forms. They should have your contact details, the book title, ISBN and price. There should be space for a date and an order reference. The buyer will need somewhere to put their contact details and the quantity they are ordering. You can put the order form on the back of your AI/flyer if you wish.

You will need a sales book in which to record:
- your customer's name
- the date of the order
- the order reference
- the quantity
- the type of order (online, phone, by post)
- the date the order was dispatched
- the date of invoice
- the date of payment.

When you send out your orders, add a delivery note. This is basically the same as the order form except you should have a line for a signature (plus printed name) and date that says 'Received by…'

Payment and bad debt

It is worth stating what your terms are for payment of invoices; many companies have 30 days. At the end of each month, go through your invoices and check that they have been entered into your system. If there are any unpaid invoices that are now outstanding (i.e. unpaid over 30 days), you should first send a reminder. If you have the customer's contact details that can involve a quick (polite) phone call, email or fax. Non-payment is often due to forgetfulness, so a gentle reminder can solve the matter.

If, despite the polite reminder, the invoice is still unpaid, you can either write it off as a bad debt (especially if it is small amount of money) or you can threaten to take them to the small claims court. If you chose to go down the latter route, you need to send a letter stating quite clearly that, if payment is not received within a set time, legal action will be taken.

The small claims court deals with disputes involving sums of under £5,000. Hearings are informal and you do not need to use a solicitor or barrister. You will need:

- a standard claim form, which is available from www.hmcourts-service.gov.uk
- guidance notes (also available from the website)
- copies of all written documents relating to your case.

The court serves your claim on the person who owes you money; they have 14 days to reply. If they dispute your claim, you will both be asked to attend the court. Both sides will be asked to give their evidence. You should be brief and state your case clearly. A judge will hear both sides of the argument and then make a ruling.

The price of a book – where the money goes

When a book is sold, the author will only get a percentage of that money as will the publisher. The price of a book has to cover:

- manufacturing costs
- royalties
- distribution and marketing
- publishers' overheads
- trade discount
- publishers' net profit.

Even if you are self-publishing, you should take into account costs such as distribution and marketing (review copies, postage, driving to a talk and selling books afterwards) and overheads if you want to get a true picture of how much profit you are making.

When publishers are pricing a book, they will calculate the likely orders from their various customers. We looked at setting the price of your self-published book in Chapter 6. If you have been taken on by a publishing house, they will set the price of your book and you will have no input on this.

 Carole Welch, publishing director, Sceptre

www.hodder.co.uk

'With literary fiction there isn't the expectation that an author will turn a book out every year on a strict timetable, but we

don't like to have long gaps between books either because people's memories are short. In the past it was easier for writers to start modestly, with the idea that their career would develop over several books. Although that does still happen, I think it is much more difficult nowadays. Apart from anything else, publishers find it a great deal harder with each successive book to change perceptions if the previous ones haven't really sold well. Booksellers can now look at precisely what they sold of the last one and, generally (though not in every case) will take a huge amount of persuasion to support a new one if the last one didn't do very well. Literary editors also become progressively less interested, so it just gets harder each time. Unless an author writes a very different book (by different I mean on a different level) and then we can go to the booksellers and say "We know the last one only sold x but, believe us, this is a huge leap forward, read it and you'll see."'

Timing

Certain books do well at particular times of the year so, if you want your book to do well, you can tie it in to a season that could dictate the timing of when you make your book available for sale. Publishers are very aware that timing the publication of their author's work can be critical to it selling successfully.

A lot of new books are brought out in October and November, ready for the Christmas market. That means there are a lot of new titles competing for attention – new titles that have the backing of large publishing houses. Conversely, fewer new books come out in the New Year, apart from the 'traditional' New Year's resolution titles of health, diet, travel and personal development. You could, therefore, consider bringing out your book when there is less competition; that's what Heinemann did in 1998 with their then new author Kathy Reichs' first book, *Déjà Dead*, which got to number one.

Timing is also important if your book is tied into the academic year. Schools will be looking at their budgets at the beginning of the year and deciding what to buy.

The trade will be working about six months in advance. So buyers will be looking at the December market in May/June. If you are selling your books, you will have to work ahead as well. To get an idea of the timings, get hold of wholesalers' catalogues.

Getting your book stocked in a book chain or supermarket

 Mo Smith, author

www.lazycookmosmith.co.uk

'All major supermarkets and book chains buy through companies who store and despatch the orders. I had to open an account with Gardners, the people who supply books to Waitrose and other major stores. They dictate the discount (at that time 52.5 per cent), and all orders are placed on a "sale or return" basis. So you could get an order for 1,000 copies but get 999 unsold copies returned and you've got to take them. I also had to cover cost of carriage, and settlement was made 90 days following the date of my invoice. But I needed these people: they were my introduction into many stores countrywide, and they were always so helpful and surprised at the success of a self-published book.'

For the big booksellers, there are usually four key points they look at when considering whether to take a book on:

- track record
- support from the publisher
- market context
- pricing and the cover.

The actual contents and quality of the writing is not a key consideration.

The big chains and supermarkets have buying departments which specialize in particular categories and genres. The buyers, based at head office, are the ones who make the decisions as to what books are taken on and sold in the high-street stores. Buyers will specialize in particular genres (children's fiction, cookery, etc.). With the large numbers of books being printed each year, it is impossible for the chains to take on every book that is published, so do not expect to walk into a book store or supermarket and expect them to stock your book. Discounts, as discussed, are expected.

Key idea

There are certain areas in a bookshop that are regarded as prime areas: the window, the front of the shop and by the till. Publishers will pay to get their books in these spots. It is unlikely that a self-publisher will be able to afford to participate in a similar promotion.

As a self-publisher, you may not be able to get your book into a book chain or supermarket as a stock item but you can hope to make it available on special order or on the store's core stock catalogue. In the United States, Barnes & Noble review over 100,000 submissions from publishers each year. Most of those books are added to the chain's database and a small order placed for their warehouse. The Small Press Department of Barnes & Noble will consider books from small presses (i.e. small publishers and self-publishers); they like to see a finished copy with marketing and promotion plans, trade reviews, suggested retail price and information on what makes the book unique and different from the competition.

At Waterstones, which has a central buying system, the buyers will decide which books to take and how to promote them (for example, as a window promotion). Like Barnes & Noble, Waterstones have a department that deals with independent and small (self-)publishers and advises them on how to get books into the Waterstones system. That can result in a book being ordered centrally to any number of stores or to a select few with a particular strength in one area.

Local Waterstones stores can also select and buy titles themselves, so it is a good idea to make friends with your local store managers. Send them your AI or flyer, explaining why you think it would be suitable for their store and whether you are prepared to do signing events.

If you would like your book to be considered for central buying/core stock in Waterstones, it will need an ISBN, have a Waterstones-recognized book distributor (like Gardners or Bertrams) and have the title information on Nielsen BookData. It can then be stocked on waterstones.com. When you have all of those elements, you can submit your book for consideration for the actual high street stores. All the details are on the Waterstones website.

Waterstones, along with other major book retailers, will only take ebook submissions through OverDrive. They distribute digital content for more than 2,000 publishers to libraries, schools and retailers worldwide. Find out more information from their website (www.overdrive.com).

If you go to the websites of any of the big book chains, there will be a link for independent publishers with information on what is required to stock your books. Most book chains expect you to have an ISBN, a recognized book distributor and details of your book on Nielsen BookData (or Books in Print for the United States).

Even when your book is taken on by a major chain, they can still return unsold books (around a fifth of all books are returned to publishers). The terms can state that you have to accept returns 90 days after the shops received your books.

 Key idea

Bookshops do not have unlimited storage space; they will have spare stock of the big sellers but not much else. Do not be surprised if your book is not stocked in every bookshop you go into; they don't have the space. They need convincing that they should stock your book.

Getting your book stocked in an independent bookshop

 Alex Milne-White, proprietor Hungerford Bookshop

www.hungerfordbooks.co.uk

'The large chains can be quite hard to get a book into because a lot of it is about central buying. It's not impossible but it's not that easy. The advantage of independent bookshops is that you'll meet the manager probably straight away who will be able to make a decision, probably on the spot, and hopefully it will all work out fine for both parties.

'We have to know our market – the sort of books that are likely to sell, that will be good for our area, our customers and our shop. We see some reps from the publishing houses, like Penguin and HarperCollins. Other than that, we look at the catalogues of new titles from our wholesalers which come out each month;

most of our backlist comes from Gardners. We'll go through the catalogues and pick out the books that will suit our market.

'With an independent shop like ours, an author could approach us and ask us to stock their book. We do our best for either local authors or authors writing about the local area we're in. We'll generally stock those... unless they're complete rubbish! As long as they have some relevance, it's worth it for us.

'If the books are about the local area, they are quite likely to sell. There's an important distinction between a local author and local subject. We'll try local authors but possibly on a 'sale or return' basis because you just don't know how it will go at first. It does depend on the individual book; they only tend to sell if the author is quite good at promoting themselves. For example, we have one local author, a lady in her 80s called Iris Lloyd, who is writing a series of novels that are self-published. Her friends and people she's given talks to come in and buy them and those do very well.

'We do quite a lot of events ourselves – readings, sometime just a signing or the occasional launch. We're a very small shop so we use lots of other venues. For instance, Iris Lloyd did a talk for us; about 20 people turned up but that still made it worth doing, especially if they all tell a friend about the book.'

Around 150,000 books are published each year in the UK. There are around 2 million books in print. Bookshops need to stock a range of backlist titles and new front list titles. Choosing which books to stock can be quite a balancing act. In Chapter 8 we mentioned AI (advance information) sheets, which publishing houses send out to bookshops, libraries and wholesalers. It is a good idea to produce your own if you are self-publishing and send them out to retailers.

Independent bookshops may buy their stock directly from you; many of them will also use the big wholesalers and distributors (see below).

The Booksellers Association represents all booksellers in the UK, including the independent stores. They have a database of over 3,000 shops. You can buy mailing lists (either as a printed list or in the form of labels) from them. The printed list includes telephone and fax numbers. You can choose from a number of categories (such as geographical location, subject group membership and so on). For all details, go to the Booksellers Association website (www.booksellers.org.uk).

Key idea

Make sure that you are a customer at your local bookshop; they are more likely to want to support you if you support them.

Distribution and wholesalers

Many bookshops will not buy direct from authors or small publishing houses (which is what you effectively are as a self-publisher). It would be a nightmare for a bookseller to have to process thousands of purchase orders from publishers, both small and large, so they prefer to source their books from one place. You will have to open an account with a wholesaler – and offer them discounts – if you want your books distributed in this way.

You will see references to wholesalers and distributors and there is a difference between the two:

BOOK DISTRIBUTORS...
- buy books from the publisher and sell them on
- take orders from both bookshops and wholesalers
- will also hold all of the publisher's stock
- have sales reps that visit retailers and actively 'sell' books
- expect a percentage of the revenue received from the retailer.

Many of the big publishing groups own distributors (the distributor The Book Service (TBS) is owned by Random House, for example) and book chains like Barnes & Noble have their own warehouse and distribution systems. Book distributors in the States include: Ingram Book Company, Small Press United and Consortium. In the UK: TBS, Bookpoint Ltd, GBS, Littlehampton Book Services. It is unlikely that a distributor will take on a sole book from a publisher.

Smashwords, BookBaby, Lulu and other online ebook self-publishing companies will distribute ebooks. The service can be expensive; for example, Smashwords takes 20 per cent of the net book sale as a distribution fee. But, if you don't wish to handle distribution yourself, this is one option.

Distribution is just another name for posting your print books out to customers, so you could handle this aspect yourself. The advantage of selling your books yourself is that you can sell them for the full price and not at the discount demanded by the retailers. Encourage these sales! Give some added value by signing every book you send out.

If you decide to do this yourself, you will need:

- somewhere to store your books
- stationery (padded envelopes, parcel tape, address labels)
- promotional material – to include with the book
- postage – stamps
- an ordering system – to process orders, check names and addresses, and take payment against orders.

If you are sending out one or two books, now and again, the distribution should not be a problem. It can get complicated when orders flood in. You have to process the orders accurately, parcel them up and then get them to the parcel company.

If you think you are going to be sending out a lot of parcels, look at the services offered by the parcel companies; they often offer a discount for large numbers of parcels.

BOOK WHOLESALERS...

- offer a service for publishers by taking orders from retailers, whether that is an independent bookshop, library, a national chain of bookstores or a supermarket
- stock books that are in demand
- agree terms with retailers, take orders and ship those orders to the retailers
- handle the returns and manage any disputes with bookstores etc.
- expect a discount off the cover price for supplying a book (around 55 per cent); publishers have to pay postage to deliver copies to them

Books are listed online on the wholesaler's website and in their printed matter. They will either stock the book physically in their warehouses or just list them in their sales catalogue. Some wholesalers in the States will only cover a specific region (e.g. Southern California or the Tri-state area), so be aware of that if you wish to use one, especially if your book has a regional focus.

The big wholesalers in the UK are Gardners, Marston Book Services and Bertram Books; in the US, they are Baker & Taylor (B&T) and Ingram. Around 30 per cent of their sales come from independent bookshops. Wholesalers can also act as distributors for small publishers and they are increasingly offering POD as an additional service.

Advantages of using wholesaler:

- You lower the cost per book by cutting out the distributor
- You know what you ship out and what condition the returns are.

Disadvantages:

- If the orders add up to just a few a month, it will not take up too much time of your time but, if sales start to increase, you can spend a lot of time shipping books out to the wholesaler
- You have to chase up invoices/payment
- You may have to store your books somewhere yourself, especially if they are only listed rather than stock items.

Wholesalers do not just take on any book. For the big publishers, such as Penguin, wholesalers will usually buy anything they publish; that includes the high-end, education/higher education academic books that go for hundreds of pounds or dollars. The big, well-known publishing houses are 'stock publishers'.

Some wholesalers will only deal with a new publisher/author if they place four or more titles with them or if they have a strong track record of previous sales. Companies like Baker & Taylor and Gardners are more open to smaller publishers but they will not stock your book unless there is proven sales activity.

Gardners currently stocks nearly 1 million titles (including print-on-demand lines, listed not stocked lines and 50,000-plus DVDs), even though there are far more books in print. In the States, Ingram works with over 25,000 publishers and imprints.

Wholesalers will physically stock a book only if they think it has 'got legs' – that is, that they can sell it because they have a customer or an outlet that would take it. One buying manager estimated that around 98 per cent of what they are shown from the small or one-man band publishers is turned down. They do not stock a book just because it has been physically published; they only stock books to customer order. In other words, they stock books that are selling.

Wholesalers will agree how many copies they are going to take (for example, 50 or 100 copies) from the publisher but they remain the property of the publisher. At the end of every month, the wholesaler sends a statement showing any copies sold to the publisher, which then invoices them for those books.

 Key idea

If you are a self-publisher and a wholesaler agrees to stock your book and asks for 500 copies, do not assume that you have 'sold' them. They can be returned to you at any time if they are not bought up by any of the retailers. And you have to take them back (the publisher pays for carriage/postage on returns).

A self-published book of memoirs, written by Joe Bloggs, would most likely be a non-stock item. In other words, a wholesaler will not physically have the book in their warehouse but they will have it listed – as long as that title is registered with Nielsen BookData and has an ISBN. So, if anyone (a bookshop or Amazon, for example) places an order for that book, the wholesaler will pass the order on to Nielsen, which in turn sends the order to the publisher; the publisher then sends the book to the wholesaler who sends it on to the customer. That is a special order service. For the majority of self-published authors, that is what happens to their books.

If you wish to try to get your book on to a wholesaler's list, check before you send a sample copy of your book for consideration. Very few wholesalers will take copies and, in many cases, actively discourage authors/publishers from sending them in. If you contact Gardners, for example, you will be asked to email them the details of your book. Every book they don't have in stock but they have ordered to customer demand is recorded. You will then get a response that says they will monitor the book's sales. Wholesalers will regularly check their SOS (special order service) bestseller list. If they see a sales increase over the next three to six months, they will contact that author again to discuss the possibility of being listed and/or stocked.

Here are some additional tips to remember:

- Don't hound wholesalers if you have sent a sample copy in; reading books is not their job.

- If a wholesaler orders four copies from you, four copies is what they want because they've had four orders – no more than that. Don't send 50 extra copies 'just in case'; they have nowhere to keep them.

- Wholesalers deal with enormous amounts of stock all the time (Gardners get 300-plus pallets of stock a day). Don't expect someone to go rifling through them to find one padded envelope with your submission in it

- November and December are the busiest months for wholesalers and distributors; warehouses are a hive of activity as books are loaded into boxes and shipped out. Avoid this time of the year if you are trying to get a response.

- Wholesalers order books to customer demand.

Key idea

If you do manage to get your book stocked by a wholesaler, you still have to keep up the publicity and marketing pressure; otherwise an awful lot of your books will come back to you. Wholesalers (like retailers) won't hold on to them for ever and you still own those books, even when they are sitting in the wholesaler's warehouse.

However, wholesalers are always on the lookout for possible good sellers. For example, one wholesaler picked up on a halogen oven cookbook before Christmas. Even though it was not produced to the highest standard (it was black and white and the photos were unappetising), it was the only one of its kind on the market so the wholesaler stocked it and sold thousands. That was at the beginning of November; by the end of December, 4,000 copies had been sold. The wholesaler spoke to the publisher, told them it was selling well but that it was being let down by its poor quality. They suggested adding some extra colour and an additional £1 on the price; the publisher took that advice, gave the book a new ISBN and they sold a further 6,000 copies in January.

The same thing happened when the *Pass the Citizenship Test* book came out; it was the only book of its kind so a wholesaler went straight in, ordered thousands and did extremely well. The book flew off the shelves. There is always a chance that a book might get picked up in that way but they are few and far between. The wholesalers know the market and what can sell. They also know what doesn't sell.

If you work hard at pushing your sales, people like Gardners, B&T and Bertrams will notice. They cannot take a book from scratch and do the sales and marketing for you. When you've proved that your book will sell and that people want to buy it, you can then approach the wholesalers.

If you are accepted by a wholesaler like Bertrams or Gardners, you will:

- need to open an account with them
- offer a large discount
- cover the cost of postage yourself
- accept any returns.

Go to your local retail outlets where books are sold (independent bookshops, supermarkets, etc.) and find out which distributors they use.

Mo Smith, author

www.lazycookmosmith.co.uk

'A friend passed the new book to the editor of YOU magazine. I was delighted and thought it would be a wonderful way to promote the book. As a distraction from the excitement of waiting for the feature to appear, my husband and I went off for a short holiday. On return, the first thing I found was an email from the Sainsbury's distributor – subject: "Book Returns". They requested the return of 1,500 of the 4,000 books originally ordered. I didn't know what I was going to do with all those books. I rang the distributor but was reminded of the terms of "sale or return". Even so, I was a bit confused because the supermarket buyer had been so positive and confident about sales. I rang her but she'd moved on to another area and the fellow who'd taken over wasn't the slightest bit interested in my books. This is what happens so many times. You just get in touch with the person you need and they move on.

'I didn't have the nerve to ask my printer to take these returns, so I cleared a space in the garage for them. My heart sank, but was lifted when I received an unexpected call from The Book People who said, "We understand your book is being featured in YOU magazine; would you like us to handle your sales?" I asked how many they thought would sell "It just depends on the subject and the feature," they replied, "We've handled Nigella's latest book and she sold 1,000 copies." I thought that I might sell about fifty, a hundred if I was lucky.

'The magazine came out with three pages of copy and photographs of me and my food. I was delighted. The following Monday I received my first order by email; by the end of the week, I'd sold 3,000 books. It was going so well that titles were beginning to run out and it was now my turn to contact anyone who might have unsold copies to return them and I also managed to empty the garage of the Sainsbury returned books. That one magazine feature resulted in sales of 6,000 books.'

Selling to libraries

Libraries do not buy directly from the publisher; they use specialize library suppliers. Like wholesalers and retailers, the library suppliers will want information well in advance of publication. Send your AI and a covering letter asking whether they will stock your book and on what terms; do not send a copy of your book.

Library suppliers in the UK (some of which are also active in the United States) are:

- Askews & Holts Library Services
- Blackwell
- Coutts Library Services
- Peters Library Services
- OverDrive.

The Chartered Institute of Library & Information Professionals (CILIP) has mailing lists of all the libraries in the UK which you can purchase and use to send out your AI sheets to librarians round the country (contact details are in the appendix).

 ## Todd Armstrong, senior acquisitions editor, Communications and Media Studies, SAGE Publications

www.sagepub.com

'We market to professors who we hope will adopt a book for a course. Sales reps go around and knock on doors and try to catch professors in their office, saying "Let me tell you about this Principles of Economics *book; you're using the McGraw Hill one – here's why mine is better." It's exactly like drug companies; you're not selling to the end user, you're selling to the person who "prescribes" the book.'*

Selling print books online

Amazon is the leading online bookseller in both the UK and the United States. All print books that have an ISBN will appear on Amazon. When an order comes through Amazon, the information linked to the ISBN will be checked and the order passed on either to you directly or to a wholesaler.

If you are the publisher, you can contact Amazon and get an enhanced listing. The more information a book has on Amazon, the more it sells. If you are not a major publisher, your book will be listed but shown with a delivery time of one to two weeks. Joining the Amazon Advantage programme means that they will hold a few copies of your book in stock and make it available for next-day delivery. However, like other book retailers, you will have to give a considerable discount (currently around 55 per cent) off the cover price. You will need to ship enough copies to Amazon so that they can meet the orders and you will have to accept returns (paying for their shipping). They will contact you via email when you need to send them more books. Information on Advantage can be found on the Amazon website.

Amazon will pay after the book has been bought and shipped to its customer. As the publisher, you are paid on a monthly basis, 30 days after the end of the month in which the book is sold. You can access sales and inventory reports for your book online. Joining the Advantage programme currently costs around £23.50 (including VAT) / $29.95 for annual membership.

Alternatively, register yourself as a Marketplace seller, which means you send out the books to customers yourself. Amazon charges a listing fee (only if the item is sold) plus a percentage of the sale price (currently 15 per cent). If you are selling online, get a Paypal account (which is free). If you are selling abroad, you can leave your money in this account until the exchange rate is favourable.

Join the Amazon Associates programme and you will get 5 per cent of anything that anyone buys after following a link from your website. The percentage increases after 21 items.

Make sure that you:
- review your own book on Amazon
- get your friends and family to review your book
- get friends to buy a bestseller and your book
- feature your book on Listmania; don't put your book first on your list. Get friends to list your book on their Listmania; frequency builds presence online
- add your book to your wish list
- add your book to 'Search inside' because books that have this facility sell better on Amazon.

Selling ebooks online

The major online ebook sellers are Amazon (Kindle Store), Apple (iBookstore), Barnes & Noble (via the NOOK), Google (Google Play) and Kobo. They are the easiest way for self-publishers to sell their ebooks online. Amazon is the dominant book retailer online but you don't have to restrict yourself to just selling on Amazon.

You can sell your ebooks directly, through sites such as Gumroad. com, E-Junkie, ClickBank and Ganxy. This is very straightforward and can offer a good profit for each book sale. The downside is that you have to drive people to that website in order to make the sale. The advantage that online sellers like Kobo or Amazon have is that they already have potential customers browsing their digital bookshelves. As with selling anything yourself, it is your responsibility to keep a record of sales for tax purposes.

One advantage of selling your ebooks online is the royalty rate. Traditional publishers will pay authors a rate of around 10–15 per cent on sales of their books. Online retailers pay higher royalty rates to authors for their self-published books (for example, Amazon pays 35 per cent or 70 per cent depending on the price of the ebook; Apple pays 70 per cent).

Amazon's Kindle Direct Publishing (KDP) allows authors to self-publish their ebooks on the Amazon Kindle Store. Books can then be read on the various Kindle devices or via the Kindle app (for Macs, BlackBerry, Android, iOS and Windows devices). It is open to writers from around the world and books can be sold in all territories that you hold the rights for.

ROYALTIES

Amazon offer two royalty rates, 35 per cent and 70 per cent. If you choose the 70 per cent option, the book has to be priced between $2.99 and $9.99 (US dollars – Amazon will either convert the price to your own currency or you can choose to set the price in your own currency and see if it qualifies for the 70-per-cent rate); there is a delivery charge based on the file size of the book (not a problem if your book is a reasonably length novel but can be pricey if you include lots of images, tables, diagrams and/or your book is exceptionally long) and it applies only to books sold to customers in certain countries. The 35-per-cent rate has no delivery charge and the book is available in any territory. The size of the book file determines the price range you can use. Amazon pays authors monthly.

KDP monitors the price of your book on other online retailer's sites and will match their price automatically.

Amazon will pick a few books for its Kindle Daily Deal where books are heavily discounted (70 per cent or more) for one day. It is a great way to attract new readers to attractively priced books.

There are Kindle Daily Deals in Romance, Teen, Science Fiction and Fantasy. It is not known how Amazon chooses these books.

Apple's iBookstore is the second largest platform for selling ebooks (both 'traditional' ebooks and Multi-Touch ebooks that only work on iPads and contain interactive media). You register your account via the iBookstore before uploading your book. You will also need to set up an account on the iTunes Content Provider which manages sales tracking and bank account details. Royalties are set at 70 per cent.

Barnes & Noble calculate royalties based on the price of the ebook. Between 1c and $2.98, the royalty is 4 per cent. That rises to 65 per cent on books priced between $2.99 and $9.99. Books priced over $10 receive a royalty of 40 per cent.

Kobo allows authors to sell their ebooks through other online retailers. The royalty rate is 70 per cent for books priced between $1.99 and $12.99; otherwise the rate is 45 per cent.

Google Play allows you to set the ebook price, like other online resellers, and the sale price is divided 52/48 between you and Google Play.

Smashwords is predominantly a distributor, although you can buy direct. It allows you to set the price and purchasers buy the book directly either from the Smashwords website or from other ebook retailers (such as Sony Reader, Palm Doc, Apple's iBookstore, Kobo, NOOK). Smashwords is the authorized ebook distributor for most of the major online ebook retailers. It does not distribute to Kindle. It takes a percentage from every sale (usually around 15–20 per cent). Smashwords allows you to generate promotional coupons and/or make your work free.

BookBaby is similar to Smashwords but has a different pricing structure. Rather than take a percentage of each sale, it charges a flat fee up front (the standard set up fee is $99 plus an annual fee of $19). So this is perhaps not the first option for a new author who may not sell many books at first, but is certainly worth considering if your sales are relatively healthy.

Independent Publishers Guild (UK)

The Guild (www.ipg.uk.com) runs seminars, has a spring conference and, most importantly, has a stand at the leading book fairs (including London and Frankfurt). You would have to pay money to be featured on their stand but it is considerably cheaper than having to buy a space on your own at such prestigious book fairs.

There are different categories of membership. As a self-publisher, you would be interested in the Full Membership (for publishers who have published three or more publications) or Non Voting Membership (for publishers who have published fewer than three publications). Price of membership is based on turnover; for example, if your turnover is less than £100,000 a year, membership currently costs £205 (plus VAT).

In the States, the Independent Publishers Group (IPG) fulfils much the same function. For more information, go to www.ipgbook.com

 ## Orna Ross, founder and director, Alliance of Independent Authors

www.allianceindependentauthors.org

'We have a campaigning role, too. "Open Up to Indie Authors" tries to encourage the publishing industry and the trade – libraries, festivals, bookstores, prizes, reviewers – to include author-publishers in their selections. Doing so can be a challenge for the industry; we don't want to minimize that in any way but we also want to say, loud and clear, "Others are finding room for author-publishers and you need to start doing it too. You've got to find a way."'

Left-over books

Publishing houses, usually because they want to clear storage space in the warehouse, regularly sell off large quantities of their unsold books at heavily discounted prices. This is called 'remaindering'. They will only do this if they feel that the books are no longer being bought; therefore the cost of storing them outweighs any income they might be bringing in.

There are various companies that buy up remaindered stock at very low prices and sell them on in discount bookshops. If no one buys the stock, the books are pulped.

If you have a garage or spare room full of books that you need to clear (in order to store copies of your next book perhaps), you could consider remaindering your books. Only do this is you really do not want to put the effort into publicity and sales or your book is seriously out of date.

Rather than trying to sell them off, consider donating them to a charity. For example:

- Book Aid International (www.bookaid.org)
- Book Trust (www.booktrust.org.uk)
- BTBS The Book Trade Charity (www.booktradecharity.wordpress.com)
- The Paul Hamlyn Foundation (www.phf.org.uk).

Case study: Sally Bee

The Secret Ingredient, *The Recipe for Life*, *Have Your Cake & Eat It Too* (all HarperCollins)

www.sally-bee.com

'I had a personal reason for doing my first book. Out of the blue, I suffered three massive heart attacks at a relatively young age. Having survived, I became a spokesperson for the British Heart Foundation and gave counselling sessions to other heart patients. What struck me very quickly was that people were not being given the right help when it came to diet and recipes. So I started handing out a few recipes to people and the results were coming back that they were working for them. So I wrote more and more.

'At the same time, I was looking to get back to work in television. I was going to be on a series for Channel 4, along came the credit crunch and the plug got pulled on it. I'd done a lot of work on a book of recipes that was to have accompanied the series so my husband suggested that I should go ahead and publish the book anyway.

'Now, my mum had self-published a book; she'd written a story about my life, about the heart attacks. She raised some funds to publish the book herself, took them to the British Heart Foundation (BHF) and they sold them, making about £12,000 for the charity.

'I needed something positive at that point so I got on with self-publishing my book. I did the layout myself and went to the same printers my mum had used and sat with their designers for a few days. I did look at the other books for ideas but there are so many different recipe books out there. As a self-publisher, it's important to have the courage of your convictions. A lot of what people will tell you is their opinion, and opinions differ. You can't listen to everyone. I had so many different mock-ups of the front cover; I'd lay them out and I asked everyone who came to house which one they liked. Well, they all chose something different. You have to go with what you like best at the end of the day.

'I didn't have a clue how many I should have had printed. In the end, 1,000 was the best value at the price I could afford. We brought the books home and I put a few in my shopping bag but I was really embarrassed to get them out. Nobody judges you when you are writing the book. Once you print your book and put it out into the world, you are open to everybody's opinion. What if they didn't like it? But then someone asked me if my book had been printed, I pulled one out and they just started selling.

'This was initially to people I knew but my stock of a thousand books was going down which gave me the confidence to create some publicity about it. I did local papers at first and it just grew from there. I had a website built and I continued with my talks to medical and patient groups.

'I had a very strong conviction that I was writing something that people needed. I suppose that conviction made it much easier to promote the book. Every mouthful I eat has to nourish me because I have a very poorly heart and nourishment is the only thing that keeps me healthy. Yet I have three small children at home and I want them to grow up loving food as I always have. The book is very marketable because it's something everybody wants to know – how they can eat well but be healthy. I am proof that it works. I have chronic heart failure but I have no symptoms at all. Journalists know that it's a story that people want to read.

'I soon realized that when I did some PR, I'd sell books. I'd stop the PR, the sales would stop. It's that black and white. If I do a radio interview, the counter thing showing hits on my website will be racking up; then it will slow down and by day four, it will have finished if I haven't done any more PR. And whether you're selling on Amazon or through your own website, you can see immediately the response that you are having to different campaigns.

'I had to be very proactive keeping up to date with my press releases. I'd look at the number of books I had in stock, see there were only a few hundred and think that I should slow down on the publicity front a bit until I got some more printed. And then, when there were enough in the garage, I'd do another news item.

'That's the other thing that people don't always realize. People who self-publish and need to promote their book mustn't feel embarrassed about getting in touch with the media. Remember that journalists need stories; so just give them what they want! There's nothing to be embarrassed about at all. That's one thing I learned – to be proactive on your publicity. Constantly.

'I wanted to get the book in Waterstones so I phoned their head office and spoke to the person who deals with independent publishers which is what you are if you self-publish. He told me they couldn't even consider it, let alone stock it, unless I went through their supplier, Gardners. So I phoned up Gardners, sent my contact there the book, kept badgering him but couldn't get anywhere. Then I found out he was going to be at the London Book Fair so I told him I'd find him and prod him in the back with a pink fluffy pen to make sure he would remember me. Sure enough, I went to London, went to the Book Fair, found him and prodded him with the pen. The next week, I rang him and yes, he remembered me! However you have to do it, you have to make proper contact with these people. There's a whole host of books out there. They will only know about yours if they listen to you and in order for them to listen to you, you have to get in under their skin. They were now listening to me. I then got back in touch with the man at Waterstones, told him the fluffy pen story and said Gardners wanted to stock my book. I then told Gardners that Waterstones wanted to stock my book… finally, Gardners said I could send 50 of my books.

'I went into my local Waterstones, and said I wanted to do a book-signing event, which they agreed to. So immediately, Gardners had an order for those 50 books. Gardners came back to me and said they'd need another 50. Make it a 100, I said, I'm doing a book signing in Nottingham where I grew up. OK. Next phone call: send 200 because I've got a news item coming out. So I just kept chipping away at it until it got put into the Waterstones system; not because they wanted it, they didn't, but because there was a demand for it. As a self-publisher, you are in charge of creating your own demand and the booksellers and distributors will look at it because they have to.

'Bookshops love events. When I did the signing in my local Waterstones, I took in a few bits of food and we made quite an event of it. I just invited all my friends because I didn't know if anyone would turn up! We sold a few but, more importantly, it meant that I was able to have a poster in the shop window for a few days leading up to the event which increased people's awareness of the book. They also put the book at the front of the shop so shoppers could see what was being talked about. Booksellers are very open and they love anything local. So authors must go into their local bookshops and ask if they can do an event. Then it's a case of contacting local radio, local newspapers, making sure they cover it when it comes out and just create as much hoo-ha as possible. It's all about building a story. You write a book; you know you want to sell it. A journalist doesn't want to help sell a book; they want a human interest story. So, if you've got a book that you want to sell, it helps that if alongside it you've got a story that the journalist can write about.

'I didn't make money myself from the first book (the proceeds went to the BHF charity) but then that wasn't my intention. I covered my expenses, such as cost of the book, the postage; I wasn't out of pocket or anything. I did intend, however, to use the book as a stepping stone to get back to work. I decided early on to concentrate on the food and I wanted to do something cheery and positive because all people ever wanted to talk about were my heart attacks and I wanted to move on. So it wasn't completely selfless because I was using it as a vehicle to help me move on. And it's worked.

'Someone I know told me her sister's friend, who lives in Austria, has my book. I don't know the sister or the friend so I have no idea how the book got there. Another friend was in New Zealand and found himself talking to someone who was trying to order a Sally Bee book. The book is definitely out there! It's amazing where your books end up.

'The order from The White House came out of the blue. At first, I thought it was the White House café in Keyworth where my mum lived. But it was the White House in Washington, DC. I immediately sent a press release out saying 12 books had been ordered by the White House.

'The newspapers picked it up big time. I was quite happily tootling along with the story and having a bit of fun. Then I started to get phone calls and emails from publishers and agents, asking me to meet with them. I found out that my book had reached number one on Amazon in the cookery section; I knew I was selling lots of books but I thought you had to sell something like 50,000 for it to be considered a success. You don't. If an unknown first book sells 3,000, it's deemed a success. I had no idea. I thought I was doing small fry but I was up to 8,000 or 9,000 by this stage.

'When I first had the idea for the book, I'd gone round agents and publishers to see if they were interested but nobody was. I'm so stubborn. I felt that if they didn't want to talk to me before, why should I talk to them now? I'd done very well, thank you, and I'd just go and publish my next book on my own again. But then I had a call from this one literary agent. I was really busy when she rang but she promised to be quick. She had three children like me; she didn't mess about; she understood I was busy and got to the point. She asked to represent me and find me and my books a really good home. She said she wouldn't get me the biggest advance but that, if I wanted a career out of this, she could really help. I really liked her and got on with her. And so, over the phone, before even meeting her, I said, "OK, let's do it."

'I was in the enviable position then of people chasing me and I think that's the position you have to be in; to be able to pick and choose. I was in a very different position now. In the past, when I'd been knocking on the doors of agents and publishers with ideas for books I wanted to write, it was impossible. Now, they invited me in; they wanted to see me. Clare, my agent, got a meeting with HarperCollins. I was very cool at first because I knew I had a proven sales record. I had the attitude that I didn't need them; they needed me. Actually, since then I have realised that I do need them but at that time, I was quite happy with the way things were.

'HarperCollins is definitely the best home for me. They identified with me about building a brand, which I'm very interested in. I have a very clearly defined idea of how I want my next five years to be. I know that I don't want to work for years and years because I won't be able to. Now is my time. My twenties were spent having fun and working; my thirties were spent having babies and heart attacks; now in my forties, I'm in the best health that I'm ever going to be, my children are old enough; who knows what the future holds for me health-wise, so I know I've got a five-year window where I want to work.

'What HarperCollins offered me was support for that plan. They would take this book on, relaunch it and make it better. Then we would do another book after that. They promised me that as long as the book was successful I would have a home with them for five years and we'd build the brand together.

'I love working with an editor because I've become a better writer. She makes me justify and quantify everything. I love the fact that she hasn't messed with any of my creative writing but she has asked questions of me about what I had written ("Why did you finish it that way? I felt I was left hanging at this part"; that kind of thing). I haven't necessarily changed those things but it has made me think about how I write. My editor is a person whose opinions I do listen to because I trust her judgement.

'Also, as far as recipe writing goes, I have full support from the publisher. So I write my recipes and other people come along and do all the technical stuff; for instance, the book has had to be Americanized because it's going to be sold there – they've done all that. They paid a fantastic photographer to do the food pictures, the family pictures and the cover shot. They didn't give a huge advance but they have invested a lot of time and money in the project which my agent says is the best way. I've had input on the design and I've enjoyed everything they've thrown at me. So, I love having the support, having worked on my own for so long.

'But I am also glad that I self-published first. I had a very clear idea of how I want to appear and present myself and my book. I've been able to prove that it works because I self-published. The good bits about self-publishing are that I have been able to have the courage of my convictions and it was under my control. I haven't waited for anyone else; I've done things when it's been right for me to do them. It's a great achievement, I feel. I've published my own book.'

Focus points

- The big bookstores look at an author's track record, support from the publisher, the market context, pricing and the cover. A book's actual contents and quality of writing are not key considerations when deciding whether to stock a book or not.
- Retailers and wholesalers get high discounts (up to 70 per cent) off books from publishers. Books are taken on a 'sale or return' policy.
- A lot of new titles come out in October–November; the New Year is relatively quiet for book sales, which can be a good time for new authors and self-publishers to bring out a book. There is less competition.

Next step

Being able to sustain yourself as a writer is just as important as being able to write well. In the next chapter, we will look at what you need to help you keep writing and publishing books.

10

Being a writer

'I never had any doubts about my abilities. I knew I could write. I just had to figure out how to eat while doing this.'
Cormac McCarthy

Should you give up your day job when you successfully publish a book? Writing is not well paid, so, if you want to do it again, you will need an income and be able to pay the bills while you write. While publishers and agents would love you to devote all your time to writing your next work for them, they are not keen on the idea of needy authors. You need to be self-sustaining and practical in your approach to your writing career.

Annie Ashworth, author

www.anniesanders.co.uk

'I think authors like J.K. Rowling and Dan Brown have done us all a disservice in some ways because people do perceive book sales in huge terms. Someone who works with my partner saw The Xmas Factor *for sale in a supermarket and commented that the royalties must be rolling in. A lot of people have this belief that it's an easy way of making money. Book writing has never been a guarantee of making money. It's like acting; there are a handful of people who are making a living out of it.'*

You need a substantial financial cushion behind you if you want to do this full time. Forget the articles in newspapers and magazines about six- and seven-figure advances for books; the majority of writers do not make huge amounts of money. The top 10 per cent of authors earn more than 50 per cent of the total income earned by authors. In 2007 a survey by the Author's Licensing and Collecting Society found that a UK author's average earnings were around £16,500 a year but the typical earnings were more likely to be £4,000.

Even if you are paid a handsome advance for your book, you will not receive that amount as a lump sum. It will be paid out over a period of time (minus any agent's commission and income tax), and, as you must always remind yourself, it is not a grant but an advance against any royalties earned on the book. There is always the chance that the book will not go on to earn its advance and that will be the only amount of money you earn from that title.

 # Key idea

Ideally, you should not go into this for the money. The main reward should come from creating something and then seeing your work in print. At least to start with, regard it as a part-time job.

Record income and expenditure

You need to declare everything you earn, even if it isn't much to start with. Initially, your outgoings may exceed your income as a writer. If you do not need to have a full- or part-time job to support your writing, you could register as self-employed and claim tax rebates against certain expenses. If that is the case, keep a record of transactions and receipts so you can claim; estimates will not be acceptable. It will be up to you to declare your income and expenses.

Allowable expenses are those incurred wholly and exclusively for business purposes. The Inland Revenue makes distinctions between 'capital allowances' (like computers, fax machines, photocopiers, etc.) and 'expenses' (outlay occurred in the day-to-day running of your writing business) – for example:

- proofreading, typing, researching
- stationery

- printing
- postage
- telephone calls, faxes
- subscriptions to societies and associations (e.g. Society of Authors)
- advertising
- travel (meeting with agent, publisher, interviews, research, etc.); use of car/taxis for your writing
- accountancy
- working from home: a percentage of the cost of heating, lighting, etc. (do take advice on this as it could affect your home's exemption from certain tax liabilities).

Royalty statements

Royalty statements are not easy to read, let alone understand. Even publishers admit that. It is not helped that they are produced by computer programs. It is high time that someone came up with a program, used by all the major publishers, that produces straightforward, clear and easy-to-read statements. No one is out to consciously hide information from you, but do not be surprised when you struggle to make sense of what it is telling you.

If there are figures that you do not understand, contact the royalty department of your publisher and ask them to clarify things. If you have an agent, you can ask them to explain what the figures mean. Alternatively, go to the Society of Authors (in the UK; the Authors Guild in the US) for help. Send a query (email is probably best) clearly stating what points you would like clarified. Keep to the point and be polite.

An author is paid when a retailer buys a book. However, if that book is returned (because the bookshop did not manage to sell it to a customer), it will affect the next royalty statement. If the returns are greater than the sales, the royalty statement could show a negative. It does not mean that the author has to return the money from the previous statement.

Royalty statements are sent out either every six months or once a year. Payments are usually made within three months of the statement date. Make sure that the payments are received; if not, contact the royalty department.

If you have a literary agent, you will receive your royalty cheque from them. They will also list any charges that they have incurred as your representative; it may be that the agreement with the agency states that the author will cover the cost of postage for the manuscript. This should be agreed at when you are taken on by an agent. If there is anything on the list of fees that you do not understand or feel should not have been charged to you, discuss it with your agent immediately.

Sub-licensed editions (such as foreign or audiobook versions) sometimes are left off royalty statements by mistake. If you are concerned that this might happen to you, get a clause put in your contract that says you are entitled to a free copy of any new edition of your book.

Bryony Pearce, author

www.bryonypearce.co.uk

'Luckily, I am not the main breadwinner; otherwise I would still be doing my job as a research professional and writing in the spare time that it allowed, which is what I did the year before I had my first child. I worked three or four days a week and then wrote the other days of the week. I'm hoping that the writing will bring in enough money to let us have luxuries; you know, pay for a holiday or two, maybe get the downstairs toilet redecorated, buy a new oven, that sort of thing. I'm not expecting to be able to buy a castle in the Scottish Highlands.'

Register with the ALCS (UK)/ Authors Registry (US)

The ALCS/Authors Registry manages the collective rights for writers, making sure that they are compensated if their work is copied, broadcast or recorded either at home or abroad.

You need to register with the ALCS/Authors Registry to get a share of royalties that relate to any scanning/photocopying or use of your (copyrighted) printed words.

These organizations collect payments for photocopying and other similar uses of copyrighted works, carried out under national blanket licensing systems. Each organization charges a commission for payments distributed (currently 9.5 per cent for members for the ALCS and 5 per cent for the Authors Registry).

Go to www.alcs.co.uk / www.authorsregistry.org for further information.

For photography and artwork, register with DACS (www.dacs.org.uk).

Join a writer's union

The three main organizations in the UK are the Society of Authors, the Writers' Guild of Great Britain and the Alliance of Independent Authors (ALLi). They describe themselves as trade unions for writers. The Society is specifically for writers while the Guild represents writers who work in broadcast media and ALLi represents self-publishers (or 'author publishers').

For a relatively inexpensive subscription, the Society offers a lot for the writer. You can only join the Society if you are a published author (including self-published for profit) or have an offer of a publishing contract. It offers a contract reading service and advises on negotiating any changes for free; it produces a very good quarterly publication, *The Author*, full of useful articles and updates on the publishing world. They also produce a range of 'Quick Guides' (covering a range of subjects: copyright, moral rights, permissions, literary agents, etc.), which members can download for free, and they hold different events and seminars throughout the year. For more details, go to www.societyofauthors.org

The Authors Guild in the United States (www.authorsguild.org) performs the same function as the Society.

 ## Orna Ross, founder and director, Alliance of Independent Authors

www.allianceindependentauthors.org

'The Alliance of Independent Authors (ALLi; www. allianceindependentauthors.org) offers information, advice on contracts and rights, networking with other independent authors around the world, and much more free to members.

'[The Alliance of Independent Authors] is the voice of the author. We do everything we can to help writers who want to publish their own work to do it well. We basically pass on information, knowledge and wisdom on author publishing from those who are already doing it and teaching it.'

Be versatile

The main source of new books is a publishing house's existing authors. A reliable writer who has a proven track record of titles that sell is a valuable asset to both agent and publisher. It is only when you become really successful as an author that you become a recognizable brand; in other words, readers know exactly what they are getting when a new book by Dan Brown or Clive Cussler comes out. Fans of writers like that probably don't even bother to read the blurb on the back of the book; they know the brand, they know they like it and so they will buy it.

> ## Key idea
>
>
> Try to be versatile with your writing. You have successfully published one book but be open to experimenting with your ideas and style. Continue to read widely and expose yourself to new writers and new genres. It may open up new avenues for you to try.

The discipline of being a writer

Waiting for inspiration to strike is not the road to getting published. You need to have a discipline and structure in place to help you write. Set aside time to write and regard it, not as a hobby, but a job of work. You have to be ruthless with yourself and your available time. Here are some key pieces of advice:

- Avoid procrastination, answering emails, buying things from Internet sites that you don't really need.
- Practice self-discipline – don't answer the phone or the door bell when you are writing.
- Set yourself a target of a certain amount of words before you can either get up and have a cup of tea or stop work for the day. Like exercise, you can start with a modest amount a few hundred words and gradually increase the amount.
- Find a place to write. J.K. Rowling famously wrote the first 'Harry Potter' in a café. It does not matter where you choose to write; the space in your head is what counts but you need to feel comfortable in order to get to that place.
- Work out when you can write – most writers have an optimum time of day when they can write. Make sure you take advantage

of that time. If you cannot choose a time, experiment to find out when you are at your most creative and can concentrate (the hour before everyone else in the house gets up; the hour after they've gone to bed; during school hours). Get the time right and you can be most productive in a short space of time, rather than staring at a computer screen or sharpening pencils.

- Practise – and aim to get your words into print, even if it is just in the local church newsletter.

Writer's block

You don't hear about 'nurse's block' or 'accountant's block', so why should writers be any different? If writing is your business, you cannot afford the luxury of 'writer's block'. You may need to experiment to find a strategy that will help you remove that block; here are a few suggestions:

- Consider the problem, write down a few questions – then leave it alone overnight or a couple of days. Don't think about it. Then, look at the questions and write down the first thing that comes into your head. Very often, this can produce the answers you were looking for.
- Rewrite your last page to pick up the momentum again.
- Don't stare at a blank screen or page; write anything down – you can always delete it the next day.
- If you have an agent/editor, talk to them; if you don't, talk to a friend.
- Go for a walk or do something mindless and let your mind wander while you do it.
- It can be important to stop at the right place; picking up the narrative the next day or whenever you get back to your work can be made easy or difficult depending on where you leave it.

Tools of the trade

Carpenters have their chisels, planes and rasps; chefs have their favourite knives. Whatever the profession, we all have tools of the trade that help us to do our job. Writers are no different.

Always have something to write on wherever you are so you can scribble down a thought or an observation when it strikes you.

Jacqueline Wilson writes her books by longhand into notebooks, only typing them up on the computer when she's finished. Frederick

Forsyth reputedly bought the whole stock of a certain type of paper he favoured when the company that produced it went out of business.

Whether you have embraced the computer age or prefer to write longhand at first, make sure you are comfortable with what you write on. If you are working on a computer:

- back up your work
- keep up to date with anti-virus/anti-spam protection
- and back up your work!

> ## Key idea
>
> Don't share your computer with anyone. A rearranged desktop can throw you and there is a danger that you could lose your work to an accidental delete or virus. One writer I know writes on a laptop without Internet or email to minimize the risk.

A writer's tools also include a desk or table and something to sit on. Unless you can happily write on the bus or in a café, you need to make sure that your work station is set up so that you help protect your back, neck and arms. Even if you work from home, set up your work area professionally and be comfortable at the same time.

If you are using a computer:

- make sure that your arms are at a relaxed 90-degree angle
- the top of the monitor screen should be at eye level
- the monitor should be at arm's length
- feet should be flat on the floor.

There are numerous online tools that are useful for writers. For example:

- **Scrivener** is a word-processing program for writers. It's a management system which can be used with Word to help with outlines, taking notes, planning structure and keeping track of your research.
- **Dropbox** is a free file-hosting service that offers cloud storage and file synchronization. Dropbox lets you create a special folder on the hard disk of any computer you use. Anything that is added to the folder (new material, amends, rewrites, research) is immediately copied to Dropbox's cloud computers as well as any other device on which you have installed Dropbox. So you can work on your laptop one minute and change to your main computer the next without having to copy files. You can also access your files through the Dropbox website and mobile phone app.

- **Evernote** is designed for note-taking and archiving. It lets you file notes, ideas, clippings from documents, emails and websites. It's useful for planning and research and it's free.
- **Hightail** (formerly YouSendIt) is a cloud service. It's a handy way to transfer large files from one place to another. You upload your copy and then send a link to whoever you want to receive it (an editor or designer, for example). They then access the file to download it. You can also restrict the number of downloads or set a time limit on downloads.

Support network

 ## Annie Ashworth & Meg Sanders

www.anniesanders.co.uk

AA *'I always think it's quite funny when you email an author how quickly you get a response. Every writer is just dying for someone to divert them. When that little symbol pops up on your computer, you just have to deal with it!'*

MS *'Yes, they're all on Twitter wasting the day. You do have to ring-fence some time and make it your job – even if you are doing another job as so many authors have to.'*

Family and friends are important for a writer. They are your support network but they also need to know when to leave you alone. Draw up some guidelines as to when you can or cannot be disturbed when you are writing.

Writing is a solitary business, so it is good to have a network of people round you that you can talk to, interact and bounce ideas off. Friends are especially useful if you are having a hard time with your writing and writing retreats can be supportive places to write; everyone needs buoying up and encouraging.

There are numerous online communities for writers as well. For example:

- **Wattpad** helps writers feedback to each other using crowdsource editing. It offers data on how many people are reading your writing and how many are finishing it.
- **LinkedIn** has many different communities and self-interest groups, including those for writers.

- **ReviewFuse.com** enables writers to review each other's work and give feedback.
- **Figment.com** allows writers to share their work with readers and gain feedback.

Age

At a publishing workshop, there were a couple of questions from writers worried that they were no longer young and therefore were concerned that publishers might think they were too old and not worth investing in.

The answers from agents and editors were encouraging. They felt that it is hard to write about a range of people and their emotions when you were very young; it is much easier when you are 60. Mary Wesley had her first adult novel published when she was 71; she went on to have ten bestsellers and sold over 3 million copies of her books. Angela Waller and Mo Smith, interviewed for this book, would be the first to admit that they were not in the first flush of youth when they self-published their books. Readers enjoy good books, regardless of the age of the writer. Publishers are looking for authors who can say something and be promoted – age does not come into that.

Mo Smith, author

www.lazycookmosmith.co.uk

'My motivation has never come from how much money I might make; as long as I had sufficient funds to pay for the printing costs that was all that mattered. For me, it is a hobby that I love and an opportunity to promote my recipes to the public at large. But you've got to enjoy it otherwise you'd give up. Sometimes I think I must be mad, as I make my way to give a talk with heavy boxes of books to transport, it's pouring with rain and I've got to find my way down dark country lanes, but after my talk follows a grateful and enthusiastic vote of thanks and a round of applause. My spirits are lifted and I'm eager for the next assignment. Take it from me, if you have complete confidence in your work, give self-publishing a go.'

Conclusion

It is an exciting time to be a writer. New formats are constantly being developed which push the creativity of writers and readers. Self-publishing has become a force to be reckoned with, offering a viable route to seeing your book in print. However, whether you find it easy or not to get published, what matters in the end is the quality of your writing.

You are a writer because you write, not because you have been published. Nigel Watts, author of *Write a Novel – and Get It Published*, talks about the importance of writing for love, not money: 'If your first goal is to be published, such ambition will likely taint what you are writing and ironically reduce your chances of a sale.'

So write for yourself first and foremost; write because you have to. Mastering the techniques of that craft and improving your writing talent should be the goal of every writer. If you do that, then you can think about getting your book published. In order to see your book in print, you will need hard work, determination, perseverance and a dose of good luck. Sometimes it seems that the odds are stacked against you. The only sensible thing you can do is to write because you love writing. Write the kind of book you would pay good money for.

Case study: Harriet Goodwin

The Boy Who Fell Down Exit 43, *Gravenhunger*, *The Hex Factor*, *The Hex Factor: Dark Tide*

www.harrietgoodwinbooks.com

'I think I had always known that I could write – but up until a few years ago I didn't have the spark of a fantastic premise. I have four children and am also a professional singer, so I had my work cut out juggling things as it was.

'Then, just two weeks after having my fourth child, I had a dream. I dreamed that a boy crashed through the surface of the earth and fell down a tunnel into a ghostly underworld populated by a colourful collection of spirits. The tunnel (which I somehow knew was called an 'Exit' – a connecting place between the worlds of the Living and the Dead) was ringed with golden ladders and peppered with luminous green algae. In the morning I remembered the dream and scribbled the gist of it down on a piece of paper.

'Dreams usually fade – but this one didn't. It wasn't in the least bit bothered that I had a new baby and that time and energy were in very short supply. It seemed to be telling me, "Here you are – here's your idea. Sit down and write!" And so I did!

'At first I managed only ten minutes each day. I didn't know how to use a computer back then, so wrote in longhand. I still have the A4 notebooks in which I wrote the first draft, and very much enjoy showing these off when I go on school visits.

'After about eight months of writing, which I did completely in secret, I decided to find out whether or not what I had written was any good – so I sent the manuscript to Cornerstones, the London-based literary consultancy.

'I got back a nine-page report; they had read it really thoroughly. The first thing they said in the accompanying letter was that I shouldn't leap straight into revision, that I should put the manuscript away for six weeks and let things mulch around in my head. There were also some suggested areas of reading at the end of the report, including Teach Yourself *Write a Blockbuster – and Get It Published* (the only 'how to' book I actually read). This book explained all sorts of techniques which I had never come across by name before (e.g. "show don't tell"): and learning about them was extremely useful.

'The report was positive but I am immensely self-critical, and once I started the revision process I set about ripping my manuscript to shreds! I rewrote whole chapters and let nothing slip through the net. The characters were developed; the plot became more streamlined; wherever I found a "was" or a "were", I tried to replace it with a strong verb. Suddenly the writing was springing off the page – and it was incredibly exciting.

'I spent four or five months revising and then thought "What next?" I knew that one option was to send the manuscript back to Cornerstones for another report, but decided to put the whole thing on hold over the summer holidays. Towards the end of the summer an email came through from Cornerstones about a fiction competition that was being run by the SCBWI. The sensible part of my brain told me that I couldn't possibly be ready for a writing competition yet and that I shouldn't leap into things too quickly. But a nagging little voice in the back of my mind said, "Just put it in the post and forget about it!" And that is exactly what I did.

'It turned out to be one of the best decisions I ever made – because six weeks later I had a phone call telling me I had been chosen as one of the winners of the competition. In the days that followed I received interest from several literary agents and remember having a conversation about the possibility of one of them representing me with my two younger children having a major Lego fight in the background. In the end, I signed with Sarah Davies of the Greenhouse Literary Agency: I liked her immediately when we met up in London and felt she really clicked with my book.

'Sarah wanted revisions – many of which were going to take a lot of thought. But it all came together gradually and I began to see that the book that was now emerging was a hundred times stronger than the old one.

'Once I had revised it, *The Boy Who Fell Down Exit 43* was submitted to various publishers and Stripes bought it in a two-book deal.

'So far, I have found the editing process to be pretty relaxed. I know it's not like this for all authors – but it yields fantastic results for me, since I never have the sense that a knife is being held to my throat. I am now revising the second book and have just got a deal for a third, *The Hex Factor*, also with Stripes. I receive my advances in parts: on signature of contract, on delivery of manuscript and upon publication.

'All my own children are now at school, so I write in my shed at the top of the garden between nine and three when there's a bit of peace and quiet. And as well as that there's all the publicity…

'When I met the Stripes team for the first time, I had to fill out a questionnaire so that they could find out whether or not I was willing to talk to schools and do interviews on the radio and TV and so on. Writing can be a very solitary occupation – so I'm always more than happy to come out of my shed and publicize my books in whatever way I can. In the beginning, my publishing team sorted me out with an intensive launch week, during which I went round six or seven schools. Now I organize the school visits myself and thoroughly enjoy them. I make sure that a letter goes out to parents before my visits, so that children have the chance to buy a book and have it signed. I am also responsible for bringing in a stock of books myself. There's a lot of organizing involved!

'I'm really glad that I invested in a website. Someone else designed it for me and I sorted out the text. It's a great too!: it means that children can leave messages on site and that I can reply to them. I run frequent competitions and have a page of "Exit Numbers around the World" which has really excited my readers' imaginations. (I bet you didn't know that Exit 35,006 is behind the biggest roller-coaster in Blackpool – or that there is an Exit in the middle of Dubai?!) The website also means that schools and libraries can get in touch with me quickly and efficiently.

'I didn't write to get published. I wrote because I had a dream that just wouldn't let me go. And what a dream it turned out to be!'

Focus points

- Join a writer's union (the Society of Authors, Writers' Guild of Great Britain, Authors Guild, Alliance of Independent Authors) and make sure you have a support network of family and friends round you; but make sure that they know when to leave you alone if you're working.
- No other profession suffers from a 'block', so why should writers? Just call it having a bad day.
- Publishers want authors who write well and have got something to say. Readers want to buy well-written books. It's never too late to start writing.

Resources

A & C Black
www.acblack.com
36 Soho Square
London W1D 3QY
t: 020 7758 0200

Agency for the Legal Deposit Libraries
www.legaldeposit.org.uk
161 Causewayside
Edinburgh

Operates on behalf of the Bodleian Library, Cambridge University Library, National Library of Scotland, Library of Trinity College Dublin and National Library of Wales

ALCS (Authors' Licensing and Collecting Society)
www.alcs.co.uk
The Writers' House
13 Haydon Street
London
EC3N 1DB
t: 020 7264 5700
f: 020 7264 5755
e: alcs@alcs.co.uk

Alliance of Independent Authors (ALLi)
www.allianceindependentauthors.org
Free Word Centre
60 Farringdon Road
London EC1R 3GA
e: info@allianceindependentauthors.org

Alliance of Literary Societies
www.allianceofliterarysocieties.org.uk

Amazon
www.amazon.co.uk / www.amazon.com
Author Central – authorcentral.amazon.co.uk/authorcentral.amazon.com
Amazon Advantage – advantage.amazon.co.uk/ advantage.amazon.com

American Booksellers Association (ABA)
www.bookweb.org
200 White Plains Road
Suite 600
Tarrytown
NY 10591
t: 800 637 0037
e: info@bookweb.org

American Society for Indexing
www.asindexing.org

American Society of Picture Professionals
www.aspp.com
117 S Saint Asaph Street
Alexandria
Va 22314
t: 703 299 0219
f: 703 299 9910

Arts Council (England)
www.artscouncil.org.uk
14 Great Peter Street
London SW1P 3NQ
t: 0845 300 6200
f: 0161 934 4426

Askews & Holts Library Services Ltd
www.askewsandholts.com
218–222
North RoadPreston PR1 1SY
t: 01772 555947

Association of American Publishers (AAP)
Washington, DC office
50 F Street, NW
4th Floor
Washington, DC 20001
t: 202-347-3375
f: 202-347-3690

New York office
71 Fifth Avenue, 2nd floor
New York, NY 10003
t: 212-255-0200
f: 212-255-7007

Association of Authors' Agents
www.agentsassoc.co.uk
David Higham Associates Ltd
5–8 Lower John Street
Golden Square
London W1F 9HA
t: 020 7434 5900

Association of Authors' Representatives (US)
www.aaronline.org
676-A 9th Ave, Suite 312
New York NY 10036
t: 212 840 5770

Association of Illustrators
www.theaoi.com
2nd Floor, Back Building,
150 Curtain Road
London, EC2A 3AT
t: 020 7613 4328
e: info@theaoi.com

Authors Guild (US)
www.authorsguild.org
31 East 32nd Street, 7th Floor
New York, NY 10016
t: 212 563-5904
f: 212 564-5363
e: staff@authorsguild.org

The **Authors Registry (US)**
www.authorsregistry.org
e: staff@authorsregistry.org

Baker & Taylor (US)
www.baker-taylor.com

Barnes & Noble (US)
www.barnesandnoble.com
The Small Press Department
Barnes & Noble, Inc.
122 Fifth Ave
New York, NY 10011

Bertram Books (UK)
www.bertrams.com
New publisher enquires: 0871 803 6666

Bibliographic Data Services Ltd
www.bibliographicdata.com
Publisher Liaison Department
Annadale House
The Crichton
Bankend Road
Dumfries DG1 4TA
t: 01387 702251

Blackwell – library services (UK / US)
www.blackwell.com
Beaver HouseHythe Bridge StOxford OX1 2ET
t: 01865 333000
100 University Court Blackwood
New Jersey 08012
t: 800 257 7341

Book fairs:
    Beijing www.bibf.net
    Bologna (children's book fair) www.bookfair.bolognafiere.it
    Frankfurt www.frankfurt-book-fair.com
    London www.londonbookfair.co.uk
    US www.bookexpoamerica.com

Bookbrunch (UK)
www.bookbrunch.co.uk
e: subscriptions@bookbrunch.co.uk

Bookpoint Ltd (distributor)
bookpoint.hachette-livreuk.com
130 Milton Park
Abingdon OX14 4SB
t: 01235 400400

The Bookseller (UK)
www.thebookseller.com

Booksellers Association (BA)
www.booksellers.org.uk
t: 020 7802 0802
e: mail@booksellers.org.uk

Bowker
www.bowker.com
121 Chanion Road
New Providence, NJ 07974
t: 908 665 6770
toll free: 877 310 7333
To register your title in Books in Print, go to www.bowkerlink.com
You will need an ISBN before you can register your details.

British Association of Picture Libraries and Agencies (BAPLA)
www.bapla.org.uk

British Fantasy Society
www.britishfantasysociety.co.uk

British Library
Legal Deposit Office
British Library
Boston Spa
Wetherby
West Yorkshire LS23 7BY
t: 01937 546268 (monographs) / 546267 (serials)
f: 01937-546176
e: legal-deposit-books@bl.uk

**Chartered Institute of Library & Information Professionals –
CILP (UK)**
www.cilip.org.uk
7 Ridgmount Street
London WC1E 7AE
t: 020 7255 0500
e: info@cilip.org.uk

Chevron Publishing (UK)
www.chevronpublishing.co.uk
Friars Gate Farm
Mardens Hill
Crowborough
East Sussex TN6 1XH
t: 01892 610 490
e: info@chevronpublishing.co.uk

The Children's Writers & Illustrators Group (CWIG)
c/o The Society of Authors (address below)

Cornerstones Literary Agency (UK)
www.cornerstones.co.uk
Milk Studios
34 Southern Row
London W10 5AN
t: 0208 9680777
e: Helen@cornerstones.co.uk / kathryn@cornerstones.co.uk

The Copyrights' Libraries Agency
100 Euston Street
London NW1 2HQ
t: 020 7388 5061

Copyright Licensing Agency Ltd (CLA)
www.cla.co.uk
Saffron House
6–10 Kirby Street
London EC1N 8TS
t: 020 7400 3100
f: 020 7400 3101
e: cla@cla.co.uk

Coutts Library Services (UK/US)
www.couttsinfo.com
Avon House
Headlands Business Park
Ringwood
Hampshire BH24 3PB
t: 01425 471160
e: salesuk@couttsinfo.com

1823 Maryland Avenue
PO Box 1000
Niagara Falls
New York 14302-1000
t: 800 263 1686
e: salesus@couttsinfo.com

Crime Writers' Association
www.thecwa.co.uk
e: info@thecwa.co.uk

Curtis Brown (UK/US)
www.curtisbrown.co.uk / www.curtisbrown.com
Haymarket House
28–29 Haymarket
London SW1Y 4SP
t: 020 7393 4400
f: 020 7393 4401

10 Astor Place
New York
NY 10003
t: 212 473 5400
f: 212 598 0917

Disclosure and Barring Service
www.gov.uk/disclosure-barring-service-check
PO Box 110
Liverpool L69 3EF
t: 0870 90 90 811
e: customerservices@dbs.gsi.gov.uk

The Eclectic Writer (US)
www.eclectics.com/writing/writing.html

Federation of Children's Book Groups (UK)
www.fcbg.org.uk
t: 0113 2588910
e: infor@fcbg.org.uk

Gardners
www.gardners.com
1 Whittle Drive
Eastbourne
East Sussex BN23 6QH
Small publisher helpline: sph@garnders.com

GBS – Grantham Book Services (distributors)
www.granthambookservices.co.uk
Trent Road
Grantham NG31 7WQ
t: 01476 541000

The Greenhouse Literary Agency
www.greenhouseliterary.com
A transatlantic agency, located just outside Washington, DC and also in London. Sarah Davies is based in the US; Julia Churchill is in Britain. They take e-queries only, send to either Sarah or Julia (depending on where you live) at submissions@greenhouseliterary.com
Sarah Davies, USA: 703 865 4990 (prefix 001 from UK)
Julia Churchill, UK: (+44) 20 7841 3959

GS1 (UK)
www.gs1uk.org
Staple Court
11 Staple Inn Buildings
London WC1V 7QH
t: 020 7092 3500
f: 020 7681 2290
e: support@gs1uk.org

hhb agency (UK)
hhbagency.com
6 Warwick Court
London WC1R 5DJ
t: 020 7405 5525

HarperCollins Children's Books (US)
www.harpercollinschildrens.com
10 East 53rd St
New York, NY 10022
t: 212 207 7000

Hilary Johnson Authors' Advisory Service
www.hilaryjohnson.demon.co.uk
1, Beechwood Court
Syderstone
Norfolk PE31 8TR
t: 01485 578594
e: enquiries@hilaryjohnson.com

Hodder & Stoughton
www.hodder.co.uk
Carmelite House
50 Victoria Embankment
London EC4Y 0DZ
t: 020 7873 6000

Holt Jackson Book Company Ltd – library services (UK)
www.holtjackson.co.uk
Park Mill

Great George Street
Preston PR1 1TJ
t: 01772 298000
e: info@holtjackson.co.uk

The Hungerford Bookshop
www.hungerfordbooks.co.uk
24 High Street
Hungerford
Berkshire
RG17 0NF
t: 01488 683480

Independent Publishers Guild (UK)
www.ipg.uk.com
PO Box 12
Llain
Login SA34 0WU
t: 01437 563335
f: 01437 562071
e: info@ipg.uk.com

Ingram Book
www.ingrambook.com
Ingram Book Company
One Ingram Blvd.
La Vergne, TN 37086
t: 800 937 8200
e: customer.service@ingrambook.com

International Standard Book Numbers (ISBNs)
www.isbn.nielsenbookdata.co.uk (UK)
3rd Floor
Midas House
62 Goldsworth Road
Woking
GU21 6LQ
t: 0870 777 8712
f: 0870777 8714
e: isbn.agency@nielsen.com

ISBN Agency (US)
www.ISBN.org
630 Central Avenue
New Providence, NJ 07974
t: 877 310 7333

IPG – Independent Publishers Group (US)
www.ipgbook.com
814 N Franklin St
Chicago
Il 60610
t: 312 227 0747 (trade or publisher enquiries)
e: mlozano@ipgbook.com
The IPG are linked to Small Press United, a distributor for start-up
and publishers with fewer than 5 titles.

John Murray Publishers (UK)
www.hodder.co.uk
Carmelite House
50 Victoria Embankment
London EC4Y 0DZ
t: 020 7873 6000
f: 020 7873 6446

Library of Congress Cataloguing in Publication
www.loc.gov/publish/cip/
Registers your book for access by libraries and government archives.

The Literary Consultancy
www.literaryconsultancy.co.uk
Free Word Centre
60 Farringdon Road
London EC1R 3GA
t: 020 7324 2563
e: info@literaryconsultancy.co.uk

The Literary Market Place
www.literarymarketplace.com
Contains a list of publishers, editors, and literary agents, along with
contact information.

Littlehampton Book Services
www.lbsltd.co.uk
Faraday Close
Worthing BN13 3RB
t: 01903 828500

Mslexia
www.mslexia.co.uk
Mslexia Publications Ltd
PO Box 656
Newcastle upon Tyne NE99 1PZ
t: 0191 233 3860

f: 0191 233 3882
e: postbag@mslexia.co.uk
Magazine for women writers; quality fiction, competition, tips on writing

National Association of Writers' Groups
www.nawg.co.uk
PO Box 3266
Stoke on Trent ST10 9BD
e: nawg@live.co.uk

National Union of Journalists – NUJ (UK)
www.nuj.org.uk
e: info@nuj.org.uk

National Writers Union (US)
www.nwu.org
113 University Place
6th Floor
New York
NY 10003
r: 212 254 0279
e: nwu@wu.org

Nielsen BookData (UK)
www.nielsenbookdata.co.uk
BookData Publisher help desk – 0845 450 0016 or pubhelp.book@nielsen.com
Nielsen BookScan (US)
Author enquiries: contact Brianna Buckley at brianna.buckley@nielsen.com or (646) 654-4778.
Publisher enquiries: contact Dennis Halby at dennis.halby@nielsen.com or (646) 654-4765

Peters Bookselling Service (UK)
petersbooks.co.uk
Specializes in children's books.
120 Bromsgrove Street
Birmingham B5 6RJ
t: 0121 666 6646
e: sales@peters-books.co.uk

The Picture Research Association
www.picture-research.org.uk
Box 105 Hampstead House
176 Finchley Road,
London NW3
t: 07771982308

Preface Publishing
www.prefacepublishing.co.uk
e: info@prefacepublishing.co.uk

Public Lending Right (PLR)
www.plr.co.uk
Richard House
Sorbonne Close
Stockton-on-Tees
TS17 6DA
t: 01642 604699
f: 01642 615641

Romance Writers of America
www.rwa.org

Romantic Novelists Association
www.rna-uk.org

SAGE
www.sagepub.com
SAGE Publications USA
2455 Teller road
Thousand Oaks
CA 91320
t: 805 499 0721
SAGE Publications UK
1 Oliver's Yard
55 City Road
London EC1Y 1SP
e: info@sagepub.com

Science Fiction & Fantasy Writers of America (US)
www.sfwa.org
5 Winding Brook Drive, #1B
Guilderland
NY 12084
t: 518 869 5361

The SF Hub
www.sfhub.ac.uk/
Science fiction research website

Small Publishers of North America
www.spannet.org

Society of Authors (UK)
www.societyofauthors.org
84 Drayton Gardens
London SW10 9SB
t: 020 7373 6642

Society of Children's Book Writers and Illustrators (UK/US)
www.britishscbwi.org / www.scbwi.org
8271 Beverley Blvd
Los Angeles
Ca 90048
t: 323 782 1010
f: 323 782 1892
e: scbwi@scbwi.org

Society for Editors and Proofreaders (UK)
www.sfep.org.uk
Apsley House
176 Upper Richmond Road
Putney
London SW15 2SH
t: 02087856155
e: administrator@sfep.org.uk

Society of Indexers
www.indexers.org.uk
Woodbourn Business Centre,
10 Jessell Street
Sheffield S9 3HY
t: 0114 244 9561 or 0845 872 6807
f: 0114 244 9563
e: info@indexers.org.uk

Society of Women Writers & Journalists (SWWJ)
www.swwj.co.uk
27 Braycourt Avenue
Walton on Thames
Surrey KT12 2AZ
e: wendy@stickler.org.uk

TBS – The Book Service (distributors)
www.thebookservice.co.uk
Distribution Centre
Colchester Road
Frating Green
Colchester CO7 7DW
t: 01206 256000

Transworld Publishers
www.transworldbooks.co.uk
61–63 Uxbridge Road
London W5 5SA
t: 020 8579 2653
f: 020 8579 5479
e: info@transworldbooks.co.uk

UK Children's Books Directory
www.ukchildrensbooks.co.uk

US Copyright Office
www.copyright.gov
t: 202 707 5959

Waterstones
www.waterstones.co.uk
Independent Publisher Submissions
Waterstones Booksellers Ltd
203 Piccadilly
London W1J 9HD
e: ipc@waterstones.com

Watson-Guptill Publishers (US)
www.randomhouse.com/crown/watsonguptill
The Crown Publishing Group
1745 Broadway
New York, NY 10019
t: 212 782 9000

Western Writers of America
www.westernwriters.org
MSC06 3770
1 University of New Mexico
Albuquerque, NM 87131-0001
t: 505 277-5234

WordCounter
www.wordcounter.com
Highlights the most frequently used words in a given text.

The Word Pool
www.wordpool.co.uk
Children's book site with information on writing for children and a
thriving discussion group for children's writers.

Working Partners (book packager)
www.workingpartnersltd.co.uk
Stanley House
St Chad's Place

London
WC1X 9HH
t: 020 7841 3939
f: 020 7841 3940
e: enquiries@workingpartnersltd.co.uk

Write4kids.com (US)
www.write4kids.com

Writers' & Artists' Yearbook
A & C Black
37 Soho Square
London W1D 3QZ
t: 020 7758 0200

Writers' Circles
www.writers-circles.com
39 Lincoln Way
Harlington
Bedfordshire LU5 6NG
t: 01525 873197
e: diana@writers-circles.com
Directory of writers' circles, courses and workshops. Free listings.

The Writers' Guild of Great Britain
www.writersguild.org.uk/
40 Rosebery Avenue
London
EC1R 4RX
t: 020 7833 0777
f: 020 7833 4777
admin@writersguild.org.uk.

WritersServices
www.WritersServices.com
Factsheets, reviews, advice, links and other resources for writers including editorial services, contract vetting and self-publishing.

The Writers' Workshop
www.writersworkshop.co.uk
t: 01869 347040

Part Two
Get Started in Self-Publishing

Introduction: Self-publishing – a revolution

One of the definitions of the word 'revolution' is *fundamental change* and that's what self-publishing is. Until comparatively recently it was an expensive process that was seen by many as an admission of failure. Self-published books were second rate and so, by implication, were their authors.

Not any more. Self-publishing, like guerrilla film-making, is rightly recognized as being just as valid as the more traditional kind. As Oscar Wilde pointed out, the thing about any book is that it's either well written or badly written and that's all.

Of course, you'll still have to market the book yourself. On the other hand, you'll have a published book to market. It puts the final decision back into your hands.

There are detractors. Dire warnings of 'diluted quality', 'bursting bubbles' and something described as 'the inevitable backlash'. We think what lies behind this nonsense is the notion that writing – like all real culture – is the domain of the privileged few and that the rest of us should know our place and be grateful for our ghost-written biographies and oceans of cookbooks.

Leave it to the experts, they seem be saying, for they know best.

On the other hand, it's significant that, at the time of writing, a major publishing house has just bought into a self-publishing company. So either the company saw it as an important investment for the future or it just did it on a whim. Which, do you think, is more likely?

There have been more than a few major success stories in self-publishing. John Locke and Amanda Hocking both sold a million copies on Kindle and both went on to sign publishing deals with major publishers. So, yes, it is possible to make money self-publishing. Artistic integrity is all very well but writers have bills to pay just like everyone else.

Of course, there's no guarantee that everyone who self-publishes is bound for glory but one thing has changed for ever. Whether or not your book gets published doesn't depend on readers' reports, the market, who you are and who you know – though, to be honest, that last one's largely a myth. Whether your book gets published at all depends on you.

What self-publishing has done is to give ordinary people – though we both believe that everyone has the potential to be extraordinary – real choice. It encourages people to think for themselves and to have confidence in themselves.

When you publish your book, you will have achieved something marvellous. Writing a book isn't easy. If it was, there would be no need for ghost-writers.

Hopefully, you'll make some money.

And another thing: you will be helping to foster cultural diversity because, just as an ecosystem needs diversity to thrive, so does a culture.

What we'll do is share our combined knowledge and experience to teach you the skills and self-confidence to:

- redraft, proofread, edit and prepare your manuscript
- find the self-publishing option, or options, that best suits both your needs and your budget
- pick a title, design a cover, fix a price
- market your book so as to maximize your sales potential.

The chapters in this book have a practical outlook, with key advice and exercises to help you put what you have learned into action. Throughout this book you will see the following icons:

 Key ideas to help you hone in on what really matters

 Snapshot exercises that encourage you to carry out simple tasks that will get you on the road

 Workshop exercises – longer exercises that ask you to do a bit more work (there aren't too many of these, you'll be pleased to know)

 Write exercises – self-explanatory

 Edit exercises to help you get into the invaluable practice of reviewing your own work

 Focus points to help you take away the main points from each chapter.

We'll also show you all the potential pitfalls and tell you how to avoid them.

We'll introduce you to other writers who have already successfully self-published.

We'll aim to give you everything you'll need to maximize your book's chances of success.

Welcome to the revolution!

1

Begin at the beginning...

Kevin McCann

I was about 14 or so when I announced that I wanted to be a writer when I finally grew up. I was told by my careers advisor in school that writing wasn't a proper job. That clinched it for me. And later, when I was a student and met professional writers for the first time, a lot of them told me it was 'better than working'. So, like a lot of people, I imagined a life of ease interrupted by the odd flash of white-hot inspiration.

I was wrong, of course. It's a full-time job. It's hard work. The money's often lousy to non-existent. But you keep going anyway because you have no choice. You're in love and logic doesn't come in to it. So let's...

Why self-publish?

Four possible reasons spring to mind straight away:

1 You love writing and you'd like to make some money.

2 You know it can take years for a book to go from final acceptance to actual publication and don't want to wait that long.

3 You've already had some work published and a book will help raise your profile.

4 You've been writing for years and now would like a book to distribute among your family and friends.

You may have already tried submitting to publishers and/or agents and been politely but firmly rejected. The rejection will probably be brief because publishers receive hundreds of submissions every week and simply don't have time to give detailed responses. But it will have been read. Publishers/agents are in the business of making money and are always on the lookout for the 'next big thing'.

Of the thousands of manuscripts submitted every year, only a small number are accepted. So being rejected doesn't necessarily mean your book is bad. It may simply be that there are other books that are better.

Of course there are mistakes – one publisher's reader famously rejected the first Harry Potter book with the words, 'I can't imagine any child wanting to read this!' – but there are no conspiracies, just human error.

What is self-publishing?

The obvious answer is, in this case, the right one. Self-publishing means taking your manuscript and publishing it yourself. You can choose either to publish it as hard copy – that is, an actual book – or digitally as an ebook. There are a number of self-publishing companies that will enable you to do both.

This last option is worth considering as it will provide your potential customers (readers) with the all-important element of choice. It's true that in the last few years there has been an explosion in epublishing and the sales potential on e-readers is huge. But it's also true that some readers prefer what they call a 'real book'. Not everyone has a computer or an e-reader, so keep your options open.

Before print on demand (POD) came into being, self-publishing was an expensive and, more often than not, soul-destroying process. You had to find a printer, pay for your book to be typeset and agree a minimum print run.

For every Roddy Doyle – who originally self-published *The Commitments* in 1987 – there were countless others who paid out small fortunes and ended up with boxes of unsold books gathering dust under their beds.

Or, worse, you might be conned by a vanity publisher who would print a limited number of poorly produced books and make a lot of promises about distribution that were never kept.

Now, for little or no initial outlay, anyone can get a book published. It will be a proper professional job and whether it gets published in the first place depends on you and nobody else but you.

But please keep the following facts in mind:

- **You'll need a computer and access to the Internet and you'll need to be computer literate.**

  In plain English, if you're a bit of a technophobe, it might be a good idea to see if there are any basic IT courses running in your local area. Using a computer is like any other skill. If it's clearly explained, it can be easily understood; and if it's constantly practised, it becomes instinctive.

- **You'll have to oversee every stage of the process carefully from first read-through to final publication.**

  Again, there's nothing to be afraid of. The old proverb about the journey of a thousand miles starting with the first step couldn't be more applicable. Think of this book as your basic itinerary with maps and the Internet as tourist information. So don't worry. Help will be there whenever you need it.

- **You'll have to promote it yourself.**

  You'll have to learn about marketing so we'll be looking at social networking, the importance of blogs and websites, limited-edition free downloads – the equivalent of a special offer – plus all the other more traditional forms of marketing.

- **You'll need to be patient.**

  There are no short cuts, no magic words, no secret formulae and no lucky charms. You must be prepared to work hard and take infinite pains. There's really no other way.

Three quick tasks

Task 1 Type 'self-publishing companies' into your search engine.

Read through the services the various companies offer and the costs involved. A lot provide a complete package – editing, proofreading, cover design – and the costs are comparatively modest.

But what do you do if even 'comparatively modest' is outside your price range?

Well, there are sites where you can self-publish for no initial outlay at all.

Task 2 Type 'free self-publishing' into your search engine.

Have a look at the sites that come up and see if it's possible to upgrade further down the line. For example, can you initially make the book available on the company website and pay for additional help with marketing and distribution later on?

If you're unsure, contact the company in question. If they're helpful and open, they're legit. If they're evasive, move on.

Task 3 Type 'self-publishing ebooks' into your search engine .

Again, have a look at the various sites that offer epublishing and see which ones offer the kind of service you're looking for. You'll notice that they all offer step-by-step instructions or tutorials to guide you through the whole process.

'But I don't know whether I'm smart enough to do all that...' On the pages of this book are individual letters. Each letter represents a sound. The letters (sounds) combine to make new sounds (words). These words then combine to make sentences. Your mind recognizes each letter, combines the sounds each one represents, reads the words produced, reads the sentences they make and then makes sense of them. It does all of that almost instantly, so following step-by-step instructions on a website shouldn't be too difficult. Try reading them aloud. I find it helps.

Remember something else as well: this whole process, from beginning to end, will involve you working in partnership both with this book and with the self-publishing company of your choice. How much or how little you spend will depend on your available funds. Of course, it would be easier to be able to afford one of the self-publishing companies that provide the full service. But if you're on a limited income it's still possible to do it all yourself and there are a couple of advantages to that:

1 The smaller the initial outlay, the sooner you go into profit (providing the book sells).

2 You will gain new skills that will in turn add to your self-confidence. That's crucial. If you don't believe in yourself, why should anyone else?

'I just want to make some money.' There's nothing wrong with that but it's not a case of either you make money or you write well. Shakespeare, Dickens and Kipling all wrote for money. The notion that the true artist is above such shabby commercial things is a myth. Nobody expects a doctor or teacher to work for free, so why should a writer?

Of course, we could argue for ever about what the difference is between a good book and a bad book. Maybe a good working definition would be: 'A good book is one the reader wants to carry on reading.'

So it doesn't matter whether it's a romantic novel, a collection of poems, a biography or whatever… it should be the best it can be. If it's a good book, it should get good reviews, people will recommend it to other readers and your sales will go up.

Feedback

Every writer needs feedback. Those who claim they don't are either perfect (unlikely) or reluctant to admit it (deeply insecure). For the rest of us, though, honest feedback is crucial.

Why? Because you're simply too close to your own work. You've devoted a lot of time – years possibly – to writing a book and you may have become so devoted to it that you're blind to its faults.

It's understandable but it's also foolish. Nobody gets anything right 100 per cent of the time.

What's good? / What's bad?

Think of two films you've seen recently – one good and one bad. Then consider these three questions:

1 *What made the good film good?*

I'd guess it had a good script, was well acted and involving, and you kept watching to the end because you cared about the characters.

> 2 *What made the bad film bad?*
>
> It probably had a bad script, was poorly acted, uninvolving and you cared so little about the characters that you stopped watching long before the end.
>
> 3 *Do you think anyone deliberately sets out to make a bad film?*
>
> Well, of course not. Why would they? And think about all the films you've seen that began so well and then fizzled out. Is it just possible that what the director needed was someone to whisper in his or her ear: 'This just isn't working!'?

No matter how good the cover is, no matter how beautifully the contents are laid out, no matter how concise and punchy the blurb, if a book is badly written, nobody will want to buy it or read it.

So there are two things you need to find out:

1 Where can you go to get honest feedback?

2 How do you deal with negative criticism?

Family and friends will, I hope, read your work and be pleased for you. After all, writing a book is an achievement in itself. But they will be prejudiced. Their natural instinct – again, I hope – will be to be as supportive and therefore positive as possible. They'll tell you you're talented and brilliant and that your book is fantastic. All of which is very nice but, to be honest, next to useless.

What you really need is detailed unprejudiced criticism and there are a number of options available for this. If you're lucky enough to know a professional writer who's willing to look at your work and offer advice, follow that route. Otherwise you might like to consider one of the following.

WRITERS' WORKSHOPS

Ideally, what you're looking for is a tutor-led workshop. The tutor should be published and offer a course that includes regular criticism of your work, though don't be put off by this. It sounds negative but in a workshop it simply means advice.

So, with criticism, every negative should be counterbalanced with a practical positive. For example, if you're told that your short story was predictable, you should also be told how to fix it. If that's not the case, move on.

Workshops to avoid...

Avoid workshops that are really nothing more than mutual admiration societies. You'll learn nothing.

Find a writing course

Type 'writers' workshops' followed by your location into your search engine.

When the results come up, read each course description carefully. Some will be for absolute beginners, some will specialize in one type of writing – poetry, for example – and some will be aimed at the more experienced writer. And they will all cost money, so you need to decide whether, at this stage, you're both willing and able to spend some cash. If you can, find a course you can afford that suits your needs.

If you can't afford to pay at this stage, don't dismiss the idea out of hand. The chances are very high that somewhere close to home there is a writers' group that meets in a local school, college or library. Keep looking until you find one and sign up because, as every writer knows, some feedback is always better than no feedback at all.

WRITING MENTORS

Mentor: Experienced and trusted advisor (*Oxford Handy Dictionary*)

If you've already attended workshops and honestly feel you've gained all you can, you might want to consider getting yourself a mentor.

Some genre groups, like the Romantic Novelists (UK), do offer a limited number of places on mentoring schemes and, if you're a member of a writers' workshop, your tutor may offer a mentoring service. However, don't assume that they do. If they say no, leave it.

Find a mentor

Type 'online writing mentors' into your search engine. Read through the results and bookmark any that look interesting. Note not only the cost but exactly what you get for your money. What you want is both a detailed assessment of your work and specific advice as to how you can improve it.

277

WRITERS' GROUPS

These can be very useful particularly if you're a genre writer – that is, you specialize in a particular type of writing such as crime, fantasy or romance. There are online chat rooms where you may find out about publishing opportunities/writing competitions as well as meeting other writers.

A lot of specialist genre groups have their own in-house publications. Some organize social gatherings, which can be great networking opportunities.

 ## Attending a networking event

Before you attend a networking event have some cards printed with your name and contact details. Take them with you and be ready to give them to anyone who asks. Not only is it easier than scrabbling round with bits of paper and a pen, it makes a far better impression. And make no mistake, networking is important. We'll discuss why in a lot more detail when we get on to marketing proper. Facebook and Twitter are all very well, but there's no substitute for personal contact. Only give your cards to people who ask for them. Don't force them on anyone and never take copies of your book to networking events to sell. It creates a lasting bad impression.

Dealing with negative criticism

How should you deal with negative criticism? The wrong way is to get angry and simply dismiss it out of hand. The right way is to think about it. Good criticism is mainly concerned not with what your book says but how it says it.

For example:

- **Your work is underwritten.**

  Your book, at the moment, lacks readability. It doesn't hold the reader's interest.

- **Your story is difficult to follow.**

  This is a very common fault which springs from the assumption that because *you* know what's going on, so will your reader. What you need to remember is that you won't be there to answer questions or clarify any aspects of your book they find confusing.

- **It's full of clichés.**

  This one often provokes a strong reaction. The usual defence is that we all use clichés all the time. And of course that's true, but in conversation we're aiming to get information across; in writing, we're attempting to tell a story in a way that's both original and emotionally involving. The use of clichés works against this.

Now it may look as though these three examples are each about different problems. Well, on the surface they are. But once you go below the surface, they're really all about the same thing: the writer's use of language.

In other words, they're technical problems, which means:

- they're solvable
- solving them will immediately improve any book.

One last point: the criticism that annoys us the most is the criticism that we know to be true. It's rarely, if ever, what most of us want to hear. We'd all much rather be told, 'Don't change a word – it's perfect.'

Take criticism seriously

Faults in a manuscript need attention and, if you're serious about writing, you'll give it that attention.

Improving your skills

Writers' groups and mentors can take you only so far. What you also need to do is begin sharpening up your own critical faculty. This is the ability to tell the difference between good and bad writing in both yourself and others. And please don't worry that you won't be able to do that. You already can.

Think back for a minute. At the beginning of this chapter I asked you to think of two films you'd seen recently: one you thought was good and one you thought was bad. I then asked you to think about:

- the stories
- the dialogue
- whether or not you cared about the characters.

What you were actually doing was examining:

- plot structure
- use of language
- characterization.

You were using your critical faculty. It's been a part of you all your life and, if you haven't started already, it's time to begin developing it. So how do you do that?

The importance of reading...

GENERAL READING

When children are learning to talk, they tend to copy the adults around them. Once they begin to develop their own individual personalities, so they develop their own way of expressing themselves. They may retain certain of their parents' mannerisms but they are not their parents. They have been influenced, not cloned.

The relationship between reading and writing works in much the same way.

If you read a lot of Raymond Chandler, you might begin writing bad Chandler pastiches. It won't last and you'll continue to evolve your own style. However, it won't have damaged you in any way. What you might gain is his ability to vividly describe a scene in three or four short snappy sentences.

So read widely and read whatever catches your eye.

 Henry James, novelist

'A writer is someone upon whom nothing is lost.'

Workshop: Brush up your reading

- What were the last three books you read?
- Of the three, how many were the type of books you have written / want to write?
- Are you a member of your local library? If not, then please join the very first chance you get. It's free and is a major writers' resource.
- Borrow a couple of books that were published no longer than five years ago.
- Read them (no need to make notes, just enjoy) and then go back and borrow more.
- When you find a writer whose work you really like, read as much as you can of that author.

MORE SPECIALIZED READING

You need to know as much as possible about the type of writing you want to do. If you don't already have one, get a copy of the appropriate Teach Yourself book. It will show you techniques to help you improve your writing immediately. It will also provide you with suggestions for further reading.

Of course, you may think you're beyond that stage. If that's the case, it would still be in your interests to at least look at the appropriate book.

What have you got to lose?

Start looking at books critically

Start looking at published books not just in terms of content but also titles, cover design, blurb and cost. Ask yourself: What is it about a particular cover or title that catches my eye? What makes me curious about a book that is written by an author whose work I don't know?

Is it the title, the cover design, the blurb or even the opening paragraph? Or is it a combination of all of these?

This is the beginning of market research, which Tom will be looking at in more detail in Chapter 2.

BACKGROUND READING

Biographies

If you're a novelist, as well as reading novels you might want to read some biographies. A good biography will not only give an account of a writer's outer life – the things they said and did – but of their inner life as well. For example, let's say you read a biography of a particular writer – someone whose work you really admire – and in it there's an extract from a letter in which they detail their working method or offer some advice on writing. Now think about that for a minute. A writer who may have been dead 20 years – as had Steinbeck when I first read *The Grapes of Wrath* – can still become, in effect, your teacher.

Critical books

Like biographies, critical books can be very useful but it really depends on your immediate needs and how deep you want to go at this stage. A good critical book should illuminate and increase your understanding. A bad one will almost always confuse.

Use your own good judgement.

Time out!

Of course, you could choose to ignore everything I've just said and go ahead and self-publish your book exactly as you wrote it because you're a genius. You know this to be true because your life partner / significant other / best pal told you so.

It's true that there are writers who have worked in total isolation and produced something utterly magnificent. You might even be one of them... but just to be on the safe side, why not get your work looked at, do some background reading and, for the moment, err on the side of caution?

Just in case you're wrong.

 ## If a job's worth doing...

The expression 'If a job's worth doing, it's worth doing well!' is a truism.

It's a truism because it's true.

Back to your book...

By this point, hopefully, your work will have been read and commented on by other writers. They may have been members of a writers' group, a tutor and/or a mentor or a combination of all three.

Hopefully the criticism has been honest though not always what you've wanted to hear. But every negative should have been counterbalanced by a positive. So, bearing all that in mind...

Workshop: Review your book

- Set the line spacing for your manuscript at one point five.
- Make sure the pages are numbered, and in the header/footer area put in your book's title, your name and the copyright symbol ©. Get into the habit of doing this with everything you write so it becomes automatic, like checking the rear-view mirror before you pull out into traffic.

- Print a copy.
- Read it. Don't worry about typos at this stage but, if you spot any, you might as well note them in the spaces between the lines.
- Ask yourself a very hard question: if this was by someone else, what would you honestly think?
- Write a short review, say 500 words or so. Remember, that for every negative there must be a positive.
- Summarize your review in two sections. In section one, briefly list your book's faults. In section two, list its strengths.

For example:

Faults:

- Story is confusing in places
- Some overlong descriptions

Strengths:

- Good ending
- Sharp dialogue

If you haven't already, go back and look again at the feedback you've already been given. Does any of it coincide with your own real feelings about your book? The chances are, some of it will, some of it won't. So, what should you do now? Well, for the moment, leave it. Put it away and go and do something else. Go out, catch up with friends and relax. You need to put some distance between you and your manuscript.

Think of it like this: next time you look at your manuscript, you'll do so with fresh eyes and a rested mind... which is exactly what you need.

In films, artists are often shown working themselves into a state of heroic exhaustion. They will then have some powerful vision and go on to produce a work of stark genius. The reality is that exhaustion leads to error. If you're driving and start getting sleepy at the wheel, you take a break.

Now, if you feel compelled to go on and begin redrafting, by all means do so. But, again, you need to be honest with yourself. If you just want to get the redrafting out of the way or you're trying to impress someone, or simply prove something to yourself, then take a break.

You don't just want your book to be good. You want it to be the best it can be.

Every book has a story

If your book is in the non-fiction genre, the above comments will still apply to what a lot of critics call a book's narrative. So, if it's a history, it's the story of a list of linked and significant events. If it's philosophy, it's the story of an idea or ideas. But the most important thing is: it needs to be as well written as you can manage to make it.

Focus points

- Find the self-publishing package that suits you.
- Minimal costs will maximize your profits once the book is published.
- Feedback can be illuminating.
- Negative feedback can be used as a roadmap for success.
- Your book needs to be well written.
- Your book needs to be well marketed.
- The last two points are of equal importance.
- Writers should also be readers, so read as much as you can.
- See reading not just as study but also as market research.
- Take your time. Hurrying any task leads to avoidable error.

Where to next?

In Chapter 2 Tom will introduce the subject of research and explore how important it is to the success of your project.

2

Research

Tom Green

Whether you are writing fact or fiction it is likely that research will be an important part of writing your book. Research might mean finding out specific things that will go directly into your book – for a local history, for example. Or it might be reading around a subject to increase your general understanding and help you shape your content.

Research matters because no one wants to publish work that gets things wrong. If people detect even small errors, it will damage your credibility as an author. If you want to be convincing, then you need to gain as much knowledge about your subject matter as possible.

In addition, it is important that you research the market for self-published books and the various services on offer.

Evaluate your research

Note down the key subject areas about which you are going to write and rate your knowledge about each one out of 10. Don't just choose the most obvious areas, include related ones as well. For example, if a character visits a psychotherapist, how much do you know about the treatment they will receive? Or, if you are writing a historical novel, consider all the aspects of people and places that you will need to know about. Be honest with yourself and where your mark is less than an 8 you probably need to do more research.

How to research content for your book

The Internet has made research much easier than it has ever been before. Huge amounts of information, opinion and analysis are available online, along with access to a large percentage of all the books that have ever been published. The key to successful research is focus.

When you first have an idea for a book your reading is likely to be at its widest. This is exciting, but it might also be daunting. On most subjects there are thousands of good sources of information and it can be hard to know how to navigate through them. It can be helpful to set yourself some time limits. Depending on how much research you think your book requires (some factual books or historical fiction might require substantial amounts), allow a certain number of weeks when you will be reading and researching.

Make sure you allow some time for general reading around the subject rather than just fact-hunting – even if you have a clear idea about your book, there's always the possibility of finding new insights that can change and develop your ideas. Once you have identified the key sources for research, set a time limit for each one. These limits should not be set in stone but they will guide you so that you do not lose yourself in one particular area and neglect another.

So, let's look in more detail at the various research resources that you can use.

Research matters

Research is an important part of the writing process for most books. Errors and inaccuracies will harm your credibility as an author. The aim should be to master your subject matter.

Research resources

THE INTERNET

It would be easy to spend many weeks researching almost any subject you can think of online. The depth and scope of information available is mind-boggling, so you will need a strategy to cope.

Search engines

For an overview of a subject, search engines such as Google or Bing will instantly list some of the most relevant and best-known sources. The results they produce are listed according to a range of factors, including relevance to your search terms and how many other sites link to them. They are not faultless, but as a starting point they are hard to beat.

Of course, what you find will depend on what you search for. These days search engines can often handle longer search terms quite well, so don't restrict your search and make sure you try different phrases. For example, if you are writing a book set in seventeenth-century France you could search on all of the aspects you feel you need to know about. So, you might start by searching on 'life in seventeenth-century France' and then move into more specific searches like 'food in seventeenth-century France', and so on. There will probably be some overlap in the results, but you will also discover new ones.

As you find relevant sites you will also want to follow links from them to other sources. As you click it's easy to get lost, so when you find a useful site make sure that you bookmark it with a note about what it contains.

All Internet browsers have bookmarks (also known as 'favourites') and it might be worth spending some time looking up how you can organize them – an Internet search on the browser name and 'managing bookmarks' will show you the way. Or you could simply copy and paste links as you find them into a document with a brief description.

Another option is to buy a project management tool such as Scrivener which has been designed to help authors manage data as they conduct research. It might take a little time to get used to, but it will help you organize your work and make it easy to rearrange and cross-reference information.

If you want to get really serious about research, you should look at the additional information search engines offer. For Google, go to www.google.com/insidesearch for advice, tips and tricks and discussion about doing searches. For Bing, visit the help section.

Video, audio and images

In most cases, search engines now include video and pictures as well as text on the main search results. However, if you want to search this content in detail, then you should visit the specific category that you want. For video, YouTube (owned and operated by Google) is by far the largest archive, and the search function works well. For sound files you might need to search a specific song or artist. You can also use Google music search www.googlemusicsearch.com. Images are probably the hardest thing to search for accurately, since the search engines rely largely on people labelling them accurately when they go online.

Wikipedia

If you search the Internet for almost anything, the Wikipedia page is likely to be one of the first results to be shown. Although, like any information on the Internet (or anywhere), it cannot be relied upon 100 per cent, for a general overview of a huge range of subjects it is hard to beat. Wikipedia pages also contain lots of links, so it is possible to read around a subject very quickly. The pages are maintained by volunteers, and it is open to abuse, but they have clear procedures to ensure as much accuracy in their information as possible.

Specialist websites

Many subjects will have specialist websites maintained by institutions or experts. These should have the benefit of being trustworthy and fairly comprehensive. They might also be able to put you in touch with people if you have specific research enquiries.

Discussion forums

Search engines often return results from discussion forums (also known as bulletin boards) quite high up their rankings and they can be excellent sources of information. There are discussion boards online for many different subjects and they are normally easy to search.

Most will have resident experts, not necessarily professionals whose opinion can be completely relied on but certainly people it is worth entering into dialogue with. And that, of course, is the benefit of discussion forums – you can register and then ask questions. As well as specialist forums, there are also general forums such as http://uk.answers.yahoo.com where you can submit any question.

Social media

Results from social media such as Facebook and Twitter won't normally show up on search engines to any great extent, but both of these sites are great places to ask questions. If you have lots of followers, you might get help directly. Or you could contact a relevant specialist person or agency via the social network and ask if they could put the question to their own followers for you. As with forums, the great benefit is that you will be able to have a dialogue with anyone who replies.

Try this

Ask a simple research question on Twitter or Facebook. If you don't get much response, search out some specialist people or agencies on Twitter and ask them directly.

Books

Despite the huge wealth of information on web pages, books and ebooks remain a great resource for research. Bookselling sites, such as Amazon, can help right from the start – their search engines tend to be very effective and simply searching on a subject will often return numerous helpful results. Some books can be browsed online, others bought. The online market for second-hand books is now vast, with Amazon and Google Books providing the greatest range. Many ebooks can be downloaded cheaply or even for free, including from the specialist free ebook site Project Gutenberg.

As increasing numbers of out-of-print books are made available on these sites, it is becoming rare for a book to exist that you can't trace online in some form. The only limits on your research are the cost of the book if it is still in copyright and the sheer scale of the task in finding the best books to read.

While you might start by browsing books, if there are too many for you to read it can be helpful to use forums on sites like Amazon, or social media, to ask for recommendations about the best books to read on the subject you are researching. Look also for books cited as sources in Wikipedia articles.

LIBRARIES

In pre-Internet days, research for writers was most likely to take place in libraries and they can still have a role to play. In the UK funding cuts have reduced library services in many areas, but they should still be able to order books you need and can often provide helpful advice and access to the Internet if you don't have that elsewhere.

Local libraries can be particularly useful for local history, since they will often have newspaper and other archives not easily accessible elsewhere. Local and regional newspapers are a fantastic first-hand source and are well worth seeking out both for specific research queries and to get useful background about a time and place. National newspaper archives are also useful

For specialist research the legal deposit libraries can be crucial. Legal deposit is the requirement for publishers and distributors in the UK and Ireland to place all published material in the six legal deposit libraries:

- British Library (London)
- Bodleian Libraries of the University of Oxford
- Cambridge University Library
- National Library of Scotland
- Library of Trinity College, Dublin
- National Library of Wales.

Each of these libraries has different regulations covering access, so you should check the website of any that you wish to visit. You will probably also need to do some planning before you visit and have a clear idea of the material you are seeking. You may need to order books in advance.

ARCHIVES

Most organizations, universities, government departments and agencies, museums and large companies will have archives of some kind. Access can be difficult, but if you are researching a specific subject then it is well worth trying to find archives relating to it. Some archives can be contacted online, although they normally charge a small fee for copying material. Others might not normally be open to the public, but if you can find the right person to contact, and can explain your interest, they might very well agree to let you see their materials.

The National Archive in Kew is the government's archive, holding information going back a thousand years. It has a huge amount of information online (including census records) at www.nationalarchives.gov.uk or you can visit them in person. However, if you are planning to visit, check the website first to see what preparation you need to do in advance.

The British Library runs the national newspaper archive (www.britishnewspaperarchive.co.uk). Work is ongoing to scan millions of pages of newspapers and the archive can be searched for free. A charge is made to download articles.

For access to the full British Library newspaper archive, you can visit the reading room in Colindale. Check the British Library site for registration details before you visit.

FILM ARCHIVES

A list of UK film archives can be found at http://filmarchives.org.uk. Film material can be difficult to access and you may be required to pay: for example, the British Film Institute (bfi) archive is available to the public by appointment and with a fee of around £10–15 per hour of running time.

INTERNATIONAL RESEARCH

The Internet can give you access to research materials around the world. Most public archives should be accessible, though you may have to pay a fee, and you should be able to find contacts in organizations or on social media sites and forums who can give you advice or answer specific queries.

For a list of online newspaper archives around the world, both free and paid-for, visit http://en.wikipedia.org/wiki/Wikipedia:List_of_online_newspaper_archives.

Make a list of possible resources

List how many different research resources you have used and consider which others might also be useful. Even if you're not sure what you're looking for, try something new. For example, do some searches on the British Newspaper Archive and the BFI National Archive and see what comes up.

Research across the board

The Internet is an incredibly powerful tool for resources but you can get overwhelmed. As well as browsing, seek out contacts in relevant organizations, libraries and archives who can help you. If possible, find people on Twitter and public forums who can advise you on where to focus your research.

Successful research methods

Whatever you are aiming to research, as a general rule it is best to start with a broad approach and then narrow down as you focus in on the most important elements for your book.

Even if you feel fairly confident about a subject, it's good to keep an open mind at the start and seek a wide variety of sources. There might be perspectives you hadn't considered before or information that causes you to rethink some of your views. Reading around the subject might also open up new areas for your work.

If you are new to a subject, the initial research is often a mix of the exhilaration of submerging yourself in new information and the frustration of having to plough through a huge amount that is, very likely, irrelevant.

KEY SOURCES

Try to find out as early as possible in your research process what the key sources are on a given topic. Sometimes you can spend ages finding bits and pieces about a subject in various sources before discovering a single text that contains all the information and could have saved you weeks of work.

Ask around online or email relevant experts to get an idea about which websites, books or other sources people think are the most important. You might not want to restrict yourself to these, but they are a good place to start.

It's important to keep good records of your research as you go. Everyone will have different methods. Some people like to underline numerous passages in a book and make copious notes in the margin. Others prefer just the occasional reference to remind themselves where to find information at a later stage. Either way, while you don't want to lose yourself in writing notes that are too extensive, you will rarely regret taking a few moments to write something down, even if you are not completely sure of the relevance at the time. As mentioned above, you can use word-processing tools like Scrivener that have been designed to help authors manage projects from research through to a finished manuscript.

Ebooks provide new tools for keeping notes and references, and on Kindle, for example, you can also share your notes with others who download the book. As well as factual notes, it can be helpful to note down your own thoughts and ideas as they develop. For example, if you are writing a novel, you might have ideas about how the subject you are researching relates to one of your characters. The acts of researching your book and writing it don't need to be completely separate – use research to inspire ideas and note them down as they come.

After reading broadly to start with, you will probably need to narrow your research down into a particular aspect of a subject or a certain timeframe.

ACCURACY

At this point, when you are dealing with specific details, accuracy becomes important. You should never trust a single source, unless it is an original source – for example, you can't trust someone saying that a certain headline was used in *The Times* newspaper on a certain day, but you can find the headline yourself to verify it. Some secondary sources – that is, those that write from original sources – will seem more trustworthy than others. You might feel, for example, that you can trust the writing of an eminent historian but would need to verify something written by an unknown blogger.

Ultimately, the amount of time you put into verifying a fact or series of facts will depend on how important they are to your book and how much it matters if they prove to be incorrect. A minor detail in an historical novel that has no real bearing on the plot or characters might be tolerated, although it's still better to avoid them unless you are changing things deliberately. However, for anything that is central to your story or your argument, it's best to seek multiple sources and, where possible, go back to the original.

Remember this

Lots of websites use Wikipedia as a reference without citing it. If the Wikipedia entry is wrong, then lots of other sites might be wrong, too. So, if possible, check the references on a Wikipedia entry, to verify its accuracy.

DIFFERENT SOURCES

While you might prefer a certain research source, try not to restrict yourself to it. You are likely to be able to find different kinds of information in different kinds of sources, so try to vary your approach. It can be helpful to try a research source that you've never considered before. Even if your work has nothing to do with film, for example, a quick online search on a film archive might turn up results that you had never previously considered and open your mind to new avenues of research.

REFERENCES

If you want to get more deeply into a subject, follow up on references, links and bibliographies. In a print book these will normally be found at the end of a factual work, whereas links often occur throughout a piece online.

 ## Be sceptical

Seeing something in print doesn't necessarily mean that it is true. Good researchers are always sceptical and look for the original sources of information so that they can judge its reliability.

 ## Keep up to date

Are you familiar with the work of current experts in the fields about which you are writing? Whether it's fact or fiction, if you require research, you need to make sure that you have read what today's leading thinkers on the subject have to say.

When research stops and writing starts

Always remember that you are researching as a means to an end: to write a book. Hopefully, research will be an enjoyable part of the process but, if you are writing a book, it is not an end in itself.

So how do you know when to stop researching and start writing?

There are no easy answers. If you have a deadline for finishing your book – either external or self-imposed – then you will first need to decide how long you will need for writing and see how much time that leaves you for research.

It should be fairly obvious to you how important research will be and therefore how much time to allocate, but the research process is not always predictable. Sometimes it can take weeks to find the right information. On other occasions a source can throw up all kinds of new leads that demand to be followed up.

Ultimately, it is you, the author, who must decide when and how to start your book.

Some writers keep the research and writing process quite separate. They will make notes as they go but, essentially, on a given day when they feel the time is right, they will put the books and Internet aside and begin to write.

For others, research and writing flow into each other. At any given point they might be furthering their research or writing, or both.

You must find the approach that suits you best.

The danger with separating research and writing is that you might not be aware of all that you need to research until you have started writing. Both factual and non-factual books can lead you in directions you don't expect and it would probably be foolish to rule out further research if you need it. You might also find it difficult to decide on the definite point where research ends.

However, if you carry on with research throughout the writing process, be wary of using it as a distraction. Most writers are good at finding anything to do other than writing and there might come a point when calling Internet browsing or half a day in the library 'research' is self-deluding.

Writing tends to be hard work, requiring intense periods of concentration. Some writers are able to switch between the writing and researching mindsets but, if you choose this approach, be aware that you might not be one of them!

Do a time-check

If you have written a book before, estimate how much time you spent researching and how much time writing. Was any of the research time wasted in self-distraction? Would you plan to spend more or less time on research for your next book?

DISPOSABLE RESEARCH

As a writer, one of the dangers of being an effective researcher is that you can find it hard not to use what you uncover. We're probably all familiar with reading novels where you can sense that the author has uncovered information they can't resist including – even when it runs to far greater length than the story requires. Some books are built on research, but be careful that you do not include information just because you have found it. Don't be afraid to leave things out. If something is fascinating but doesn't fit in the book you are working on, save it for the next one.

Copyright and plagiarism

It's important to respect copyright on any sources you use. In the UK 'Copyright is an automatic right and arises whenever an individual or company creates a work. To qualify, a work should be regarded as original, and exhibit a degree of labour, skill or judgement.' See http://www.copyrightservice.co.uk.

The duration of copyright varies depending on the form of the work, but for literary work it is 70 years from the end of the calendar year in which the last remaining author of the work dies.

Copyright law can get complicated and varies in different countries, but as a writer you don't want to risk legal action or getting a reputation as someone who breaches copyright: so err on the side of caution and always ask permission from the copyright holder if you want to quote from their work.

Copyright can be waived by the copyright holder and this sometimes happens through what are called Creative Commons Licences. See www.creativecommons.org.uk.

PLAGIARISM

Plagiarism – passing off someone else's work as your own – is a very serious issue for a writer.

Sometimes it is unintentional. For example, during your research you might note down a useful passage of text and forget to put an attribution with it. Then, weeks or months later when coming to write, you paste the text into your manuscript as if it were your own.

You might consider this a harmless mistake, but the original author will not. So you need to be very careful to ensure that work in your name is by you. Plagiarism is a kind of fraud and should be avoided at all costs.

For more information about plagiarism, see www.plagiarasm.org.

Market research

At each stage of the self-publishing process it is helpful to learn as much as you can about books you might be competing with or services you might buy. It's hard to write any book without an awareness of the market for that type of publication, and it might actually inform your work to a large degree – for example, if you can see the kind of works that have been successful or can identify gaps in the market.

Throughout this book we will also be recommending you research the market of fellow authors and service providers at every stage. For example, it is useful to see which cover designs work well, which formats suit which kind of book and how successful authors use social media.

Focus points

- Whether writing fiction or non-fiction, research matters. Inaccuracies will damage your credibility as an author.
- It's easy to get overwhelmed by the number of research resources available. If you have a publishing deadline in mind, make a timetable and restrict your research to a certain number of weeks or months.
- Start research by getting a good overview of a subject and then narrow down.
- Ask for help and advice from experts via email or on social networking sites and forums.
- Be aware of copyright laws and never plagiarize someone else's work.

Where to next?

In Chapter 3 Kevin will look at how you can improve your manuscript and develop your visual imagination.

3

Redrafting

Kevin McCann

OK, so you've read your book, spotted some typos and written a 500-word review. At this point you may be experiencing one of two dangerous extremes. You could be thinking, 'It's brilliant – I need not change a word!' or 'It's dreadful – what a fool I've been!' Both are dangerous because both invite you to ignore your own intelligence. The chances are it's not ready either for publication – yet – or the bin.

What it will need now is work.

A plan of action

When redrafting, use the following plan of action:

1 Draw up a timetable/schedule and stick to it. Ideally, it should be a couple of hours per day but no less than three sessions per week.

2 In each of those sessions carefully proofread your manuscript.

3 At this stage you're looking for typos, punctuation errors and missing words – in other words, obvious mistakes.

4 Correct as you go along and aim for a minimum word count checked per session.

5 Take a ten-minute break every half-hour or so.

Keep a notebook and pen handy. As you're checking, ideas for additional material, plot or structure changes, for example, may occur to you. Note them down for future reference and then get back to the checking. If you stop and start rewriting at this stage, you'll never finish.

If you come across a section that's typo-free but somehow doesn't feel right, try reading it aloud. I find that problems with sentence construction that can't always be seen are glaringly obvious when heard.

Write a chapter-by-chapter summary as you go along. You may think you know your book inside out already. After all, you wrote it. The problem is that you're now so involved that making an objective assessment is probably impossible. Writing a summary will give you some distance as well as a complete overview.

When you've finished, read your summary, put it away for 24 hours (at least) and then read it again.

Pause for a story

Michelangelo was buying marble from a quarry just outside Rome. After he'd selected the pieces according to size, quality, etc., he noticed a chunk that was being used as a doorstop. It was green, uneven and looked good for nothing except being used as a doorstop. He asked the quarry owner how much he wanted for it. The owner was baffled.

'Why do you want that?' he asked.

Michelangelo smiled and then replied, 'Because when you look at that marble all you see are its flaws. But when I look at it, I know there's an angel trapped inside and, with my chisel, I'm going to set it free.'

By summarizing and reading (then rereading) your summary, you should begin to see both the strengths and weaknesses in your book's plot even more clearly. You should also have realized that a good original idea is, in itself, not enough. As a creative writing tutor I've sat and listened to dozens of great ideas for stories. Then I've listened to the stories themselves and watched the face of the writer as she/he begins to realize that it's just not working. And the main reason the story didn't work was because it didn't involve. And the reason it didn't involve was because it was badly written.

So what exactly do I mean by that?

For me, it means any piece of writing that lacks evidence of either craft or talent. Now, you can't teach talent. There are no 'seven steps to true genius', but you can maximize the talent you possess.

And how do you do that?

The same way Michelangelo, Shakespeare or any other artist has done – by hard work and practice. It's true that there are no short cuts but there are any number of techniques you can use that will immediately improve your work.

For example, is your book too wordy? Are you, like me and everyone else who writes, just head over heels in love with words? Are you using whole pages where a few sentences will do?

Pause for a bad joke

The last man in the world can't stand the loneliness any longer. He climbs up to the top of the Empire State Building and jumps. As he passes an open window on the twelfth floor, he hears a phone ringing.

I know it's not exactly a thigh slapper but it does illustrate a point. The joke begins with the last man in the world. We're not told how he ended up as the last man or where he lives. We work out it's the USA because of the Empire State reference.

Workshop: Your opening pages

Take the first two pages of your book, copy and paste them into a new document and note the exact word count.

Next, have a look at your opening sentence. What you want is to grab your reader's attention and make them want to read on. An excellent example of this is the opening sentence of Graham Greene's thriller *Brighton Rock*.

> *Hale knew, before he had been in Brighton for three hours, that they meant to kill him.*

Who wants to kill him? Why? Why doesn't he either go to the police or leave town? The only way to find out is to read on.

Go back to your opening sentence. Does it make you want to read on? Is your real opening sentence further in? One thing I've noticed running writers' groups is how many people begin a story by setting the scene. They'll introduce details the reader (at that stage) simply doesn't need.

Finally, read your extract aloud and listen for the point where the narrative actually begins. You'll know it when you hear it. It'll be like that moment when a dull film suddenly, and unexpectedly, gets interesting. That's your *writer's instinct*. It's an ability we all possess; only most of us call it intuition.

 ## The first rewrite...

The first rewrite is almost always about cutting words.

Notice I've said 'almost always' because there are no absolute rules in writing and redrafting. You want to cut everything you don't need but you don't want to end up with something that reads like notes. That's where judgement comes in.

 ## Edit exercise

Go back to your extract and delete every word you don't need.

When you've finished, read it aloud. If it's awkward to say, it will be awkward to read. So:

- Are some of the sentences still just too long?
- Can you split them into shorter sentences?
- Can you delete some of them and still keep your meaning?
- Are they difficult to say because the word order is awkward?
- Does it read like a bad translation from another language?
- Does it contain more information than you need?

Go back through the extract again and, when you've finished, check your word count. You'll have lost words but the chances are you'll have gained greater clarity.

Ted Hughes, poet

'… imagine what you are writing about. See it… When you do this, the words look after themselves like magic.'

Think back to Michelangelo's angel. When he saw that lump of marble, he imagined the angel inside it. He visualized it. When you write, aim to do the same thing.

How? Again, let's think about films:

Q: How does a film tell a story?

A: By combining dialogue and action – words and pictures.

Q: How does a writer tell a story?

A: By combining dialogue and description – words and pictures again.

Anton Chekov, writer of short stories and plays

'Cut out all those pages about moonlight… Show us the moon's reflection in a piece of broken glass.'

Let's think about reading. In Chapter 1 I talked about what's actually involved in the process itself – recognizing individual letters and the sounds they represent, combining those letters into words, the words into sentences and so on.

What I want to talk about now is how words on a page interact with your imagination.

Think back to your own childhood. When you were reading, or being read to, what effect did the words have on your imagination? I'm not thinking here about the abstract – 'they fired my imagination' – but the concrete. In my case, then and now, the words on the page generated images in my imagination – my mind's eye, if you like. And the more precise, concise and exact the description, the more my imagination was stimulated.

This, in turn, affected my emotions, which engaged me even more. But if the description I was reading was vague or even confusing, then I'd have to stop and reread that section again and this created a barrier between my imagination and the words on the page.

So what you're looking for are *images:* word pictures that are immediate and vivid.

Show emotion

Think of an emotion. Now think of a character feeling that emotion. In no more than 50 words, show that character experiencing that emotion without naming it.

For example:

Mary leaned against the back wall staring out of the window. Rain fell steadily. Her students were all making notes and the room was silent. She glanced at the clock. Three-twenty. Still forty minutes to go before the lesson finally ended.

'My hands', she thought, 'look old.'

(Word count: 47)

The emotion I was attempting to invoke was depression and, apart from drawing on my own memories, I used a few cinematic devices. Think of the passage as a clip from a film.

Medium close-up: Mary leaning against classroom wall.

Cut to: View outside – rain.

Cut to: Panning shot of classroom then up to clock.

(Silence except for ticking clock.)

Voice-over: Forty minutes to go.

Close up: Mary's hands.

Voice-over: My hands look old.

F. Scott Fitzgerald, novelist

'Action is character.'

Look again at the short passage about Mary, our depressed teacher. I could have written a much longer piece beginning:

Mary stood at the back of her classroom and looked out of the window at the pouring rain. *The weather matched her mood.* She was depressed and the afternoon *dragged at a snail's pace.* Her students wrote silently and the clock's ticking *reminded her of the fact that time was passing…*

Now, apart from the fact that it's too wordy, it tells you what to feel (the weather matched her mood), it uses a cliché (snail's pace) and explains the symbolism of the ticking clock. The first version contains all the same information but in just 47 words. It also only takes about 20 seconds to read aloud, so halve that for silent reading. If the passage was twice as long, it would take twice as long to read. It would affect the pace of the story.

In a film, if the action and dialogue race along too quickly, it becomes difficult to follow and, therefore, uninvolving. If it goes too slowly, your attention wanders and you lose interest altogether. It's the same with writing. You have to vary the pace. Short sentences speed up the pace. Longer ones slow it down. So avoid:

- **Padding** This is needless detail. Try to give the reader an impression of each character but don't provide them with something that reads like a description issued by the police. In Alan Sillitoe's short story 'Uncle Ernest', we're told that Ernest makes his living as a furniture upholsterer, that he smokes and that his clothes are shabby. We're not given any more because we don't need any more. We can imagine the rest for ourselves.

- **Clichés** It's OK to use clichés in dialogue or if your main character is telling the story, but it's never acceptable to use them in descriptive passages. Either cut them altogether or replace them with better descriptive phrases.

- **Unnecessary dialogue** Dialogue requires purpose. In other words, it's no good just slotting in a few lines of dialogue every now and again to fill up another half page and get you that bit closer to writing THE END. It must all be adding to the story.

It's also important to remember that most people don't speak in perfectly formed sentences. Nor, of course, do they always get straight to the point.

If you're not sure about a section of dialogue, again, try reading it aloud. If you're having trouble following what your character is saying, what chance will your reader have?

It's equally important to remember that a story is not real life. It may be inspired by real people and events, but those real people, the things they say, and events must then be shaped into a coherent story.

Cut, cut, cut...

In your book, anything that's not needed, whether it's a page, a paragraph, a sentence, a phrase or even a single word, should be cut.

At this point you could be forgiven for thinking 'I can't do all that!' and, of course, you don't have to. You could sort out the typos, tidy it up a bit and then publish – and within six months be ashamed to have your name on the cover.

Or you could go on the Internet and cost the complete editing, design and publishing package. You could even get the whole thing ghost-written – that is, get a professional writer to rewrite your whole book for you, so that only your name appears on the cover (and you'll feel about as involved with 'your' book as a ghost feels involved with its former life).

However, there are two counter arguments:

1 You've already invested a lot of time and energy writing the first draft. Was that all for nothing?

2 Of course you can do it. You already know the difference between good and bad writing because you read. Simply put, a good (well-written) book makes you want to read on. A bad (badly written) book doesn't.

I know it looks daunting and I know I've given you a lot to think about. And I haven't mentioned the word 'inspiration' once. Don't worry, I'm getting to it.

Let's summarize the story so far:

- Check through your manuscript slowly and carefully. Do not skim or speed-read. Note all the typos, missing words, punctuation errors, and so on. In other words, start with the obvious.
- Correct as you go along.
- Summarize your book, chapter by chapter, as you go along.
- If ideas for plot changes and so forth occur to you, note them but keep going.
- When you've finished, read your summary, then give yourself a few days off.
- Go back to your book and again, slowly and carefully, cut out verbiage, clichés and padding – like Michelangelo, chip away anything you obviously don't need. Once you've done this, your angel will begin to emerge.
- Your descriptions of people and places should be precise and visual – think film here – so that your reader 'sees' the story in their mind's eye.
- Evoke emotions – don't just name them. Don't tell me that someone's depressed, make me feel their depression – let me see the world through their eyes.

- Make sure your dialogue rings true and moves the story on.
- If in doubt, read it aloud. Or, better still, record your reading and then listen to it.

Now, as I said, you don't have to do any of that. However, I'd strongly advise that you to give it a try. The first and, to me, most obvious reason why you should is that writing is a skill and, like any skill, the more you practise, the better you become.

The second reason, not quite so obvious but equally valid, is that underachievement (the thing bad teachers call failure) is almost always linked to low self-esteem. Well, the reverse is also true. If you redraft slowly, carefully and systematically, and follow the suggestions I've made, your book will be improved – and it will be you who has improved it. By doing so, you will have sharpened up your writer's instinct, gained in confidence and, most of all, made an important discovery: redrafting is hard work, very tiring, seems to take for ever and can reduce you to tears. However, when it's going well, it's exhilarating, addictive, energizing and, ultimately, profoundly satisfying.

Readability

When you're redrafting, keep asking yourself the following question: What do I want my reader to get out of this?

Whether your book is fiction or non-fiction, it's still a narrative whose aim is to fully engage the reader's intellect and imagination. Notice here that I've said intellect *and* imagination. It's not a case of either one or the other. It should always be both. If your book is a thriller, you want your readers to feel thrills. If it's a comedy, you want your readers to laugh. If it's non-fiction, then you want your readers to come away with a clearer understanding of your subject matter.

What it should never be is an uninvolving insult to the reader's intelligence.

And just for the benefit of anyone thinking, 'Doesn't apply to me. My book's aimed at five-year-olds!' think again. Young children will accept fantasy and even apparent illogic, but they won't sit still long for a story that contains no internal logic. The logic may be crazy – at night, beds fly, toys come to life when nobody's looking, monsters have big teddy bears – but it must make some kind of sense.

So what makes you start reading a particular book? What makes you want to carry on? What makes you glad you did?

I suspect that most of us would give the same three answers:

1 The book's title/blurb/cover caught my attention.
2 The first page drew me in straight away and the rest of the book held my interest.
3 I gained something by reading it.

Depending on the book, what each reader gains will be different. I gain knowledge from non-fiction and I gain pleasure from fiction. Then again, I also read critical books for pleasure and I've read novels that have increased my knowledge. I often start a particular book because I'm either researching something or it's been recommended to me, or both. But there's only ever one reason why I finish a book: because I want to.

Why do I want to? Because it draws me in and holds my attention, and what holds my attention is a lot more than just good content. A well-researched but badly written book, whether it's fiction or non-fiction, will soon be discarded.

Interestingly enough, a correctly written book, one that's grammatically perfect, contains not a single typo, and so on, but is profoundly uninvolving, will often suffer the same fate.

The thing that they both have in common is contempt for me, the reader. The badly written book assumes that I'll read any old trash to pass the time. The correctly written book assumes that I'll be so impressed by someone who can spell, I won't notice how dull and lifeless the content is. But the well-written book, the one I always finish, assumes:

- I'm reasonably intelligent and can understand most things if they're explained clearly.
- I really don't like being told what to think.
- I can tell the difference between a fact and an opinion.
- I want to feel both imaginatively and emotionally engaged with any book I'm reading.

Inspiration

There is a myth that Van Gogh was a self-taught, blindly inspired genius whose greatest works were knocked out at the rate of five or six a week. The truth is that Van Gogh was a genius and that he was prolific in the last few years of his all-too-short life. What is also true is that he spent the preceding years practising and perfecting his skills. He would paint and repaint the same landscape until he got it absolutely right. In a letter to his brother, Theo, he uses the phrase 'Now my brush stroke is sure'. What he means is that constant practice has made his craft instinctive and that now he'll be able to fully realize his vision.

So am I saying that inspiration is a myth and that all art, whether it's painting, sculpture or, in our case, writing, is nothing more than the product of techniques that anyone can learn?

The short answer is no.

We're all born a blank page and our experiences shape us into the people we become. It's true that there are common factors in the early lives of writers – they include a solitary childhood, a rich fantasy life, a near-death experience… I know the full list by heart because when I was a teenager I read *The Poet's Calling* by Robin Skelton. In a chapter called 'The Child and The Muse' there was a long list of common factors in the early lives of poets. I eagerly read through it and found, to my joy, that I had the lot.

Excellent, I thought. Everything I write will be brilliant!

Five years and several hundred rejection slips later, I decided to have a rethink. I went back to Robin Skelton's book and read the chapters I'd originally skipped. The ones about craft and study. The ones I thought I didn't need to read. Why should I? I'd scored a perfect ten on the checklist so I was obviously beloved of the gods.

So, again, am I saying inspiration is a myth?

Well, again, no.

So, if it's not a myth, what is it?

In my experience inspiration is that point in any piece of writing when craft, imagination and emotion converge and, as Ted Hughes put it, the words take care of themselves. It's the intuitive leap that bypasses logic and amazes you, the writer, as much as it will amaze your readers. It won't grow out of software or templates any more than Van Gogh's best work could have grown out of painting-by-numbers.

You can believe that it's sent by God, the muse or your subconscious; it doesn't really matter. What does matter is that you recognize it when it arrives. And when it does arrive, you'll need to have developed the necessary level of skill to be able to take that imaginative raw material and transform it, make it as real and vivid for your readers as it is for you. So:

1 Carry a notebook and pen, or something to make notes on, at all times.

2 If a sentence, phrase, description, etc., comes into your head, even if it's not apparently related to your current project, note it down.

3 When you're working on your book, if a strong idea that will take your story in a new and unexpected direction won't leave your head, go with it!

CAN INSPIRATION BE INDUCED?

The short answer is no, but you can create conditions that will make you more receptive to it:

- Continue reading widely.
- As well as the appropriate Teach Yourself book, have a look at more books on writing.

One last thing. Like Van Gogh, you will gain from regular practice. You need to 'sketch' regularly. One very simple but incredibly useful exercise is the daily haiku.

> **Haiku:** three-line non-rhyming poem originally from Japan. It is usually 15 syllables – line one is five syllables, line two is seven and line three is five again. What it aims to do is capture a moment. For example:
>
> *Clearing the bar, she*
> *Falls through silence and into*
> *All that unleashed breath.*

The beauty of haikus is that they're economical (and therefore help you practise economy), mainly visual (so sharpen up your use of visual imagery) and, if you get into the habit of writing them regularly, they will become instinctive. This, in turn, will carry over into your other writing.

There are two things to bear in mind here. Firstly, the rules regarding syllable count are blurred. If the haiku is a translation, then the syllable count can vary; but if they are new and original, as yours will be, then in my opinion it is non-negotiable. Anyone who tells you differently is, again in my opinion, simply wrong. If you stick to the rules, you'll find that working within a strict discipline will make you more, not less, creative.

Secondly, don't expect instant results. The chances are that to begin with your haiku will be very 'So what?' Stay with it and cultivate patience – think tortoise and hare here – because there is still a long way to go.

I mentioned in Chapter 1 that writers should also be readers. I'll take it as a given that you've already looked at other Teach Yourself books directly related to your chosen field. Here are two more, one technical book and one e-bulletin, that I urge you to read:

- ***The Art of Fiction* by David Lodge:** In this the novelist and critic David Lodge looks at the opening pages of 50 different novels. He analyses and explains, in an accessible and readable style, a whole range of technical terms such as magic realism and in the process will introduce you to ways of telling a story you may never have heard of, let alone considered using. Each chapter is roughly four pages long and can be read in about ten to fifteen minutes. It is one of the best books of its kind I've ever read.

- grammar.guide@about.com: E-bulletin packed with useful articles on writing.

There are some more ideas for helpful reading at the end of this book.

Focus points

- Your first redraft will deal mainly with typos and other obvious errors.
- Make notes for possible plot changes and so on as you go along but don't start the rewrite yet.
- Your first redraft will be the first of many.
- Write a chapter-by-chapter summary as you go along.
- Initially, redrafting is almost always about cutting.
- Don't tell me what to see – make me see it.
- Don't tell me what to feel – make me feel it.
- Inspiration is not enough – you need skill as well.
- So write regularly *and*
- Read!

Where to next?

In Chapter 4 we will look at how to prepare your manuscript for publication.

4

Preparing your manuscript for publication

Kevin McCann

So far we've talked about the need for economy, accuracy and precision. By now you should have read through your manuscript, checking for typos, grammatical errors, clichés, padding and every individual word you don't need. You should also have written a chapter-by-chapter summary.

So, are you finished and ready to publish? Well, the chances are, no.

Victoria Roddam, publisher

'Self-publishing should be, in fact, more beholden to the rules of quality and form than traditionally published work, as it stands alone with no marketing, "community" or author personality smokescreen.'

There will be typos and other assorted mistakes in the text that you won't have spotted yet because you're too close and too involved in the book. You may even be wondering if you really want to carry on.If that's the case, take a break. Catch up with some reading, go for some solitary walks, bake another cake and put some distance between yourself and your book.Don't leave it too long before you get back to it, though. One month can give you the objectivity you need. Three could kill your momentum completely.

Readers' groups and...

At the time of writing, a lot of libraries still host readers' groups. They meet at regular intervals, usually once a month, to discuss a book they've all read. The books are loaned by the library hosting the event. Joining one will help your development as a writer by sharpening up your critical faculty – once a month you'll be discussing plot, structure and characterization with a group of readers, so it will also be market research. What better place to find out about people's reading habits than a readers' group? You'll be introduced to writers whose work you may not have considered previously. This will broaden your knowledge and monthly meetings will provide structure to your writing life – writing is self-discipline; self-discipline grows out of structured routine.

...self-education

Back in the 1960s there was a debate going on in educational circles which could be summed up as: 'Spelling and grammar: taught or caught?' On one side there were the advocates of free learning, with the traditionalists on the other. Most practising teachers were in the middle.

Free learning meant that children chose their own topics to study, corrected their own work and were self-motivated. The traditionalists favoured grammar, spelling tests, learning by rote and lots of testing. Obviously, there was a lot more to it than that. I'm oversimplifying for the sake of brevity.

Those in the middle realized that there's no one-size-fits-all way of learning. Some of us learn by listening, some by doing and some by a mixture of both. It wasn't taught or caught. It was both, and the best way to educate the individual child was the way that worked best for them.

What most teachers did agree on was that self-discipline grew out of structured routine. Traditionalists believed that an imposed structure (and the discipline that went with it) would always be required. Progressives believed that, once children became self-motivated (i.e. they could see the point of gaining knowledge), the imposed structure would fade and be replaced by self-motivation, which would in turn lead to greater achievement. What everyone did agree on was that the purpose of education is to help the individual child realize their full potential.

> Education: From the Latin *educo* – to draw out.

That's your aim as well. You want to realize your full potential as a writer. You're both student and teacher. True, you've also got Tom and myself, the Internet, writers' groups, friends, family, a whole support network, in fact. But, in the end, it will always come back down to you, the words and how well you get on together. So you need to consciously and realistically recognize the gaps in your knowledge and address them by constant reading. As well as reading more, you should start to become more discriminating, and joining a readers' group will help you do just that.

The Irish novelist Edna O'Brien once said that if you read rubbish, you'll end up writing it. Of course you might respond with, 'And who decides what's rubbish?' The answer is, of course, that ultimately you will.

You already discriminate when it comes to films and TV shows – at least I hope you do. You begin by applying those same feelings to whatever it is you're reading.

It was, and still is, accepted by good teachers that underachievement is often the result of low self-esteem. Low self-esteem manifests itself either as 'Can't do this – I'm thick' or 'Not doing this – it's boring'. In adults this becomes a kind of militant anti-intellectualism. And, sadly, I've often come across it in would-be writers. They either put their faith entirely in inspiration or claim that reading other people will somehow dilute the purity of their vision.

It's like offering somebody a compass and detailed map showing the best route through the forest, only to find yourself glibly refused with the words, 'No thanks, I've decided to put all my faith in dumb luck.'

You may feel that you're a reasonably well-read, open-minded kind of person and that none of this really applies to you. You may even be right… but are you sure you're not just being complacent?

Go back and read the quote at the beginning of the chapter again. Victoria Roddam is not saying your book should be as good as something published by Bigname Publishers; she's saying it's got to be better than that.

So step one is to make sure that it's well crafted. You can, of course, use the spellchecker and then go back and proofread it again. A spellchecker will highlight 'teh' but won't tell you whether you typed 'pole' instead of 'pale'.

Don't use the auto-correct. This only leads to more errors as your computer (unlike you) is incapable of making informed decisions. I once used the auto-correct on an article I was writing and it altered the name of the self-publishing company FeedARead to Breastfeed.

Rely entirely on software and you'll learn nothing at all. If you're not prepared to learn, how can you ever expect to improve?

If you don't think your book is worth all that extra effort, you obviously don't really believe in it. If you don't believe in it, why should anyone else? Why should they part with money and give up their time to read something you think 'will do'?

You owe it to your potential readers, but you also owe it to yourself, not to fall into that trap. You might even tell yourself that that's the best you can do. You might even believe it. Well, for a while at least. But if you're developing your writer's instinct, you will carry on. As well as making sure that your book is free of all the obvious errors, you may begin to sense that it needs something else as well.

 ## Harriet Bourton, fiction editor

'There must be an interesting, engaging and emotive voice coming through. If I can't hear that voice in my head when I read it, I know that, regardless of how well plotted it is, I just won't love it. And if I don't love it, I won't rave about it to my colleagues, who are essentially the people who'll eventually be the ones to sign off on whether we can buy it. What's difficult is that you can't force a voice in fiction – it's either there, or it's not.'

In his essay on Dickens, George Orwell said that he always got the impression that somehow Dickens was speaking directly to him. Incidentally, if you've never read any of Orwell's essays, do so. They're not only insightful but also models of clarity. 'Decline of the English Murder' is an excellent starting point.

The point that both Harriet Bourton and George Orwell are making is this: a well-crafted, well-plotted book is simply not enough. What makes any book, fiction or non-fiction, stand out is the writer's voice.

Think of it like this. Two people tell the same joke. They both use more or less the same words and both arrive at the same punch line. When A tells it, everyone falls about laughing. When B tells it, people smile politely but no one so much as giggles. Why?

Because A knows when to pause, what to emphasize and how to bring the joke to life. B, on the other hand, merely tells you what happened. One is a living story; the other is only a description.

So how do you find your voice?

Well, as Harriet Bourton rightly points out, you can't force it but you can develop it. So as well as reading widely in your chosen field, read book reviews, magazine articles and also have a look at writers' blogs. The best ones are always interesting. You could also consider starting one of your own. If you type 'starting a blog' into your search engine, you'll find various free sites as well as online tutorials showing you how to set one up.

Tom goes into blogging in more detail in Chapters 9 and 10 so you might want to jump ahead and read that section as soon as you feel ready. Just come back here once you're done.

Incidentally, you might think that, if you've written non-fiction, all of this 'writer's voice' stuff doesn't really apply to you. You're wrong. Remember: whether you've written fiction or non-fiction, you've still produced a narrative (story). It might be the story of a specific period of history and its significance or a sci-fi extravaganza, but if it doesn't hold the reader's attention from beginning to end, then it's a failure.

Think back a moment to when you were a child. When you were listening to a story (as opposed to reading it yourself) what was it that held your attention? The content, the storyteller's voice, or both? What made A a better joke teller than B?

You could be forgiven for thinking, 'He's given me all this to think about, I'm redrafting my book and now he suggests writing something else!' What I'm actually suggesting is that you begin working on smaller projects that will complement your book and bring you one step closer to finding your authentic voice.

Because you've got one and it's exactly the voice Harriet describes. You can't force it, but you can now take further steps to help release it.

Finding your voice

One very good way of doing that is writing a blog. In fact, get into the habit of writing whenever you can. Get a Facebook page, comment on whatever you like and do so regularly. Make it part of your daily routine. I log into Facebook once a day. I try to make it roughly the same time every day and I put a time limit on myself. It's not just that I don't want to spend half my life Facebooking; it's also because time limits, like deadlines, concentrate the mind.

And, again, you're speaking in your own voice.

You might want to consider article writing. I used to write for the novelist Helen Watts when she edited educational magazines aimed at literacy teachers. I usually had a couple of weeks to get each piece written and I always had a word count of 1,500. I found writing the first one really heavy-going. A full week had gone by and I only had about 400 words to show for it. 'What the hell's the matter with you?' I thought. 'You can talk to a room full of teachers but you can't…'

That was about as far as the thought went. The key word was *talk*. Which led me to, 'Write it as if you were speaking it out loud!' which led me to finishing the first draft in one day. I went on to write more articles for Helen, and after I'd joined the Writers' Guild (more on the advantages of that later) I also contributed pieces to *UK Writer*.

Now there are three important points here:

1 Article writing didn't get in the way of my other work.

2 My prose style improved.

3 As a direct result, I gained in confidence and my weekly word count went up.

Workshop: Find a magazine publisher

If you simply type 'freelance article writing' into your search engine, you'll get dozens of results. I know. I've just done it. So narrow your search. What really interests you? What are you passionate about?

Once you've decided, search the Internet for magazines that publish articles on that subject. Once you've found one, find their submissions policy. They'll vary. Some accept unsolicited work. Some don't. Some want to read finished articles. Some want a proposal – that is, a summary of what you want to write about. Some even pay.

Once you have found a magazine that does accept unsolicited work, read a copy and familiarize yourself with the in-house style. When you find one whose style is closest to your own, contact the editor with your idea and see if they're interested.

They may have printed a similar article to the one you're proposing six months previously and so turn you down. But you've not wasted your time. You've made contact with an editor (who may suggest a different subject for an article) and you've put forward a proposal which has at least been considered.

If they accept your proposal (and your finished article), you've made a small but important breakthrough.

There are two other things to consider:

1 The editor's decision is final, so don't argue if you get turned down.

2 You're not doing this instead of working on your book. You're doing it as well. So decide how much time you want to devote to it and pretty much stick to that. I'd suggest two weeks. Not long, I know, but, as I've already said, deadlines concentrate the mind wonderfully well.

If you're a genre writer and haven't yet joined the appropriate specialist group, do so. The journal of the British Fantasy Society (*BFS Journal*), for example, accepts unsolicited work. You might also want to have a look at *Freelance Writers News* which comes out 11 times a year. At the time of writing, a year's subscription is £29. In it there are details of various writing competitions and a letters page, but what it mainly consists of is the contact details of magazine editors and the kind of work they're looking for. See www.writersbureau.com for further details.

Storytellers and storytelling

A few years ago I worked for an agency that booked me into schools. Mainly, I was performing poetry and helping children write their own. One school asked if I'd go into Reception and tell the children a story. I was happy to agree. All they wanted me to do was sit in a room full of four- to five-year-olds and tell them the story of *Goldilocks and the Three Bears*. How hard could that be?

I emerged 20 minutes later, a wiser man. It's not that the children were badly behaved. Quite the opposite. They were well mannered, polite and obviously bored rigid.

So what was wrong? I knew the story, so all the details were correct. They all knew the story and, at the start of the session, were obviously looking forward to hearing it again.

Over lunch I talked to their teacher, who said, 'When you tell a story, tell it as if you believe it's true.'

Now that's one of the best pieces of advice any writer can be given. If *you're* not convinced, how can you expect anyone else to be?

Over the several years that followed, I carried on visiting schools and I introduced storytelling into my repertoire. I learned by constant practice, rehearsals and, above all, by only telling stories that I liked.

It was invaluable.

Find your voice

Type 'YouTube – storytellers' into your search engine. Listen to any that look interesting. When you find one that you particularly like, listen to it until you're familiar enough with the content to retell it yourself.

Don't write anything down at this stage.

If possible, record your retelling and then listen to it. Chances are, you'll hear faults, but don't worry about that because you're not finished yet.

Next, take the story you've retold and write it down from memory. Double-space it. As you're writing, try to keep in mind not just what happened, but the words you used when telling it. Try speaking each sentence or group of sentences before you write them down. By doing that, you're developing your own voice. It's not just poetry that's about sound as well as sense. Everything you write is.

When you've finished, record yourself reading the story, leave it for 24 hours, then listen to that recording. Have your manuscript in front of you. When you come across mistakes, clumsy sentence construction, long-winded dialogue, etc., pause the recording and fix it there and then. Once that section is fixed, continue.

Repeat this exercise whenever you can or, better still, make it part of your working week. Even better, make it the same part of your working week. What you will find is that, sooner or later, you'll be able to 'hear' your own voice in your head as you write.

That's your *writer's voice*. Just as the tone of your speaking voice changes depending on the situation you're dealing with, so your writer's voice will vary depending on what you're writing about. The voice I use when I'm angry, and need someone else to understand that, is not the same voice I use when I'm talking to someone who needs comforting. The tone changes but it's still my voice.

Watch out for 'cultural theft'

A lot of stories on the Internet are told by Native American, Australian and African storytellers. Please be aware that to many indigenous people their stories are both part of their spiritual as well as their cultural heritage. In plain English, please do not publish your 'version' of a traditional story from a living culture. No matter how well intentioned, unless you have permission, it's still cultural theft.

Change the point of view

Retell a story from the point of view of one of the characters, for example *The Three Bears* as told by Baby Bear or *Red Riding Hood* from the wolf's point of view. Playing the villain can be very liberating. Ask any actor.

Orson Welles once pointed out that one of Shakespeare's many strengths was that he understood that everyone has their reasons. It's something you should keep in mind.

Which 'person'?

If your book is currently written in the third person, would it work better in the first?

A writing workout

Think back to an important incident from your own past. Good or bad, it doesn't matter. All that counts is that it still affects your emotions. Set yourself a 15-minute time limit and then write down what happened, but write it in the present tense. It will make the writing all the more immediate. Don't worry if you can't remember all the details. Invent. You're a writer and that's what writers do. When you get to the end of the allotted time, stop. Please don't cheat here; otherwise the only thing you'll be doing with your time is wasting it.

There are three purposes to this exercise, all equally important:

1 It concentrates your mind. Again.

2 It gives you the direct line to that part of your mind where your creativity is waiting – it's the same place your dreams come from.

3 It will help you develop your own individual style and nurture your authentic voice.

So repeat it whenever you can. In the unlikely event you've had an incident-free life, scour newspapers and magazines and write about anything that catches your imagination. It doesn't have to be something big like a riot or disaster of some kind. In fact, I'd advise against it. Look for something small scale. I won't say any more. You'll know it when you see it.

Self-actualization and the writer's voice

I've worked as a writer in a wide variety of locations – jails, community centres, closed wards, schools – and, again and again, I saw the same pattern emerge. Individuals suffering from low self-esteem begin writing: in the course of writing they 'forget' their apparent lack of ability; they are proud of their achievement; they write more.

I compared notes with other writers. They all told similar stories and I began to wonder why. Then a few years ago I was interviewed by a transpersonal psychology student who was researching the nature of poetic inspiration for her Master's thesis. She showed me a summary of her conclusions, which included the following:

 Danielle McGregor, BSc. (Hons), MSc.

'…*it is possible to conclude that each of the poets is in fact engaged in an active and ongoing quest for self-actualization.*'

[The psychologist Abraham Maslow (1908–70) defined self-actualization as 'The impulse to convert oneself into what one is capable of being.']

Earlier in this chapter, I pointed out that low self-esteem led to underachievement. In extreme cases this prompts a 'not worth even trying as I'm bound to fail' attitude in people. But it can also lead to 'That'll do'. Or, worst of all, a narcissism that fools the writer into thinking that they 'need not change a word'.

I doubt if any of you fall into either the first or last category. If you did, you wouldn't be reading this book. And hopefully, by now, if you ever thought 'That'll do', you've abandoned that as well. But you may be drawn to the final option, which is: 'That's the best I can do.'

It may even be true. Let's say, you've read and reread your book until your eyes ache. You've tracked down and corrected every typo. You've cut every word you don't need. You've rewritten great chunks of it and it really is the best it can be. Well, for now at any rate.

Or, you hope it is.

So, what now? Are you finally ready to go ahead and publish?

Before you take that final step, you need to do two very important things:

1 Get your manuscript assessed.

2 Get it proofread.

Find an assessment service

If you type 'manuscript assessment services' into your search engine, you'll get a lot of hits. Be aware, and beware, though. They tend to vary in price from the fairly cheap to the very expensive and there are several where the assessor charges by the hour. In the latter case, you have no idea how much your final bill will be, so if you do decide to use this process, it might be better for you to consider somebody who charges fixed fees for specific word counts.

If you simply haven't got a lot of cash to spare, then the assorted assessment services may not be an option. What you'll need, then, is a first reader. Your ideal candidate should be someone you know and trust – so no strangers you've met in Internet chat rooms, for example. It should be somebody who isn't prejudiced one way or the other. Someone who 'just loves your work' will be no good – they'll be prejudiced in your favour and almost totally blind to your faults.

So where else could you look?

Well, as I've already mentioned, I'd avoid strangers met in Internet chat rooms. I remember seeing an ad in one a few years back which read: 'Anyone out there willing to read my book and give me your opinion?' It was a very foolish and naive thing to do. A stranger could simply download your book, change their email and steal your idea. You'd have little or no proof. That's absolute worst-case scenario. Well, actually, that's more like an 'only a poet could come up with something that paranoid' worst-case scenario. The other possibility is that the person you send the book to might very well be someone with an agenda. The commonest being: 'You read mine and I'll read yours.' This is followed by completely over-the-top praise and you, of course, are expected to respond in kind.

So, what are you left with? You could decide on the cheaper end of the manuscript assessment services and raise the money. You could contact your local library and/or Regional Arts Board and see if there are any writers' surgeries available in your area. I've run a lot of these myself and the way it usually works is you bring along a sample of your writing and have a one-to-one tutorial with a professional writer. You may even find that the writer in question is willing – for a fee – to read your whole book. But don't count on it. It's more likely that they'll read the first few pages and then talk about your style and use of language. In other words, they'll tell you if they think it has readability.

That's why, for example, when you're submitting a novel to a publisher, they often ask for a summary plus the first 50 or so pages. Despite what a lot of people may think, that's generous. Just as you or I can usually tell after 50 pages or so whether or not a book has that quality, so can they. If it hasn't got that quality, then they won't recommend it for publication.

Whenever I've made that point to an aspiring novelist I've often been told, quite angrily as a rule, that 'That's just not fair because it might get better after that!' Which may be true. But shouldn't it be the best it can be right from the start?

So let's get back to your first 50 pages.

Find a writers' surgery

You'll also find that quite a lot of writers' surgeries offer occasional writing days and/or master classes. In my experience, they're often well worth attending. Again, look at who's running the session and, even if they're working in a genre that's not your own, consider going anyway; you can still gain a lot. Besides which, if you want to be a writer, it will help cultivate your mind and add constantly to your knowledge of the craft of writing in all its aspects.

One other thing. Often, if you're working on something in a particular genre or on a very specific subject, you get blocked. Thinking you're finished because that's the best you can manage is just as much writer's block as staring at a blank screen or page without a single idea in your head. You try everything you can think of but nothing works.

Q: What do you do?

A: Something else.

I was once asked to write some 'green' poems for children. I read a lot of stuff on the environment and I read a lot of poems but not one word came. Later that same week I went to a talk in my local library on the subject of writing historical fiction. At one point we were asked to think of a character and describe their life. The speaker had also mentioned museums.

Something sparked in my imagination and, instead of a character study, I wrote a poem about a museum in the future that contains:

> *Elephant tusks, a grey seal,*
> *White snow, green fields,*
> *The Rain Forest's very last tree.*

This was followed by another eight verses.

If that was an isolated incident, it would be possible to put it down to coincidence. But the fact is, it wasn't.

However, I digress, usefully, yet again. Back to your book. If you've joined a readers' group, is there anyone there, whose opinion you trust, who might be willing to read at least some of your book and give you their thoughts as a reader?

If you're a member of a writers' group, is there anyone there you could ask?

If the answer to either of the above is yes, then approach the person in question and sound them out. If it's a reader, what you really want to know is whether the extract they looked at made them want to read more? Did they want to know what happened next? If they say yes, ask why and then listen. If they say no, ask why and take notes.

If your first reader is a member of a writers' group, then ask them the same question but also ask them to comment on your style. And, again, whatever their response is, good or bad, listen and take notes.

If you find more than one person – that is, a reader and a writer, two readers, etc. – then don't just pick one. Give them different extracts and, if they both make roughly the same kind of comments, take note. If two people tell you your book is dull, then the chances are high that it is. So don't get too angry – though you're bound to feel a bit vexed – go away and think about it. Before you do that, ask them, calmly and politely, to say why. And then thank them.

If you are told it's a well-written page-turner, ask if they'd mind reading more. If you're lucky enough to get a yes, make doubly sure they realize what's involved and have the time to do it and then await their conclusions. If your reader likes the whole book and you trust their judgement, then you might be getting close to that point when you can seriously think about publishing.

But before you do that *read it again*!

If you have the slightest nagging doubt about so much as a single sentence, read it aloud. How does it sound? Does it ring true? Remember the schoolteacher I mentioned earlier who said, 'When you tell a story, tell it as if you believe it's true.'

Jimmy McGovern, screenwriter

'My first drafts are always full of effort. With subsequent drafts I try to make it look effortless, to make it look as if I found the story in the street.'

Look at the above quotation and now think back to the other one about telling 'a story as if you believe it's true'. One is from a Reception teacher who is talking about children's stories. The other is from an award-winning screenwriter. What they're both saying is, essentially, the same thing. Whether your book is non-fiction or fiction, sci-fi, fantasy, romance or gritty social realism, does it sound true?

Is it the book you want to write or is it the one you feel that you should? Because if it's not the book you want to write, if it's not your own authentic voice speaking, no matter how many drafts it goes through, it will never be right.

If that's the case, have you wasted your time? No, of course not. In writing, nothing's ever wasted. If your book is still not right and you know it, go back and redraft. Or even start again.

The fantasy writer Nina Allan, acting on the advice of Christopher Priest who wrote *The Prestige*, redrafts by printing out her manuscript and then retyping on to the computer from scratch. In an interview in the Autumn 2012 issue of the *BFS Journal* she said:

> *...it changed my life. The improvements were vast... Writing proper second drafts – third drafts if necessary – is now an indispensable part of my writing practice, and I know that all the most sizeable improvements in my work have come about either directly or indirectly because of it.*

You could begin a rewrite with just your summary; use that as a plan and begin again from there.

You could, as I've already suggested, try retelling the story in the first person. If you do, choose the character that interests you the most, even if it's the villain of the piece. Just remember Orson Welles' dictum: Everyone has their reasons.

If you're confident that you're getting ready to publish, then in Chapter 7 we'll talk about final preparation of your manuscript.

Focus points

- Self-published books need to be a cut above when it comes to quality.
- Readers' groups are well worth joining. They provide structure, broaden your reading habits and provide you with primary-source market research.
- It's important, whether your book is fiction or non-fiction, to develop your own writer's voice because...
  - every book's a narrative *and*
  - the best way to find your writer's voice is through writing, *so*
  - widen your net and open your mind to new influences.
- Try writing in the present tense.
- When you've done all you can, get your manuscript both assessed and proofread.
- If possible, attend a writers' surgery.
- If you get writer's block, do something else for a while.

Where to next?

In Chapter 5 Tom looks at how to publish your book the traditional way – by producing printed books.

5

Print and print on demand

Tom Green

The traditional method of self-publishing, paying for a run of printed books, remains a valid approach if you are confident that you can sell a large number of copies – at least 500 and perhaps as many as 1,000. If you don't expect to sell this many, then you should probably start with print on demand and/or ebooks (see Chapter 6).

Offset printing

Offset printing is the most common method for books with a reasonably large print run. There are different types of offset printing suitable for different kinds of book. What all have in common is that the set-up costs are relatively high but the marginal unit costs (that is, the cost of printing each additional book) are low. The more copies you print in one run, the cheaper the unit cost overall (that is, the cost of each individual book).

You cannot use offset printing for print on demand. If you want more copies, you will need to pay for a whole new print run.

Offset printing makes economic sense only if you need a relatively high print run of at least 500, or possibly even 1,000 books.

You might not think 500 books sounds like a very large number, but most self-published books sell only around 100–150 copies.

Unless you have existing orders or a strong track record, it is unlikely that you will want to use offset printing.

Digital printing – print on demand

Digital printing normally has very low set-up costs, but the costs for printing each additional book will be higher than for offset printing and do not tend to fall as the print run increases.

Because the set-up costs are lower, digital printing makes economic sense for shorter print runs – fewer than 500 copies, or perhaps fewer than 1,000, depending on the book.

Digital printing also enables print on demand. This means that, whenever a book is ordered, a copy is printed and dispatched. The set-up costs are normally captured in the selling price (of which the printing company keeps a percentage), so as a self-publishing author you will face no up-front costs for printing.

For most self-published authors, digital print on demand will be the best option. If you end up selling lots of books, you can meet the demand, or, if your sales really take off, get a larger print run done through offset printing.

QUALITY

The quality of digital printing used to be much lower than offset printing or letterpress printing (which preceded offset and is still used for some limited-edition books today). These days, the quality of good digital printing is excellent. But if you are publishing high-quality images, or wish to publish to an exceptional quality, you should speak to printers about the best options, look at samples of their work and compare costs.

Evaluate possible sales

How many books will you sell? List the possible sources of sales – and be realistic. Ask others on relevant forums and social media how many copies authors of similar books have sold. Don't be misled by the few who have had bestsellers; you can learn from them but don't assume that you will be able to emulate their success.

Vanity publishing

Before the rise of digital publishing, self-publishing was blighted by so-called 'vanity publishing' companies that frequently over-charged and over-promised. Typically, they would offer a range of publishing services that they said were essential and required a much higher print run than necessary. Rather than preying on the 'vanity' of authors, it is perhaps truer to say that they were taking advantage of ignorance. Publishing can be made to seem more complicated than it really is, and the prospect of having a book in print can be a very strong incentive.

These days there is no need to pay a company to publish the book for you, even if you want to publish via an offset press. You can contact printers, find the best price and then discuss with them how you want the manuscript prepared.

Whenever you engage a company or an individual to work on your behalf, make sure you are clear what you will get for your money. Check the terms and conditions and get reliable references from other people who have used the service. If possible, contact those people yourself to ask them about the service they have received. Alternatively, ask people on relevant forums and through social media.

Shop around

The easiest way to make sure you are not taken advantage of by a printer or self-publishing company is to compare estimates from several providers. If things aren't clear, ask for more detail. And ask other people online who have been through the process for advice.

Doing it yourself

As a self-publisher you can choose how much of the process to do yourself, and how much to pay someone else to do.

It's easy to find companies that will manage everything, taking a manuscript from you and then proofreading it, preparing it for print, laying out the text, designing the cover, and either printing the number of copies you require or setting it up for print on demand.

If you don't want to be involved in any of that work, find a company you can trust – ideally through several recommendations. If you can afford to spend what will probably be several thousand pounds, then this can be a good option. We'll discuss self-publishing companies in more detail below.

However, if you want to save money and are happy to learn about the various parts of the publishing process, then you should not find it too difficult. There may still be professional services you choose to buy, but you can pick and choose when you need them.

The most important job for a self-publisher is to make sure that your manuscript is properly prepared for print. Some self-publishers are tempted to rush through this, keen to get on with what might seem to be the more exciting work of design, layout and print. But mistakes in the manuscript are the ones that you will regret most once your book is published. Take as long as it needs to make sure you get it right.

 ## First things first...

You must make sure your manuscript is ready before you begin the printing process. It will be possible to make changes later, but it's much easier to make them at the outset (see Chapter 4).

Layout

For most books the layout of the text will be straightforward. Make sure you leave sufficient room for margins – you will be able to get advice on margin width from the printer or self-publishing service you work with.

Always number the pages.

There are common approaches to book layout that you will probably want to follow. There will normally be a half-title page (with just the title and nothing else), followed by a blank page and then the title page (containing the title, author, editor, edition number and publisher). This will be followed by the copyright page (with a copyright statement and ISBN) and then others such as a dedication page and acknowledgements (although these can also come at the end).

There are good guidelines to aspects of book layout on www.thebookdesigner.com.

If you have little experience self-publishing, it is probably best to look at the layout of a successful book in a similar genre to your own. There are many ways to handle chapter headings and section breaks, and you can see them simply by looking at books. As a general rule, keep things simple. You don't want a fussy layout to get in the way of the reader's enjoyment.

Some sites such as CreateSpace provide formatted templates that you can download and insert your text into.

Look at some 'prelim' pages

Find several books similar to yours that have been published by a mainstream publisher and look at the pages that come before the main content (called the 'prelims', short for preliminary pages). There will probably be some variation – for example, some might have a page of information about the author – but they will have quite a lot in common.

Front cover design

Your book's front cover is very important, not just as a way to advertise the work's content but also to suggest its quality. A poorly designed or printed cover can strongly influence a reader's views of the text itself.

The format for your front cover design will depend on what the printer or self-publishing service requires. Some online self-publishing companies provide tools to help you with the design and formatting for the cover, while there are also numerous companies and individuals selling design services. If you do pay for front cover design, make sure that you have seen examples of the designer's work and be clear about what you expect from them. Show them the types of cover you like for books that are similar to yours, and give them a clear brief for the dimensions and format you need, including the back cover and the spine (you will need to research this first). If possible, request sketches of several ideas so that you can choose the one you like best.

It is possible to do the design yourself, especially if you keep it simple. Ask for advice on forums and via social media and be prepared to put some time into experimenting with different ideas. You will need to have some knowledge of a design tool like Photoshop (or a free equivalent such as Gimp), or else be prepared to learn. Follow instructions closely and make sure that you are accurate in your work.

If you are using an online self-publishing company, make sure that you look at their options for cover creation. The tools offered vary between companies, and it might be a critical factor in your decision about which one to use.

Remember that the cover design needs to work well when shown in a small size. People are far more likely to encounter it as a thumbnail image on a book-retailing website than they are at a bookshop, so avoid small type or intricate images. There is more on this in Chapter 7.

Formatting

Whether you are using an online print-on-demand service or a traditional printer, you will need to format your book correctly or pay the printer to do it for you.

Online services such as Lulu and CreateSpace have detailed instructions about preparing your book before self-publishing. Though they try to make it as simple as possible, things can seem complicated if you are not familiar with the process.

You should start by asking the printer, or finding out from the self-publishing company website, exactly what the requirements are for the format of your book.

In theory, almost anything is possible. All fonts, layouts, page sizes and designs can be accommodated – as long as you set them up correctly and pay whatever they cost.

However, unless non-standard design and layout are important for your book, it probably makes sense to start with as simple a design as possible. That way, you will make the process quicker and are less likely to make mistakes.

FONT

If you use a standard font that is found on all home computers, such as Times New Roman, you will not have to pay and are unlikely to encounter formatting problems. Times New Roman is known as a 'serif' font – one that has small tails at the ends of letters. 'Sans serif' fonts such as Arial and Helvetica are plainer. It is normal practice to use serif fonts for long sections of text, as it is easier to read.

Some unusual fonts will require payment for use, and they might cause problems for your printer. If you do use unusual fonts, make sure to embed them in the pdf. Unless you have experience in this area, it is probably best to stick with one of the most common fonts. Printers and self-publishing websites will be able to tell you which fonts to use.

If you are unsure about what size font to use, ask for advice. The common sizes will vary depending on the size of the book.

PAGE SIZE

You will normally be offered a set choice of page sizes to choose from. You are likely to want the size that is most common in the market for the type of book you are writing. But you might select a size that you hope will make your book stand out. Whatever you choose, you will need to make sure that your manuscript is in roughly the same dimensions and is roughly the same size. If you are using a printer (for either offset or print on demand), they will probably help you with this if your manuscript isn't correctly sized. However, when working through an online company, unless you pay them to do it for you, you will need to get it right yourself. For example, if you select a book size smaller than your manuscript then everything will be scaled down in the printed book and the fonts might be too small.

Again, if you select a common size and shape and are using standard word-processing software, then this should not present any problems. Check the formatting instructions for your chosen self-publishing service and, if you have any doubts, either contact them directly or ask in one of the self-publishing forums.

In Microsoft Word you can change the size and dimensions of your manuscript using File > Page Setup > Paper Size. Other word-processing programs have similar menus.

Size (and shape) matters

Look at the books on your own bookshelves and think about the size and shape of different kinds of work. Do certain books have a certain size in common? What size and shape are most of the books that are similar to yours?

IMAGES

For most standard self-publishing services it is possible to include images in your book. However, you will need to be careful about how you present these images for print. If you are working directly with a printer, talk to them in detail about what they require. For online services, read the detailed instructions about the image size and layout requirements. For example, if you want images to be full-bleed (set to the very edge of the page), there might be certain formatting to undertake.

CREATING A PDF

Most self-publishing services will accept common word-processing files but recommend that you convert your manuscript to a pdf before uploading. This reduces the chance of formatting errors.

You can convert your manuscript to a pdf in most word-processing software by clicking on 'print' and then selecting 'print to pdf' or just 'pdf' from the printer options. Alternatively, you can buy Adobe software to make pdfs or download free software to create pdf files.

If you are making extensive use of colour and images, you should read the detailed requirements for preparing a pdf.

Self-publishing websites should have guidance about making pdfs. If you have problems, ask them or seek help via a forum or social media.

Paperback or hardback?

Unless you are publishing a book that you expect to sell at quite a high price – for example, one with high-quality images and design – you are unlikely to want your book to be hardback. The additional costs in production and distribution just won't be worth while.

WHAT KIND OF PAPER?

The quality of paper can make a big difference to the look and feel of the book, so it is worth asking to see samples if you are working directly with a printer, or ask in a forum or via social media if you are using an online self-publisher. Unless you are printing high-quality images or require premium quality, for example, for a commemorative book of some kind, then you are unlikely to want the highest-quality paper.

However, the lowest-cost options can sometimes feel cheap, so it is worth finding out more about them first.

Again, unless you are producing a premium book of some kind, you should probably use whatever the normal paper is that the printer or self-publishing service recommends. If you have photographs or graphics, seek advice about what weight and type of paper you will need.

BINDING

For paperbacks, the most common option is 'perfect binding', where the cover wraps around the pages. You might also consider 'saddle stitch', if you have a small number of pages, or 'spiral bound', if you are printing something more like a manual.

For hardbacks the binding is normally 'casewrap', which you will find used for hardbacks on your bookshelf. You will probably also have the option to put a dust jacket over that, on which the cover design is printed.

ISBN

An ISBN (International Standard Book Number) is a unique code for each book (or ebook) that booksellers or the public can use to identify it. It will normally be shown as a barcode on the back of the book.

It can be difficult to sell a book without an ISBN as both major online retailers such as Amazon and bookshops require them. ISBNs are not always required for ebooks, but if you do get an ISBN for an ebook it must be different from that used for a print version of your book.

Only one agency in each country is authorized to issue ISBNs although many self-publishing companies (including Amazon CreateSpace) will offer them to you either for free or as part of a package you purchase.

You can get more information about ISBNs and how to purchase them in the UK from Neilsen www.isbn.nielsenbook.co.uk. However, you can only buy ISBNs from Neilsen in blocks of ten, with the price currently at £144. So, unless you are planning to publish a number of books, it probably makes sense for you to get one from a self-publishing company.

The only problem with this is where you want to create your own publishing 'imprint' – that is, a brand name under which you publish. Normally, if you use an ISBN from a self-publishing company, they will be listed as the publisher. If this matters to you, then, unless the self-publishing company offers a 'custom' ISBN, you will need to purchase a block of ISBNs yourself.

Note that if you are reprinting a book without changes, then you must use the same ISBN. But if you are printing a new edition, then a new ISBN must be obtained.

Pricing

The price you set for your book will probably depend on a number of factors, including:

- what the typical market price is for this kind of book
- how much the book costs to produce
- how much money you hope to make
- how many copies you hope to sell.

It will help if you produce a simple business plan setting out your estimates relating to all of these things so that you can estimate how much money you will need to invest and how many copies you will need to sell to break even. Be realistic when you do this, basing all of your estimates on evidence rather than aspiration. Selling books is rarely easy and the market is extremely competitive.

Research the going price

Search online for books similar to your own and note down the prices. It's likely to be difficult for you to sell books that are much above the market rate, unless you have a unique proposition. Most self-published books sell fewer than 150 copies, and even this number can be hard to achieve. When estimating your sales and revenue, be realistic and try to base estimates on evidence from market research and what self-published authors of similar work have achieved.

MARKET PRICE

As a self-published author you will be in competition not just with other self-publishers but also books published conventionally. There is likely to be a typical market price in the genre your book fits into, but there will probably also be numerous discounts and special offers. Lesser-known authors might price their work lower than those who are more established, although sometimes established authors can use economies of scale (i.e. printing large numbers of books) to achieve a lower price. If the market for your book is specialized, you might be able to set a higher price. Indeed, sometimes a higher price can help establish the credibility of your book. Remember that you are also in competition, to some extent, with ebooks, many of which are priced at less than a pound.

Production costs

Unless money is no real concern, keep your production costs as low as possible. With digital printing-on-demand they could be almost zero if you have expertise in book production and design or can get people to help you for free. But if you do need to pay people for things like editing and front cover design, the costs can soon mount up. With print on demand the costs of printing are included in the price of each book sold. Your share will be whatever is left over from the sale price once those costs are covered. Other retailers, online and offline, will have different models for pricing and payment. For offline sales you will probably need to pay to have stock printed, and it is very unlikely that retailers will pay for anything unless they are likely to sell it.

HOW MUCH MONEY YOU HOPE TO MAKE

If you are planning to self-publish a printed book to make money... good luck! The competition across the publishing industry is intense and it's very hard to break even, let alone to make money. Unless you have a proven track record, it's probably best to exercise caution at the start rather than investing large amounts of money up front. Spend what it is required to produce the book you want, and then proceed cautiously. Print on demand means you don't need to spend a lot, you can test the market and can respond as your sales increase. Don't be tempted to push the price of your book up in the hope that it won't affect sales – it will. Unless you have a special selling point, you are unlikely to sell many copies above the market rate.

Start small

It's difficult to make money self-publishing because the market is so competitive. Be ambitious, but start small and avoid risking money you can't afford to lose.

HOW MANY COPIES YOU WISH TO SELL

For some authors it is more important to reach a wide audience than to make money. If this is true for you, then you should consider producing an ebook as well as (or instead of) a printed book, as electronic publishing offers lower prices and far easier national and international distribution. Maximizing sales will depend significantly on your marketing, the quality of your book and keeping the price down. A low price on its own will not be sufficient. There is no shortage of very cheap books and free ebooks, so very few people will be tempted by price alone.

Distribution and retail

Before the widespread use of the Internet and print on demand, distribution was one of the biggest challenges for self-publishers. If you take an independent route and work by yourself with a printer, you will still need to overcome this. Where will you keep your stock? How will you deal with enquiries? How will you process payments? How will you distribute books? It's not impossible, but it's not straightforward, either.

Online self-publishing companies can manage most of this for you. With print on demand there is no need to keep surplus stock and all sales can be processed by the retailer. There are different models of distribution, so check what the different self-publishing companies offer.

Bookshops, though far less important than they used to be, can still play a part in selling your book. Local stores, in particular, can be receptive to special events and book signings. However, shelf space in the big retailers is extremely hard to obtain unless you have a proven track record and a very strong proposition.

Revisions

With print on demand it is normally quite easy to revise your manuscript after publication. Your book might become unavailable for sale while the new version is uploaded, but that should be the only disruption. If the changes are significant, it is normal practice to number the book as a new edition.

Self-publishing companies

Services offered by self-publishing companies have been mentioned throughout this chapter. It is still possible to do everything independently, working with freelance specialists such as editors and designers as required and then finding a printer to produce the books. However, it is far from straightforward and, unless you have a particular desire to learn about and manage the entire process, you are probably better off working through a self-publishing company.

A quick Internet search will show you just how many companies there are, from big multinationals to small local companies.

Some companies focus on selling a package of self-publishing services for a fee up front. This might suit you and, once you have established the company's credibility and, ideally, heard from authors who have used them, you might be happy to pay it. However, be very clear about, what they are offering before you commit to them and be wary of additional services that make publishing more expensive than it needs to be.

Some of the best-known international self-publishing companies such as Lulu and CreateSpace don't require up-front payments. They do offer a range of editorial, design and marketing services that you can buy, but it is not required. They make their money from a proportion of the sales price of each print-on-demand copy that is sold. Lulu offers sales through Amazon, which is by far the most significant book retailer in the UK and internationally. CreateSpace is owned by Amazon, so offers the best integration with Amazon sales. Both CreateSpace and Lulu also make it easy to monitor your sales and earnings.

Services and requirements for all self-publishing companies differ, so take the time to do research and find out which one is best for you.

Tax

You are liable for tax on any profits you make selling books and ebooks. All earnings must be declared as part of your tax return. Because some of the biggest self-publishing companies (notably Lulu and CreateSpace) are based in the United States, royalties on their sales might attract an automatic tax from the American Inland Revenue Service (currently 30 per cent). However, this is not always the case and, if you complete a W-8BEN form, which is available on self-publishing companies' websites, UK self-publishers (and those from many other countries) will be exempt from this tax on all sales apart from those that take place via American-based websites or retailers.

If you have queries about the tax treatment of your royalties, consult a tax expert, or the help section of the relevant self-publishing service.

Know what you're getting

If you spend money up front, make sure you know what you are getting in return. Take time to do research into the various different companies. Read articles online and try to make contact online with authors who have self-published with different companies so that you can learn from their experience. Bear in mind that services change and develop, so a comment or complaint made by someone a year or two ago might not still be relevant.

 # Focus points

- Unless you are confident of sales exceeding 500 copies, then print on demand will be the best option.
- Print on demand companies will usually also process sales and manage distribution.
- Preparing and formatting your manuscript correctly are key.
- Take time to learn about formatting and cover design, even if you then decide to pay someone to do this for you.
- Be realistic with your business plan, and don't spend more than you can afford on production in the hope that your sales will be high.

Where to next?

In Chapter 6 we explore what is today the usual option for those self-publishing – the ebook.

6

Self-publishing ebooks

Tom Green

The market for ebooks has grown hugely in recent years and the ease of publication, combined with the low cost of production and distribution, means that ebooks are now the most common self-publishing option to take.

Ebooks can come in many formats, for many different kinds of devices and readers, but they are all delivered electronically rather than being printed on paper.

Why self-publish an ebook?

It has been possible for years to self-publish documents, for example in Word or as pdf files, which can be sold via email and websites, but the reading experience has been poor. Conventional computer screens, because of the technology used, are not comfortable to read for long periods, so few people chose them for book-length work, even where it was available.

The big change came with the development of e-readers designed to create a comfortable reading experience and to enable anyone to download books easily without having to worry about the technology behind them. Books were now available in formats that looked similar to the printed version, and the devices were able to store and index them effectively.

Buy an e-reader

If you haven't got some kind of e-reader yourself, buy one! It's a necessary investment to find out what the market is like, and to test the publication of your own book. If you're strapped for cash, you could buy one second-hand or, if you really can't afford it, borrow one from a friend or colleague.

The companies behind these e-readers, like Amazon, also put a huge amount of effort and money into marketing them and ensuring that popular books in all genres are available.

Thus, while some people still prefer a conventional printed book, there is no longer any stigma attached to publishing ebooks, and many people prefer to read them.

A growing market

Ebooks are the simplest and most convenient way to self-publish and the market is growing for all types of content.

Once the ebook has been created it can be distributed more or less without any cost. Although you might have to pay the distributor in certain ways – for example, Amazon takes a share of each sale – there are no printing or postage costs, so publishing for ebooks is much cheaper than for conventional books.

Another advantage is that you can update a text and republish it. This can cause complications and confusion if you do it too frequently, but if new information comes to light it is relatively easy to publish an updated edition, whereas in conventional publishing (although not print on demand) you would have to wait until the first print run has been used up.

Perhaps most importantly for the self-publishing author, especially those without a track record, ebooks are the most dynamic sector of publishing. There are numerous Internet forums discussing the process and the works themselves, and the market, while extremely competitive, is also more accessible than for print books. You might choose to set your price very low or even at zero to start with, but you should be able to find people willing to sample your work and say what they think about it.

There are still traditionalists among readers, authors and publishers who think that a book is only a real book if it is made from ink and paper. But for everyone else, even if you also choose to publish a hard copy, the ebook offers an exciting and accessible way to bring your work to the widest possible audience.

What are the main formats for ebooks?

AMAZON KINDLE

Although ebooks look quite similar on different readers, they use a variety of formats. Requirements for different readers change as new products develop, so you will need to check the relevant websites before uploading.

The most popular ebook reader is the Amazon Kindle. You can now publish to Kindle, using Kindle Direct Publishing from Microsoft Word (doc or docx), HTML, Mobipocket (MOBI), ePub, Plain Text, Rich Text Format and Adobe pdf.

However, for best results they recommend that you upload from HTML. You should be able to convert most documents from Word (or a similar word-processing program) into HTML quite easily, but to ensure best results follow the detailed instructions outlined at a specialist website (for example http://kindleformatting.com). This will help strip out some of the excess code included in Word files that might otherwise spoil the layout when you publish to Kindle.

If your HTML content contains images or other files, they need to be saved separately in a single .zip file with no sub-folders.

You should follow the detailed instructions for this on the Kindle website.

If you are familiar with HTML, you will be able to add certain HTML tags. Amazon recommends that you use only the supported tags rather than stylesheets and other formatting that the Kindle reader might not support.

If you have problems converting to HTML, it's probably easiest to upload direct from Microsoft Word or, if you don't have Word, the simplest option is to save it as a text file.

Always check the formatting of the new file before you upload it. For example, saving a Word document as a text file will remove much of the formatting, so you might need to add it to the document.

There is a maximum size for a file you can upload (currently 50MB). A text file is unlikely to exceed this amount, but if you have a number of images you might need to reduce their size or compress them to make the files smaller.

KINDLE FIRE

In 2011 Amazon launched Kindle Fire, a colour version of the ebook reader with a multi-touch screen and Android operating system that makes it, in some respects, a competitor of the iPad. Kindle Fire uses a publishing system called Kindle Format 8 that allows for a far greater flexibility in formatting and layout.

To publish for Kindle Format 8, it is recommended that you start with a Word file, follow the detailed formatting instructions and then convert the file to HTML or HTM. For more information, search online for 'Kindle Format 8' or download the free ebook 'Building Your Book for Kindle' available from Amazon.

The sales process for Kindle Fire is the same as for the conventional Kindle.

KOBO

The Kobo reader was introduced after the Kindle, but has significant support from certain publishers and retailers. Their publishing system is called Kobo Writing Life and it supports uploads in Microsoft Word (doc or docx), OPF, HTML, Mobipocket (MOBI), ePub, Plain Text, Rich Text Format and Adobe PDF.

Whichever format you upload in will be converted to ePUB. Therefore, Kobo recommends that, if possible, you upload an ePub file or an OPF file because this will result in the cleanest and most accurate conversion to the Kobo reader. If you use Apple's Pages software, you should be able to save a file directly to ePub format. However, it's not straightforward if you are using Microsoft Word (although you can download converter programs).

If you aren't able to convert your Word document to OPF or ePub format before uploading, follow the tips to formatting Word documents in the 'Uploading' section of the Kobo user guide. This will help ensure that the finished ePub file looks as close as possible to how you would like it. This includes guidance on how to format images that appear alongside the text.

A video about uploading to Kobo along with frequently asked questions and the Kobo user guide are available for free at https://writinglife.kobobooks.com/learningCentre.

Research your target audience

Contact at least ten people who might be a target audience for your book (by email, on Twitter or Facebook), to ask which e-readers they have and what were the last three ebooks they downloaded. Ask them roughly what they would expect to pay for a book of the type you are publishing. Although it's a small sample size, this research is still worth doing – the more you can talk to your potential audience the better.

APPLE IBOOKS

You can self-publish ebooks for Apple devices, including iPad, through Apple's iBookstore. Before you start you will need to create either a Paid Books Account, which allows you to sell books and offer them for free (and for which you will need to provide banking and tax information), or a Free Books Account, if you are only going to give books away. A Free Books Account cannot be converted into a Paid Books Account later on.

In order to create a Paid Books Account you need a US tax ID so that you can process sales taxes – you should be able to obtain this from www.irs.gov.

Uploads for iBooks can only be done as ePub files – as mentioned above, these are relatively easy to create from Apple word-processing software but you will need to search for a convertor to download if you are using other software.

Apple also offers special self-publishing software called iBooks Author, which creates books in what it calls Multi-Touch format. This has a particular focus on creating text books but can be used for any book, offering templates and tools to create extra functionality within the book that can help make the most of the interactivity available to iPad users. However, if you publish from iBooks Author you can only distribute the book (in any form) through Apple devices.

The iBookstore works through Apple's iTunes system, so if you do not already use this, or have an Apple ID from elsewhere, you will need to download iTunes to get an ID. You can do this for free. For more information, see: www.apple.com/itunes/content-providers/book-faq.html

NOOK

The NOOK e-reader, distributed by the American bookseller Barnes & Noble, was first sold in the UK in 2012. Its market share in this country is still small, but it has had considerable success and backing from major publishers in the US.

The publishing system for NOOK is called NOOK Press (replacing their previous system, PubIT!). Uploads can be in ePub, Microsoft Word, HTML or text. For more information and updates about using the system in the UK, visit www.nookpress.com.

GOOGLE PLAY AND GOOGLE BOOKSTORE

Most devices running the Android operating system can download the Google Play Book Application, which will give them access to the Google Bookstore (also accessible through a web browser on any device) containing a huge range of out-of-copyright books that Google has scanned, digitized and made available online. Content can also be transferred to many other devices, including the NOOK and Sony Reader. Current books are also available for sale and for free and it is possible to submit your own printed work to be digitized or to publish an ebook.

Once you join the Google Books Partner Program – there is no fee but you must agree to the terms – you can send either hard copy or digital content of published books to be displayed in-part online with a link to other retail sites. You can also sign up for a share of the Google Ads revenue generated by pages featuring your work.

You can also upload ebooks for sale via the Google Bookstore. Again, you must join the Google Books Partner Program and the section specific to ebooks. You will then be able to upload your work in either pdf or ePub format. The formatting for the reader is likely to be much better if you use ePub.

OTHER DEVICES

You can publish an ebook in some format to almost any kind of electronic device, even if it is just as a pdf. They key thing, as with the systems outlined above, is to check the format requirements and seek support if you get stuck. There are also a number of services, often called aggregators, which manage the publishing process for you. Some devices, such as the Sony Reader, require you to publish through an aggregator.

Use the right formatting

You must format your work correctly before uploading. Take time to read the detailed user guide and preview your work before publishing it. Even though you can make corrections later on, it creates a bad impression if you have errors at the start. If you find formatting difficult, keep it as simple as possible in your original text.

How I do publish through an aggregator?

Aggregators are online services that help you publish and distribute your ebook. Some of the main ones are:

- Smashwords
- BookBaby
- Lulu.

These sites have a similar uploading process to those outlined above, and then export your work into a format that will work on various devices. For example, Smashwords supports distribution to Apple iBookstore (in some countries), Barnes & Noble, Sony, Kobo, Baker & Taylor, Diesel and Page Foundry.

Some, like Smashwords, take no fees up front, but take a royalty on sales; a royalty is also taken by the online retailer. You will need to work out whether this represents good value for your ebook. Others, like BookBaby, take a fee up front to help you self-publish but do not take royalties.

How are ebooks sold?

Unlike conventional books that can be bought and read by anyone, ebooks are often dependent on specific devices. This is partly for technical reasons as different devices use different formats and it's not possible to move content from one to another. It is also because the manufacturers of the devices tend to want to keep sales of ebooks created on their publishing platform within their own systems so that they can take a share of any sales.

It's a similar concept to print-on-demand books – you tend not to pay anything up front, but give a share of any sales to the vendor. This works differently for the different devices, and you will need to decide which gives you the best deal.

In general, there is nothing to stop you publishing the same content on different ebook platforms for different devices. It's just a case of you taking the time to format and upload them, and then managing your various accounts.

Another possibility is to publish for one of the major platforms and then also create a pdf file that people without that device can buy from you directly – perhaps from your website using an online payment system such as PayPal. You are unlikely to generate many sales, because buying pdf files has not tended to be popular with readers, but it would allow anyone with a strong desire to buy the book, but without a device to read it in the format you have chosen, to buy a copy.

Perhaps the most important decision you will make is how much to charge for your ebook, although the different platforms might impose their own restrictions. You are usually able to change the price after publishing whenever you wish.

Research your competitors

Visit the Kindle bestsellers list in the category of ebooks you are working on. Ignoring those by famous authors, what stands out about the successful books? Do certain themes predominate? What about cover designs? You don't have to follow what other people do but it's helpful to know what can succeed.

AMAZON KINDLE

The greatest benefit of publishing for Kindle is the easy access to a listing on the Amazon website, the largest ebook retailer in the world. It has an excellent search function and allows considerable user interaction.

Their standard royalty payment in the UK is 70 per cent of the cover price (they keep the other 30 per cent), but to qualify for this the list price must be at least 20 per cent below the lowest price for the printed book (if there is one). Amazon sets a minimum and maximum price, and there is also a 35 per cent royalty option for certain circumstances – for example, if you are publishing a book already in the public domain or if you want to set a very low sale price.

After a process of review by Amazon your book will then be made available in the Amazon store and will be available to purchase. Royalty payments will be made to your account.

The only way that you can set a price of zero, which some ebook authors do for a period of intense marketing to generate reviews and interest, is by joining the Kindle Direct Publishing Select scheme. Joining will enable you to enroll in the Kindle Owners' Lending Library – and receive royalties for loans taken out – and take part in free promotions. There is no cost, but you must commit to publishing a given ebook only through Kindle Direct Publishing and not on another platform.

KOBO

Kobo ebooks are sold through its own website bookstore and, perhaps more significantly, through a series of retail partners. The most important of these in the UK is WHSmith, although the scale of stock and sales is far smaller than for Amazon Kindle ebooks.

Pricing and royalty payments for Kobo are along very similar lines to the Kindle. There are minimum and maximum prices and a main royalty rate of 70 per cent. As with Kindle, payments are made directly into your account and VAT payments are processed for you.

APPLE IBOOKS

iBooks are sold through Apple's iTunes – an application with a national and global reach comparable to Amazon, although not yet as well established for books and ebooks. Ebooks bought in the iBookstore can be downloaded and read on any Apple device belonging to the purchaser.

Remember that before you can sell books through iBookstore, you need to get a US tax ID from www.irs.gov. You can go through one of the aggregator services, which should take care of this for you.

Pricing and royalty payments and arrangements through iBookstore are normally in line with those for Kindle and Kobo.

NOOK

Royalty payments for NOOK sales are generally 65 per cent of the sale price, or 40 per cent for books sold at low prices. Books are sold mainly through the Barnes & Noble website which is well known in the US but doesn't have the same profile in the UK.

GOOGLE PLAY

If you sell ebooks through Google Play, you will, under normal circumstances, receive a royalty payment of 52 per cent of the cover price. This is considerably lower than other major online retailers and, if it does not change, you might want to consider whether it is worth while for you. Google Play does have a huge potential market, however.

SONY READER AND AGGREGATORS

The Sony Reader has an online Reader Store for sales of eBooks, but the publishing process is required to take place through aggregators such as Smashwords and Author Solutions. Most aggregators pay higher royalties than standard on sales from their own sites and slightly lower on sales through other sites. Their services, terms and conditions vary so you will need to check the details carefully. In August 2014 Sony announced that it would not be bringing out a new e-reader.

How do you decide which format and platform is right for you?

The choice of which platform and device to choose for your ebook will probably depend on which one you think will lead to most sales. For standard ebooks Amazon Kindle has by far the greatest market share and the Amazon website is a dominant force in ebooks retail. They offer good support and there is the large and vibrant online community discussing and promoting their ebooks. The widely used Kindle App also makes your work available on a wide range of devices, not just the Kindle.

The biggest danger is probably that of being lost amid the sheer number of titles, but unless you have a built-in preference for a niche product you would need a good reason to choose another device for your ebook.

The role of WHSmith in selling Kobo devices and titles might influence you. If you think your ebook will appeal to the Smith's audience – and, therefore, the retailer might even choose to promote the title – then they would be worth considering.

Google Bookstore will certainly be hard to ignore, simply because of Google's huge reach across the UK and the world. But the uploading process is a little more difficult to follow than with the other major sites and, most importantly, the royalty payment is considerably lower.

Take your pick...

If you want 'rich content' with lots of images and interactive content, you should publish for devices like the iPad and Kindle Fire. If it's just text, then simpler devices like the Kindle and NOOK are probably best.

The Apple iBookstore is likely to be tricky for those who are not already familiar with Apple products and services. If you are, then the big appeal of publishing an iBook is likely to be its reach across the iTunes store – and the reach to that market – and the ability for your ebook to be downloaded to a variety of Apple devices. If you want to add richer content to your ebook such as graphics, animations, high-quality images, and so on, then the iBook is probably the best option, especially given that you can download and use iBooks Author for free.

Another option for richer content and greater functionality is to upload for the Kindle Fire. There is no iBooks Author equivalent but the publishing system it uses works with Word documents if you follow the formatting instructions. Kindle Fire sales are a small fraction of those enjoyed by the iPad, but it is growing in popularity and would be worth investigating if your book requires richer content than just text.

Using aggregators is probably best if you find the process of self-publishing an ebook complicated or time-consuming and prefer the idea of someone doing it for you in return for either an up-front fee or a share of your royalties. They should also ensure that you get your ebook across a number of formats and devices.

If you do favour Amazon Kindle, then the big question you will face is whether to sign up to their Kindle Direct Publisher Select scheme – to do so brings advantages in terms of flexibility of pricing but means that you must agree not to publish the work on any other platform.

Every e-reader is different

Each e-reader has slightly different requirements in terms of format and terms and conditions. Do your research before deciding which to upload to and ask other people on social media sites and discussion boards about their experiences.

How much technical knowledge do you need?

It's impossible to explain the ebook publishing process without using some technical language. As mentioned above, if you find that off-putting then you can opt to pay (via an up-front fee or a share of royalties) to get parts or all of the process done for you.

However, if you can get past any unfamiliar language, the various processes should be relatively easy to understand. The main technical requirement is the formatting. It's worth spending some time trying to get your file in the format the publisher prefers – if you get stuck, seek help from one of the many self-publishing online communities. Even though most devices support a variety of formats for uploads, the danger is that there will be formatting errors.

These can also be avoided simply by following the instructions in the relevant user guide. Both Kindle and Kobo have particularly clear instructions about formatting that do not require any real technical understanding except when it comes to HTML. Indeed, working with HTML is probably the one area that does require some specialist knowledge and you should consider doing some background work or seeking specialist help if your ebook has layouts or functionality that require accurate HTML.

What help is available – free and paid for

The best sources of help are the sites where you are uploading your ebook, but the processes change and the sites can be a little complex so take your time to navigate the relevant sections of the site and to read the user guide.

You will also find numerous articles online and videos on YouTube explaining each step of the process.

Weigh things up carefully

As well as choosing the device that best suits your work, you should choose the one with the most appropriate market. Amazon's Kindle is the dominant e-reader, but the iPad and Kindle Fire are gaining popularity and other devices also have factors in their favour. You can publish for more than one device unless you sign an exclusivity agreement.

Social media and discussion forums can also be a huge help – just make sure before posting a question in a forum that you have searched that forum to see if the question has already been answered.

If you are prepared to pay for help, then you will find a range of companies and freelancers advertising online to help with each part of the process. Before paying someone, try to understand as much as possible about what you want them to do, what the desired outcome is and what you will pay them. Get references if possible and perhaps discuss what you are planning for in a discussion forum to see what other more experienced self-publishers think.

Many of the e-reader self-publishing websites list companies that can help you through the process, and they might even offer their own service.

Uploading isn't as hard as it seems

Don't pay a freelancer or company to upload your text until you have tried yourself. The instructions can seem daunting and complicated but online self-publishing systems have been designed for users without technical experience. If you follow the instructions carefully, you should be fine.

How do you design and lay out an ebook?

The basic layout for an ebook does not vary much. The key thing is to get the formatting correct before you upload so that you do not get errors. However, for more sophisticated multimedia devices like the iPad and Kindle Fire, you can use a variety of templates to vary the design.

AMAZON KINDLE, KOBO AND OTHER TEXT E-READERS (INCLUDING FOR GOOGLE BOOKSTORE)

If you are able to upload and tag html files, then you will be able to select some simple styles covering elements such as fonts, heading styles and page breaks.

If you are uploading from Word or ePub, most simple formatting should be retained, especially if you follow the detailed instructions on the relevant device website. Most e-readers will support a range of fonts and you should be able to use different styles of headings.

Pdfs might give problems, depending on how well the site is able to convert them. Sometimes, for example, the text uploaded from a pdf will not 'flow' in the e-reader, but remain as fixed pages.

For your first ebook, however, it is probably best to keep the formatting as simple as possible or else to seek specialist help. Otherwise, be prepared to spend plenty of time researching online as you encounter a variety of formatting problems once your text is converted.

Bear in mind that there are now many different versions of each of these devices, with more new ones in the pipeline, and the functionality for each will vary. While you can use a preview tool before you publish, it probably also makes sense to try something relatively simple first of all so that you can see it published on different versions of the chosen device.

Although some e-readers automatically skip past the front cover, it is still an important part of the design of your ebook. It is what readers are likely to see in publicity and listings, and it therefore needs to give them a clear idea of what your book is about.

The user guides for different devices explain very clearly how to upload your front cover artwork, and the restrictions in terms of size and colour.

Most of the self-publishing systems make it relatively easy to change the cover at any point. You can also change the text and some – for example, Amazon – offer to email everyone who has bought the book with any significant updates.

iPAD AND KINDLE FIRE

Layout and design for devices with more interactivity, such as the iPad and Kindle Fire, can also be kept simple if your ebook is primarily text. If you want to make more of the functionality they offer, then the process is more complicated. Both of these devices offer systems to make it easier for non-HTML specialists (iAuthor for iPad, Word documents with KindleGen for Kindle Fire), but you will still need to develop some knowledge of design and layout if you are to make the most of what's on offer.

Again, it probably makes sense to start with something relatively simple and then gradually build and develop your expertise.

What are the different processes for publishing an ebook?

The publishing process for most e-readers is relatively similar and quite straightforward. The user guides will take you through step by step, including with regard to the following aspects:

- **Formatting your text**   As discussed above, this really is the key step!
- **Confirming rights and suitability**   You must own the rights for whatever you publish in all the territories in which the ebook will be published. The self-publishing site from which you upload will explain which these will be. Your work will also need to conform to the terms and conditions regarding things like explicit images and libel. Again these will be set out as you go through the self-publishing process.
- **Entering title and summary**   These are required for the book listings on the relevant sales websites.
- **ISBN details (if you have them)**   An ISBN (International Standard Book Number) is a unique code for each book (or ebook) that booksellers or the public can use to identify it. Not all e-retailers require an ISBN: Amazon does not, for example. If you choose to get an ISBN, it must be different from that used for a print version of your book. Unfortunately, you can only buy them in blocks of ten, with the price currently at £144.

Remember...

Remember, you can get more information about ISBNs and purchase them from www.isbn.neilsenbook.co.uk.

- **Select pricing and royalty levels** – and confirming bank and tax details if your ebooks are for sale.
- **Uploading your text (and pictures)** – with the opportunity to review and make changes before it is published.
- **Publishing your ebook**   There will normally be a period of review before the work is available for sale.

Tax

You are liable for tax on any profits you make selling ebooks. All earnings must be declared as part of your tax return. Because some of the biggest self-publishing companies (notably Lulu and CreateSpace) are based in America, royalties on their sales might attract an automatic tax from the American Inland Revenue Service (currently 30 per cent). However, if you complete form W-8BEN – which is available on the self-publishing companies' websites – UK self-publishers, and those from many other countries, will be exempt from this tax on all sales apart from those that take place via American-based websites or retailers.

If you have queries about the tax treatment of your royalties, consult a tax expert or the help section of the relevant self-publishing service.

 Focus points

- Research the different e-readers available and decide which one best suits your work.
- You will not have to make payments up front unless you choose to contract a company or freelancer to publish your work for you.
- The standard royalty payment is about 70 per cent of the sale price.
- You can publish for more than one e-reader, unless you sign an exclusivity agreement, but you will need to upload your work in a variety of formats.
- Rich content with images and interactivity works well on more sophisticated devices like the iPad and Kindle Fire.

Where to next?

In Chapter 7 Kevin will look at some of the finer points of publication.

7

Publication

Kevin McCann

Up to this point you've researched, written (or vice versa), redrafted, proofed, redrafted again and maybe even made a decision regarding your preferred publishing package. Now it's at this point that mistakes most often get made. After all, you're almost finished, aren't you? There's the cover, title, blurb and author biography left to do, but you can rattle through those in a couple of hours. In a day at the most!

Well, no, actually – now read on.

Before you take the final step and publish your book, you'll need to ask yourself some crucial questions:

- Am I satisfied that this book is the best it can be in terms of content?
- Has it been carefully and accurately proofread to the point where there are no obvious typos, grammatical or punctuation errors?
- Do I have any nagging doubts lurking in my mind?

If the answer to all three is an honest (as opposed to a wished-for) yes, then we're ready to proceed.

Tom touched on cover design in Chapter 5 but there are also other things to consider:

- the title
- the contents page
- the blurb
- the author biography.

Title

This is often the last thing to be chosen. If you still haven't thought of a title that you like, don't worry about it. Give your book a working title, for example *My Novel*, and turn your mind to something else. Keep a notebook and pen or an iPad – whichever you prefer – with you at all times and jot down anything that comes to mind.

Never assume that you'll remember a possible title and be able to write it down when you get home. You may not. Besides which, you're a writer, *so write*.

A lot of writers use quotations from other works for titles, for example:

- *Something Wicked This Way Comes* by Ray Bradbury (*Macbeth*)
- *The Mirror Crack'd from Side to Side* by Agatha Christie ('The Lady of Shalott').

Or they'll take a well-known rhyme:

- *Tinker, Tailor, Soldier, Spy* by John Le Carré (seventeenth-century nursery rhyme)
- *All the King's Men* by Robert Penn Warren (nineteenth-century nursery rhyme).

You'll have noticed that John Le Carré has changed the quotation slightly, replacing 'Sailor' with 'Spy'. Ian Fleming did something similar when he took part of the old adage 'You only live once so make the best of it' and altered it to get *You Only Live Twice*.

Another way is to take the name of your central character and make that the title, for example:

- *David Copperfield* by Charles Dickens
- *Doctor Zhivago* by Boris Pasternak.

Or take the central character's name and combine that with the theme of the book:

- *Alice in Wonderland* by Lewis Carroll
- *Harry Potter and the Philosopher's Stone* by J.K. Rowling.

Or zero in on the theme of the book:

- *Catch-22* by Joseph Heller
- *The Hound of the Baskervilles* by Sir Arthur Conan Doyle.

Or even its geographical location:

- *Salem's Lot* by Stephen King
- *Wuthering Heights* by Emily Brontë.

The variations are endless but in the end what you're looking for is a title that's eye-catching. You'll know it when it comes to you. Just don't settle on the first thing that does. When you think you've picked a title, check on the Internet and make sure no one else has used it recently.

Two last points on titles before we move on. In non-fiction it has become the norm to keep it simple and fairly obvious. Charlie Chaplin's autobiography was called *My Autobiography;* Stephen Hawking's history of time was called *A Brief History of Time* … and so on. But it's not legally binding.

George Orwell's report on poverty in 1930s north-west England was called *The Road to Wigan Pier;* Laurie Lee's account of his travels in Spain during the build-up to the Civil War was called *As I Walked Out One Midsummer Morning.* The title comes from the first line of an old folk song 'The Banks of Sweet Primroses'. Both are intriguing titles and, in my opinion, a lot snappier than *Poverty in 1930s Lancashire* or *My Travels in Pre-Civil War Spain.* So, if your book is non-fiction, try to sidestep the obvious.

If your book is a collection of short stories, consider taking the title of the strongest story in the collection and making that your title.

Contents

Will your book have a contents page? Does it need one?

Well, again it depends on the kind of book you've written. In non-fiction it's not only the norm, it's common sense. If you pick up a history, you'll want to know what it covers and where, in the book, it is covered. Ditto for biographies, science books, memoirs, and so on.

On the other hand, if it's a novel, unless your chapters have titles, why do you need to list them?

However, if your book is short stories, you may want to include a contents page.

Check the page numbers

If you have chosen the print-on-demand process, after you've uploaded make sure that the page numbers in your contents still match the page numbers in the book before you click Publish, especially if you have changed the page or font size.

One other thought, with regard to short stories. How have you decided on the running order? One tip I was given concerning poetry collections – and which I know from experience also applies to short stories – is to begin with a strong story and end with the best one in the collection.

Save the best until last

In a collection of short stories, never begin with your best story – the rest of your book will feel like an anti-climax.

When James Joyce put together *Dubliners*, he began it with 'The Sisters', which concerns a recent death, and ended it with 'The Dead', which also concerns a death but not so recent. It's not only a strong story, but it ends with this astounding passage:

> '...*snow was general all over Ireland. It was falling over every part of the dark central plain, on the treeless hills, falling more softly upon the Bog of Allen and, farther westward, softly falling into the dark mutinous Shannon waves. It was falling too, upon every part of the lonely churchyard on the hill where Michael Furey lay buried. It lay thickly drifted on the crooked crosses and headstones, on the spears of the little gate, on the barren thorns. His soul swooned slowly as he heard the snow falling faintly through the universe and faintly falling, like the descent of their last end, upon all the living and the dead.*'

Now that may be the best last page I've ever read. Try it for yourself. Read it out loud and you'll see what I mean.

Another approach that's sometimes possible is chronological. Put simply, if you have stories set in different time periods, begin with the one furthest back in history and work forward to the present; or begin with the present and work backwards; or group the stories thematically; or if they're a mixture of very serious, semi-serious and humorous try alternating – for example, precede a very serious story with something humorous and follow it with a semi-serious story.

Again, the variations are endless.

One other tip: if you've done all that and yet... try taking the first and last stories in the book and swapping them round. To be honest, I've no idea why this works but I know it often does.

Front cover

As Tom mentioned in Chapter 5, some publishing companies provide tools to help you design a cover and/or offer a choice of generic covers – that is, something eye-catching but not specific. So you might get a cover with two colours, the title, your name and the whole thing edged with a simple design.

Or, of course, you can pay someone to do it for you, but, again, as Tom has pointed out, you could end up with a bill that runs into thousands. Now, if you can afford to do that and want to, go ahead.

However, if you either can't afford it or simply don't want to spend more on the cover than you have on the book, then there are a number of alternatives.

You've already looked at book titles, now have a look at their covers.

- Which ones catch your eye and, more importantly, why?
- Which ones don't you like and, even more importantly, why?

You need to know not just what you like (and why) but also what you don't like (and why). You've got a critical faculty which you can apply to writing. You can also use that same faculty to think about graphic art. And let me be really clear here. Whatever image you decide on, it must be something appropriate but it must also be something you like. So you don't have to pick the kind of image everyone else is choosing.

Three quick points to note here:

1 By all means be inspired by what you see but never just take a design from somewhere else. It's an infringement of copyright.

2 Always check that an image you've found on the Internet is in the public domain. Don't just assume it is.

3 Never use clip-art: it will make your cover look cheap and therefore sends out the wrong message.

So, where does that leave you?

Well, maybe what you need is an image that is original to you and therefore not infringing anyone's copyright. One obvious solution is to do it yourself.

If you've looked at lots of different book covers, you could be forgiven for thinking that, unless the cover is artwork, it won't do. That's simply not true. Let me explain. Whether you go for print on demand and/or epublishing, the cover is the first thing your potential readers will see when they go on to your sales page. The cover consists of a design plus title and your name. We've already talked about the importance of finding a good title that catches the eye. The same applies to your cover design. And just as a book is either well written or badly written and that's all, so a design is either eye-catching or it isn't.

It doesn't matter whether it's a photograph, line drawing or painting, collage or abstract. All that matters is that it's right for your book.

So, to begin with, you need to think about your book's theme. What's it about? How would you sum it up? *The Call of the Wild* by Jack London, for example, is about the wolf that is buried inside every domesticated dog. Now, take that sentence you've just read. Does it suggest an image to you?

Workshop: Developing cover designs

Either write a brief description of a cover design for *The Call of the Wild*, or draw it or Photoshop it. It doesn't matter if you haven't read the book – although, if you haven't, I recommend that you do. What we're thinking about here is imagery. What we're looking for, specifically, is one image that suggests an entire book. Notice I said 'suggest' there and not 'summarize'. How could you summarize *Oliver Twist* in one image? You can't but you can suggest it by using an image that's now so well known, it's almost a cliché.

Let's take two more very well-known titles:

- *Dracula* by Bram Stoker: the first images that will spring to most people's minds are: old castle; man in an opera cape; male/female vampire lying in a coffin.
- *Frankenstein* by Mary Shelley: old castle/tower and lightning; mad scientist and/or monster.

Now think of two images, one for each book, that suggest the story but don't use any of the elements I've listed. Again, don't worry if you haven't actually read them. If you type 'Dracula by Bram Stoker – Wikipedia' into your search engine, you'll get a summary of the plot. The same applies to Mary Shelley's *Frankenstein.*

Try repeating this exercise using other books you're familiar with. In each case, ask yourself 'What is this book's theme?' and then take it from there.

Finally, go back to your own book and repeat the exercise as many times as you need to until you come up with an image that:

- fits in with your book's theme *and*
- you can produce using either original artwork or a photograph.

Don't just settle on the first thing unless you're absolutely head over heels in love with it. Each time you do this exercise, the image that is perfect for your book will become more and more clearly fixed in your visual imagination. The exercise is like a lens bringing a blurred picture into sharp focus.

Think photographs

Unless you have complete confidence in your own abilities as a visual artist, think photographs here. I've seen more than one self-published book cover in the last few years ruined by what was obviously amateur artwork.

And, as I keep saying, your cover and title will be the first thing your potential readers will see. If it's your first book and you're not yet a 'name', it must have something that makes it stand out from all the others in your field.

Once you know the type of image you want, go out looking for it. Get yourself a digital camera and start taking photographs. But remember, you're not just looking for a good image, you're looking for a good image that fits your book. If it doesn't, you might as well have saved yourself the bother and just used one of the generic images provided by a self-publishing company.

There's something else to consider. If your book is set on the coast, then a photograph of the sea is perfectly acceptable. If it's about a horse, then a photo of a horse will do nicely. But, again, you can sidestep the obvious and go for an image that suggests something in itself.

I've got a copy of *The Spy Who Came in from the Cold* by John Le Carré whose front cover consists of a black-and-white photograph of a man in a long coat and wearing a trilby standing on a small jetty, looking out to sea. He has a briefcase and there are seagulls flying all round him.

It's an evocative image and suggests a story in itself. In other words, it would work as an image on its own. So aim for that.

If you've decided on one image and then see something else that grabs your eye, give it serious thought, even if it's nothing like the image you originally had in mind. The best ideas frequently spring out of an intuitive leap of imagination.

Become visually literate

Familiarize yourself as much as you can with visual imagery. As well as looking through photographs, look at film posters.

Look at film posters for inspiration

Type 'twentieth-century film posters' into your search engine. You'll find a lot of examples. See where your intuition leads you. And remember, it doesn't have to be a complex image – just the right image for your front cover. You'll know it when you see it.

The blurb

This is also known as the contents description. What you're aiming for here is somewhere between 70 and 100 words that give your readers just enough information to make them want to read more. So, as well as looking at book covers and titles, you need to familiarize yourself with blurbs. From there, either go straight into writing the blurb for your own book or, just to loosen you up a bit, try writing a couple of blurbs for books that you've both read and enjoyed.

Write a blurb

Write your own blurb, but don't worry about the word count of your first draft. Once written, aim to get it down to no more than 100 words. Use complete sentences – no notes or bullet points – and when you've finished, put it aside for 24 hours, then go back and see whether you can reduce the word count even more without losing the sense. When you've got to the point where one more cut would begin to make your description incomprehensible, stop.

Author biography

Don't undersell yourself but don't exaggerate either and, like the blurb, keep the biography brief and to the point. It's also worth remembering that you don't have to include one at all. If you've set up a website, you may just want to put the link to the biography in brackets after your name.

So, can I publish now... please?

Well, the short answer is 'Yes, of course you can!'

The sensible answer, however, would be 'Not quite yet... Let your first reader(s) have a look and get their opinion.' What you want to know specifically is whether the cover is eye-catching and/or the blurb arouses their curiosity. As always, listen without interruption or prejudice. In short, listen to what they've got to say and don't get annoyed if they're not keen. Because if they're right and you can suddenly see they're right, they've done you a huge favour.

If you don't agree, again, there's no harm done. You've asked for an opinion but it's your book, so if you don't agree, you don't have to change anything.

One tip here, though. If someone were to say 'I think the cover's dull', ask them why. Ask them what they'd change. Note the points being made, even if you don't agree with any of them, and then sleep on it.

You may find that your design wasn't quite right but neither were their suggestions. You may also find that a solution, often involving only a small change, will then present itself which will improve your cover out of all recognition.

This is known as tweaking and it is just as important as every other phase of the writing process. After that, you can finally publish your book, get marketing and set up your website.

Focus points

- Don't publish until you're completely happy with the content.
- Both your title and blurb need to be eye-catching and intriguing, so give them just as much thought as every other element in your book.
- Your biography should be the unvarnished truth. Don't lie or exaggerate because, when you're found out, your credibility will be shattered.
- Ask for second (and third and fourth) opinions regarding the cover, title and blurb *and then*
- Listen and take notes!

Where to next?

In Chapter 8 we will read the experiences of three authors who have self-published.

8

Case studies

Tom Green

Many self-publishing authors are generous with their time and advice. If you are new to the process, then it makes sense to learn from their experiences. In this chapter, three authors explain why they chose to self-publish and share the lessons they have learned.

Martin Cloake

Martin Cloake has self-published two mini-books in a series called Spurs Shorts that he launched with his writing partner, Adam Powley. One is about Danny Blanchflower, the other concerns Arthur Rowe. They have also republished the first full-length book they wrote, We Are Tottenham, *as an ebook after the rights reverted back to them.*

WHY DID YOU CHOOSE TO SELF-PUBLISH?

I'm a journalist and I've worked in production for years. I'm also interested in technology and the media business, an area I covered as a journalist. So I've been interested in and involved with new publishing platforms and methods for years. Digital publishing has changed the game in so many ways, one of which is to change the view of, and the opportunities offered by, the self-publishing route. Essentially, digital makes the whole process more nimble. The idea for the shorts series came from the kind of thing the *Atlantic Review* was doing in the US, and *The Guardian* in the UK. Those publications are mining their archives to produce collated volumes on particular subjects.

Adam and I were both published authors through the traditional print route, and we are both experienced journalists. So we had already built a bit of brand awareness, if you want to call it that.

We wondered if we could monetize some of the writing we were already doing, while at the same time building on the profile we already had. We decided to produce books of about 6–8,000 words – not long enough for a conventional book but longer than a magazine article. The Spurs Shorts idea was based around profiling famous players from Tottenham Football Club's history, but adding some original angle and analysis so readers could find out about a player and get some original, considered analysis, and access that on mobile devices or their desktop for a short read. We wanted to offer quality and originality at a fairly low price, but a price we felt reflected the effort we put in.

The longer-term aim was to build up a critical mass of titles, and possibly to branch out into other areas under the Sports Shorts branding. A lot of the ideas we have wouldn't ever be ideas you could pitch for a full book, published traditionally. So this gives us the opportunity to publish some longer-form journalism, and to potentially make some money. Hopefully, as we put out more titles, the back catalogue will continue earning. One of the beauties of digital self-publishing is that once the initial work is done, that's it – there's no stock ordering or extra effort over the normal process of publicizing the books.

My Arthur Rowe book started life as an extended piece for *The Blizzard*, a quarterly football journal. I did a deal whereby the article was available exclusively in *The Blizzard* until the next issue came out, at which time I published a slightly fuller version as an ebook, running an ad for *The Blizzard* in the book. The deal with *The Blizzard* is that writers write for free, but get a platform and any money made is redistributed according the contribution authors make if there's a surplus. Writing for something like *The Blizzard* provides a good platform, and authors always have the option to use their material how they want after first publication.

Keep your rights

Publishing a short article magazine or website can be a launching pad for a longer piece to self-publish. So make sure you keep the rights for pieces you write for other people – especially if you aren't being paid.

Publishing the full-length book was a slightly different proposition. We'd originally been published through an established publishing house. They did want to digitize the books in their back catalogue, but the offer we were made just didn't stack up. So when the rights reverted to us, we decided to self-publish as an ebook. Over the years, since the print run sold out, we'd frequently been asked if there would be a reprint, so we thought the demand might be there. For a traditional publishing house it's more of a risk to take the chance that people saying they will buy something will convert into them actually doing so. For us, it was less of a risk.

We'd already written the book, we'd already published ebooks, we had established a bit of a name for ourselves. But we wanted to offer something more – to maintain brand quality. So we wrote a new foreword and reinterviewed many of the people we'd spoken to in the original book. That way we could push a quality product, and give those who'd purchased the original book something extra if they decided to repurchase.

Look after your brand

As a self-publisher you need to look after your 'brand'. Make all your books as professional as possible and try to add value when you republish, by updating content and adding extras like a new foreword.

Various options are likely to open up in the future. We want to do more short books on a greater range of subjects. Some of those, if they sell and/or attract the attention of a traditional publisher, might lead to more traditional commissions. And we've also got the option to do full-length books that are attractive to a niche market – the sort that would not stack up economically for a publisher having to commit to a print run and production costs, but which might be viable for an individual writer.

Having a production background also helped. Many writers, quite understandably, just want to write, and when the creative part is over they prefer to hand the work on to someone else. I quite like the production side too, so something that offered greater control of pretty much the whole process appealed.

HAVE YOU USED PRINT ON DEMAND OR EBOOKS?

Ebooks seemed simpler and more direct. The short-form books are also written with a view to them being quick reads on mobile devices.

HOW MUCH DID YOU RESEARCH INTO THE PROCESS?

I've been a journalist and subeditor for over 20 years, so I know a fair bit about production techniques. Constructing an ebook is more complex than you're led to believe, but it's also a case of thinking in a different way in order to work through the process. Having to construct books in a slightly different way for different platforms is also a bit of a pain. I did a lot of research on the Web, and through face-to-face chats and email conversations. The Scrivener software was really useful for organizing that research. Online communities are very useful, too.

I also did a fair amount of research on pricing, and on the tax situation with ebook royalties, which is quite complicated. Being a journalist who works in the finance field also means I'm taking in a lot of detail about all this on a daily basis, so the 'research' is actually me just being interested in and aware of what's happening in my trade.

DID YOU GET PROFESSIONAL HELP PREPARING YOUR MANUSCRIPT?

No. I didn't need to as I am a journalist and subeditor. Adam and I bounce ideas off each other, and it's great having a writing partnership where we can both be constructively blunt and honest about ideas and execution.

WHAT WERE THE MOST CHALLENGING THINGS ABOUT THE SELF-PUBLISHING PROCESS?

Adopting the different mindset required for digital as opposed to print throws up some challenges. For example, worrying about formatting concerns like widows and orphans and hanging lines is pointless when people read the pages on different-sized devices. Unless you publish in pdf format, you don't have the same degree of control over how the product is served up, because the accessibility of digital, particularly on mobile devices, is largely about the reader deciding how to read, rather than receiving what they are given. I still find it irritating that I have to compromise on some aspects of formatting, but the point is that it just doesn't matter as much.

Format your book for a mobile device

Download a free ebook to a mobile device such as a phone or tablet. Does the formatting work OK? How easy is it to read? Think about how your book formatting might need to be adapted for mobile devices, perhaps by simplifying the layout and adding more paragraph breaks.

Making sure you meet the many and complex regulations required to get an ebook published is also quite demanding, especially when many of the aggregators seem incapable of communicating in plain English.

And ensuring you don't get a double whammy on tax is also a laborious and complex process. In a nutshell, because companies such as Amazon are based in the US for the purposes of author earnings (but not, interestingly, when it comes to the company's own earnings!), earnings UK authors make through Amazon, etc., are taxed in the US, and then taxed again in the UK unless the individual applies for an opt-out. [See Chapter 6 for information on opting out.]

WHAT DID YOU LEARN?

I'm still learning. I know how to use several new bits of software, how to solve some basic problems, and most of all I'm constantly learning about good methods of marketing the content. Each book has been slightly easier than the last, as the process becomes more familiar. So I like to think I'm constantly honing my technique.

HOW DID YOU APPROACH MARKETING AND SELLING YOUR BOOKS?

I'd already done a lot of work on marketing and promoting the books I'd had published by more traditional routes. Again, my background in journalism helped, as did Adam Powley's background working for some of the big publishing houses. Many writers, quite understandably, just want to create the product and leave it to others to market. We felt we could offer a more complete package, and that's helped in our relationship with publishers. We bring a similar approach to our own books. We both use social media a lot, and the advantage of writing, as we have done, about sports and particular sports clubs means we can involve ourselves in the various online fan communities and put the word about. We also negotiate deals with various websites and magazines, providing extracts in return for a plug and link to the book.

I have a static website that I set up as a showcase that works as a kind of online CV: www.martincloake.com. I created it myself using a piece of software called Rapidweaver, which is available for about £35. I used it to find out how to put a website together. It's a time-consuming process and I wouldn't pretend to be a web designer, but I feel I know a bit more than the basics about how to put a decent site together and what works.

I blog regularly at blog.martincloake.com.

I promote all my books through the blog, and I write about sport, journalism, media and technology and occasionally a bit of music and politics. The blog started as a way of raising my profile and demonstrating what I could do when I was preparing to go freelance. There's also a line on my profile page that talks about a journalist not blogging as a bit like someone not using electricity, and I'd stick by that.

I also use Twitter a lot, again for professional purposes, but the nature of it means there's inevitably going to be some more personal stuff. Twitter is great for networking, getting information out and, if you're following the right people, for finding out about what's going on and keeping up with the latest thinking and the latest trends. I've also got a LinkedIn profile, and I knit that network of platforms together.

On Facebook I find it's harder to maintain a divide between the personal and the professional – there's a lot of 'noise' in comparison to Twitter and LinkedIn, and I don't like the way they keep changing the interface after you've set stuff up as you want it. It's also probably a product of my being from an older generation – I noticed when I was teaching how the students pretty much lived on Facebook, and use it very effectively both personally and professionally. So I'm conscious I should probably do more on Facebook, but I find it difficult to find the time or the inclination.

Give Martin a tweet!

Look at Martin Cloake's website, blog and Twitter profile. Can you see how they all connect? Is it easy to find the books he has published, their content and tone and how to buy them? Send Martin a tweet to let him know you have read this case study.

DID YOU HAVE ANY EXPECTATIONS FOR SALES, AND HAVE YOU MET THEM?

Adam and I started the ebooks strand to test the water. We knew it would be a long-term project, building up a number of titles and hopefully capitalizing as the mass created its own momentum. We deliberately didn't entertain any wild ambitions about making money; we saw it as a side project. Because we both do other work, we don't have to rely on this as an income stream. That also means we don't feel the same pressure to drop the price that someone dedicating themselves to the marketplace would. We price the books based on the effort we've put in and what we think they are worth, as well as with an eye to what the market will sustain.

ARE YOU PLANNING TO SELF-PUBLISH AGAIN?

Yes. We want to expand the range of subjects we cover. We've also thought about offering to help other writers use the same concept, but that needs a bit more careful thought. And I've been (cliché alert!) toying with some ideas for a novel for a while (I'm a big reader of crime fiction) so there's a possibility there – although fiction is a whole different, er, ball game.

WHAT ADVICE WOULD YOU GIVE TO ANYONE ELSE PLANNING TO SELF-PUBLISH?

- Believe in what you're doing.
- Be honest about what you're doing and what you can do.
- Work out what you can do well yourself – you'll be surprised at what you don't need to buy in.
- Get real experts to do the stuff you can't do, for example, cover design. Amateurism doesn't sell and it doesn't promote quality. You might be able to barter expertise, but always remember you're not the only person who needs to make money.
- Be prepared to put lots of time in.
- Network, market, publicize.

Mel Sherratt

Mel Sherratt has self-published a crime thriller, Taunting the Dead, *and three books in a series called The Estate:* Somewhere to Hide, Behind a Closed Door *and* Fighting for Survival. *She has also published two other books under a different pen name.*

WHY DID YOU CHOOSE TO SELF-PUBLISH?

I tried for 12 years to get a book deal and in the past two years had an agent trying to place my books without success. So I studied the Kindle markets for a few months, watching authors such as Kerry Wilkinson hit the top of the charts, and decided to give it a go for myself. I also knew self-published author Talli Roland who became a huge help to me. I am now mentoring two other writers in the way that she helped me.

HAVE YOU USED PRINT ON DEMAND OR EBOOKS?

Primarily I use ebooks but I did use print on demand for one of my books, *Somewhere to Hide*, because I want it to be available for people who can access a digital copy. The profit I make is minimal. The majority of my sales will always be digital, but to enable readers to purchase a print copy, which is obviously more expensive, I decided to keep my price as low as I could rather than add a couple of pounds, profit.

HOW MUCH DID YOU RESEARCH INTO THE PROCESS?

I watched the Kindle sales charts for months to see who was selling, who wasn't, what genres were selling, the prices, etc. Then I read an ebook on how to create the document and upload it on to Kindle Desktop Publishing. I worked out my own strategies and pressed upload.

Check out what's selling

Follow Mel's lead and look at the Kindle sales charts for books in your genre. Make sure you have read most of the bestsellers and have learned lessons from their content, format and design. It's also worth investigating how they have been marketed. What is it that has made them a success?

DID YOU GET PROFESSIONAL HELP PREPARING YOUR MANUSCRIPT?

I didn't pay for editing or copy-editing for *Taunting the Dead* but for all books after that I paid for copy-editing and then proofread it several times myself. Any book I bring out in the future will always have a professional copy-edit – you can't see your own mistakes.

DID YOU MANAGE THE SELF-PUBLISHING PROCESS YOURSELF?

Yes, with a little help from my mentor.

WHAT WERE THE MOST CHALLENGING THINGS ABOUT IT?

Uploading the document and getting the formatting perfect were the most difficult. Once I'd done this the first time, it became second nature, but it is fiddly to learn to get it right. Also, ensuring that the work was to a standard where a reader would take a chance on an author they had never heard of.

A mentor is invaluable

Advice from someone who has already self-published is invaluable. See if you can find someone, through personal contacts or by asking around online, who is willing to help guide you through the process.

WHAT DID YOU LEARN?

Everything! But there's a great sense of achievement to see it all done.

IS THERE ANYTHING YOU WOULD DO DIFFERENTLY?

I'd hire a copy-editor for my first novel! I also tried various sales platforms for about six months and they were far less cost effective for the time it took to create and upload the documents to specifications, and then also to get them distributed.

Match your genre to the right platform

Which retail platforms are most worthwhile? Search around online communities and ask on social media to see which genres seem to do best on the different platforms.

HOW DID YOU APPROACH MARKETING AND SELLING YOUR BOOKS?

Before I self-published, I hosted a blog called High Heels and Book Deals and for two years I absorbed myself into indirect networking. I interviewed authors and reviewed books for publicists who I met online through Twitter, and then tweeted out the posts I did to all those involved – the author, the publicist, their agent, the publisher, etc. They in turn would retweet them. In between these posts, I wrote a few about my writing journey. I then started to attend crime festivals such as Theakstons Old Peculier Crime Writing Festival in Harrogate and Crimefest in Bristol and events like Crime in the Court. This meant I started to meet the people I'd known via Twitter, plus lots more. This all took up a lot of time – I did it for at least 20 hours a week – but it was great fun. And it gave me a good network when I came to self-publish my own work.

For this reason, and because of strong word of mouth, *Taunting the Dead* went into the top 100 after five weeks.

For The Estate series I created a new website and Facebook author page and set up a newsletter. Then I added the cover to my website one month before it was due to come out, then the prologue, the blurb and the first chapter in intervals to create a buzz. All three books came out over six months. *Fighting for Survival*, the third book, was released on 21 December 2012 and by New Year's Eve it was number one in thrillers and suspense and had sold 1,000 copies.

I have a website (www.melsherratt.co.uk) that I created myself, and I also write guest blog posts or complete Q&As most weeks. I've recently started High Heels and Book Deals up again, with different topics to cover this time.

I only use social media to interact with people and readers. I tweet out my blog posts occasionally and I have a Facebook author page to chat to my readers. I think social media is useful for helping the book to get seen but not necessarily for sales. I think word of mouth is always the best thing for that.

Give Mel a tweet!

Visit Mel's website, Twitter profile and Facebook page. Are they well connected? Do they give a clear idea of the books she publishes and how to buy them? Send her a tweet or a Facebook comment to let her know you have read this case study.

DID YOU HAVE ANY EXPECTATIONS FOR SALES, AND HAVE YOU MET THEM?

Obviously I wanted to do well, but I had no idea how quickly it would take off. *Taunting the Dead* took five weeks to get into the top 100 Kindle bestsellers. It went to number one in police procedurals, number one in thrillers and number one in mysteries. It stayed in the top 10 for four weeks, hitting its highest point at number three and stayed in the top 100 for three months. It also became one of the top ten best-selling Amazon.co.uk KDP books of 2012. I never would have anticipated that!

I've recently signed a two-book deal for world English rights with Thomas & Mercer, Amazon Publishing's mystery, thrillers and suspense imprint. The two books in the deal are *Taunting the Dead*, which will be repackaged for the US market and my new novel, *Watching over You*. Self-publishing has got me this far but it's great now to have this support. Finally, I can say those magic words: I have a book deal!

WHAT ADVICE WOULD YOU GIVE TO ANYONE ELSE PLANNING TO SELF-PUBLISH?

- Make sure the decision is the right choice for you.
- Make sure the product, because it is a product, is the best you can make it – an eye-catching cover, an intriguing blurb and ensure that the copy inside is perfect.
- Don't oversell on social media – it doesn't sell books; it only makes readers aware of them.

Olivier Nilsson-Julien

Olivier Nilsson-Julien has self-published The Ice Cage, *a Scandinavian thriller, as an ebook through Kindle Direct Publishing (KDP) and* Significant Others and Possible Selves, *an academic book on French-Canadian cinema, using print on demand through Lulu.*

WHY DID YOU CHOOSE TO SELF-PUBLISH?

In the case of the academic book, a top German academic publisher wanted my book in a series including world-leading scholars in the field of film and media, but they asked me to pay for a print run, which I wasn't prepared to do. And, as a freelancer, I didn't have an institution to pay for the publishing. There was also the fact that an academic career wasn't my priority. I was teaching screenwriting, creative writing and doing lots of translations. So when the publisher question dragged on too long I simply put it on Lulu. Done.

HOW MUCH DID YOU RESEARCH INTO THE PROCESS?

With the academic book I kept asking the publisher offering me the deal why they couldn't do print on demand. When they said they couldn't, I did some limited research online, but really I just wanted to make the book available. I had no expectations whatsoever in terms of profit – it's a very niche book. I just wanted to get it out and move on.

The thriller was a different prospect. It had been picked up by a big literary agency and I'd worked on it for considerable time, on my own and later with the advice of the agent. In spite of the agent's encouragement and ultra-positive outlook no publisher took the book. A few really liked it but passed in the end. At this stage the agent offered to publish it under her imprint. The agent had already done that with some back catalogues. I was flattered, but when I looked closer at the imprint it didn't even have a website and the covers weren't impressive. I also checked the ranking and exposure of their most successful author.

After a few weeks of reading and research I concluded that I could do just as well, while also maintaining the rights to the book, because I'd been offered a deal whereby I would sign off my rights for 15–20 years for free, with no real opportunity to break the contract in case of bad sales. I did try to negotiate, as I wanted there to be some incentive for the publisher to sell my book, but the agent insisted on getting the rights for nothing.

I felt I needed to go at it on my own, but still wasn't sure if I'd missed anything, so I did a weekend self-publishing workshop with *The Guardian*. It was brilliant and very inspiring, covering development, pitching, market positioning and practical ebook publishing.

Coming out of the workshop I felt I could do it, and it also totally freed me from the misplaced stigma of self-publishing as a form of vanity publishing. As it turns out, self-published authors often earn more than their traditionally published counterparts, especially if we're talking books of comparable quality and genre. After the workshop I also read a few books on epublishing and marketing on Amazon. I chose to publish the thriller as an ebook because one platform was said to be more efficient in terms of rankings. I would like to offer the book as print on demand as well but haven't got round to it. I've been too busy with the sequel and other projects.

DID YOU GET PROFESSIONAL HELP PREPARING YOUR MANUSCRIPT?

I had help with the editing, but mainly from friends and my agent. Also, my wife is a writer and we always give each other feedback. As for proofreading, this is something I would recommend. I didn't use a proofreader. Several people read the manuscript to help me pick up typos but there are still a few left.

Employ a proofreader

Proofreading is harder than it sounds! If at all possible, get someone with some professional experience to proofread your work before you publish.

WHAT WERE THE MOST CHALLENGING THINGS ABOUT THE SELF-PUBLISHING PROCESS?

I should have been much more active on blogs, Facebook and Twitter but I only did the basics. I started tweeting after the *Guardian* workshop, but I'm not sure to what extent it has had an impact on book sales. Whenever there's a sudden surge of sales I try to see if it's anything to do with a tweet pattern, but I can't say I've discovered a magic solution.

The most challenging part will always be the writing. If you write a good book, the readers will come.

 Attend a course

If you are serious about self-publishing, it might be worth attending a short course or workshop. Find out as much about the people running it as possible first, and try to get independent recommendations. Speaking to experts face to face can be a great help, whether you have some publishing experience already or are a newcomer.

WHAT DID YOU LEARN FROM SELF-PUBLISHING?

That you can do it yourself, be just as successful and earn more in the process without all the hassle of negotiating and being rejected.

Without self-publishing my book would still have been in the drawer. Now it has earned me £10,000 in nine months and given me a sense of empowerment. More than 22,000 people have downloaded the book. So it has done better than most traditionally published books.

IS THERE ANYTHING YOU WOULD DO DIFFERENTLY NEXT TIME?

I'd take a bit more time before publishing, but at that point I just wanted to get it out, so hindsight doesn't really mean much. It was the right thing at the time. Maybe I would work on hard copies and do some book signings in bookshops. Not that it would necessarily boost sales but I think it's nice to have a real-life anchoring. But if I do hard copies I want them to offer something extra, a tactile and visual dimension a Kindle book can't offer.

HOW DID YOU APPROACH MARKETING AND SELLING YOUR BOOKS?

I used KDP Select, mailings to friends and contacts. I was also fortunate that my book tapped into an established genre – the Scandinavian thriller.

DO YOU HAVE A WEBSITE?

Yes, but I took most of the pages down when I self-published, as they were CV-like and focused on selling myself as a screenwriting/writing tutor. Instead, I just pasted some reviews and added a contact page, which has meant that I've received a lot of comments from people who liked the book.

Invite comments

Make sure you invite people who visit your website to comment on your book. Make it easy for them and reply to them when they do.

DO YOU USE SOCIAL MEDIA?

Twitter has sucked up a lot of my time, but it also allows direct feedback. Not sure if Amazon reviews count as social media but the immediate feedback there and through email (via my website) and Twitter has been great. Of course, you get a lot of bad reviews but the good ones make up for it. It has also taught me a lot about pitching, price, etc. Readers react to price (too cheap, too expensive, impossible to get it right), references (if you compare your book to a hit book they'll tell you it isn't the same). These are all aspects I'm taking into account when writing my second book. The reviews have definitely influenced the way I approach the second book.

Give Oliver a tweet!

Find Olivier's book *The Ice Cage* on Amazon and look at the comments to see what he might have learned from them. If the book appeals to you, buy it and leave your own comment behind. You might also like to tweet him @icecageolivier.

DID YOU HAVE ANY EXPECTATIONS FOR SALES, AND HAVE YOU MET THEM?

I didn't really have any expectations. I thought maybe a couple of thousand in the first year. That turned out to be very pessimistic, as when I put *The Ice Cage* on free for a weekend in September 2012 it reached number one in free Kindle books, which set it on a roll. After that the initial target was met within the next couple of weeks.

ARE YOU PLANNING TO SELF-PUBLISH AGAIN?

I'd love to work with an editor or publisher as teamwork is always going to benefit the book, but it would have to be a good offer, because as things stand a traditional publisher would have to offer double my current sales figures to match the income of self-publishing. It might be a better idea for me to develop as a publisher – but the problem is that when you're doing everything it leaves less time to write.

WHAT ADVICE WOULD YOU GIVE TO ANYONE ELSE PLANNING TO SELF-PUBLISH?

It's much more positive and empowering than anything you will encounter in the traditional publishing industry. Maybe it will change but there's a real pioneer spirit if you attend events organized by Byte the Book at The Ivy, or just follow self-publishing discussion online.

However, beware of self-publishing companies grabbing half of your revenues to make a cover. Fill in some metatags and upload your ebook on Amazon. Formatting is much easier than people think.

What's also clear is that even authors published by traditional publishers are required to do the same social media marketing work as self-publishers. Before going with a publisher, I recommend having a good look at what they do to give their authors and titles exposure. It doesn't take long and certainly reinforced my decision to self-publish. How many hours a day is a publisher going to spend on your book? How much will you pay the publisher (percentage of royalties)? Publishing is changing and maybe it's already becoming a sustainable model, but from what I've seen in the last year there's no way a publisher can give a small writer what self-publishing can give when it comes to value for money. And empowerment – positive as opposed to negative energy.

Self-publishing is about the book; publishing is about maintaining an industry. I'm just trying to make a living as a writer, so I know where I stand. Of course, this is a generalization and hopefully there will be more flexible publishers realizing that we need to put the story and the writer first, not the industry. Writers produce US TV series; maybe a similar model needs to be applied to publishing. Fundamentally, it's about people sharing stories and that's what we should be focusing on – nothing else. But of course I'll always be open to offers I can't refuse.

Where to next?

In Chapter 9 Tom looks at how you can market your book effectively.

9

Marketing your book

Tom Green

For many writers the business of marketing their book is the hardest part of self-publishing. However painful it has been researching and writing the text, however much they have had to learn about editing and proofreading and formatting a manuscript, none of it seems as daunting as telling the world that the book is now on sale, and persuading people to buy it.

This is often due, in part, to the insecurity that often comes with a creative endeavour. For writers without a track record it can be very intimidating putting work on sale for the first time. And even established writers are often unsure about their latest book and would prefer it to speak for itself rather than having to promote it.

However, for all publishing, marketing is crucial. There's no need to think of it as a cynical process or something that will make you feel uncomfortable. It's about giving your book the best possible chance to reach an audience.

Why marketing matters

If you write and publish a book to communicate with other people, then the actual writing is only the first part of the process. There's no point publishing something that no one reads.

Equally, there's little point thinking that a readership will somehow find the book themselves once you have listed it on Amazon. There are hundreds of thousands of books and ebooks published in the UK each year – you would have to be incredibly lucky for many people to stumble over yours unless you do something to draw it to their attention.

This doesn't mean that you must aim for record-breaking sales that shoot you to the top of the bestsellers. You can find remarkable self-publishing sales success stories online, but these are the tiny minority. Most self-published authors without a track record should be aiming for sales in the hundreds rather than the thousands. Nothing says you can't exceed this, and you shouldn't limit your ambition, but as a self-publisher it makes sense to be realistic and build step by step.

If you aim too high, there is a danger that you will feel deflated when you don't reach the targets you set. Also, you might be tempted to splash out too much on consultants in the hope that a sales boost will cover the cost.

So be realistic. Marketing is a huge area covering advertising, social media, press, film, reviews, word of mouth, pricing strategies and much more. Make a plan that you will be able to deliver and learn as much as you can as you go. Remember that every lesson learned can be applied when it comes to marketing your next book.

What matters most...

What matters most of all is the content of your book. The better your book, the more work your readers will do for you: making recommendations in reviews, on social media and through word of mouth.

Research sales

Log on to self-publishing forums online and see if you can find out how many copies books similar to yours have sold. If no one has spoken about their sales figures, politely ask if anyone is willing to share – either on the forum or privately via email.

> The more information you can find, the more realistic you can be about your own sales. If you find self-published books similar to yours with high sales, see what you can find out about how they were marketed.

A marketing plan

The amount of detail you put into a marketing plan ahead of publication will probably depend on how experienced you are. If you've never marketed a book or anything else before, then it's best to keep things simple and learn as you go. But even a simple plan will be useful, helping you to plan what marketing activity you can undertake and reminding you of what needs to be done in the midst of the excitement of getting the book ready for sale.

HOW MUCH TIME DO YOU HAVE?

If you are working full-time and have three young children, then you probably feel that you simply don't have time to devote to marketing your book. However, if you have found enough time to write it, then you should be able to find time to help sell it. Remember, that's at least part of the point of publishing. Most self-publishers find themselves stretched for time, since most are doing it in addition to other work or responsibilities. You should, of course, be realistic about how many hours a week you can devote to marketing, but don't use your busy schedule as an excuse for not getting stuck into the business of promoting your book. If you really don't have time, but do have some money, then consider contracting out marketing to a consultant. (See the end of this chapter for more on this.)

> ## Fit marketing into your schedule
>
> Sketch out a timetable of your week. Where could you find time for marketing? Once your book is finished, could you use what was once writing time as marketing time?

Countdown to the launch

In publishing, the launch of a book really counts. That's not to say that your marketing should stop once the book is out, or that you shouldn't try to build an audience over time – you should. But the launch is an event that media and readers can latch on to. Pick a date that will give you the best possible opportunity to get attention for your work, and when you will have some spare time to handle enquiries. Certain times of year might suit certain types of book – for example, diet and exercise books normally come out in the New Year when people have made fitness resolutions. But sometimes avoiding those popular times can give your book more chance to stand out.

Once you have picked a date, count backwards and plan your marketing activity week by week. If you haven't left yourself enough time, either consider pushing back the launch date or, if that's not possible, see if you can concentrate your marketing into that timeframe.

Remember, the launch date doesn't need to be when the book is actually published. In fact, it's better to wait for at least a few weeks after that (perhaps more) to allow time to check for problems, send out review copies and get your other marketing activity done.

If possible, try to organize some kind of launch event that will appeal to your target audience and provide an opportunity to sell books. People will expect you to do a short reading from your new work and to talk a little about it... and to have a drink or two. Think carefully about what budget you have for the event and whether the prospective sales make the spending worth while. It can be difficult to judge, but make sure you don't spend more money than you can afford to lose.

Make sure you invite media contacts to the launch and use social media to generate interest. Arrange for someone else to take photographs and then share them online afterwards. It's all about creating a 'buzz' – the sense that your book is being read and talked about.

 ## The launch is crucial

The launch of your book is likely to be your best opportunity for marketing. People are attracted to something new, and you should do everything possible to generate interest in the launch and be prepared to deal with enquiries, comments and purchases.

Target audience

Some writers will have a target audience in mind right from their book's conception. For others, a book is entirely personal and they give no thought to whom it might appeal to.

When it comes to marketing, however, identifying the target audience is key. Once you know who they are, you can work out how to reach them.

Your target audience is likely to be people who have bought similar books in the past or have an interest in the subject you are writing about. You will find them in online forums, on social media and through specialist publications and websites.

In some ways it is helpful if your book has the potential to appeal to a very wide audience. An historical novel, for example, could be read by hundreds of thousands of people. But this also presents a difficulty. It takes huge amounts of money, contacts and expertise to target a broad audience, and even then a book is often lost in the crowd.

It's far easier to target smaller groups of people with specialist interests. That might be obvious if your book is non-fiction. But even with fiction try to narrow things down – perhaps there is a genre, theme or a setting or character that might appeal to a certain audience you can target.

Narrowing down the audience for your marketing doesn't mean that the book won't have a chance to appeal more broadly. In the end, the book's content will determine how widely read it is. But the more that you can focus your marketing effort at the outset, the more likely you are to get some momentum and begin on the road to selling hundreds of copies rather than just a few dozen.

Endorsements

Even established authors frequently seek endorsements for a book from fellow authors or experts in the relevant field to help promote their book when it is launched. If you don't have a track record, then you will find it difficult to get well-known people to read your work, let alone recommend it, but that doesn't mean you shouldn't try.

More realistically, try to think of someone to read and endorse it who would appeal to your target audience.

For example, is there another self-published author in the same genre with a good sales record whom you could approach? Even if they are only known to a few thousand people, those people will be part of your key target audience.

Another idea is to approach well-respected local writers or booksellers. They might be more willing to read your work and their endorsement will mean something to people in your area.

Social media and blogging

One of the main drivers behind the rise of self-publishing has been the spread of social media like Twitter and Facebook. Mainstream publishers used to have a massive advantage because of their access to the printed media and radio; it was very difficult to get any coverage without having some kind of personal contact. Now, even the biggest publishers find social media a significant marketing tool. Authors, whether first-timers or Man Booker Prize-winners, are expected to be active tweeters and, though there are a few who still opt out, most realize that social media are an invaluable tool for promoting their work.

It would be a mistake, however, to see social media purely as a marketing tool. It can be used that way – making posts about your upcoming work, book deals and positive reviews – but Twitter and Facebook are most effective when they are used genuinely socially. That means reading and responding to other people's posts, interacting whenever possible, and posting about a wider range of topics than just your work.

 ## Think before you post

Laws of libel and copyright still apply on Twitter and Facebook, and even if you delete a post someone might already have saved it (and it will be saved on the host company's server). So, while informality and strong opinions are normally welcomed, you should still think before you post.

TWITTER

A Twitter profile, which is free to sign up for, is like having a web page on which you can make short 'posts' of no more than 140 characters. Unless you protect your profile (which, as an author seeking publicity, you are unlikely to do), it can, in theory, be seen on the Web by anyone anywhere in the world.

In practice, it will usually only be seen by people who choose to 'follow' you. You see every post made by someone you follow – and you can follow as many people as you like. Unless they 'protect' their tweets, you can follow anyone you like – but remember that other people can see who you follow and who follows you.

When you first join Twitter it can feel overwhelming. There are millions of Twitter profiles from all over the world and some people seem to make a new post several times a minute. The best approach is a gradual one. Use the Twitter search box to find some people you know you would like to follow – perhaps well-known authors, or publishers, journalists, friends or family – and get used to how it all works. You don't have to post at all until you're ready, but people will probably only start following you when you do.

If you put someone's Twitter name in a tweet – for example @stephenfry – they will be notified in the 'connections' part of their account. Very famous people are unlikely to respond due to the sheer volume of tweets they get, but with the less celebrated it can be a good way to connect. You might want to tell an author how much you enjoyed their book, or a theatre how much you liked a play.

Normally, after a few weeks people start to find Twitter addictive. Once you are following more than a few hundred people – and Twitter makes continual suggestions about whom you might follow, based on whom you follow so far – you'll find that rather than trying to read every tweet that comes your way, you need to dip in and out.

There are lots of ways to manage your Twitter use, using lists and apps for your phone or PC. Once you've mastered the basics, start researching online if you have any problems or difficulties.

From a marketing point of view Twitter has two main functions.

The first is as a kind of broadcaster to your followers so that you can tell them about your book. Unless you are already well known, it will probably take many months to build up more than a few hundred followers, so time spent on Twitter is a long-term investment. But these followers are likely to be your prime audience; people who have shown an interest in you and might be interested in buying your book. Don't bombard them with self-promotion, but don't be shy of letting your Twitter followers know about your book launch. They are then likely to be your first target for ongoing promotions such as discounts and giveaways.

The second use of Twitter is for making new contacts. As mentioned above, you can tweet anyone. They might not respond but, if you can identify them as part of your target audience, then it's worth a go.

FACEBOOK

A normal Facebook profile shares many similarities with Twitter. It's about connecting, interacting, commenting and sharing. Facebook has always been more about 'friends', however genuine, and online conversation but you can still use it to help market your books.

The biggest difference from Twitter is that you can only be someone's 'friend' – the equivalent of following them on Twitter – if they give permission. On the plus side that means that connections can be more genuine, but it also means that it can be hard to build up connections with people outside those you already know.

For your book you could create a separate Facebook Page – these are used by organizations and companies and can be 'Liked' by anyone, without permission. Creating a Page can help separate your personal life from your publishing life, but it's also an extra element to maintain.

Facebook can certainly be a fantastic marketing tool, especially if you have events to publicize and pictures and videos to share. But if you're not already a regular Facebook user then for marketing purposes you are probably better off sticking to Twitter.

BLOGGING

Blogs – simple websites in a diary format with the newest post at the top of the page – have been somewhat overshadowed by the rise of social media. But they remain a key tool for the self-publisher, and one that can interact with your other marketing devices.

If your main website keeps most of the same content from month to month (information about you and your work), and your social media changes every day or even every hour, a blog can fit somewhere in between. You might make a new post every week or so, perhaps a reflection on something you have been writing about or something you have read.

The tone is often informal, and blog posts can be any length you choose, but they are a chance to publish at greater length than the 140 characters of a tweet.

From a marketing point of view, blogs are a shop window into your writing and you as a person. If you can engage an audience, they will be much more likely to buy your book, even if your blog posts are not directly related to it.

If you are good at writing short blog posts and articles, you should also enquire about contributing to other magazines and blogs.

Many of them won't be able to pay you for articles, but if you have something interesting to say they might be willing to provide you with a platform.

As with all marketing activity, don't spend more time on this than you can afford!

Don't get bogged down in blogs!

Time spent on social media and blogging can be time well spent. But don't forget that the main thing writers need to do is write!

Reviews

Unless you are an established author, you are unlikely to get reviews in the mainstream press. If appropriate, you should send review copies to specialist and local press, once you have made contact to establish who would be the best person to send it to. But in the main you will rely on reviews by readers.

Reader reviews have been the cause of much controversy in recent years. With so many sites, most notably Amazon, using prominent rating systems, authors have tried many ways of influencing them in order to promote sales.

The simple truth is that reviews, especially on Amazon, really can make a difference, but it's a mistake to try to trick the system. For example, creating fake profiles to post positive reviews will, if discovered, seriously undermine your credibility – it is known as 'sock-puppeting' and amounts to committing fraud. Of course, you can invite friends to post reviews in the hope they will be positive, but on the whole you just have to accept whatever gets posted.

It can be worth while sending out free review copies in the hope that people will read the book, like it, and post positive reviews in time for the book's launch. This has certainly worked for some established self-publishers with a strong following, but it might be less easy to orchestrate if you don't yet have a track record and a readership.

Another approach is to try specialist self-publishing sites. A good list can be found in this article and in the comments beneath it: www.guardian.co.uk/books/booksblog/2012/nov/19/self-published-books-where-to-find.

Get into the reviewing habit

Get into the habit of reviewing books yourself for online communities and retail sites. If you make a real effort to be fair, and to understand the author's intentions, it can be a great way to get yourself thinking more deeply about what you read. It will also introduce you to the huge community of online reader reviewers and you might be able to make some useful contacts who will review your own work.

Price-cuts and giveaways

As self-publishing ebooks has grown in popularity there has been a general acceptance among authors that free giveaways are a vital part of building an audience. The idea is that by giving away one book for free, you generate interest and reader reviews.

If you have published other books, then it might also make people more likely to buy one.

For ebooks this is possible (if the retailer / self-publishing company allows it) because there are no production costs. With printed books you're unlikely to be able to afford to give many away for free, but you could consider offering discounts.

Amazon, the largest retail platform for ebooks, has changed the way it governs pricing and at the moment you can normally give books away for free only if you join the Kindle Direct Publishing scheme. See the chapter on ebooks for more information about how the different self-publishing platforms approach pricing.

If you are going to give discounts of any kind, it's best to make them time limited and to promote them as much as you can without annoying people! You might start with a reduced price to generate interest, then go to the standard price and then return to a discount when the initial interest has flagged.

Stick to your pricing plan

Have a plan for pricing your book and stick to it. Don't chop and change every few days just to try to generate interest or it will seem unprofessional.

How to commission marketing support

There are lots of companies and consultants advertising marketing support, and some self-publishing companies offer it as part of a package.

As with any commissioning, establish very clearly what you will get before you sign up. Shop around to compare prices and services and ask to have contact with people they have worked for already.

Don't be blinded by jargon that might sound more impressive than it actually is. And, when it comes to the bottom line, try to estimate how many sales the money you will spend might deliver. If possible, ask other authors who have commissioned similar services how it has worked out for them.

Review your progress

Whether you are a marketing veteran or a complete novice, make time to review your progress at regular intervals.

It can help to do this with someone else, explaining what you've done so far, what you hoped to achieve and how the results have panned out. Even if they lack expertise, they might have a different perspective that proves useful, and sometimes just having to explain something can make it clearer for you.

Another way to do this is online. If you can connect with other self-publishers online, it can be really helpful to post updates and self-assessments of your progress and then to ask questions. A blog can be a good place for this, and if you are happy to share your experiences, you will probably find that other authors are interested to see how your approach has fared.

Although in some sense self-publishers are in competition, in practice you will find that many people are happy to co-operate and help one another to improve.

You should also make time to read up on the subject of marketing; like all aspects of writing and self-publishing, there are always possibilities for improvement. There are lots of interesting articles you can find online, but two authors you could start with are Tim Ferriss and Seth Godin. Both are American, and both have had huge success as self-publishers. Don't feel you have to try to emulate them, or follow their methods, but both have interesting insights into marketing and self-publishing.

Focus points

- Don't be shy about marketing. The point of publishing is to get people to read your book.
- Draw up a simple marketing plan before you start.
- Make the most of your launch, even if you don't have money for a launch event.
- Get active on social media as soon as possible. The more you put into them, the more benefit you will gain.
- Use price discounts and giveaways, but don't chop and change your price so much that you confuse people.

Where to next?

In Chapter 10 we look at how you can set up and run an author's website – another crucial way in which you can promote your work.

10

Setting up and running a website

Tom Green

While at one time setting up a website was expensive and running it required specialist knowledge and training, it can now be done for free.

A number of online tools exist that aim to enable non-experts to create professional-looking websites. There are also numerous paid-for services both online and via companies and individual consultants. If you are thinking of paying to help set up your site, make sure you check out the free sites first to make sure any expense incurred is necessary.

Do you need a website?

There are various places you can create web pages without having to set up a whole site. They include Amazon Author Pages, Lulu Storefront and other pages provided by self-publishing services or retailers.

It is certainly worth making use of these pages, and, if you have limited time or expertise, you might decide that one or more of these is sufficient. They will provide a place online for people to find information about you and a link you can give for people to see your books. They are free, easy to use and, in most cases, easy to update.

However, your own website allows you to impose your own personality online and to create the environment that best suits your books. You will have more flexibility in terms of design, content and additional 'plug-in' content like YouTube videos and Twitter feeds.

A website can establish your identity as an author, becoming the single authoritative place where readers, potential readers, media and retailers can find information about you and your work.

Assess some authors' websites

Do a web search on some of your favourite authors including self-published authors working in the same genre as you. Can you find their websites? What features do they have? Do you think they promote the author's work effectively?

How to set up a free website

Popular free website-building services include Moonfruit, Weebly and Wix. A web search will also reveal several others. If you are looking for a free service, check the terms and conditions carefully before you commit yourself. For example, some sites charge for hosting – that is, for providing an online space for your site.

The aim of these services is to make it easy for people with little or no web expertise to set up a site.

All you need to do is sign up with your email address and you will be able to select from set designs into which you can put your own images and content. You will be able to modify the design elements to varying extents, depending on your technical proficiency and the flexibility of the various services. For example, Weebly allows full editing access to the style sheets containing the code that creates the page.

One of the great things about these services is that it is very easy just to sign up and have a go. Although once you publish the site it will be online for all to see, it's very unlikely that anyone will find it at first unless you send them the link because it normally takes search engines several weeks to index new sites. So you can play around, experiment with different layouts and designs and try the different tools. You can also get feedback, both in person and by sharing the link via social media.

How to get the right domain name

Many of the free sites make their money by selling you a domain name. Typically, they will offer you a free one that involves their domain name, for example janesmithauthor.weebly.com.

There is nothing wrong with those free domains, but if you want something similar such as janesmithauthor.co.uk then you will have to pay for it.

Only one person can own a domain name at any one time, so if someone has beaten you to it then you will just have to wait until it becomes available. If your first choice – normally involving your name or the title of your book – for either a free or paid-for domain is not available, then think creatively for a version of the name. Try to keep it short and, as far as possible, ensure that it makes sense to someone seeing it for the first time.

Buying a domain name

Free website-building sites normally offer an easy way to get your domain name – you buy it through them and they automatically assign it to the website you build with them. However, while this is the most convenient way to get a domain name, you will probably find it cheaper to buy it elsewhere from one of the many domain registration services such as www.123reg.co.uk. They have easy-to-follow instructions and prices are normally low for .co.uk domains. But you will need to work out how to connect your site to this new domain.

The service you use for your free site should explain how to transfer it to an external domain, but the terminology can vary so you might need to get help from a friend with some web experience or else by asking via social media or on one of the many forums dedicated to the popular web-building tools.

Research a domain name

Go to www.123.reg.co.uk and use their search tool to find out which domain names relating to your name or the title of your book are available, and how much they cost.

Domain names ending in .com are normally more expensive than those ending .co.uk. Unless you have realistic aspirations to sell internationally, you should probably stick to .co.uk (.org domains are for organizations).

Simple tips for website design

When designing your own website it makes sense to follow one of the templates that is provided. Unless you have real skills in design, and can make something unusual and striking, the key is to organize content on the page in a way that is easy to read at a glance.

People tend to browse on the Internet, flitting from site to site, so you have only a few seconds to make it clear who you are, the title of your book, what it is about and why they should buy it.

That doesn't mean that you need to SHOUT IN CAPITAL LETTERS and use lots of exclamation marks!!! Nor should you splash colour and moving text all over your site. And under no circumstances have music playing automatically when people arrive.

All of those things are likely to annoy people and make them leave your site straight away.

Think carefully about the most important information you want to provide and organize it on the page in a clear way that suits the tone and genre of your book. Use appropriate colours and images and always get copyright clearance for any images you use.

Match your website with your book

Your website is a tool for selling your book and so should embody the qualities, genre and tone of that book. Make it easy for people browsing the Web to understand what your book is about and why they should buy it. Think about colours, fonts and overall style for your site in the same way that you do for the cover of your book.

Try not to put too much content on each page. Even people interested in your work probably won't scroll far down on their screen, and some might be using small laptops, so keep the most important information high up.

Don't be afraid of white space. Lots of very professional websites use lots of white space to help the rest of the content stand out and to give the impression of a calm and measured design.

Workshop: 'First impressions'

Search for the websites of five authors working in the same genre as you. If possible, find a mix of corporately published and self-published. Consider your first impressions of the sites. Before you even read the words, what impressions do the sites create? Does the tone and feel of the site tell you much about the author's work?

Now think about the tone and feel of your own work and consider what elements on your website will help convey that. For example, what colours will you choose, what images and what style of font?

The importance of 'usability'

'Usability', as you might guess, refers to how easy a website is to use. As mentioned above, a great-looking website is not the first priority – it's no good at all unless people browsing the Internet can find what they want from your site.

As well as clear and well-organized design, usability is also improved by the language you use, the structure you give your site and how you use links.

LANGUAGE

The general rule for websites is to say what you mean, especially with headings and titles. While newspapers and magazines often use clever titles with puns and intriguing language, when reading online people are not normally willing to invest the time to find out what you mean. They want to scan the page and understand whether it is worth their while reading on.

Of course, you might want to challenge this conventional wisdom, especially if your book is unconventional. But if not, use clear simple language. Try to use as few words as possible, but if you need to use an extra word to make things clear, then use it.

Because people tend to scan web pages at speed, headings and subheadings are particularly important. They give the website user something to focus on. So do images, as long as they relate closely to the content of the text.

STRUCTURE

For a website relating to a book, or even a series of books, the structure of your site is unlikely to be complex. We'll discuss some of the key content for your site later in the chapter, but whatever you include, make sure it is easy for the first-time visitor to your site to see clearly where everything is. If there are processes for them to go through – for example, to contact you or to buy your book – these should be clear and intuitive.

LINKS

You should use links in moderation, but they can be very helpful. From your homepage, you should link through to key content on your site. For example, you should have at least one link that takes people straight to somewhere they can buy your book. You will probably also want a link that takes them to more information about the book. There will already be links in the 'navigation' at the top or by the side of the page, but it's still a good idea to make these important links prominent elsewhere on the homepage.

You should also offer links to other sites, where appropriate. If there are positive reviews of your book, then you should both quote from them and link to them. If there is a good reason – for example if they are relevant to the research or background of your book – provide some links to external sources; they will help establish the credibility of your work.

Any web-building tool will show you how to make web links and will automatically make them stand out in bold, a different colour, or underlined, or some combination of those three. It's important that visitors to your site can identify links quickly, so don't make any text that isn't a link either bold, a different colour or underlined.

Key content on an author's website

Most good authors' websites have much the same kind of content. You will certainly need the following features:

HOMEPAGE

This is the 'front cover' of your website. It should give a clear and appealing impression of your work and should contain links to key content within the site, especially to where people can buy the book.

YOUR BOOK TITLE

If you have published several books, you can give each their own section or put them all under one heading. Give a concise summary of the contents, along with recommendations, positive reviews and links to where the book can be bought. Underneath this you might like to add something longer about the background to the book and how you came to write it.

ABOUT ME

Whether you have had an ordinary life or an extraordinary one, readers tend to want to know something about you. If biographical details are relevant to the book, then you can go into some detail. And, if your life story is remarkable in some way, don't be shy – let the world know!

CONTACT ME

If you put an email address on a website, it will attract spam, but it is important that people can get in touch if they need to. Many email clients these days are good at filtering out spam, so it need not be a problem. If your email address gets clogged up with spam, consider creating an email with another free provider such as Google's gmail.com which has a good spam filter.

PRESS AND REVIEWS

Here you can list positive feedback. Don't quote reviews or comments at length unless there are no web links for them.

NEWS

If you have news to report on a reasonably regular basis – about once a month – then you can create a news section for updates about any book signings or promotional activity.

TWITTER AND FACEBOOK

If you have social media accounts, you should be able to embed them in your website. That means your status updates and tweets can appear automatically in a box on your site. It's a good way to connect your different online activities. Follow the instructions from Twitter and Facebook about how to do this, and also look in the 'Help' section of the website-building service you are using.

Your website is your hub

Your website should be a central place connecting all of your online activity. Make it easy for people to find what they want.

How to use a blog

In addition to the content above, you might also choose to create a blog. Most free website tools offer a blog that can be a part of your website, so it should be easy to set up.

Blogs allow you to upload content – text, photos or video, or some combination of the three – that is automatically dated and archived. This means the newest content you upload is always at the top of the page. Older content gets pushed down the page and neatly stored.

Blogs are often written in quite a personal way, emphasizing the author's opinions and experiences. But you can write yours in any way you choose. However, if you are writing your blog on a site whose main purpose is to promote your book then you might want to restrict your blog content to something related to that book, or to your experiences as a self-publishing author.

Assess some authors' blogs

Type 'author blogs' into your search engine and read a selection of the sites you find. Note down which ones appeal to you and why. Are the posts always directly related to the author's own book?

Connecting your website with social media

One benefit of writing a blog is that it gives you fresh content to promote via social media. You can't keep repeating posts on Twitter and Facebook promoting your book – people will soon get bored and annoyed – but you can post about new items on your blog. You will need to invest time and effort in writing the new content, but it's a great way of showing people how you think and getting them to your website from where, hopefully, they will buy your book.

As mentioned above, you can also 'embed' your tweets and Facebook updates into your site. They won't always make sense out of context, but they will add freshness to your website (as long as your social media content is updated every few days) and encourage people to connect with you.

Selling books from your website

It is quite easy to sell books directly from your website. Many free and low-cost sites have 'shopping cart' functions that you can use. If you are only selling one or a few books, then this should be quite easy to set up, with payments normally made through an online system such as PayPal.

The main reason for doing this will be if you are self-publishing without support from a company that will process and fulfil orders. If you choose to do this, then it is easier than ever to manage the online sales process yourself.

The main challenge is likely to be fulfilment – that is, wrapping and despatching the books to customers. You will need to decide how much to charge and make sure you have enough time to deal with orders.

One possible drawback of selling directly from your own site is that potential customers might be wary of making payments if you have no track record. So make sure you are very clear about who you are, how they can get in touch with you if they have problems, and how the payment and fulfilment process will be carried out.

Bear in mind that people are used to prompt despatches from sites like Amazon, so might be unhappy waiting for more than a few days. You will also need to work out what to do if people say that books have not arrived or if they arrive damaged.

However, if you are familiar with a site like eBay, then none of this will be new to you.

Even if you are self-publishing independently, you might still decide that you don't want the hassle of processing orders. In that case you can simply point people towards a retail site where your book is listed.

Ways to improve your search rankings

'Search ranking' refers to how high up the page your website comes when someone searches for a certain thing. The aim is to come as high up as possible so that there is the greatest chance that someone will visit your website.

For general searches, it is unlikely that you will get much benefit from search engines. For example, if you have written a contemporary love story, there will be many thousands of search results for 'contemporary love story' from bigger sites and more established writers that will come above yours.

But with more specific searches you might fare better. If people search your name or the title of your book, then you want your site to figure prominently in the rankings. And searches might also be beneficial in relation to specific aspects of your book. For example, if it concerns a particular place or a particular issue, then there is a chance you might be able to build a good ranking if you can set your site up well and make it popular.

Setting up your site

Most website-building services will automatically prompt you to do certain things that work well with search engines. These include giving your site a title and naming individual pages. Make sure you include a clear summary of your book in text on the homepage so that search engines can pick that up as well.

CONTENT

Search engines tend to like 'natural language' content – that is, words you write that are genuine rather than attempts to repeat lots of key words in the hope that search engines will notice them. Natural language headings and subheadings are also important. Try to avoid repeating content on different pages, other than for small sections such as quotations from reviews that might appear on both the homepage and inside.

NEW CONTENT

The more new content you can add, the better. That's why blogs are good. Don't sacrifice the quality of your site for the sake of adding content but, if you can, regularly add relevant blog posts – it will definitely help your search ranking.

LINKS AND INTERACTIONS

The more you can get people to link to your site and comment on your blog, the better. Don't sign up for any link exchange programs, as search engines hate those and might even blacklist you. But if you let people know about your website and, most importantly, create interesting content that prompts them to visit and post links on their own site and on social media, then your search ranking will rise.

METADATA

On a small website, metadata – text that doesn't appear on the published site but is used to inform search engines – will not matter too much. But most website-building tools give the chance to use metadata and it is worth doing. Simply follow the instructions to add simple text describing your site and, if possible, each page.

PAID-FOR SERVICES

There are lots of companies that offer to improve your search ranking. Some will do a good job, but proceed with caution – if you follow the instructions above you will have done most of what is possible. If you do commission someone to do this work, ask them to be explicit about what they will do and remember to be wary of any tricks such as 'link farms' or 'link exchanges' that might improve your ranking in the short term but could end up getting you blacklisted from search engines.

Try this

Do an Internet search on a subject relating to your book. Which sites come top? Is there any way you could persuade them to feature or promote your work?

Google Analytics

Google Analytics is a free tool that enables you to monitor how many people come to which parts of your website, which sites they were referred from, which search terms were used and many other things besides.

It's normally relatively simple to install. Just check the help section of the website-building tool you are using. It can seem complicated to use at first, but it can be interesting to see how people are finding your site and which bits they are reading.

If you are running a well-planned marketing campaign, then it allows you to see which parts of it are proving most effective at bringing people to your site.

Setting up web pages on other websites

Whether you set up your own site or not, you should also set up a free page on any other retail or listing site where it is available. If you are offered the chance for a paid-for page, be careful before you commit and check with others who have used the service to see whether it is worth while.

The templates for free pages will be more restrictive than your own website, but your approach should be similar. Communicate clearly and concisely in a style and tone that reflects the content of your book and acts as a strong advertisement for it.

Commissioning a website

If you can afford it, there are many individuals and companies whom you can commission to build a website for you. The following is useful advice:

- As with all services you commission, shop around and try to get personal recommendations either from people you know or other authors you connect with online.

- Ask different companies or consultants to submit a proposal and a budget as well as references and links to sites they have previously built.

- Be clear about what you want. Do you just need some help with design? Do you need someone to help you through the whole process? Will you be able to update the site yourself, or do you need to pay someone to do it?

- If you are going to do the updates yourself, ask to try out the editing system that will be used – there are many different ones – so that you know you will be able to do it.

- Be sure to ask about the costs of hosting and make sure you have access to the site where your site's domain name is registered. If, for some reason, you lose contact with the person who built the site you still want to be able to access the domain name.

- Also be clear about any ongoing costs for updates or maintenance, and be clear what these will entail. Try to ensure that you will be able to take the website to another company in the future if you choose to do so and are not locked in with the company that built the site, even if their prices rise.

Focus points

- Experiment with a free website tool. You might find it easier than you think.
- Keep the content and design for your website clear and concise.
- Have prominent links to the most important content.
- If you can find the time, create a blog and write new posts at least once a month.
- Connect your social media and blog with your website.

Where to next?

In Chapter 11 Kevin will look at what happens after your book is published.

11

Post-publication

Kevin McCann

Well, it's decision time again and the question is: what next?
Do you want to carry on writing and, if you do, do you want
to continue developing your skills as a writer?

If the answer to these questions is yes, read on.

If the answer's no, read on anyway. You might change
your mind.

In his poem 'Flying Crooked', Robert Graves compares the flight of a butterfly – by implication – to the mind of a poet. He was not the first writer, nor will he be the last, to point out that creative thinking and logical thinking are, apparently, two entirely different things. This has led to the idea that creative people are impractical, illogical, exotic beings who can't think straight. And, contrariwise, that logical people can only think in straight lines, are good at things like maths but are hopelessly dull company.

This led to the notion that there were two types of thinking, and in the 1950s the psychologist J.P. Guilford coined the terms 'convergent' and 'divergent' to differentiate between them.

> **Convergent thinking:** thinking that brings together information focused on solving a problem, especially solving problems that have a single correct solution. A good example of this would be a maths problem for which there is only one correct answer.

For example: In a group of four people, A weighs 120 pounds; B weighs 140 pounds; C weighs 200 pounds and D weighs 130 pounds. What is the average weight of the group?

The correct answer, if you care at all, is 147.5 pounds, and to get the right answer you need to follow a logical sequence – that is, add the four weights together and then divide by four.

There is a set method and only one correct solution.

> **Divergent thinking:** thinking in an unusual and un-stereotyped way to generate several possible solutions to a problem. Or, thinking that moves away in diverging directions so as to involve a variety of aspects which sometimes lead to novel ideas and solutions; often associated with creativity.

Divergent thinking is also known as lateral thinking, a term coined by Edward De Bono in 1967.

This apparent split has led many people into a kind of either/or mentality – that is, you're either one kind of thinker or another. Ask any experienced teacher and they'll tell you that's nonsense. In reality, we're all a mixture of the two and most of us can switch between types of thinking depending on the task in hand.

If you're writing a poem, you tend to think divergently, but not always. Your poem has to have what I call a poetic logic so that your reader may not be able to explain the poem's literal meaning, but they can still understand it emotionally. The line 'Macbeth hath murdered sleep' is a logical impossibility – how can you kill sleep? – but anyone who's ever had a sleepless night brought on by stress knows exactly what it means.

Even cartoons have an internal logic – characters run off cliffs but never fall *until* they've looked down.

If you have a series of maths problems to solve, you'll probably think convergently; on the other hand, if you're launching a new business or book, you may follow all the tried-and-tested marketing strategies… and then come up with something new that nobody, as far as you know, has tried before.

As a self-published (and therefore self-promoting) writer you need to be convergent or divergent depending on circumstances.

Albert Einstein, theoretical physicist

'Creativity is the residue of time wasted.'

I suspect Einstein was being heavily ironic in the same way Oscar Wilde was when he claimed that 'All art is quite useless.' It all depends how you define your terms.

Anyway, let's get back to time wasted – for me, time wasted is when I expend a lot of energy on something that isn't of the slightest importance and, in the end, just wears me out.

Time not wasted is time spent enriching my life. So time wasted could be, for example, writing sarcastic comments on Facebook about some politician or other. It's often – no, scrub that – it's always an excuse not to start writing.

Time spent usefully could be reading, walking, writing letters, listening to music, baking a cake… the list goes on and on. The point is this: deep down, you know the difference between meditation and procrastination. You know it the way a small child trying to postpone bedtime knows it.

Prioritizing and time management

If you're serious about building a career for yourself as a writer, you need to start organizing your time around your writing. How much or how little time you've got available obviously depends on your personal circumstances.

If you've got a job and/or family commitments, finding the time and energy to write as well is very difficult. And as I've already mentioned, the 'heroic exhaustion leads to glorious visions' myth is just that: a myth, and a dangerous one at that.

We all need balance in our lives so what you need to do is sit down and draw up a schedule for yourself that's realistic. And don't worry. There are lots of ways you can use your downtime to help your writing.

SLEEP ON IT

For as long I've been writing, I've had the habit of rereading the last page I wrote that day just before going to bed. I've often found that when I go back to it the next day, I get much more written than if I simply 'forget it' until my next writing session. My own theory is that, while I'm sleeping, the part of my brain where my dreams come from is active – I dream a lot; meanwhile, my conscious mind has all but completely closed down. But not completely; one small part of it spends the night mulling things over.

HAVE A FEW LAUGHS

I found that when I was working on a particular piece and was feeling either completely blocked, too stressed to cope or just generally riddled with self-doubt and whining self-pity, that a few laughs really helped.

I began to realize that it wasn't just the rush of energizing endorphins that helped; it was also the divergent thinking found in really great comedy, whether it's visual like Keaton or Chaplin, or verbal like Tommy Cooper or Groucho Marx, or both. Humour often describes a world in which the laws of logic don't apply. It's a world we all need to visit from time to time, not just because it does you good physically but because it aids your creative faculty. In humour the only limit is your own inventiveness.

It's something that is being rediscovered by psychologists but has been known by supposedly primitive people for ever. Hence the tradition of the sacred clown because:

 Black Elk, Lakota shaman

'Laughing or crying, it's still the same face.'

DO SOME HOUSEWORK

Again, my own experience coupled with conversations with other writers has confirmed that such humble tasks as ironing, washing the dishes and peeling potatoes during your downtime enhances your work.

I think there are two reasons for this.

Firstly, your intellect as well as your body needs rest. If you never switch off, you'll end up either physically or mentally ill. A quick word of warning here. There are people who think that what they call 'madness' actually helps creativity. They're the sort who believe the 'Van Gogh blindly inspired genius' myth. Now it is true that a lot of artists – I'm using the word to cover everyone who creates, so that includes musicians, visual artists and so on as well as writers – suffer from mental illnesses of one kind or another. I think that it's also true that, in many cases, creativity helps the individual cope with the illness. It's the thread that leads out of the maze. I speak here from personal experience.

Secondly, it's good to remind yourself that being a writer does not make you better than other people nor does it absolve you from the ordinary mundane tasks. Taking your turn emptying the waste bins is not only helpful, it keeps you grounded. I've noticed that the self-appointed literary genius whose artistic temperament puts them above the rest of us is often, in reality, a terrible writer and a dreadful human being.

No surprise when you think about it: how can you write convincingly about people if you think most of them are beneath you?

GRAB SOME SOLITUDE

Everyone, whether they write or not, needs time to themselves. How little or how much time depends on individual circumstances. If you live alone, you can have all the solitude you want. If you don't, you have to adapt.

I tend to get up early and once I've fed the cat I can spend an hour daydreaming before I start work. I never open a newspaper, listen to the radio or watch breakfast TV. I find them intrusive and irritating.

I've discovered that, by doing this, I get much more written every day. I've also discovered that I write best in the morning.

FIND THE BEST TIME TO WRITE...

As I've pointed out elsewhere, there's no one-size-fits-all method when it comes to writing. Find the time that suits you best and fits in with the rest of your life and then begin to build a schedule round that.

If you have a job and/or family commitments, then sit down and work out a realistic schedule. Ideally, what you're after is a working week that includes your non-writing commitments, your downtime and regular set periods when you can work uninterrupted.

Once you've done all that, as much as possible, stick to it.

Extending your network

As well as your website, blog, Facebook and Twitter, you should also plan out a strategy for extending your local network. I'd begin with local radio and newspapers.

For local papers, start with a visit to their website. Find the name of the appropriate contact, which you will probably find listed under features or local news, and send them a brief email introducing yourself, telling them you've just had a book published and asking if they're interested.

Make a note of the date and if you haven't heard anything after a week or so, resend the same email and ask politely whether they've had time to consider your proposal. If you don't get a reply to that one, forget it. They're not interested.

The chances are that someone will get back to you. Local dailies have to be filled six days a week, so, if it's interesting, they'll probably want to cover it. If they do, don't expect this to be the start of regular local press coverage. It won't be. What it will be is a chance to publicize your book locally.

Local radio stations are usually happy to get as many studio guests on as they can and in my experience, are always helpful and encouraging.

 ## Research local media

Before you contact either local radio or newspapers, do some research. Have a look at their respective websites and see if there's a specific journalist/presenter who deals with local interest/arts events and contact them directly.

 ## Jonathan Dean, radio producer

'Essentially the book needs to be interesting and relatable to the audience. The author needs to be able to speak well in a conversational style and react to the dialogue without the need for notes – otherwise it can just sound staged – it's all about being as natural and as interesting as possible.'

If you're invited to appear on local radio, don't forget to Facebook and tweet the date and time. Do the same if you're going to be featured in the local paper.

Don't expect to be paid

You won't be, but you may gain in other ways.

My one appearance on Radio City (Liverpool) led to me being asked to write ghost stories, which were then featured on City Talk… which led to me publishing a collection… which was then promoted by Pete Price (the host on City Talk)… which led to a selection of the stories being recorded and remastered by Jonathan Dean (a producer at Radio City) and then sold as downloads… which in turn raised my profile considerably.

However, don't assume that one appearance on local radio will suddenly change everything. Most of the time, once you're finished it'll be 'Thanks very much… Here's the exit' and that will be that. It's not because media people are shallow – it's because they're busy and you're one of maybe a dozen studio guests they've looked after just that week. So don't start asking when you can be on again.

If you do have an idea that you think they might be interested in – new short stories, local history, folklore, theatre reviews and so on – get back in touch. Again, I'd suggest an email.

You might also want to look at community radio as a place where you can both raise your profile and gain some valuable broadcasting experience. Go on to the Internet and find out where the nearest station is, contact them, tell them about your book and ask if they're interested. If you are interviewed, ask if you can have a copy and put it on your website as an mp3.

If you have a good 'radio voice', publicize your book every chance you get. It may lead you into more work.

LIBRARIES

If you're already a member of a readers' group, you can publicize your book there. Find out if there are other groups within a reasonable distance of where you live and see if it's possible for you to visit them as well.

If your book is print on demand as well as epublished, take a few copies with you to sell. By all means, offer a small discount if you can afford it but don't give them away. It makes you look desperate.

Take business cards giving your contact and website details and give those out. It could lead to further invitations from other readers' groups, writers' groups and even from librarians looking for speakers for the next World Book Day.

INDEPENDENT BOOKSHOPS

A rare breed these days but they do exist. If you know of one and have a print version of your book, I'd suggest an initial phone call to see if they'd be interested in taking some copies on sale or return. If they're willing, agree what their share of the cover price is going to be – most of the ones I've dealt with take a third – and how long they'll keep them for (they can't take up shelf space for too long if they're not selling). Then get something in writing formalizing your agreement. It's standard practice and doesn't imply a lack of trust. If a bookshop owner implies it does, walk away.

As your book is already on sale on the Internet, you may think this is a waste of time. It's not. You're competing against literally thousands of other titles so you want to make your book not just available but visible in as many places as possible.

Professional associations

If you haven't already done so, consider joining a professional association. The two main bodies in the UK are the Writers' Guild of Great Britain and the Society of Authors. Go to their respective websites and have a look at criteria for joining and then apply to whichever one suits your needs best.

The Society of Authors has very specific criteria for membership and, at the time of writing, will accept self-published writers only after they've achieved minimal sales of 300.

The Writers' Guild will accept you as a candidate member whether you've sold 300 copies, 30 or none just yet. At the time of writing you can join as a candidate for £100 a year. For that you get all the advantages of full membership – although no vote at the AGM – plus a weekly e-bulletin, *UK Writer* magazine to which you can submit articles and the chance to attend networking events.

My own experience of the Guild has been very positive and it was an article I wrote for *UK Writer* (edited by Tom) that led to this book being commissioned.

Income tax...

These are two words that can cause a lot of needless anxiety. I remember getting very stressed about keeping accounts and filling in a tax return when I first started earning money as a writer. This was because I'd listened to the people who'll tell you that all tax officers are heartless bloodsuckers. My actual experience was quite different and I found, as you will, that it's all pretty straightforward.

All you have to do is keep an accurate record of all your income as a writer and keep receipts for all those things you are able to claim for and set against tax. For example, you might be paid £100 for giving a presentation to a writers' group but have to pay £20 train fare to get there. So you'd deduct £20 from your fee and pay tax on £80. Just make sure you keep the train ticket as proof.

So keep both records and receipts and add them up every month.

If you go on the Internet and type 'tax advice for authors' into the search engine, you'll find general advice plus web pages for accountants who specialize in tax advice for writers. They will charge for their services, so weigh up your options. If your income at this stage is still low, you could contact the Citizens Advice Bureau for general free advice. You can also contact the tax office direct by phone or email if you need further help.

The most important thing to remember is this: declare every penny you earn, only claim back what you're actually entitled to. If in doubt, ask.

Focus points

- You need a schedule that you are able to keep to.
- It must reflect a balance between your writing time, other commitments and your downtime.
- Try to make your writing times coincide as much as possible with the time of day you write best.
- Start extending your network via Twitter and Facebook.
- Start to build up a network of contacts in the local media.
- Seriously consider joining a professional association such as the Writers' Guild.
- Get into the habit of keeping accurate accounts.
- Declare every amount you earn as a writer.
- Never get creative with your claims for amounts to be set against tax.
- If in doubt, ask for help – you will get it!

Where to next?

In Chapter 12 we will consider how you can develop further.

12

The continuing need for self-development

Kevin McCann

Good writing, in my opinion, is – among other things – about self-development. It sets progressively higher standards, refuses to make do with second best and lowers your boredom threshold to almost zero.

Like all good relationships, it requires work and real commitment.

It's not always easy or even ultimately successful.

We write anyway because, in the end, we don't really want to do anything else.

And our best book will always be the one we write next.

Post-publication pitfalls

Once you've published your book, there are two major pitfalls you need to avoid – the smugs and the blues:

- **The smugs:** the belief that you can do no wrong, that everything you write will be brilliant and that all criticism of your new work springs from vile jealousy. When this wears off you may very well suffer…
- **The blues:** total depression characterized by excessive self-pity and melodrama. This can in turn lead to **writer's block:** the inability to write a single word down.

In my opinion, all three are different aspects of the same thing: fear of failure and/or fear of success.

What if… the book doesn't sell… it gets bad reviews or, worse yet, no reviews at all… Or it gets great reviews, it sells really well, everyone loves it, so the pressure's on. Or…

You could go on for ever, and being a writer – so probably a tad obsessive-compulsive – will be tempted to. You can analyse your feelings, talk things through, get in touch with your inner child… You could waste months of your life or you could recognize that depression almost always follows exhilaration and that the only way out of the maze is work.

So the first thing is: stick to your schedule. Yes, have a break from it all for a week or so. You've worked hard and achieved a lot so relax for a while. Just don't let a week turn into a month.

Secondly, when you do go back to your schedule, use your writing time for writing. I've found, for example, I can waste hours happily Facebooking, tweeting and generally losing myself in the Internet. It's marvellous in one way because you really can fool yourself into thinking that you're working. Of course, in a way, you are. You're marketing – but unless it's part of a thought-out pattern of activity, it will be about as much use as sharpening all your pencils and then colour-coding your socks.

Because you need to start writing again.

If a new book is already taking shape in your mind, then great. Get going. If not, don't despair. It's there but maybe needs a little coaxing.

So how do you write if you haven't got a single idea in your head?

Ways to start writing again

FREE-FALLING

This is also known as automatic writing. The method is very simple. You get either a notebook and pen or a screen and keyboard and then begin to write. Write the first thing that comes into your head and follow that with the second, then the third and so on. Don't plan what you're going to say in advance, well, not consciously anyway. Give yourself a time limit of ten minutes and stick to it.

At the end of the ten minutes read aloud what you've produced, but for the moment don't tinker with it. Just keep it safe.

THE FILM SCORE

Take any piece of instrumental music, play it and imagine it's part of the soundtrack of a film. Write the scene it goes with. I'd suggest you listen to it once, ponder for five minutes and then play it again while writing. In this case, your writing time will obviously be dictated by the length of the music.

LAST AND FIRST THOUGHTS

Keep a notebook by your bed. For about five or six minutes each night before you go to sleep, write down any thoughts that are going through your head. Repeat the exercise in the morning and then again that night and so on for about a week. Before you write each thought or thoughts *do not* go back and reread your last entry.

SERENDIPITY

Open a book, newspaper or magazine at random. Pick a sentence, close your eyes and then put your finger down on the text. Write down the words you've landed on and carry on from there. Again, give yourself a ten-minute time limit.

When you've finished these four exercises, read back through them all. Are there any common themes and/or images that occur in all four? If the answer's yes, as I suspect it will be, then that theme or image could be the starting point for your next book.

And while you're getting on with all that – or when you want a break from it – you might want to consider other ways of combining the need to raise your profile with your continuing development as a writer.

COMPETITIONS

Writing competitions generate very strong feelings in some people, though I really don't know why. At worst, you'll lose your entry fee and get very bitter when you read the winning entry. On the other hand, if you win or at least get placed, it will give your self-confidence a mighty boost and help get your name that bit more widely known.

There is often a set theme, a maximum word count and a closing date. Three factors guaranteed to focus your mind.

It's also worth remembering that, while not all competitions require an entry fee, most do, so never pay more than you can happily afford to lose.

E-ZINES

In Chapter 4 I mentioned freelance article writing, but just in case you haven't got round to that yet, I'll mention it again.

 Victoria Roddam, publisher

'When it comes to non-fiction writing, and areas of "expertise" like knowledge of the publishing industry, or a psychology background, or a health expert background, it is useful for authors to raise their profile by contributing articles, or blogs, to specialist publications or online sites. Non-fiction publishers will often read or buy publications in the area in which they're looking to commission, and I would also say that online is probably the first port of call for many in this instance. Also, networking with others in the same field (so, comments on blogs, reviews, etc., as well as more traditional forms of networking) is useful because many publishers use recommendations, so the more people you know the better.'

What you need to be developing now is a portfolio – a selection of articles, reviews and so on which you've had published. Keep a record of where and when each was published – don't think you'll be able to remember, you won't – and as and when you come across magazines that you'd like to write for, contact the editor and ask if they'd be interested in seeing a sample of your work.

Keep a record of editors/magazines you've contacted and note the title of the sample piece you sent them. Also note the date you sent it and give them a realistic turn-around to get back to you.

When you find magazines that will take your work, stay with them and develop a good working relationship with your editor. Never miss a deadline, never be either over or under the word count, rewrite if you're asked to and always be polite.

Three last tips

1 Don't try to fake it. Write about topics that you've a genuine interest in and passion for. If you simply look at what's big right now, you could probably produce something that was informative and competent. If, on the other hand, you write about your passions, your work will have the potential to be so much more than that.

2 Be prepared to write for deferred payment, i.e. nothing in the short term. A small fee is always better than no fee at all, but in the long term a raised profile that could lead to you being talent-spotted is worth much more.

3 If you're unsure, ask for advice either publicly through online chat rooms or privately by contacting the Writers' Guild. In the end, though, trust your instincts.

Writers' retreats and residential courses

I've attended three of these and found them incredibly useful. Their main value was being away from the everyday world for five days and writing, sharing my work and worries with other writers and getting detailed feedback from a course tutor.

The only drawback is that they can be very pricey. However, if you live in the UK and want to attend one of the courses run by the Arvon Foundation (www.arvonfoundation.org), you might be eligible for a grant to help with the course fees. These grants are awarded on the basis of need and not your publishing record.

Find a writing course

Type 'writing courses' into your search engine followed by your location. List the ones that look the most useful and/or interesting. Give priority to your own type of writing – for example, if you're a novelist, attend novel writing courses – but include at least one that's dealing with a type of writing you've never tried before.

Then go to as many as you can. The day you think nobody can teach you anything is the day the writer in you expires. In fiction, brilliant people are almost always cutting, scornful and know everything. In reality, the best writers I've ever met have always been open-minded and curiously self-effacing.

Websites and blogs

Update both regularly and don't forget to put the link for your blog on the website and vice versa.

Raise your profile... but keep your credibility

Put the links for both your blog and website under your name whenever you send out an email. People do look and it can lead to work.

In the 'About me' section of your website never lie, exaggerate or spin. If you do and get found out, your credibility will vanish.

And there's another reason too, although it's purely a personal opinion. I believe that when Shakespeare said, 'To thine own self be true', he wasn't just mouthing a platitude; he was sharing an insight. Now we all know that your truth and mine may not coincide. Ask any police officer who's collected witness statements related to a traffic collision and they'll tell you that, if there are five witnesses, you'll get five different versions of the truth. What is important is that you, as a writer, remain faithful to your truth and tell it as best you can – so be honest in every aspect of your writing life.

Primary sources

As a child I was fascinated by my parents' and grandparents' tales of what I called the 'olden days'. I was given eyewitness accounts of among of the things, the 1914 Christmas Truce, the General Strike and the Blitz. And what had made these stories lodge in my mind was their human perspective.

At the age of 11, for example, I had only the vaguest understanding of the causes of the First World War but I did know that on Christmas Day, 1914, my granddad and his mates climbed out of their trenches and walked into no-man's-land.

His stories and those of my grandmother, mum and dad began as entertainments to while away wet afternoons in the days before daytime television. Their importance as my first encounters with story didn't become obvious until years later when I took part in a writing project based in Lancashire Archives.

I'd assumed before the project began that the archive itself would consist mainly of birth, marriage and death certificates and other official documents. I couldn't have been more wrong.

There were last wills dating back as far as the sixteenth century, postcards sent from France during the First World War, records of the local assizes, music – hall programmes, a thirteenth-century almanac, guest books from theatrical boarding houses ('Very many thanks, sincerely Harry Houdini') and the one that grabbed my attention – the patients' ledger, Lancaster Asylum, 1890.

I opened it at random. There was a full-page report: a name, an age, a description of the patient's condition on admission – 'imbecile' – a record of his stay and in the top left corner, his photograph. And, because he was looking straight at the camera, he now seemed to be looking at me. I turned the page to find a brief account of his sudden deterioration and death the following year.

I turned over to the next page. Above the name and condition – 'melancholia' – were two photographs. One of a smiling girl wearing a straw bonnet decorated with flowers. The other of an almost fleshless face framed by lank hair. It was mentioned in passing that she'd been force-fed daily.

Before this I'd seen archive material as nothing more than a research tool. The thought that it could act as a primary stimulus had never occurred to me. I started writing. Six poems about the patients in Lancaster Asylum came in as many days. I hadn't written so much in the last six months. And these were followed by another 30 on a wide variety of subjects. They weren't all prompted by the stories I'd heard as a child. Just the overwhelming majority of them.

The archive material had not just given me a starting point; it had reminded me of why I started writing in the first place. It wasn't for money or fame – though I wouldn't turn my nose up at either – it was because I felt passionately and wanted to express that passion through words. It had reawakened in me a point of view that apparent cynicism had all but totally obscured. And, of course, the apparent cynicism was just my cover story.

The simple truth was that I hadn't written anything for over six months. The result was that I had become very depressed and convinced that the rest really was going to be silence. Now, suddenly, the words were flowing and the poems more or less writing themselves.

I compared notes with other writers on the course and they all told the same story. Not only were they suddenly writing more, the quality of their work was, in many cases, better than it had ever been. This got me thinking.

Usually, when I need information I google in a few key words and see what comes up. If I want to know about conditions in nineteenth-century asylums, I can access, almost instantly, dozens of eyewitness accounts as well as extracts from official reports, annual death rates and so on. Or I can do what I actually did.

I can go to the main archives and look at the Record Book for the year 1890. I can feel the weight of it. If I press my face close enough to the pages, I can catch a smell, even if it's only imaginary, of carbolic. The same smell that would have filled the wards. I can look into the eyes of the inmates and imagine their lives all the more vividly.

I think I'd fallen into the error of thinking that, because I was now a published writer, I needed to concentrate my attentions not on those things I wanted to write, but on the things I felt I ought to write. I'd been deliberately suppressing anything that I thought wasn't worth my attention, which of course was everything in the end.

So, by all means, seek out gaps in the market, sit down and plan out a strategy – I do both – but write your passion, craft it, publish it, market it and hope it sells. No matter what else, write what you love to read.

And if, like me, you find yourself blocked, apart from the writing exercises to loosen you up, go to primary source material – old letters, diaries, news clippings... – and just start reading until something grabs your imagination. You'll know when it's happened because nothing else you try to read after that will go in.

Visit an archive

Type 'archon' into your search engine. This will lead you to the ARCHON Directory, which will give you the location of every archive in the UK, plus related archives in other parts of the world including the 275 to be found in the United States. Find your nearest archive and visit it.

Don't just go in and ask if you can have a browse. The material in archives, is stored and can only be initially accessed by archivists, so, when you go, have a specific area you want to look into. Phone or email in advance and find out what the archive's system is. One very good way to start is to see if it has back copies of local newspapers. If so, pick a month and a year and start reading through. You'll find something. I guarantee it.

One picture is worth...

I've already mentioned the link between the written word and film (see Chapters 1 and 3) – how the fact that you can tell a good film from a bad one shows that you have a critical faculty which you must now develop and how a great deal of prose writing borrows from film to achieve its effects. Remember our bored teacher, Mary, leaning against the back classroom wall and feeling old?

I later went on to talk about the need to make your reader see whatever it is you're writing about and how all writing, whether it's fiction or non-fiction, contains a strong visual element.

Try this

Type 'scripts online' into your search engine. Two sites that are well worth a look are www.lazybeescripts.co.uk and www.simplyscripts.com.

Get into the habit of reading scripts regularly and, when you're reading them, as well as looking at the visual imagery start thinking about structure – that is, the way the film tells its story. Ask yourself questions such as:

- Is it a linear narrative that begins at the beginning and then goes through to the end in a straight line?
- Does it begin with a series of flashbacks?
- How does the script draw you in and then keep you interested?

Now, obviously, not all cinematic techniques will translate into prose. Could you describe slow-motion in a story? Probably not, but could you slow-motion your prose in any way to create that effect? Remember: long sentences slow the pace of the story down; short ones speed it up.

If you're drawn to non-fiction, type 'online documentaries' into your search engine. You'll get a lot of hits and, again, as well as the choice of images, look at the way the story is told.

As well as film/documentary scripts, look at theatre scripts. On stage, unless it's some overblown musical, you're going to get a story that centres on dialogue and character. You can't hide behind special effects and cameos from big names. What you've got is an audience and an acting area.

The audience has paid and expect their interest to be held for anything up to three hours. So when you're reading stage scripts, look at the dialogue and how it's used to push along the story while simultaneously maintaining the illusion that what you're seeing are real conversations between real people.

Finally, go to www.bbc.co.uk/writersroom. As well as TV scripts, you'll also find radio scripts. Again, get into the habit of reading them regularly. Radio depends on sound, so, as well as voices, it uses sound effects. These combine with the listener's imagination and create the story. Read a couple of radio scripts and see how the writer makes it possible for the listener to keep track of who's talking at any one time. How is sound used to create atmosphere? Is there anything you can learn from that and apply to your own writing?

One last thought. Have you considered adding scriptwriting to your repertoire? Breaking into film or TV is very difficult but you might want to consider writing for the radio. The BBC Writersroom will read unsolicited scripts and their website regularly posts details of writing opportunities for aspiring scriptwriters.

Dealing with 'failure'

Let's suppose you've done everything right. Your book was edited, proofread, had a great cover, a snappy blurb and was well marketed but still isn't selling. What do you do?

- **Option 1:** Give up the whole idea and quietly withdraw.
- **Option 2:** Ask yourself why?

A good place to start is with your book itself. Reread it critically. You've now put enough distance between your manuscript and yourself to be able to do so objectively.

- What are its main strengths but, more importantly, what are its faults?
- Why did you write that particular book? Was it because you had to or because you felt you ought to?
- Why do you write at all?

HAD TO VS. OUGHT TO

A book or story, poem, script and so on should, ideally, be something you write because you feel compelled. The story won't leave you alone. It intrudes into your mind whether you want it there or not.

A book you feel you ought to write is one that you hope will impress people and make you famous. Nothing wrong with that, but has it got in the way of your own good judgement? Are you a novelist who really should be writing short stories? Or vice versa? Are you writing in the genre you're most passionate about? Maybe you've looked at what's selling, decided on, say, crime fiction, read a couple, drawn up a plan and then followed it. Slowly and laboriously and with no real joy at all.

Go back to basics here for a minute and ask yourself two simple questions.

1 Who are you?

2 What do you want?

Let's take the second question first. What I want is love, financial security and to write. And not just that, but to write well. Notice that I've mentioned money, because, in the real world, I need it to survive. And we all need love because, deep down inside, we're all just a bit insecure. But, above all, I want to write well. I want each thing I produce to be better than its predecessor. That's it.

Now, if I was answering the first question, my answer would be Kevin Patrick Michael McCann, aged well over 21, whose main passion in life is writing.

Which would lead me back to, *Why do you write?* And my answer to that would be because I have to.

Which prompts one last query: *How do you choose what to write?*

Well, the short answer is: I don't – it chooses me. However, I'm aware that sounds glib and evasive, so let me put it this way. When I'm writing something I want to write, I can't wait to get back to it. Anything else is a monumental effort that always sounds a false note.

Over the years I've tried out a lot of different types of writing apart from poetry – my main passion – and have made some interesting discoveries.

I started off wanting to be a serious poet (and, to some extent, I am) but for years I dismissed children's poetry as trivial, something only written by people who couldn't produce the 'real thing'. When I was finally challenged to produce some good children's poems, I discovered how wrong I was.

I found writing for children was a technical challenge I really enjoyed – they love rhyme but not jingles – and that editors liked my work. Now, I could go on and give you other examples but I don't have to because my point is simply this: for years I stubbornly refused to try my hand at particular kinds of writing because I wanted to be a serious writer and considered such trivialities as beneath me. It was only when I finally deigned to give it a go that I discovered:

- I was quite good at it and
- I really enjoyed it and, most important of all,
- my other work improved – considerably – because I'd reopened what was a closed mind.

So, if you haven't already considered it, how about now?

Writing for children

There's really only one good reason for writing for children: because you want to. If you think it's going be easy and very well paid and that you could end up doing a J.K. Rowling, you're probably going to be bitterly disillusioned.

The simple truth, as I discovered, is that children are far more discriminating than most of us give them credit for. They know when they're being patronized, they hate being preached at – don't we all? – and they can be very perceptive.

If they don't like something, they'll tell you. If you ask them why they don't like something, they'll tell you. One other thing as well – they're usually right.

The same applies if they do like something.

So what do children like?

In my experience, they want a good story that is well told, has believable characters, even if it's a fantasy, and holds their attention. So the first thing you need to do is read lots of children's books. Go into bookshops and see what's both currently being published and selling.

ᵕ into libraries and talk to a librarian. Find out what's being
ᵒowed and what isn't, and then read the work that's popular and
ʰat makes it popular. Do the same for the books that aren't
ᵘut and see if you can work out what's wrong.

ʳas a teacher – I taught 11- to 18-year-olds – I discovered
f the books aimed at the children's market were very
ᵃined strong moral messages and, for the most part,
ᵛ rigid. I remember one class of adolescents who would
ʰeir books at me if they weren't gripped within two
ᵛsperation, I tried them with *The Call of the Wild*
ʰey loved it.

Now, on one level, it was simply because the central character was a dog. On a deeper level, it was because it was about a dog that was brutalized and in the end became savage before being finally rescued by a decent man. The message – brutality creates savagery – was one they clearly understood. The story rang true and the ending gave them consolation.

I think that's the key even when we're talking about fantasy. In the Harry Potter series Hogwarts is a dream school for apprentice wizards and witches who, just like any other school students, moan about their homework and dread exams. But it's also a place where people die, evil is real and it's OK to be scared. Just like the real world that children know exists because they see it on television every day.

Books about children's books

As well as reading books for children, read a few books *about* books for children. Apart from *Writing for Children* by Allan Frewin Jones and Lesley Pollinger, which is excellent by the way, have a look at J.R.R. Tolkien's essay 'On Fairy Stories'.

One last point here. I mentioned earlier in the chapter how much I, as a child, enjoyed hearing about what I called the olden days. When I first started writing for children I used my own childhood as a starting point. I realized that, while the trappings of childhood change, the emotions don't. So I avoided specific contemporary references and concentrated on events and the emotions they generated.

When I was eight we had two TV channels, both black and white, and there were no such things as computer games. On the other hand, 'it' hurt just as much then as it does now – 'it' being anything from being ridiculed by a bully to the grief felt when someone you love dies. Children's emotions may be more magnified than those of adults – well, most thinking adults anyway – but they're just as real.

You might find it interesting to read *The Lore and Language of Schoolchildren* by Iona and Peter Opie. It was first published in 1959, so a lot of the material is out of date, but it's still one of the best insights into the way children think that I've ever read.

Focus points

- Fear of failure, fear of success and writer's block are all aspects of the same thing.
- The only way forward is to keep raising your profile!
- Use archives not just as a source of research but also as a source of ideas.
- Continue reading.
- Look at different approaches to narrative, so read scripts as well as novels, short stories, biographies and so on.
- Ask yourself: Am I writing what I want to or what I feel I ought to?
- Consider writing for children, although you should bear in mind that it's not as easy as it looks. If you have the knack, however, it's incredibly rewarding.
- Keep writing!

Where to next?

In Chapter 13 we will consider how you can build and extend your writing career.

13

What next?

Kevin McCann

One thing I've learned is that, when it comes to writing, there's very little that can be just written hastily. Well, I suppose that's not quite true. Some things have almost written themselves and some would never have been written at all if it hadn't been for a magazine editor with a specific request. And when I was a student, I wrote thousands of words on subjects that didn't always set me on fire. I suspect it showed.

Everything I've ever written, whether it's been for money, love or both, has required effort and commitment. The more committed I am, the better – in theory – the writing becomes.

What I also discovered was that it was possible to write for money and produce work I was and still am proud of. I don't have an artistic hierarchy and I don't believe that my children's poems or articles for educational magazines get in the way of my adult poems and short stories.

Quite the opposite, in fact. It's all writing, and the different strands are no more separate than the threads that make up a spider's web are ultimately separate.

Writing to order (i.e. to a deadline with a specific word count) taught me the self-discipline I needed. It's the difference, I think, between being 'a writer' and writing.

Let me briefly explain.

In Liverpool we have a saying: 'If you can't fight, wear a big hat!' It's a saying I've often applied to the kind of people who read lots of books about writing, talk about the daily struggle with language, and their poor suffering souls, etc. I also found, oddly enough, that they all subscribed to the 'I can't get published because I didn't go to Oxbridge' conspiracy theories.

In my time, I've met dozens of them in the various writers' groups I've tutored. I discovered that their work rarely matched the build-up they gave it. I also discovered the person I call 'the quiet one at the back'. She or he would attempt all the writing exercises I set – but sometimes a bit quirkily – had done a lot of reading, rarely repeated a mistake and in the end, while agreeing with my criticism of their work, would often come up with a solution that was far better than mine. It was better than mine because it was a conclusion they'd arrived at by combining their own intelligence, their own experience and their own critical faculty.

It was always a moment I enjoyed because I knew they'd found their own voice and no longer needed either my approval or guidance. I'd also know that it wouldn't be much longer before we had the 'thanks for everything' conversation followed by the final parting of the ways. When that came, my last words to them were always: 'Will you carry on writing?'

That was an easy one and I always got a resounding yes.

The second and final question was always: 'And what's your ultimate ambition?'

You now have to answer the same two questions. I'm hoping that, having been through so much, the answer to the first question is yes. But what about the second question? What is your ultimate ambition?

Well, the answer I heard most frequently was: 'To be a full-time writer.'

If that's your ambition, good luck to you, but be realistic. You'll have to make money because you have to live. If you're making money, it's great. If you're not, it's sleepless nights, cheap but filling food and no social life. So, ideally, you're looking for the kind of writing that both pays and you're passionate about. Pash plus cash.

So, the next question is: can you make enough money to live on?

If not – well, at this stage anyway – can you combine a number of elements that together will give you enough of an income to get by? If you're lucky enough to have a full-time job, can you reduce your hours and give yourself more time to write?

If you're on your own, your decision affects nobody but you. If you share your life with somebody else, what are their thoughts? Because it's all very well being prepared to go without and sacrifice life's little luxuries, but it's not quite so good to expect other people to just blithely go along with you. Where I come from, that's called selfish. That's the polite version anyway. You could be lucky and your partner says – as mine did – 'Go for it!', but you need to have a plan:

- Make sure your income will still exceed your outgoings.
- Don't get a credit card and assume you'll be able to pay it off once the money starts rolling in. It might not.
- Try to build up a list of editors who both like your work and pay.
- Never assume that any magazine will last for ever.
- Look around for other sources of writing-related income.

Writers' workshops

If you've been a member of a writing class, then you'll know how they work and what people expect. So, could you run one? Now bear in mind that you're looking for income here as well as accolades, which means you'll have to charge.

So, do you know enough and, just as importantly, do you have enough natural authority to deal with the dynamics involved in keeping order? Do you have the patience to deal with the really difficult customer? Would you pay to be taught by you – if you see what I mean?

If the answer to any of the above is no, then you might want to seriously reconsider. For the moment, at least.

Unless you've already had some teaching experience, in which case all this will be blindingly obvious, I'd hold back and begin by getting some practical experience.

If you're a member of a group run by an accredited tutor who is being paid, then asking them whether they'd mind letting you practise chairing with a view to taking their job is probably not advisable. However, there's nothing to stop you observing their method and noticing how the session proceeds:

- Do they limit the time for each discussion on each piece of work?
- How do they deal with difficult students?
- Does the session include writing exercises?
- If so, when are they attempted? During the session or during the week?

If you're a member of a more informal group, ask if you can chair it. Do the same if it's a readers' group. In fact, if you're involved in any kind of group/organization that holds meetings, volunteer your services as chair.

And keep one very important fact in mind at all times: good teaching opens minds and bad teaching crushes potential. So it's not just a case of being confident enough to teach a group, it's also about having confidence in what you are teaching. It's no good having all the knowledge if you can't communicate that knowledge. It's no good having the gift of the gab if you've got nothing to say that's worth listening to. You need both.

 Remember this...

Good teaching like great acting looks effortless. It's not!

HOWEVER...

If you still want to try your hand at running a writers' group, you could set up some sampler sessions and see how things go. What you'll need initially is a free location (i.e. no fee for the use of the room) and a title that plays to your strengths. So, if you've published a novel, it's 'Writing a Novel: Getting Started'. If you write short stories, it's 'Writing Short Stories' and so on.

You already know how important a good eye-catching design is for a book cover, so apply the same knowledge to your poster. Ideally, what you want is something clear and concise. The title of the session, where it takes place, date and time (finish time as well as start time), your name and what you've published. I'd make it a one-off session to begin with and, initially, I'd make it free.

If things go well, you can look at setting up more sessions and maybe even charging a token fee to cover your expenses. At the time of writing, I know of a couple of groups that do just that. They meet weekly for two hours and each member pays £2 per session. The tutor obviously isn't making much money but isn't out of pocket either.

Scout a location

Find out if there are any writers' groups in either your local library or community centre. If there are, look further afield. The last thing you want is a feud with some already established group or groups. If you find a suitable location, approach the head librarian / centre manager and offer to run a free one-off sampler to gauge interest.

If this is agreed upon, have a look at the room you'll be using. Make sure that it's in a quiet location and that tables and chairs are available. Obvious, I know, but you'd be amazed how many times I've arrived somewhere and found four barstools and a coffee table next to the pinball machine.

Running a group

If you do get a group up and running, I would urge you to set out a few basic ground rules and stick to them:

- Comment on the work but not the individual.
- Don't insist on 'positive comments only' but do encourage the notion that negative comments should include a suggested improvement.
- The writer whose work is being discussed should only speak in response to a direct question but will get their chance to respond at the end.
- Speakers should never interrupt each other.

With regard to that last point, you must be able to direct the conversation. If everyone just jumps in as and when they feel like it, you'll end up with chaos. A number of years ago I was invited to a talking circle on a Native American reservation and saw the talking stick used very effectively to solve this problem. In that case it literally was a carved piece of wood. While someone was talking they held on to it, and when they'd finished they passed it to the next person in line.

It worked very well and I've used a similar device myself. Only in my case, it was a 12-inch ruler. It did work, though!

Before we move on, here are a few helpful tips:

- Good teaching is like good cooking – it's all in the preparation – so go into each session with a writing idea just in case no one has brought any work to share. And have a backup… just in case they do the first piece of writing in ten minutes flat.
- Don't just recycle other people's ideas, come up with new ones of your own. But remember, if you do use someone else's idea, acknowledge them.
- Remember that people soon tire of gushing praise, so don't be afraid to be critical of a piece even if everyone else claims to love it. Your praise when it comes will carry more weight.
- Don't get involved in arguments about content. It's either well written or it's not. There are obvious exceptions to that suggestion. I once had a student read out a piece that was an incitement to race hate. So I talked about both content (vile) and style (crass).
- Make sure you set the agenda. Most students prefer it that way.
- Be consistent, don't play favourites, and hide any dislike you may feel towards individual students.
- By all means ask for feedback but don't keep asking for it. It may be a good idea to ask for something in writing at the end of your final session. It's often very useful.

One last thing. Not everyone can teach so, if it's not working out, walk away once you've fulfilled your commitments. But never walk out on a commitment unless you have absolutely no choice. You're only human, so nobody should expect you to be perfect, but they have a right to expect you to be reliable.

Here's a quotation for you to ponder:

 Chas Parry-Jones, Ucheldre Arts Centre, Holyhead

'A good workshop leader needs to be a good and swift judge of character of his or her students, picking up their abilities and evaluating both their learning and listening capacity.'

Community arts

Find out what, if any, community arts projects are taking place in your area and try to get involved. You may not make any money but it will raise your profile, add to your experience, go on your CV and improve your chances of getting paid work further down the line.

If you haven't done it already, start subscribing to Arts Council England's jobs bulletin (www.artsjobs.org.uk). Apart from paid work, you'll see opportunities to get unpaid work experience. Now I subscribe to the notion of being paid for any work I do but I'm also prepared to work for no fee if it's for charity or if I'm likely to gain valuable experience.

Writer-in-residence

I've been a writer-in-residence several times. It's a position that can be useful for two main reasons:

1 It's usually paid *and*

2 It's often paid quite well.

That may sound cynical but, actually, it's not. It's realistic. The fees from a residency can buy you the peace of mind you need to get on with your own writing. The myth of the starving artist whose best work is forged in the white heat of poverty and noble thought is just that. What actually happens is that writers who are poor get on with their writing despite being poor, not because of it.

It's true that a good few years of going without can help you appreciate what life is really like for far too many people. George Orwell actually chose to live as a tramp and wrote up his experiences in *Down and Out in London and Paris*. He saw it as completing his education, but he also recognized that being poor is something to be endured but not desired.

Be warned, though. For every residency there will be dozens of applicants. They will all have track records in both publishing and community arts of one kind or another. So think of this as a long-term goal and start building up both your publishing record and your experience in running writers' groups.

If you manage to get the job, you'll find it very demanding. However, it will be valuable experience and, again, it adds to your credibility. One thing, though: read the terms and conditions very carefully. Make sure your hours and duties/responsibilities are clear. As a general rule, avoid anything that's open ended, for example '… and any other duties the line manager sees fit to designate'. All that really means is more work, same money. Ask any teacher.

If in doubt, get the contract looked at by an expert, so make sure you're in a professional association like the Writers' Guild before you sign. If whoever's managing the residency is insulted when you tell them you'd like a third party to look at the contract, assume they've got something to hide... so think hard before proceeding.

Don't let yourself be exploited

If the contract is fine but later on in the residency you feel you're being exploited, go straight to your professional association and ask them for help and advice. You'll be doing yourself and every other writer a huge favour.

Approaching publishers

Have a look at the home pages of publishers that are interested in the kind of books you've either already written or want to write. Check what their submissions policy is. Some will want sample chapters plus a synopsis of a finished book but others will just want a proposal.

This, initially, would be a brief synopsis plus a short covering letter with some background information about yourself. Again, having a track record will help, but that, in itself, won't be enough. What you'll also need to do is convince a publisher to spend their money publishing your book.

So who is the book aimed at? The temptation here is to respond, 'People who can read!' – very witty, very unhelpful. So think carefully about this one. We'll come back to it in a minute.

What will make your book different? How will you make it stand out from its competitors? What you're looking for is a both a gap in the market and an original approach.

Do your market research

If you have an idea for a new and original book, do some market research before you start writing. Somebody else may have had the same idea and already written and published it.

Back in 1969, for example, George MacDonald Fraser published his first Flashman novel. He took the historical novel as his form and then proceeded to mix fact and fiction. The facts were his carefully researched accounts of actual events (First Afghan War, Indian

Mutiny) as seen through the eyes of Harry Paget Flashman, the infamous bully who appears briefly in the almost unreadable *Tom Brown's Schooldays*.

His approach was to make Flashman a liar, cheat, racist, sexist lecher who fools everyone and ends up winning the Victoria Cross. The novels are Flashman's secret memoirs in which he tells nothing but the unvarnished truth.

The Flashman novels have three great strengths. They're meticulously researched. They're beautifully written and the first one was published in 1969. This was the year of Monty Python, Woodstock, the first Moon landing and riots in Derry. It was also a time when England's imperial past was no longer being seen as a source of pride.

Then along came Flashman, who was about as far removed from the 'play with a straight bat, stiff upper lip' myth of the British past as it was possible to get. Readers lapped it up. Of course, there are some who assume that, because Flashman's a racist, the books are racist. They judge Huck Finn in the same way and simply can't see that the device being used here is irony.

Literary agents

If you've approached an agent or agents in the past, you'll already know all the dos and don'ts. But if you haven't…

Find an agent

Type 'literary agents' followed by your location (UK, USA, etc.) into your search engine. Go to each agency's home page, find their submissions policy and read it carefully.

If they clearly state that they don't look at unsolicited manuscripts, move on. Never write and ask whether they'd be willing to make an exception in your case. They won't. Not because they're being pedantic but because an agent can represent only a finite number of writers. There are, after all, only a finite number of hours in a week. It's as easy as that.

If they take unsolicited work, see if there's a reading fee. If there is, move on.

Of the agents left, find the ones who represent the kind of book that you've written. List them and then read their submissions guidelines – carefully! – and then stick to them.

> The chances are they'll want a section of the manuscript (e.g. first three chapters) plus a brief summary of the plot. 'Brief' means about a thousand words or less. So you don't need to put in every tiny detail, just the main points.

Begin your brief summary with linked headings showing the flow of the narrative.

For example:

> Red Riding Hood sets off for G/ma's house – meets wolf in forest – wolf goes on ahead – eats G/ma – wolf disguises himself as G/ma – RRH arrives at cottage – wolf about to attack – huntsman bursts in & kills wolf – slices it open & out pops G/ma – all live happily ever, etc.

Now, as somebody who's told that story, I know that the above are the barest of bare bones so in order to turn it into a synopsis, I'd now need to flesh it out.

> Red Riding Hood sets out for Grandma's house – needs to deliver food as G/ma is sick – takes path through forest where she meets wolf, etc.

Again, as far as your covering letter goes, keep it brief and relevant. You might want to start by giving a brief outline (about 200 words) of your writing career to date (publications, your first book) but don't waste words – limit yourself pretty much to that. When you're talking about your book, you need to talk about its main theme (e.g. it's a crime novel that explores a moral dilemma), your target readership (teenagers, general readership, etc.) and point out why it's different from every other book already published in the same genre.

 ## Have a finished book

Only approach an agent if you have a finished book. If all you've got is an idea/outline plus the first chapter and don't want to write the rest on spec, go back to publishers who are interested in proposals.

And remember, whether you've got a finished book or just an outline, a good track record will help enormously.

If you're turned down, move on, but don't slam the door on your way out. Reply to your rejection with a quick note thanking the agent for their time. You never know when your paths might cross again.

Publisher seeks new writers...

Also be very aware that vanity publishers haven't gone away. They dress themselves up as more plausible outfits these days but they're still the same as they've always been. As a basic rule of thumb, anything that involves buying advance copies of your own book and claims about epublishing being just a craze should be avoided.

The story so far

If this was a one-to-one surgery, I'd pause at this point, glance at my watch and then begin summing up. Before I do that, I've got one last thing I'd like you to do.

Workshop: Assess your self-publishing skills

From memory, write out a list of all the skills you've acquired in the process of self-publishing your first book. I want you to do it from memory because I suspect that, as the list grows, it will have more impact than if you'd merely copied out the highlights of the chapter contents. Don't worry about getting them in chronological order. That's not the point of the exercise. What I want you to realize at this point is that with some help and advice from Tom and myself you've learned how to...

Now make that list.

When you've finished that, make a list of everything you've published or had published to date. Again, do this from memory.

Finally, look back through the contents section of this book and see how your memory compares with the full list of all the things you've actually learned.

Compare your list of remembered publications with the actual list on your CV.

Now, let's analyse the results and ponder their implications.

SKILLS

That should be a pretty long and impressive list by now. If, as I suspect, your memory fell short of your actual achievements, then so much the better. It only further reinforces my point that you probably know considerably more than you give yourself credit for. Now pause for a minute and think about that.

Whether you found the whole process comparatively easy – in which case you have natural ability – or quite hard work – in which case you're not one of those people who want it all on a plate – the fact is, you've written, edited, proofread and published a book.

That's a hell of an achievement so be proud of yourself – just don't get arrogant!

Publications

If your list of publications consists of nothing but your first book, then you do need to start doing something about that. Or, rather, if you want to move into the world of professional writing, you'll *really* need to start doing something about that. It very much depends on what you want and you simply may not want to go through all that again. Well, not yet anyway.

Or you may have a full-time job that you love and are perfectly content to self-publish every few years for a comparatively small readership.

The most important thing of all is this: write your passion and don't just hope for the best – strive for it.

If your first book was fiction but you've developed an interest in a non-fiction subject and want to write about that next, then go for it. It's not that art is better than academe or vice versa. They're both equally important. The academic explains how the world works. The artist interprets it. Value them both.

And finally...

Always remember that books like this one are helpful in showing how to take your knowledge and experiences and apply them to a practical end. In this case, writing and self-publishing. They will often confirm what you've suspected all along. They help you avoid mistakes and guide you to a successful conclusion, but they can never be a substitute for knowledge and experience.

You need to acquire that for yourself.

Now take everything that you know and keep writing.

And good luck.

Resources

Ebooks

Publish on Amazon Kindle with Kindle Direct Publishing (free ebook)

Smashwords Book Marketing Guide: How to Market Any Book for Free (free ebook)

How to Self-Publish: A Guardian Masterclass (Guardian Shorts, ebook)

Websites

Self-publishing showcase: www.theguardian.com/books/series/self-publishing-showcase

Design: www.thebookdesigner.com

Guidance on writing, publishing and self-publishing: www.authonomy.com/writing-tips

Publishing and self-publishing news: www.publishersweekly.com

Marketing discussions and ideas: http://sethgodin.typepad.com

Reading (compiled by Kevin McCann)

The list that follows is not meant to be seen in any way as an *ignore-the-rest-because-this-is-best*: it's entirely personal. As I have already stated, if you write you should read, and read widely. So, as well as making use of libraries and bookshops, scour the shelves of charity shops. Follow your own passions, but maybe try some of the following as well:

Dictionary of Literary Terms and Literary Theory (published by Penguin) One of the most useful and illuminating books I've ever come across.

Writing a Novel by John Braine

Becoming a Writer by Dorothea Brande

On Writing by Stephen King

The Art of Fiction by David Lodge

Four excellent books – all very readable and all very useful. However, don't take my word for it. Read them and then make up your own mind.

Nights at the Circus by Angela Carter   Excellent introduction to magic realism – if you don't know what that term means, look it up – and a page-turner to boot.

Heart of Darkness by Joseph Conrad   This is worth reading for the descriptive passages alone. Try reading them aloud.

Great Expectations by Charles Dickens   I think this is Dickens' most subversive book – which is probably why I like it.

The Great Gatsby by F. Scott Fitzgerald   Beautifully written – again, try reading it aloud. On the surface it's about a doomed passion but there's much more than that going on.

I, Claudius by Robert Graves   Excellent example of first-person narrative and a page turner to boot.

Catch 22 by Joseph Heller   Any book whose title becomes part of the language has to be worth looking at. Although it's set in World War II, it has an oddly contemporary feel.

The Perfect Spy by John Le Carré and *Mother Night* by Kurt Vonnegut   Try reading these back to back. On the surface they're both very different books but in terms of theme... well read them and, again, decide for yourself.

The Call of the Wild by Jack London Simply   excellent. If you enjoy it, try *White Fang* and then round off with *Tarka the Otter* by Henry Williamson.

Doctor Zhivago by Boris Pasternak   Everyone who's either seen the David Lean film or the TV version thinks they know what this book's about. They don't. Read it for yourself and find out why.

Wuthering Heights by Emily Brontë   Her only novel, this owes a great deal (like so many others) to both folk and fairy tales.

On Fairy Stories by J.R.R. Tolkien This is a very readable discussion of fantasy/fairy tales that analyses both how and why they appeal. It contains the best reply to people who dismiss escapist stories I've ever read.

Danse Macabre by Stephen King   There's an extensive watch this / read this list at the back which is well worth a look... even if fantasy isn't your genre. For example, find out what King means by the phrase 'phobic pressure points' and then see whether it might apply to your own work.

The Haunting of Hill House by Shirley Jackson   One of the best, if not the very best, haunted house novel ever written. There's an interesting story about how Shirley Jackson got the idea in the first place which you may find useful.

The ghost stories of M.R. James   These stories are masterpieces of subtlety and suggestion that set a standard for everything that followed.

The Book of Fantasy, edited by Jorge Luis Borges, Silvina Ocampo and Adolfo Bioy Casares   Unlike most genre anthologies, this isn't simply a rehash of all the others and includes some genuine rarities.

The Fall and Rise of Reggie Perrin by David Nobbs   This is a classic – to 'do a Reggie Perrin' has now entered the language – just read it.

The Hard Life by Flann O'Brien   This includes a character who runs correspondence courses in Tightrope Walking – which should give you a clue. If you enjoy this, try *The Third Policeman*.

Decline of the English Murder by George Orwell   This begins with a short essay on murder (and our fascination with it) that's as relevant today as when it was first written. It also contains essays on Dickens and Kipling that make for excellent introductions to their work. Also, try tracking down Raymond Chandler's essay 'The Simple Art of Murder' and, again, read the two back to back.

The Big Sleep by Raymond Chandler   Phillip Marlowe is the archetype of all private eyes and you'll either be confused or hooked by Chapter 5. It's beautifully written, although Chandler has been criticized for being too poetic… which is like criticizing strawberries for being just too delicious.

The Night of the Hunter by Davis Grubb   Most of you will know this through the film version starring Robert Mitchum. The book is well worth tracking down. Again, it's wonderfully well written and is in a direct line of descent from every big bad wolf story ever told.

Red Harvest by Dashiell Hammet   Hammet had actually been a private investigator, so his stories have that extra whiff of seedy authenticity. Unlike Chandler, his prose style was very simple. He proves that really great writing is not about using extraordinary language; it's about using ordinary language to do extraordinary things.

Voice of the Fire by Alan Moore   Short stories all set in and around Northampton – beginning about 4000 BC and ending in the twentieth century.

Metamorphosis by Franz Kafka   Kafka's name alone scares off a lot of people – they imagine something so highbrow as to be almost unreadable – they're wrong. Try this story as an introduction to his work. It's a direct descendant of many a folk tale and is the ancestor of horror films like *The Fly*.

Index

academic publishing, 13
accounts, 87
acquiring editors, 11
advance on royalties, 82
aggregators, 345
anniversaries/tie-ins, 44
archive material, 428–30
assessment services, 323
auctions, 12
authonomy, 8
authors, *see also* writers
author's biography,
    39–40, 367
author's copies, 87
author's questionnaire,
    173
author's rights, 237, 367
authors' websites, 182–
    3, 381, 399–410
    content, 404–6
    language, 403–4
    links, 404
    search rankings,
        407–8
    structure, 404
    usability, 403–4
    website design, 402–3
automatic writing,
    424–5

backlists, 7–8
barcodes, 94
biographies, 281
blurbs, 366–7
boilerplate agreements,
    89
book binding, 337
book contents, 361–2
book distributors,
    214–19
book fairs, 18–19
book packaging, 13
book sizes, 132
book title, 39, 360–1

books, and research, 289
bookshop publicity,
    188–91, 420
budget, 127–9

Cataloguing-in-
    Publication, 95
cheap editions, 85
children's publishing, 13,
    434–5
clichés, 305
Cloake, Martin, 370–6
commissioning, 410
commissioning editors,
    11
competing works, 87
consumer publishing, 12
contracts, 81–3
convergent thinking, 414
copyright, 78–81, 103,
    296
costs, 127–9
cover design, 133–5,
    333–4, 363–66
critical books, 281
cultural theft, 322

deadlines, 107
deferred payment, 427
design, 113, 132–37
dialogue, unnecessary,
    307
digital printing/
    publishing, 6–7,
    330–1
distribution, 115, 340
divergent thinking, 414
DRM (digital rights
    management), 90
dropped capitals, 137

e-readers, 344
ebooks, 6–7, 151–67,
    3413–58

aggregators, 349
Amazon Kindle,
    155–6, 345–6,
    350–1, 355–7
Apple, 156–7, 347–8,
    351, 355–7
Bookbaby, 159
cover image, 161
dashboards, 162
design, 355–7
Diesel, 158
formats, 352–4
Google, 348, 352
help available, 354–5
keywords, 161
Kobo, 157–8, 346–7,
    351, 355–7
Lulu, 159
manuscript
    preparation, 154–5
NOOK, 157, 348,
    352
online sales, 221–2
pricing, 162–3
publishing processes,
    357
royalties, 162
sales of, 350–2
Smashwords, 158
Sony, 158, 352
tags, 161
tax, 358
technical knowledge,
    354
editing own work, 59,
    130–1
editions, 340
editors, 5, 11, 68–9,
    116, 130
educational publishing,
    13
emotion, 304
endorsements, 391
epublishing, 1, 159–70

feedback, 61–2, 109–13, 275–8
fiction categories, 19
fiction synopsis, 42
film archives, 291
film posters, 362
film scores, 425
first drafts, 57
font, 136–7, 3324–5
formatting, 334, 373
free giveaways, 396
free-falling, 424–5
friends/acquaintances, 130
front lists, 7–8

genre categories, 19–20

illustrations, 137
images, 335–6
imprints, 6
indexes, 131
industry classifications, 92–3
inspiration, 308–11
Internet publicity, 180–8
Internet resources, 287–9
ISBN (International Standard Book Number), 93–94, 337

lateral thinking, 414
launch dates, 391–2
left-over books, 228–34
libel, 91
library book deposits, 96
library research, 290
library sales, 219–20
list building, 11
literary agents, 5, 6, 8, 14–18, 20–2, 31–5, 65–8, 85
literary consultants, 62–5
literary festivals, 192

manuscripts
  assessment services, 323
  design, 113
  ebooks, 154–5
  feedback, 61–72, 109–12
  pdf, 336
  preparation, 106–7, 154–5, 313–28
  professional help, 373, 377, 381
  proofs, 112
  redrafting, see redrafting
  stages at publishers, 108–9
market potential, 43
market price, 338
market research, 297
marketing, 374, 378–9, 387–98
  in-house, 171–2
  and promotion, 133–4
  target audiences, 347, 390–1
marketing plans, 389
marketing support, 397
media publicity/reviews, 175–9, 395
moral rights, 81

negative criticism, 280–1
negotiation, 88–9
net sales revenue, 128
networking, 60–1, 418–20
newspaper publicity, 177–8
Nilsson-Julien, 380–5
non-fiction categories, 19–20
non-fiction synopsis, 42

offset printing, 330
option on next work, 87–8

packing, 115
padding, 305
page layout, 135–6, 332–3
page size, 335
paper quality, 336–7
paperback/hardback choice, 336–7
payment date, 85
permissions, 91
persistence, 53–75
plagiarism, 91–2, 296
POD (print on demand), 141–3, 330–1, 372, 376
point of view, 321
post–publication, 414–21
presentation copies, 87
price cuts, 396
price setting, 338
primary sources, 428–30
print runs, 138–9
printing, 114–15, 138–9, 329–42
prioritizing, 415–18
production, 114–15
production costs, 339–40
production process research, 372, 377, 380–1
professional associations, 420
progress review, 397
promotional material, 173–75
proofreaders, 130, 381
pseudonyms (pen names), 97
publicity, 6
  in-house, 171–2
  Internet, 180–8

libraries, 419
in media, 175–9
venues, 188–95
publishers, 1–3, 5, 6,
9–11, 20–2, 30–1,
69–71
publishing publications,
17–18, 32

readers' groups, 314
readership, 43
reading
background, 281–2
general, 280
importance of, 280–2
specialized, 281
recording thoughts,
425
redrafting, 299–311
action plan, 300
inspiration, 308–11
readability, 307–8
word-cutting, 302–5
rejection
dealing with, 432–4
preparation for, 55–6
reasons for, 56–48
remainders, 85
research, 285–97
accuracy, 293
content, 286
disposable, 296
references, 294
sources, 287–93
successful methods,
292–4
when to stop, 294–5
reserved rights, 87
reversion of rights, 86
reviewing book, 282–3
rights, 78
royalties, 84–5, 162,
222–3, 234
royalty statements, 236

sales, 115–126, 203–31
bad debt, 207–8
bookshop chains/

supermarkets,
210–7
discounting, 203–5
expectations, 331,
339–40, 375, 379,
384
independent
bookshops, 210–11
library sales, 219–20
net sales revenue, 128
online, 220–2
overheads, 208
payment, 206, 207
price-setting, 127–9
record keeping, 207
retail, 340
returns policy, 206
royalties, 222–3
timing, 209
on website, 407
sample chapters, 44–7
search engines, 287–8
self-actualization, 322–7
self-development,
continuing, 423–36
self-editing, 130–1
self-education, 314–18
self-publishing, 1, 6,
123–49, 272–5, 332
case studies, 369–85
companies, 340–1
considerations, 126–7
courses, 382
POD (print on
demand), 141–3,
330–1
providers, 14
total revenue, 128–9
using experts, 129–30
sentence length, 305
serendipity, 425
Sherratt, Mel, 376–80
similar titles, 44
social media, 184–6,
289, 383, 3932–5,
405, 406
social networking sites,
187–8

STM (scientific,
technical, medical)
publishing, 13
storytelling, 319–22
subject knowledge, 427
submissions
accuracy, 47
author biography,
39–40
book title, 39
guidelines, 31–8
introductory/covering
letters, 34, 37–8
keeping track of, 36–7
multiple, 35–6
unsolicited, 8, 27
subsidiary rights, 86–7
subsidy epublishers,
160–1
synopsis, 40–52

tax
ebooks, 358
income tax, 421
writers' earnings,
341
television/radio
publicity, 179
textbook publishing, 13
time management,
415–18
timing, 23
trade publishing, 12
typefaces, 136–7
typesetting, 114, 139–40

vanity publishing,
140–1, 333

waiting for replies, 54
websites see authors'
websites
widows and orphans,
137
word count, 98
writers
age of, 243
financial support, 234

income and expenditure recording, 235–6
self-discipline, 239–40
support network, 242–3
tools of the trade, 240–2
versatility, 239
see also authors

writers' associations, 420
writer's block, 240
writers' groups, 278
writers' retreats, 49
writers' surgeries, 323
writers' union, 238
writers' workshops, 276–7

writing
for children, 13, 434–5
craft of writing, 58–9
writing competitions, 425–6
writing courses, 49
writing mentors, 277
writing skill improvement, 279–80

Acknowledgements

The authors of *Get Started in Self-Publishing* would like to thank the following people: Nina Allen, Harriet Bourton, Martin Cloake, Jonathan Dean (Radio City, Liverpool), Phillipa Fawcett, Vicci McCann (Senior Archivist, Lancashire Archives), Jimmy McGovern, Danielle McGregor (BSc. Hons, MSc.), Olivier Nilsson-Julien, Chas Parry-Jones (Ucheldre Literary Society, Holyhead), Victoria Roddam and Mel Sherratt.